INSIDE THE
HOUSE

Former Members Reveal
How Congress Really Works

EDITED BY

Lou Frey, Jr. and Michael T. Hayes

U. S. Association of Former Members of Congress
and
University Press of America,® Inc.
Lanham   New York   Oxford

Copyright © 2001 by
University Press of America,® Inc.
4720 Boston Way
Lanham, Maryland 20706

12 Hid's Copse Rd.
Cumnor Hill, Oxford OX2 9JJ

Library of Congress Cataloging-in-Publication Data

Inside the house : former members reveal how Congress
really works / edited by Lou Frey, Jr. and Michael T. Hayes.
p.   cm
l. United States. Congress. I. Frey, Lou. II. Hayes, Michael T.
JK1021 .I57   2001   328.73—dc21   00-066604 CIP

ISBN 0-7618-1937-1 (pbk. : alk. ppr.)

⊖™ The paper used in this publication meets the minimum
requirements of American National Standard for Information
Sciences—Permanence of Paper for Printed Library Materials,
ANSI Z39.48—1984

The nonpartisan United States Association of Former Members of Congress was founded in 1970 as a nonprofit, educational, research, and social organization. It has been chartered by the United States Congress and has approximately 600 members who represented American citizens in both the U.S. Senate and House of Representatives.

The Association promotes improved public understanding of the role of Congress as a unique institution as well as the crucial importance of representative democracy as a system of government, both domestically and internationally.

For more information about the Association, please visit our Web site at: www.usafmc.org.

Copyright Acknowledgments

Contents

Preface

Lou Frey, Jr.

My good friend and former colleague, Congressman Barber Conable, wrote me that this book was taking more time than the birth of an elephant. As usual, Barber was right. The idea for this book came about when I started a congressional intern program in 1969. Under that program, each high school elected one junior to spend eight days with me in Washington. I had over 30 high schools in my district and thus over 30 high school students in groups came to Washington to see and learn first-hand. In a newspaper article in 1974, I stated, "Our intern program allows these young people to see first-hand what they have been studying in their classes, and I learned by just listening to their views and opinions." As a result of the success of this program, I began to teach in every high school in my district and in area colleges.

Later, after I retired from Congress, I became involved in the U. S. Association of Former Members of Congress and helped develop their Congress to Campus Program. The Congress to Campus Program is a partnership between the Association of Former Members and the John C. Stennis Center for Public Service. I would like to thank the staff of the Stennis Center for all that they do to make the Congress to Campus Program a reality, coordinating visits and providing transportation for former members to colleges and universities. This book is an outgrowth of that Program.

During my many trips to college communities, I learned that there was no one book that gave the reader an inside look at the Congress from a personal viewpoint. Both teachers and students asked me to put together a book that incorporated the information they obtained during our informal lectures and talks. On one of these trips, to Colgate University, I met Professor Michael Hayes. He and I decided to work together to produce such a book.

After spinning our wheels for more than a year trying to co-author a book on Congress, we realized that what we *should* be doing was drawing on the lectures developed by the various former members who had participated in the Congress to Campus Program. I began contacting former members in 1996. The end result, which you see here, is 44 chapters on Congress written by 34 former members of the U.S. House, the spouse of a former member, one former staff member, one former lobbyist, and a Canadian scholar. The list includes men and women, Republicans and Democrats, and members whose careers span the last four decades.

I would like to give special thanks to Professor Michael Hayes, Chairman of the Political Science Department of Colgate University, my alma mater. He has labored long and hard on this project, and it has been his guidance and wise advice that have molded this book. He has edited and helped structure every chapter. Michael has a wonderful sense of history and love for our institutions of government. I have had the privilege of teaching in his classes and know how well received he is by the students at Colgate University.

I also want to thank all my colleagues who wrote chapters for this book. I know some wrote a chapter because they just did not want to hear from me anymore. I am proud of the job that each of them did and believe that this book will make a significant contribution in understanding how and why our government really works.

Finally, I would like to give special thanks to my partners at my law firm, Lowndes, Drosdick, Doster, Kantor & Reed, P.A., in Orlando, Florida. They have encouraged me to take on this task and have supported me even though it has taken time from the law practice. Everyone should be so lucky in their choice of friends and partners.

I confess to having a love affair with our country and our system of government for many years. I make this confession with all my senses left, knowing full well where politicians rank in terms of prestige and believability. A survey in May 1989 showed approximately one-third of the American people felt that congressmen were dishonest. This is not a new phenomenon. H. L. Mencken, the "sage of Baltimore," was one of America's greatest satirists writing about the American scene from the early 1900s through the 1950s. His hard-hitting reporting of politics and politicians is still unequaled. In a 1924 essay entitled "The Politician," he said, "If the American people could only rid themselves of another and worse false assumption that still rides them—one that corrupts all their thinking about the great business of politics, and vastly augments their discontent and unhappiness—the assumption, that is, that politicians are divided into two classes, and that one of these classes is made up of good ones. For if experience teaches us anything at all it teaches us this: that a good politician, under democracy, is quite as unthinkable as an honest burglar."[1]

As much as I enjoy reading H. L. Mencken, I am in deep disagreement with him on this issue. There is no question that some people in the political system do not measure up. However, the majority do. The sad part is, if you kiss your wife it is not news, but if you shoot her, it's front page news.

This book will take you behind the bare bones outline of how Congress works and how a bill gets passed, to look at how real people, your friends and neighbors, react and act when they are in the toughest political league in the world—the United

States Congress. Although Congress has changed in many ways over the years, the practical, personal, and political problems remain the same. No one should ever think that politics is not a full contact body sport. It is not a place for wimps or the fainthearted. However, it is a place for those who want to make changes and want to exercise power in a responsible way.

The United States Congress is described in some textbooks as an orderly place where well intended men and women pass laws that are good for the country. But in reality, Congress is a complicated body where issues are seldom clear cut, where only a handful of the thousands of bills introduced each year become law, and where most laws are passed in a form that only vaguely resembles what their sponsors intended. Yet our system works and will continue to work as long as the American people believe in and understand our system of government.

I had the fortune (or misfortune) to be one of the Republican leaders during Watergate. I saw our system under severe attack. But I also saw that our Constitution worked, not only when times were good, but when times were bad. We owe a great deal to those who wrote the Constitution and to those who served in the Congress over the last 200 plus years keeping our country free. Governmental service is an incredible challenge and opportunity. Hopefully, this book will give you a better feel for the people who make it work and the problems they face.

Notes:

1.H. L. Mencken, *Prejudice: Fourth Series* (New York: Alfred Knopf, Inc., 1924; renewal copyright 1952 by H. L. Mencken).

Introduction

Michael T. Hayes
Colgate University

As Lou Frey observed in his Preface, the American people don't appreciate the contribution Congress makes to our system of government. Opinion surveys show that many Americans have lost confidence in their government in recent years. They distrust politicians and Washington in general. They are impatient with gridlock, and they believe something happens to corrupt, or at least coopt, good people once they get to Washington. They see an "Inside-the-Beltway" mentality that is out of touch with the people, and they feel government can no longer be trusted to do the right thing most of the time.[1] A piece of irreverent graffiti I read recently expresses this attitude well: If pro is the opposite of con, then progress must be the opposite of Congress.

This attitude is not confined to the layman. According to many reform-minded political scientists, our system of checks-and-balances makes it impossible to meet the serious challenges our nation faces today. James MacGregor Burns is the most prominent contemporary advocate of reforms that would make the U.S. political system more like the British parliamentary system, either by moving toward a system of ideological, responsible parties or by strengthening the presidency at the expense of Congress.[2]

The case for majoritarian democracy can be traced back to Woodrow Wilson in the late 19th century. Like Burns, Wilson favorably contrasted the British parliamentary system with the American system of "congressional government," calling for a strengthening of the presidency through a variety of measures designed to reduce the independence of Congress. He also called for a strong rhetorical presidency in which the president, as the sole elected official representing the entire nation, would champion the larger, national interest against narrow special interests and the local constituencies represented by individual legislators.[3]

Wilson's case rested on the assumption that all any legislative body can really do is approve or withhold approval from initiatives advanced by the executive. Although this may seem like a very limited and reactive role, Parliament nevertheless performs a vital function in the British system, educating the public and legitimating government policy by subjecting legislative proposals to open and principled debate. By contrast, the American system, in Wilson's view, is inevitably dominated by strong committees that are typically responsive to narrow, special interests; such a system fails to advance or debate any coherent program. To the contrary, the legislative program in any given Congress consists of nothing more than the sum of the initiatives flowing out of the various committees. To make matters worse, the constitutional division of powers between Congress and the executive makes it impossible for voters to hold anyone accountable for performance in office.

Wilson, and more recently Burns, correctly identify the drawbacks of the American system. The case for the superiority of the parliamentary system has been advanced eloquently by a number of writers over the years, including the late Eugene Forsey, whose work, *How Canadians Govern Themselves,* remains the definitive treatment of the Canadian constitutional system.[4] Chapter 17 of this volume provides a discussion of party government in Canada, adapted from Forsey's work.

If legislatures are to be judged by their capacity to approve or withhold approval of initiatives originating with the executive, as Wilson suggests, it is worth asking in this Introduction which system actually permits the legislature to say no to the executive and prevail. Within a two-party parliamentary system like Britain's (or Canada's much of the time), passage of the Cabinet's program is virtually automatic. Indeed, this is the basis of its appeal to reformers like Wilson and Burns. If rank-and-file members must vote with the party to have any chance of advancing to leadership positions, and if a defeat of a major government initiative forces dissolution of the government, then the parliament will be extremely reluctant to say no to the executive.

By contrast, within the American system, Congress is well-positioned to block the president's program, even where both houses are under the control of the president's party. The defeat of President Clinton's comprehensive health care reform in 1994 is only one of many examples that could be cited in this regard. Here, the government does not fall when Congress defeats a presidential initiative, and members of Congress are nominated and elected locally, effectively removing them from control by the president or party leaders.

The net effect is to enhance the role of deliberation and reduce the role of coercion within our system. Where individual members of Congress are free to vote their consciences, they must be persuaded, or at least induced, to go along with the president's program. By contrast, where career advancement is controlled by party leaders, as in the British and Canadian systems, backbenchers have little choice but to vote with their party. The threat of coercion may be implicit, but it is still there. In the words of one Canadian Member of Parliament, backbenchers fall in line like trained seals.[5]

Where a parliamentary system fosters accountability by presenting voters with parties that promise to vote together as teams in support of a common program, the

American system makes it hard for voters to hold anyone responsible for policy outcomes. Indeed, within the American system it is often difficult, if not impossible, to say definitively just who "the government" is. However, by forcing presidents and party leaders to rely on persuasion rather than coercion, our system encourages a genuine deliberation on the merits of public policy proposals in a way the parliamentary system does not.

To return to Wilson's criterion, within our system, the legislature is truly free to say no to the executive. When Congress says no to the president, it is merely saying no to a particular initiative. Because we have a system of fixed terms, the government does not fall. The president will continue in office until the next election, as will the individual members of Congress. There are distinct limits to what party leaders in Congress can do to affect the career advancement of maverick members, and the president is without any power at all to inflict punishment on dissenting members.

Moreover, within the American system, the president has no monopoly on the legislative initiative. The president's program is only one part of Congress's agenda, albeit an important one. Much legislation originates outside the party leadership with individual members.

If there is one theme that recurs throughout the chapters of this volume, it is this sense of having made a difference in the lives of people and the affairs of our nation through legislative service. Without exception, the contributors to this volume, like Lou Frey, have a love affair going with our country and our system of government. Many express a sense of awe upon seeing the Capitol building for the first time. Most never lose this sense of awe. They combine this reverence for our system with a practical sense of how an individual person—as Lou Frey puts it, your friend and neighbor—can go to Washington and make a difference. They want you to understand that you can make a difference in the same way, and they want to encourage *you* to become involved as they did.

The chapters in Part One all focus on how individual citizens can make a difference through involvement in our government. The chapters in Parts Two and Three address the practical problems of getting elected, settling into Washington, and finding a niche. Parts Four and Five provide perspectives on the two major institutional forces shaping the policy decisions of Congress: political parties and congressional committees. Part Six focuses on key elements in the members' environment: interest groups, constituents, and the media. The chapters in Part Seven provide personal accounts of how individual members can have an impact on domestic and foreign policy. Part Eight concludes the volume with a variety of perspectives on how Congress has evolved over time and whether it might function better if organized differently.

Congress is the greatest deliberative body in the world, and the delay and compromise that Americans dislike so much are the prices we pay for a system that enhances persuasion at the expense of coercion. Voters are notorious for hating Congress and loving their congressman. Hopefully this volume will encourage you to appreciate both.

In addition to reading and commenting on the chapters, Lou Frey worked tirelessly to urge former members to contribute to this volume; publication of this book is a tribute to his energy and enthusiasm, as all the contributors recognize. I would like to thank each one of the contributors to this volume for their understanding, patience, and cooperation. Without exception, they put a great deal of time and thought into their chapters. Many have rewritten chapters in response to my suggestions—some more than once. All have accepted without complaint the need to edit and shorten chapters in order to reduce the overall length of the book and keep the final product affordable for students. It has been a real pleasure to work with each of these authors. Special thanks are due also to Linda Reed, Executive Director of the U.S. Association of Former Members of Congress, who provided invaluable assistance at key points along the way.

I would also like to thank three people at the University Press of America: Peter Cooper, who recognized the potential of this project very early on and was a consistent source of advice and encouragement, and Beverly Baum and Helen Hudson, who guided me through the process of producing camera-ready copy.

Finally, I would like to thank our departmental secretary, Cindy Terrier, who made an enormous contribution to this book, particularly by scanning and converting these chapters into a common word processing format and by managing my correspondence with this very large number of authors. Without her help, this project could not have been completed.

Notes:

1. See John R. Hibbing and Elizabeth Theiss-Morse, *Congress as Public Enemy: Public Attitudes Toward American Institutions* (New York: Cambridge University Press, 1995).

2. James MacGregor Burns, *The Deadlock of Democracy: Four-Party Politics in America* (Englewood Cliffs, N.J.: Prentice-Hall, 1963); James MacGregor Burns with L. Marvin Overby, *Cobblestone Leadership: Majority Rule, Minority Power* (Norman: University of Oklahoma Press, 1990). More recently, see James MacGregor Burns and Georgia J. Sorenson, *Dead Center: Clinton-Gore Leadership and the Perils of Moderation* (New York: Scribner, 1999.)

3. Woodrow Wilson, *Congressional Government: A Study in American Politics*, 15th ed. (Boston: Houghton, Mifflin and Company, 1885); and *Constitutional Government in the United States* (New York: Columbia University Press, 1921).

4. Eugene A. Forsey, *How Canadians Govern Themselves*, 3d ed. (Ottawa: Public Information Office, House of Commons, Canada, 1991).

5. Gordon Aiken, *The Backbencher: Trials and Tribulations of a Member of Parliament* (Toronto: McClelland and Stewart Limited, 1974).

Part One

Making a Difference

While the contributors to this volume differ in many respects--political party, ideology, district composition, and gender, among other things--they are united in their sense that serving in the House of Representatives enabled them to make a difference in the lives of people. The selections in Part One all illustrate this theme.

Romano Mazzoli describes the many jobs performed by members of Congress. In addition to lawmaking, members must also engage in "casework," solving problems for constituents. If they do their jobs properly, they also educate citizens as to how the legislative process works and why it sometimes works better than others. Finally, members also must be successful politicians inasmuch as reelection is a prerequisite to all the other ways in which members serve the public. Mazzoli also reflects on the various lessons he learned from his years in the House, centering on the importance of friends, families, learning from ordinary people, and humility.

Elizabeth Holtzman tells what it was like to be the youngest woman ever elected to the U.S. House and describes her struggles to make a difference as one of only a few women serving in the House. Representative Holtzman did not consider herself a feminist when she first entered the House; she believed in equality for women, but had never really experienced discrimination. Serving in the House educated her as to the extent of discrimination against women, and she tells how she was able to make a difference on a number of women's issues. She also tells how she was able to play a major role on other issues as well: ending the Vietnam War, deporting Nazi war criminals, and participating in the impeachment of Richard Nixon.

In a similar manner, Robert Garcia became increasingly aware of his Hispanic cultural heritage through his service in the House. He recounts his efforts to make a difference for his constituents both through legislation and by expanding and empowering the Hispanic Caucus in Congress.

Finally, Denny Smith tells us what it was like to take on the Pentagon, not as a liberal instinctively distrustful of the military, but rather as a conservative Republican seeking genuine military preparedness with a minimum of waste and corruption.

Chapter 1

Ron, What Really Did You Do All Those Years in Washington?

Romano L. Mazzoli (D-Kentucky)

The most frequently-asked question I have confronted since retiring from Congress after 24 years of service in the House of Representatives is: "Ron, we know you were in Congress in Washington for a long time - 20 years or something like that. But, just out of curiosity, what did you do while you were there? In other words, Ron, what did you do for a living?"

At first, I was a bit nonplused by this kind of question and by the frequency of it. But, then it dawned on me that what I did - and my colleagues and I collectively did - in the Congress was and remains a bit of a mystery to even the most informed and conscientious citizen/voter among us.

THE MEMBER WEARS MANY "HATS"

I usually have responded to this question along the following lines: I can best describe what I "did for a living" while in Washington by characterizing my activities as "hats" which I wore sometimes consecutively and sometimes simultaneously.

The Legislator as Lawmaker

The first "hat" which I wore was that of a lawmaker. At the root and core of what an elected legislator in any assembly—and, certainly, any elected member of the U.S. Congress—does is to make law. We lawmakers do not make law individually, of course, but we make laws in the context of an assembly or a congress (small c) in which members come together from various constituencies, backgrounds, and regions of the country representing a bewildering variety of viewpoints. In that complex and confusing context, we create laws which will apply to all of our constituents and all of the citizens of the United States.

I explain that laws are made in the U.S. Congress, and in most other legislative assemblies, via the committee system. In the House of Representatives, there are 19 standing committees representing all of the various activities and constitutional powers of the central government. These 19 committees deliberate and decide upon legislative proposals falling within their jurisdiction. Proposals, which are approved by the standing committees following lengthy hearings, debates, and mark ups, will then be reported through the Rules Committee to the full House of Representatives for further debate and for ultimate acceptance or rejection. (The Senate's system is different but similar.)

What the House of Representatives and the Senate working separately and together do with respect to legislation is, however, not the final word. The genius of our nation's founders was that they established a government of checks and balances with built in "deliberativeness," a term which is used repeatedly in texts—such as the one recently co-authored by former U.S. Representative Abner Mikva—describing the legislative process. Deliberativeness means essentially that the combination of a bicameral congress and the presidential veto slow the lawmaking process down and make it more deliberate and, in that process, deliberativeness, hopefully, makes the final product more likely to be a product of genuine consensus and, therefore, more likely to be acceptable to the American people if it becomes the law of the land.

I also tell my questioners that laws are made in a setting in which members of the House and Senate are "juggling lots of balls" in the air at the same time. Among these balls is a packed schedule of office appointments, committee meetings, constituent briefings, staff meetings, White House conferences, fund-raisers, and frenzied trips to the airport to catch planes. And, each year as the member or senator gains seniority and increased committee responsibilities, the schedule becomes even more demanding and frenetic.

Even as a member is in his or her office on the Hill, constituents drop by (sometimes with and sometimes without appointments) who must be seen and accommodated, though these moments interrupt the tempo and pace of business. Even as a member is in his or her committee room attending a hearing and trying to concentrate on the statements of the witnesses, the bells ring signaling a vote which triggers a headlong dash of members of Congress and senators to the subways and through the tunnels and garages and across the sidewalks and lawns of Capitol Hill to reach the respective floor before the end of the allotted time for the vote.

These treks to the floor are not just journeys, but "seminars on the run," as the member or senator tries to determine the nature of the upcoming vote from notes stuffed in his or her pockets, from briefing books, and from whispers-in-the-ear by a staff member racing to keep up with his or her boss. Even as a member or senator is on the floor trying to get last-second information before voting from colleagues who sit on the committees or who have taken part in the debate, a page or a floor attendant will tender a note that a phone call is waiting in the Cloakroom from his or her staff, from a constituent, from the White House, from the press, or a trade group representative. Also, a member or senator while on the floor is often summoned by a doorkeeper to meet a staffer or a reporter or a constituent in the outer hall adjacent to the House floor who needs a moment or wants a quote.

Even as a member or senator leaves home in the morning expecting the day to be tractable and expecting a reasonable adjournment hour allowing time for family and children or an early flight back to the home district, a call comes from leadership that important votes have been added to the day's agenda. Then comes a mad dash to the telephones to reschedule family events, receptions, and airline reservations with all the attendant apologies, explanations, and red faces which ensue.

This is not to say that a member of Congress is more harried or harassed than a business executive, an entrepreneur, or a working mother or father, but it is to say that the lawmaking "hat" which members wear can sometimes be a tight fit. And it also suggests that, given this kind of ambience for lawmaking, the miracle is not that an occasional bill will become law which is not well thought-out and does not have all of the t's crossed and i's dotted, but that the bulk of the laws which Congress passes and which are signed by the president into law are, in fact, well thought-out and do have the t's crossed and the i's dotted.

The Legislator as Caseworker

I then tell my listener that a second "hat" which I wore when I served in Congress was that of caseworker. Casework is the term used on Capitol Hill to designate the kind of problem-solving, red tape-cutting, free-up-the-log-jam type of work given to a member or senator by constituents and others to which staff time and energy and, of course, the legislator's time and energy must be devoted.

It was once said by a congressional critic that if government worked the way it was designed to work, members of Congress would need fewer staff and would be less harried because they would not have the casework to shoe-horn into an already busy lawmaking and travel schedule. This may be true, but, in the imperfect world in which we live, there will always be governmental slip-ups, foul-ups, snafus, and assorted glitches and mistakes which a member of Congress will be asked to correct for his or her constituents or for some person or entity in need.

One of the few pledges I made in my first congressional campaign in 1970 was to open my congressional office in the Federal Building in Louisville (which, due to the great generosity and kindness of my colleagues, has now been named the Romano L. Mazzoli Federal Building) in order to be at the hub of the federal "wheel" and, thus, be where people come to seek redress for problems and grievances with federal agencies and federal programs.

We had no sooner opened our new federal office in January 1971 than my first administrative assistant—and my late and very dear personal friend, Cecil Noel—got a call from a constituent with a passport problem. Cecil and I solved that problem, and we earned for our office and ourselves a reputation, in that very early moment of my career, as an office which worked hard for the people and which got the job done. And because there is such a thing as "word of mouth advertising" even in the congressional realm, our office became the popular port of call for all manner of casework from all kinds of people including those who did not even live in the district.

If the truth be known, I was happy to be known as the "casework congressman." I derived more personal pleasure and satisfaction and fulfillment as a member of Congress from the opportunity that my office and my vote gave me to help people with their various and legion problems than even from the opportunity to initiate, or help craft, a piece of legislation which had national or even international implications such as the well known Simpson-Mazzoli Immigration Bill of 1986 (on which I worked for three Congresses with my dear friend, Senator Al Simpson).

This may or may not have been the best way to organize my office. And, casework may or may not have been the correct priority for my time and energy as a member of Congress. However, I always had a belief and a feeling that the people were entitled to a government which operated as it was designed to operate. And, when government failed to operate in that fashion, I felt that the nation's elected representatives and senators had the obligation to rectify the situation to the extent they could.

Members of the House of Representatives return to their home districts frequently—quite often weekly—despite sometimes great distances and many time zone changes. Since my district was only an hour away from Washington by air and because I maintained a home in Louisville during all the years of my service in Washington, I was home virtually weekly. Accordingly, I heard from constituents frequently and face-to-face about what pleased them so far as my service was concerned.

Consistently, what seemed to please my constituents and to earn applause for my office was the way we handled casework and our success rate with it. I believe our success stemmed more from hard work and determination than from special insight or sophisticated knowledge of bureaucratic functioning. But, certainly, now that I am back home and living every day among my former constituents, I am very pleased that our office emphasized the human dimension of government and the personal dimension of representative democracy.

The Legislator as Teacher

I also tell my questioners that a third "hat" which I wore as a member of Congress—again, sometimes these hats are worn sequentially, but often they are worn simultaneously—was that of communicator, teacher, elucidator, and commentator. By this I mean that one of the hats which I wore rested upon the head of a person whose responsibility it was to explain the governmental process to constituents, taxpayers, citizens, students, and the general public—and not only to explain the process but also to explain why it seemed to work better on some occasions than on others.

Many of us wore this hat by holding frequent meetings with constituents—the famous town hall meetings. I would sometimes approach this function quite simply by setting up a table in a concourse of a shopping mall. On other occasions, I would convene formal meetings, in large meeting halls with microphones, story boards, and cameras preceded by mailed announcements to constituents of the time, place, and location of my meeting. But, whether these meetings were informal or quite formal, their essence, as I saw it, was to demystify and demythologize government and to inform the people about their government and about the issues.

Perhaps my decision to leave a very fine law firm here in Louisville, which I joined after retiring voluntarily from Congress in 1995, to become a full-time teaching Fellow at the University of Louisville stems from the delight and pleasure which I derived from all my town hall meetings over all the years and from my frequent visits to classrooms, from kindergarten to postgraduate, while in office.

I don't think members of Congress have a special gift for teaching. However, all of us who have ever served in Congress have had an intense experience with both the process and the substance of our form of tripartite government. Because of this matchless experience, I believe members and former members are invaluable resources to the nation's educational institutions and to their students, particularly those students who may have some desire or inclination to enter public life. For example, I particularly enjoy the Congress to Campus Program jointly sponsored by the U.S. Association of Former Members of Congress and the John Stennis Center for Public Service at Mississippi State University. I have taken part in several of these programs in which bipartisan delegations of former members of Congress spend a day or two on a college campus to speak with students, faculty, and administrators on topics involving government and politics. This is a perfect example of a win-win program.

One of my responsibilities at the University of Louisville is to teach in its Louis D. Brandeis School of Law. I endeavor each semester to feature guest lecturers—including former and sitting House and Senate colleagues—from the legislative and executive branches of federal, state, and local government.

Inevitably, at the end of the semester when the course evaluations are submitted by the students, they comment that these classroom visits by those who have "walked the walk and talked the talk" have provided immeasurably effective and gainful learning experiences for them.

It is also fair to say that a former member is able quite often to evaluate and comment upon a public policy issue raised by a student with more candor and balance than when that man or woman actually served in the Congress, since the constituent pressures and the parochial and local interests are no longer factors in framing a response to a particular question.

The Legislator as Politician

I also tell my questioners that yet another "hat" which I wore as a member of Congress was that of a politician. Obviously, in order to wear the hats of a lawmaker, a caseworker, or a communicator, one must be elected. So, one must always wear the hat of the politician, even as the other hats are being put on and taken off. A member has to stay in touch with the constituency, has to be aware of movements and changes within it, has to be alert to both partisan and nonpartisan political activity in his or her community and throughout the electoral district, and has to maintain cordial and professional relationships with organized groups and political forces in the district or the member will not remain in office. Then, off will come all the hats.

In one respect, it is a bit easier for members of the House of Representatives to keep their political hats firmly on their heads because members of the House, with two-year terms, are traditionally more prone to either maintain their homes in their districts—never moving their families to Washington—or to make frequent, even weekly or biweekly, trips to the district.

Each such trip offers up a broad menu of civic and political events to attend. Each of these is an opportunity for the member to address certain issues of interest, concern—even alarm!—raised by constituents, to be visible to a particular interest group which can be influential in an election and, most of all, if the member or senator has his or her eyes and ears open, to return to Washington armed with ideas to be developed into legislation and with problems which need to be solved.

Unfortunately, from the time that I was first elected to Congress in 1970 to the time that I retired in 1995, the "political hat" was resized—dramatically—by money and the quest for it in the form of campaign contributions in order to stay in office. Accordingly, more and more over the years I served, the member wore the political hat to "dial for dollars" or to plan various fund-raising events for past as well as prospective future donors.

My wife, Helen, and I began our political campaigns literally over a card table and under an incandescent light bulb in our basement on Ardmore Drive. We had no money, but we did have a host of loyal friends who spread the "good news" about Ron Mazzoli. We mounted the quintessential grassroots campaign which involved a lot of people, not all of whom were of the same political persuasion and not all of whom held to the same political philosophy. The glue that held our grassroots campaign together was not political orthodoxy, but boyhood or girlhood palship, church affiliation, or school, family, or neighborhood ties. Unfortunately, nowadays, it seems that the only glue which binds campaigns together is money and the things money can purchase in the form of polls, focus groups, campaign managers, and media coverage. It's a whole lot tougher for young people to get started in politics these days, and that is quite a shame.

I tell my listeners that these four hats do not exhaust the number of hats that a member can wear in the course of his or her career. Sometimes you wear the hat of an advocate for a cause, sometimes you wear the hat of a negotiator or conciliator, and sometimes you wear the hat of the deal-maker trying to pull together the various financial strings needed for a major economic development project to move forward. But, one way or the other and of one description or another, a member of Congress wears many "hats."

A MEMBER LEARNS MANY LESSONS

After I complete my "hat trick" and explain to the questioner what I did for a living while I was in Washington, very often my questioner will shift gears and ask: "Okay, Ron, now that we know what you did those years in Washington, can you tell me if you learned anything of value while you were there?"

I try to answer this profound question in a fairly simple way by referring to the famous book written by Robert Fulghum called *All I Really Need to Know I Learned in Kindergarten.* This is to say that life's most important lessons are usually self-evident and simple and, in fact, they're pretty much known to us in early stages of our life, if not actually in kindergarten. This is also to say that sometimes we look at life in a much too complicated way and we lose life's essence in the midst of all these abstractions and complications. This is the "can't see the forest for the trees" syndrome.

Lesson 1: The Importance of Family, Faith, and Friends

So to answer the question of what, if anything, I learned in Congress, I usually resort to something along the following lines: Well, the first thing I learned in Washington was that family, faith, and friends are the most important factors in life and, paradoxically, they are the very factors, despite their importance, which we tend to reject, ignore, shortchange, or generally de-emphasize in the course of our carving out a career in public life.

I should add that any of these lessons which I will discuss in this chapter are as applicable to a career in public accountancy, medicine, carpentry, or plumbing as they are to a career in public life. Life today is very complicated and complex, demanding and time-consuming no matter what one does for a living. But, despite our opportunities to do immense good for an immense number of people, at the end of the day, in whatever profession or pursuit we choose, our attainments should not come at the expense of family, faith, or friends.

I recognize that many members decide to keep their families at home for various reasons. However, for Helen and me that was not a real option. We desired very much to have our family together as a unit during those early years when Michael and Andrea were young and needed the nurture and the comfort that parents alone can provide. Accordingly, despite the financial burden, we moved our family to the Washington area—precisely Alexandria, Virginia—in the late summer of 1973 following two-and-a-half years of weekly commutes between my office in the Longworth House Office Building on Capitol Hill and our home on Ardmore Drive.

Having the kids with us through the week enabled us to have a more normal family life. We could and did take full advantage of PTA meetings, sporting events, and musical activities in which Mike and Andrea took part while in grade and high school. Being together as a family also, I believe, kept my feet on the ground and enabled me to retain a better perspective on the real priorities of life compared to the priorities which a congressional life emphasizes. While what worked for Helen and me might not work for others, I am content that we made the right decision.

In context of priorities, I could never forget the statement that my former House colleague, friend, and paddleball partner Paul Tsongas made upon his retirement from the Senate because of an illness (which many years later took his life). Paul said that on one's deathbed one never says, "I wish I'd spent more time at the office." The temptation in today's world of public life with its immense pressures and its intense pleasures is to "spend more time at the office" than one should. This is a simple lesson, but a profoundly important one which I learned pretty quickly in my congressional life.

Lesson 2: Don't Let Your Status Go to Your Head

Another of my lessons learned in Congress is that one should never succumb to the temptation to be smug. There is nothing less elegant and unseemly or more off-putting and truly foolish than to be smug. I think all of us who have served in Congress have heard the famous—and perhaps apocryphal—story about the new member who upon first meeting a veteran but rumpled and unprepossessing colleague in the House or Senate will say: "I wonder how he (or she) ever got here." Then, as the story goes, a few months later, upon finding that the very colleague who failed to make a memorable initial impression turns out to be an adroit and effective legislative tactician, a skilled debater, and an insightful legislator, the new member will muse: "How in the world did I ever get here?!"

The reason why it is so foolish to be smug is that around the next corner in Washington (or Frankfort, Springfield, or Sacramento) is someone who is a better speaker, who is more intelligent, and who is a better legislative strategist. So it pays to be modest in the correct sense of that word: Do not overestimate yourself and certainly do not underestimate your colleague either.

Lesson 3: People Are Prophets, so Listen to the People

There is another lesson which I learned while in Congress. This lesson is that "The words of the prophets are written on subway walls and tenement halls." This is, of course, a line from "Sounds of Silence" by the duo of Paul Simon and Art Garfunkel, who performed mainly in the 1970s and '80s.

We are familiar with the words of the prophets such as Micah, Ezekiel, Jeremiah, and Isaiah. We also are familiar with the fact that the words of these prophets repose in the Bible, with ornate pages illumined by the monks during the Dark Ages, in the Torah, kept in a very sacred place and opened only amid great ceremony and solemnity, and in the Koran, where they are treated with reverence and respect as sanctified writings.

Why then would Simon and Garfunkel have suggested that the words of prophets would be found on subway walls and tenement halls where only the poor, the dispossessed, and the homeless live and frequent? I suspect that what Paul Simon had in mind—he wrote most of the lyrics for the group—is that we all tend to overlook the wisdom, insights, and inspiration that come to us from very common people in very common situations. For example, from the barber, the hairdresser, the cab driver, the storekeeper, the clerk of court, and the passerby as well as the panhandler.

For my part, I always made it a point while in Congress to talk with the Capitol Police and the Doorkeepers, the Clerks, and the waiters and waitresses. I always spent time with the Democratic and Republican Cloakroom staff and with my Pages and interns. I never came away from these exchanges empty handed.

This is certainly not to say that I did not learn from the great and wise leaders of the nation and world who spoke to Congress in Joint Session, including U.S. presidents—going back, in my case, to President Nixon. Nor did I fail to gain immensely from the testimony of witnesses in Committee hearings and from conversations with colleagues and committee staff. But if we only look to the great and the talented and the renowned and the accomplished for our wisdom and information, we will lose out on many opportunities to gain both insight and information from the simple, the uncomplicated, and the common people around us.

I am reminded of a story I heard once from a political consultant who was jetting from coast to coast handling the campaign of a major political figure. She jumped into a cab at the hotel bound for the airport. She had her cell phone and briefcase out for some last-minute work, but the cabby attempted to start a conversation. She emphatically brushed off the cab driver and turned to her work. It happened that the candidate whose campaign she managed lost.

I have no idea if the cab driver would have been able to tell this campaign consultant anything of value regarding the way the campaign was going or regarding the way the candidate was handling the issues. But it is at least arguably possible that a few minutes conversing with the cab driver might have been more profitable than sorting through her e-mail and returning her phone calls. Often, the cab drivers, the hairdressers, and the convenient shop clerks know more of what is happening in campaigns than do the candidate and his or her workers. So, the lesson is to keep our ears and eyes open. There is much wisdom we will glean that can be put to good use for ourselves and for our country.

Lesson 4: Everyone Has to Carry Out the Garbage

Another lesson I learned while in Washington was that in life, one has to carry out the garbage.

In our career in Washington, Helen and I were invited to two State Dinners at the White House. One was when the president of Italy, President Francesco Cossiga, came to Washington and the other was when then-Prime Minister of Canada, Brian Mulroney, was in the United States for discussions with the president. A State Dinner is an absolutely elegant occasion. Those invited are treated royally. They are met at the White House entrance portico and assisted from their automobiles by attendants in uniform. Then the guests in tuxedos and ball gowns are shown into the White House to the melodies of chamber music. The guests are escorted to the receiving line to meet and greet the president, the first lady, and the visiting heads of state.

Then come the scintillating pre-meal conversations with talented and accomplished people from the world of public service and from every possible discipline and pursuit. In addition, there is the beautiful silverware, the sparkling crystal, the spotless linens, the gourmet meal, and the table talk. Following the meal, there are elaborate and witty toasts from the president of the United States and from the foreign leader to the assemblage. Following these memorable toasts, the group leaves the State Dining Room and reassembles in the East Room of the White House for the after-dinner entertainment, which is always top caliber. Then there is dancing with one's spouse in the magical and lyrical setting of the White House with its magnificent decorations and historical ambiance.

When the evening is over, the member and his spouse move down the hallway to the portico and the awaiting car. The doors are opened and the attendants assist you into the car—the '85 Chevy Cavalier seems oddly discordant with the elegant setting—and soon you are driving across the 14th Street Bridge still in your tuxedo and your wife still in her beautiful ball gown thinking of the wonderful experience of a few minutes earlier with all its drama, glamour, and festivity. The memories will live forever.

Soon the car nudges into the familiar driveway in front of the familiar home in Alexandria. The key is turned in the ignition. The engine is silent. The doors are opened and the member still in his tuxedo and his spouse still in her ball gown step out onto the driveway. They then come to the sudden realization that "tomorrow is garbage day." Accordingly, the member in his tuxedo and his spouse in her beautiful ball gown carry the garbage out to the curb.

This is a true story, and it does illustrate many things beyond the literal fact that the garbage has to be taken out to the curb or it will not be picked up. The essence of this story is that, unless in life one is willing to do the routine, the "scut work"—the carrying out of the garbage, if you will—then one probably is not going to be invited to the Big Dance.

It was once said by a pop philosopher that life is 90 percent showing up. Which is to say that life is not always intellect, insight, and analysis. It is simply getting up in the morning, grabbing one's lunch bucket (or briefcase, laptop, wrench, or other tools of the trade), going down to the corner, grabbing the bus (or getting into the Lexus, Mercedes, Explorer, or chauffeured car), and punching-in for another 8, 10, 12, or 15 hours of hard work, most of which is unheralded and basically unnoticed except to the individual doing the work. It is, however, in this rather undramatic, lack7luster, commonplace, and routine setting that we gain the knowledge, experience, and substance to move forward in life and to do things of value for ourselves, our families, and our fellow man and woman.

In this context, I always think of my late friends and former Kentucky delegation colleagues, Congressman Carl Perkins of Hindman and Congressman William Natcher of Bowling Green. Both of these men were giants in the legislative arena: Congressman Perkins in education, labor, and human resource-related matters and Congressman Natcher in identifying and funding the nation's needs. If alive today, both readily would agree that their success in Congress came not solely—or even strongly—because of their intellect or their strategic legislative knowledge, but because of their ability to put in hour after hour, day after day, month after month, year after year of hard, dry, and routine committee work to lay the predicate for the relatively brief but dramatic, exciting, and scintillating experience later on the House floor when a bill passed or in the Rose Garden when it was signed into law.

There are many, many illustrations of the adage that one must be prepared to "carry out the garbage" if one expects to do anything of value and worth later on. But, it is an oft-forgotten message and an oft-ignored admonition. Precisely because we are always more prone to look for the glitz and glamour than for the "garbage," we are the poorer as individuals and as nations.

Lesson 5: Life Is About Making a Difference

My final lesson also falls into the above category of being simple and not original. It is that life is not just for making a living, but it is for making a difference.

Fortunately, during my career in Congress, my family and I were able by reason of our background and family experience to live within my congressional salary. We had no "toys" before coming to Congress. We acquired no toys during my career. So, I was able to make a living for my family and me, and, in the process, also to make a difference.

I know of no profession other than the ministry or, perhaps, medicine that enables a man or woman to be more closely involved in the welfare and well-being of his or her fellow. Because, as I mentioned earlier, one of the major elements of congressional life is casework—that is, problem-solving for constituents—members of Congress have a wonderful opportunity by the use of their office and by the devotion of their staff's time and energies to solve numerous problems and cut through miles of red tape to benefit their constituents.

Each time a case is solved or a check released, a difference is made in someone's life. Some of these differences are not monumental nor are they permanent. Some of these differences may not be essential nor even deserved. But, differences are and were made, people are and were touched, and lives are and were affected. I believe that this is why I loved and enjoyed my 24 years in the House of Representatives so much. Even as I was making a living, I was making a difference.

I did not feel this same sense of making a difference when I joined a law firm soon after my retirement from Congress. As I became more active at the University of Louisville, my law school *alma mater*, as a visiting professor, as a member of the school's Alumni Association, and as a member of the university's Board of Overseers, I found again that sense of "making a difference." So, I left the law firm and joined the University in a full-time capacity as a Fellow in Law and Public Policy.

There will probably never be in my lifetime an opportunity similar to the one I had while a member of Congress to make a difference for the good for my fellow man and woman. But, I am finding, quite happily and most refreshingly, that in working with students at the University in a teaching, mentoring, and nurturing capacity, I am again making a difference.

The moral here is that there is "life after Congress."

Chapter 2

The Youngest Woman
Elected to Congress

Elizabeth Holtzman (D-NY)

I was elected to Congress in 1972, in the midst of the Vietnam War. I had run on an anti-war platform, and rode the surge of protest to victory in the Democratic primary. (In my moderately liberal Brooklyn, New York district, winning the primary was tantamount to winning the election.) My victory was a great upset, since I defeated the 84-year-old dean of the House of Representatives, Emanuel Celler. No one had given me a chance of winning because I was unknown, underfunded, a woman, and young. (I was so obscure, that the newspapers didn't even use my name in headlines announcing my victory; "Celler Foe Wins" is what they trumpeted.) My campaign was also desperately underfinanced. I had only just started practicing law (taking off a couple of years to work as an assistant to New York City's mayor), *and* my parents were not rich. With a bare $36,000 in campaign funds, we couldn't afford any polls or television ads. But with lots of shoe leather and volunteers, I was able to stitch together a serendipitous triumph.

Winning the election was one thing; being a congresswoman was something else. One of my first tasks involved finding a place to live—both in Washington and in New York. Before I ran for Congress, I had moved in with my parents; but the state legislature, to help my opponent, drew new congressional lines that put my parent's house outside the district. So, I had to find a place in the district. With the help of a campaign aide, I was able to locate a relatively nice one-bedroom apartment close to my district office. In Washington, the search was not as successful. A friend had hosted a welcoming party for me at her house in Georgetown. I was smitten. A house, I thought to myself, that is really what I would like. But with a salary of $42,000 and all my savings used up in the campaign, buying a house seemed out of the question financially. So I settled on a sterile apartment whose main attraction was its proximity to the Capitol; naively, I thought I could walk to work. But, it turned out to be far too dangerous to walk home at night, although I sometimes walked to my office in the morning. My Washington apartment came furnished, so it never really felt like home. At least in Brooklyn, I had my books and records and all my own things.

Living in two apartments at once proved to be something of a nightmare. I could never keep straight where the milk was fresh. Although I kept some clothes in Washington, I generally brought several outfits down with me each week. But that was always a precarious gambit; somehow, something wasn't there that I needed—a piece of jewelry, a different blouse, or, simply, pantyhose without runs.

The schedule, too, was exhausting. When Congress was in session, I would come down on to Washington on Tuesday morning and return to New York on Thursday night. But often I had to leave on Monday and return on Friday. When the House Judiciary Committee took up the impeachment of President Richard Nixon, it was a round-the-clock timetable.

But it wasn't as though being back in New York was a vacation. Fridays to Mondays in my district were filled to the brim with appearances at community and citywide events. Also, on Sundays, I had office hours—my constituents could come to see me without an appointment. (I did this because the Brooklyn Democratic machine was out gunning for me. I won on a reform ticket and knew that if I didn't strengthen my ties with the people in my district, I would lose the next election.) During my first term in Congress, I was on the go constantly. Every minute counted. I would drive helter-skelter to and from the airport, catching the planes by the skin of my teeth. I perfected the dash up the steps to the Capitol in very high heels, always arriving out of breath, but generally in time for the first vote. And, even though my work on the Nixon impeachment solidified my standing among the voters of my district, I never really let up.

In fact, the only breathing space I had was on the rare weekends that I decided to stay in Washington. Then, there were no constituents, no events, no press calls tugging at my free time. I could sightsee, read, go to the movies, or visit with friends. I remember taking some wonderful trips on those rare stolen weekends: to Thomas Jefferson's home in Monticello, to civil war battlefields in Virginia, and to the North Carolina coast. Also, once every two years, when I was not up for re-election, I could really take off for the month of our summer vacation. I remember blissful long weeks on Nantucket or Martha's Vineyard. But inevitably, those vacations would get interrupted. Once I had to fly from Martha's Vineyard to Chicago to do the Phil Donahue show.

But don't get me wrong. Those were heady and exciting days; and I was young enough to withstand the incredible pace. Trying to cope with living and working in two places on a frantic, hectic schedule just didn't bother me. Somehow, I knew things would work out—and in general they did.

When I came to Congress in 1973, it's fair to say I wasn't a feminist. Of course, I believed in women's equality. My mother had been a college professor and she, as well as my father, who was a lawyer, made it clear that as a woman I could follow whatever path I chose. But I didn't realize that many people didn't feel that way and so I wasn't really conscious of the discrimination that was so prevalent. After all, I had gotten into one of the country's best colleges and law schools. I was hired by two of New York's finest law firms and got elected to Congress. How serious could the barriers be? When the Harvard College Library excluded all women, my Radcliffe classmates and I ignored the discrimination and pretended that other libraries on campus would do. I never rebelled against my professor at Harvard Law School who refused to call on the women in his class, making us go up to the front of the class on "Ladies Day" to answer his humiliating questions. But neither did any of the other women, including my classmate Elizabeth Dole. I guess I refused to see that these incidents were signs of deeply seated gender bias. Nothing was going to crack the rose-colored glasses with which I was viewing the world.

Being in Congress educated me about the plight of women. What I could push away when it had to do with me personally, I couldn't when it came to my constituents. They taught me through their personal pain, in ways I couldn't ignore, about discrimination—in jobs, in credit, in pensions and insurance— and about violence against women. I also learned from looking around me. In one respect, women were equal in the House: that is the seniority system, by which one rose through the ranks to subcommittee chair and committee chair, was gender neutral. You could be the chair of a committee if you lived long enough and got re-elected enough times. But, there were no women in the House leadership, which required election by one's peers, and the gym, where critical informal contacts with colleagues took place, was off limits to women. We didn't dare make an issue about the gym then, fearing we would be ridiculed.

After a while, I realized that if the congresswomen worked together, we could make more progress on women's rights. In those days, the Congress was much less partisan than it is today. Peggy Heckler, a Republican from Massachusetts, and I decided to form the Congresswomen's Caucus. Soon, all the congresswomen, Republicans and Democrats alike, joined. We tackled lots of issues, including domestic violence, the extension of the ratification deadline for the Equal Rights Amendment, and discrimination against women in the military. It was an important beginning. One of the nice things about the Caucus was that the women got to know each other a lot better, and there were strong, important leaders, many of whom became household names, such as Barbara Jordan, Shirley Chisholm, Pat Schroeder, Barbara Mikulski, Olympia Snowe, Bella Abzug. A number of congresswomen even undertook a humanitarian mission to Cambodia to persuade the government to allow food into the country to feed huge numbers of starving children. It was heartbreaking to see the condition of the children, but we felt tremendous pride when the Cambodian government agreed to our request.

What the public does not often realize is how hard it is to be a really responsible member of Congress. There is so much information you have to master. Every member has to vote on hundreds of bills, not to mention dozens of amendments to those bills, almost all of which will affect people's lives. I had to learn about everything from agricultural subsidies to public works projects around the country. I had to familiarize myself with dozens and dozens of issues, including taxation, education, housing, military weapons, foreign policy, and the environment, just to name a few.

Voting on legislation was only one part of the job. Coming up with your own proposals—making law—was another. Being in Congress allows you to be creative and to find areas where you can get things done. Forming the Congresswomen's Caucus to advance the status of women was one example. Working on Nazi war criminals in the United States was another. In my first term in Congress, someone knowledgeable about the U.S. Immigration Service told me that the agency had a list of Nazi war criminals living in the United States, but was doing nothing about the problem. At a hearing in 1974, the Immigration Commissioner conceded to me that there was such a list. After looking at the files, I learned that nothing was being done to bring these mass murderers to justice. I started a campaign to end this. By the time I left Congress in 1981, I had been able to force the government to create a special Nazi-hunting unit and place it in the Criminal Division of the Justice Department. I also was able to get a law passed (that carries my name) authorizing the deportation of anyone engaged in persecution under the Nazis. As a result, more than 50 mass murderers have been located in the United States and expelled from our country. Our efforts have created a model for the rest of the world.

Other issues that I worked on also produced results. Enlisting the help of a conservative Congressman from Georgia, Billy Lee Evans, I was able to write a federal rape privacy statute, protecting women who are rape victims from being humiliated by cross-examination at trial about their past sexual experiences. It became a model for state efforts. Despite State Department objections, I was able to persuade the government of Vietnam, after the war, to allow refugees to leave by plane from that country instead of having to risk the dangers of fleeing in flimsy boats. The orderly departure program then put into effect in cooperation with the United States saved thousands of lives.

And there are other ways to make a mark. One of the first things I did when I came to Congress was to keep my pledge to oppose the Vietnam War. But what could one person do? I joined with my colleagues and spoke out frequently, but then a unique opportunity arose: I was asked to join four Air Force pilots to bring a lawsuit to stop the bombing of Cambodia. I did. We won the case in the lowest federal court, because Congress had never authorized the bombing and actually had specifically barred it in law after law. The case went to the Supreme Court and Justice Douglas granted an injunction against the bombing. I was thrilled. Unfortunately, Justice Marshall allowed the bombing to go on and the issue became moot before the whole Court could consider it. But it became an important precedent in legal questions about presidential war-making powers.

Without any question, one of the most important and historic aspects of my years in Congress came about through sheer luck. When I won my election, I did not want to be on the House Judiciary Committee. My predecessor, whom I defeated, had served on the committee for 50 years. I wanted to break new ground and do something different. But I couldn't persuade the powers that be, and I was placed on the House Judiciary Committee against my wishes. I was terribly disappointed, and remembered thinking that this loss was not an auspicious beginning to my congressional career. Barely a year later, however, to my amazement and that of my colleagues, we were thrust into historic roles. In October 1973, President Nixon ordered Archibald Cox, the Watergate Special Prosecutor, fired for seeking White House tapes. The Attorney General and Deputy Attorney General of the United States resigned rather than carry out Nixon's order, but an underling fired Cox anyway. These events, known as the Saturday Night Massacre, triggered a huge public outcry, and impeachment proceedings against President Nixon commenced. The House Judiciary Committee and its members became the center of attention.

Impeachment involved an immense amount of work. I had to master the constitutional questions about the meaning of a "high crime and misdemeanor." That meant reading many books and articles about constitutional history. Then there was a huge amount of evidence to study and absorb. Eventually, it became clear to me that the evidence against the president was overwhelming. Voting for his impeachment, however, was a sober and awful responsibility. No one—not even the most partisan Democrat took any pleasure from learning about the great abuses of power and criminal conduct in which our president engaged. We were saddened as well as dismayed to find President Nixon ordering the CIA to stop an FBI investigation into the Watergate break-in, offering presidential pardons to the burglars for their silence, and authorizing the IRS to audit his political enemies. Casting the first vote for impeachment was an extremely unpleasant task for me. The chair of the Judiciary Committee, Peter Rodino, said that after the vote, he went back to his office and cried.

The country accepted the verdict of the House Judiciary Committee. We were fair; Peter Rodino wisely insisted that we bend over backwards to be evenhanded. We were bipartisan—a majority of Republicans joined all the Democrats in voting for impeachment. (Ultimately, when the smoking gun tape was released, every Republican on the Committee publicly supported impeachment.) The chair of our committee understood from the start that the country would not accept a partisan impeachment. We were thorough. The process that started in October was not concluded until the following July. We amassed an enormous amount of evidence, including tapes and live witness testimony.

From the perspective of history, it was particularly dismaying to see the House Judiciary Committee act on the impeachment of President Bill Clinton in an entirely different fashion. The Hyde Judiciary Committee praised our work and promised to follow our example, but ignored our precedent. This proved a disastrous mistake. Ultimately, the Senate and the country rejected the partisan impeachment. The unfair and inadequate work of the House undermined the public's respect for the House and discredited the process so that it may be much more difficult in the future to invoke the impeachment powers even in the face of serious, Watergate types of presidential abuses. Ironically, the impeachment created a new media role for me; with my "niche expertise" on impeachment, I became a "pundit," appearing on endless television programs on the subject. So, you never know where your congressional years will take you.

When I was in Congress, civility generally marked our proceedings. Republicans and Democrats had differences, often strong ones, but we worked to find the common ground. That happened not only during the impeachment process, but in many other circumstances.

The House of Representatives is "the people's house." Every two years, Americans can make their views felt directly in government. Every two years, all House members stand for election. In 1974, in the aftermath of Watergate, Americans wanted to defeat Republicans. In 1994, in the wake of the Clinton Administration's health care fiasco, the people voted Democrats out of power.

Because it is the "people's house," members of the House of Representatives have a special duty to stay in close touch with their constituents and represent their needs—and not the special interests. But in too many instances, that is not the case. The cost of elections has become astronomically high, putting a congressional seat out of the reach of too many. Indeed, if I were starting out today instead of in 1972, I could never get elected. A congressional primary in Brooklyn now costs about $500,000, a sum that would have been impossible for me to raise.

Perhaps that is the reason that my record as the youngest woman ever to be elected to Congress has not been broken yet. (I was 31 when I took office; many younger men have been elected.) Until we have serious campaign finance reform and reduce the costs of running for office, young women, mavericks, idealists, people who have not sold their souls, people who are not rich will have an inordinately difficult time winning a seat in the House. That is a loss for the country; we need the talents of a variety of people in Congress. The large amounts required for congressional campaigns also creates the appearance, if not the reality, that officeholders are beholden to their large contributors. This engenders a dangerous public cynicism about government and helps explain the smaller and smaller number of people voting in congressional elections. The high cost of elections also helps incumbents. More than 70 congresspersons were not even challenged in the 1998 election. Opponents, although unpleasant for the incumbent, help to preserve a vigorous democracy. If anything, campaign finance reform is central to creating a House of Representatives that can truly be, in Abraham Lincoln's words, of the people, by the people, and for the people.

Chapter 3

Constituencies within Congress:
The Experience of an Hispanic Congressman

Robert Garcia (D-New York)

My journey to Congress was anything but typical. I was elected in a special election in 1978 to fill the remainder of the term of my immediate predecessor, Herman Badillo. The newly-elected mayor of New York City, another former member of Congress, Ed Koch, asked Herman to become Deputy Mayor. He accepted, and his seat was open.

I had never aspired to go to Washington. I had a terrific job in the New York State Senate, where I was Deputy Minority Leader. I knew and liked Albany, having served there for 12 years. In addition, as a Deputy Minority Leader, I was not just a rank-in-file member of the Senate. I was a respected member of the Senate leadership. I was so much a part of the action that I was given the "honorary" title of "Conscience of the Senate" by my colleagues for my up-front defense of the poor and disenfranchised. I co-founded, with Assemblyman Percy Sutton, the Black and Puerto Rican Legislative Caucus and through this union found an effective way to get legislation passed through mutual cooperation.

Finally, I love New York. While Albany was not New York City, it was certainly an important part of the State's political culture. Why would I want to go to Washington where I would 435th in seniority and far from the hustle and bustle of the exciting New York politics?

What drove me to go to Washington was my love for the Bronx. I was born and raised in the South Bronx. It had always been home. I went to school and worked there—even sold peanuts at Yankee Stadium. It truly boiled down to the inescapable fact that I sincerely wanted to make a bigger difference in the quality of life of the people who lived there. They were more than just constituents. They were my friends and neighbors. They were my family. The Bronx was home.

While I worked hard to make a difference in Albany for the Bronx, I was intrigued at the possibility of doing more in Washington. In the 1970s, the Bronx was such a symbol of abject urban poverty and decay that some referred to it as a third world country inside the United States. In 1977, President Jimmy Carter came to the South Bronx and talked about putting together a major urban renewal project that would help places like the Bronx. I wanted to be part of that effort. So, after some initial hesitation, I decided to run for Congress.

As difficult as it was for me personally, deciding to run turned out to be the easy part of getting to Congress. Mind you, the Bronx at the time was 93 percent Democratic, and I was a Democrat who had been reelected 13 times by a large portion of the constituency that made up the 21st congressional district. The problem was, I was part of the "new" breed of New York politician. I was a reformer, and as such, I did not always have the support of the local Bronx Democratic party leadership. They were the ones who determined who would get the party's nomination. I knew that I would not get the support of the party machine. I had not been particularly supportive of them, and I didn't expect they would be of me. When it came time to pick the Democratic nominee to fill Herman Badillo's seat, I received a total of two votes out of 35 from the local Democratic Party.

Fortunately, the Republican County Leader from the Bronx, John Calandra (who was a friend of mine from the New York State Senate), offered me the Republican line in the special congressional election. He had no candidate willing to run since no Republican had won in that district in over 100 years. I officially ran as a Republican, as well as on the Liberal Party line, in my first congressional election. It was the right thing to do, but it made for interesting campaigning. My usual staunch Democrats, especially some of the little old Jewish ladies, would shout at me, "You should break my arm I should ever vote Republican!" Apparently, they did because I beat the Democratic candidate by more than a two-to-one margin. I was off to Washington, albeit as a "Republican."

Upon arriving in Washington, my first order of business was to officially align myself with the Democratic Party. This involved getting the Democratic Caucus of the House to accept of me as a Democrat on their records. While I was truly grateful to my Republican friends for their support, in all honesty, my politics, philosophy, and policy inclination lay with the Democrats. But the support I received from my friends on the other side of the aisle underscored a lesson I had learned in Albany as a Deputy Minority Leader. The only way you get anything done is by working with the consensus of both parties. Partisan politics can only go so far. For years after my initial win, I ran with the endorsement of all three parties.

After properly identifying myself with my rightful party, I had to pick the right committees. As a freshman, my choices were quite severely limited. At that time, seniority ruled implacably and it was unlikely that I would be able to get on the powerful Ways and Means or Appropriations Committees. Those were plum assignments usually reserved for members who had been around much longer. But no matter, I was focused on another committee that I believed would enable me to help the City of New York.

When I arrived in Congress in 1978, the most pressing business for all members of the New York City delegation was helping the city to secure a loan from the federal government. New York was effectively bankrupt and was near default, and it sorely needed the federal government's assistance. So, I decided to take the committee assignments of my predecessor, Herman Badillo. He was a member of the Banking, Housing, and Urban Affairs Committee, which in addition to having some say over a federal loan to the City of New York, also had jurisdiction over federal housing programs and other related urban issues. Urban revitalization was obviously to me the bread and butter of helping the Bronx. I accepted this new assignment with great enthusiasm.

During this time, I was becoming increasingly aware of my own cultural heritage. Of course, I knew that I was Puerto Rican, that Puerto Ricans were Hispanics, but I had always looked at myself primarily as a New Yorker. I had to make an emotional and philosophical quantum leap connecting me to the larger Hispanic community across the nation. It was a great revelation to me at the time that I could be a New Yorker, a Puerto Rican, and a member of America's Hispanic community. And I was not so unusual. The actual word "Hispanic" was not one we liked as a collective label. If any such identification was needed, most if not all, of us preferred to be called Latinos generally speaking, but were singularly identified as being of a *specific* ethnic origin. Non-Hispanics began to use this term for us collectively as a convenience because to them we were really all alike in that we were Spanish speaking and culturally or geographically identifiable.

The U.S. Congress had an "Hispanic Caucus," the concept originally being the brainchild of Rep. Ed Roybal, but it really existed in name only. Since there weren't many Hispanic members of Congress, the Caucus was virtually in an incubator and just trying to get off the ground. To me, it was a question of numbers and, therefore, to increase our clout, we had to increase our numbers in Congress. But we also had to learn that in unity there is strength. Whether Mexican-American, Puerto Rican, or from elsewhere in the Caribbean, we were going to be stronger only if we had the numbers and if we were able to work together to target our mutual agenda cohesively. It was clear to me that we could find unity in our diversity by working together on common problems. But first we needed to increase our political clout, and that meant increasing our numbers in Congress and in state and local legislative bodies.

At this same time, within that first year, I became a member of the House Post Office and Civil Service Committee and was assigned the Chairmanship of the Subcommittee on Census and Population. Now this seemingly obscure subcommittee actually was the beginning of my successful efforts to work with minority communities at the national level, especially Hispanic communities. Counting America's citizens was not only a useful exercise, it was and is a politically important function. Population apportions congressional districts, and federal aid programs were dependent on accurate census data. My goal was to get every person counted. This was a somewhat daunting task with minority communities like my own in the Bronx because there was such an innate fear and distrust of government—federal, state, and local. While state legislators draw congressional districts, the federal government does determine size by population, and federal law—the Voting Rights Act—offered some protection for minorities. As a direct beneficiary of the Voting Rights Act, I was committed and personally determined to help more Hispanics come to Congress and to see our numbers increase. This became my passion and my intense focus for the next two years.

The other rule of politics that I was learning, in addition to the need to work with the other side, was the need for people to vote and make their voices heard. The first step for the Hispanic community in making their voices heard was getting counted. The second step was making sure that Hispanics would get elected to political office. It was a lesson I would never forget. So, with this goal in mind, I set out across the country and held a record-making series of 26 congressional field hearings on the census, earmarking the minority communities and trying to educate people on why they needed to respond to census takers.

One of the most unique tools that Hispanics had at their disposal, but was virtually untapped at the time, was a network of low-powered Spanish language television stations throughout the United States. Then it was called Spanish International Network (SIN), as it indeed had affiliates in Central and South America. The head of this organization, Rene Anselmo, who shared my vision of awakening the "sleeping giant of the Hispanic population" to the reality of their own political strength, wholeheartedly put his many resources to the task of improving Hispanic image and quality of life.

He agreed to broadcast a weekly report from the Congressional Hispanic Caucus concerning all issues and agendas affecting Hispanics at the congressional level. His only requirement was that everything had to be in Spanish, which almost excluded me, as my Spanish was so poor as to be practically non-existent. Although my parents spoke Spanish, as the youngest and last child, I spoke only English, although I did understand Spanish. In my determination to make this thing work, I enrolled in the School of Foreign Languages in Roslyn, Virginia that trains our State Department diplomats.

Rene then personally committed himself to working closely with me and the U.S. Census to get the word out. He expended a lot of energy and resources with a specially designed programming series called *Destino 80* focusing on every aspect of the census to answer all possible questions and fears in the minds of Hispanics about being counted. The resulting barrage of up-to-date, reliable, and official information that was now available to the community helped to galvanize the success of the 1980 Census and directly manifest itself in the next congressional election. One can never be absolutely certain about the effect one's efforts have, but by 1982, we were able to increase the number of Hispanics at the federal level by five new congressional seats. Four were elected in the 1982 election following the re-apportionment mandated at the completion of the 1980 census. Representative Matthew Martinez of California was elected in a special election several months preceding the November general election, but this was a result of the same re-apportionment. Although we were still undercounted, the results were spectacular for our cause.

To put this into proper historical perspective, when I was first elected in 1978,

I was only the 13th person of Hispanic heritage to have a vote on the floor of the U.S. Congress. New Mexico and Louisiana were the only states to send Hispanics to Congress until 1961, when Rep. Henry B. Gonzalez of Texas was first elected. It is fair to say that Representative Gonzalez was the first member to really open up Congress for Hispanics, chairing the banking committee and proving that Hispanics could earn the respect of Wall Street and other prestigious national institutions.

Our numbers slowly increased. In 1962, the next great Hispanic leader in Congress in the modem era, Rep. Ed Roybal, was elected to Congress from California. He was followed by Rep. Kika de la Garza of Texas, the third member of the Hispanic triumvirate that changed the role of our community in Congress. These were my role models to follow.

With my arrival in February 1978, as a result of the special election, the nascent Congressional Hispanic Caucus now had five members. The additional colleague from that Congress was Rep. Baltasar Corrada del Rio, the Resident Commissioner and Delegate from Puerto Rico. This did not include the sixth Hispanic, Rep. Manuel Lujan of New Mexico, the sole Republican, who was elected prior to my arrival but did not join the Caucus until after 1980.

Our work was definitely cut out for us. While we were about ten percent of the population in 1978, we only had one percent of the votes in Congress. I was determined to change this with the help of my friends on Capitol Hill and other activists in our community. After being elected to my first full term of Congress in November of 1978, I became very visibly and actively involved with the Hispanic Caucus, first as Vice Chair. I was then elected to two successive terms as Chairman from 1979 to 1983. These were critical years for us as Hispanics, and I was very aware of where I wanted to go. The first step was unity, and I worked very hard to get my colleagues to forge a common agenda.

Fortunately, in 1982, I also was elected by the New York delegation to represent them on the powerful Steering and Policy Committee. The main function of this committee, made up of the House leadership, was to help members get the committee assignments of their choice, if possible. I was in the right place at the right time to help the newly-elected wave of Hispanic members secure the committee assignments they wanted.

During this period, I sponsored the Garcia Amendment to the Civil Service Reform Act that mandated the federal government to *recruit* minorities for jobs in the Civil Service. I continued my work with the Census Subcommittee and forged a strong relationship with another minority activist in Congress, Rep. Mickey Leland of Texas. Mickey was an African-American and as concerned about making sure his community was represented as I was with mine.

Working with people like Leland, as well as private voluntary and non-governmental organizations like the League of Latin American Citizens, the National Council of La Raza, the Mexican American Legal Defense Fund and its counterpart, the Puerto Rican Legal Defense Fund, made me aware that we had the power base, we simply had to realize it. So, we began to work together–all Latin

Americans really for the first time–with the common goal of trying to advance our community as a whole, and piece by piece, in places like the Bronx, Miami, Los Angeles, San Antonio, Puerto Rico, Chicago.

We picked our issues carefully. The first key battle we fought was over the renewal of the Voting Rights Act and the Act's bilingual provisions. We won a major victory for the community when the Act was renewed and the bilingual provisions were left intact. We also fought for other issues along the way on subjects like bilingual education and urban development, the latter issue being extremely important for my district and me personally.

Shortly after coming to Congress, actually in 1980, and crossing party lines, I began working with a young dynamic Republican member of Congress from Buffalo, New York, Jack Kemp, to find a way to benefit districts like ours that were poverty stricken and "red-lined." (Red-lining was a practice commonly in use by insurance companies to penalize landlords of tenements that abandoned them once they were destroyed. Insurers would refuse to insure them and the landlords would be unable to rebuild or repair as the case might be.) We drew on the experience of Puerto Rico's Operation Bootstrap, and we even traveled to England to study first hand a similar idea. As a result, we co-sponsored the Garcia-Kemp Bill to Establish Urban Enterprise Zones, an idea that was finally realized later on a national level with the establishment of the Clinton Administration's Empowerment Zones.

I am also very proud to have played a major role in enacting the long-overdue Martin Luther King Holiday Bill. Because all commemorative legislation had to pass through the Civil Service and Post Office Sub-Committee, which I chaired, I was Floor manager when it came to the House floor for final passage. It was a wonderful way to do favors for other members, as virtually all of them had a request for special legislation to commemorate something in their districts. This in turn helped me when I was looking for help for my poverty-stricken district's needs.

But perhaps the biggest issue for the Hispanic community in the 1980s was immigration reform. In the early '80s, Senator Alan Simpson, a Republican from Wyoming, and Representative Ron Mazzoli, a Democrat of Kentucky, began to work together to put in place a new immigration policy. Since we were the largest immigrant community at the time, Hispanics were very concerned about the details of the legislation. I worked with members of my community to make sure this legislation would not discriminate against Hispanics. Employer sanctions and a national ID card were the two ideas that we fought hard against. We made alliances with the business community, civil rights groups, and others in our fight to try to get the immigration bill fair and right. The immigration bill that finally passed in 1985 was shaped at least in part by the Hispanic community. In many ways, the immigration bill gave us our voice. We showed that we could not be ignored where legislation had a direct impact on our community.

The other key issue of the '80s that helped bring us together as a community was U.S. policy toward Central America. The Hispanic Caucus and individual leaders like Bill Richardson and I fought hard to develop a policy toward the region that was fair and long term. One of our biggest concerns was to make certain that our policy focused on the long-term development of the region both politically and economically. This was for our community the first time that we shifted to the area of international policy making. We all learned to compromise—Republican and Democrat, liberal and conservative—to try to find common ground on this most difficult issue.

I also was involved with the North Atlantic Assembly, a body made up of parliamentarians from NATO nations. NATO and transatlantic affairs was not traditionally an area where minority members of Congress were involved. I was skeptical of what the utility of my involvement would be for my community and me when I went on my first trip to Europe as a member of the U.S. delegation.

I learned that there was a role for someone like me in all aspects of international affairs. It was very important that, as an Hispanic, I show our friends in Europe and even some in Congress that we are not one-dimensional. We can and should make a contribution to all aspects of public policy, including national security policy. My tenure as a member of the Assembly was so successful that I eventually became chairman of its Civilian Affairs Committee.

As part of my overall work, I encouraged Spain to become a permanent member of NATO. I had met former Spanish Prime Minister Felipe Gonzalez when he was a minority politician and believed that with individuals like him active in Spanish politics, Spain was more than ready to be a full-fledged member of NATO. I wrote an op-ed article to that effect for the International Herald Tribune. Spain became a member of NATO, and while I take no credit for that, I believe that I did show that an Hispanic member of Congress was very capable of taking on a wide array of issues both national and international.

In this same spirit, I undertook to be helpful on another important international issue: Spain's recognition of Israel. Under Franco, Spain did not formally recognize Israel. In the post-Franco era, there was no reason that this should be continued. Nonetheless, getting this policy changed would not be easy; I wanted to be part of the effort to make this happen. I worked with my colleagues in the Congressional Hispanic Caucus, and put together a letter signed by all the Caucus members to the prime minister of Spain, asking that Spain recognize Israel. In addition, at every opportunity, I would talk with friends and colleagues from Spain, both in the government and in the private sector, asking them to do what they could. Eventually, Spain did recognize Israel, and I once again felt that I had represented my community well by showing that we could reach beyond what was normally seen as our traditional role.

I like to think that my work, and that of others in the Hispanic Caucus and community, on international issues paved the way for our involvement in national security concerns at the highest levels of government. Years after his hard work in Congress, Bill Richardson became the first Hispanic to be our Ambassador to the United Nations. It was a tribute to him and to all of us who believed our community could help our nation in many different ways.

All of these issues were not only important substantively for the Hispanic community, but also were important politically. That is to say, we found our voice as a community the more we worked together in common purpose. I was fortunate enough to have been the chairman of the Congressional Hispanic Caucus for those exciting four years during the early 1980s. In a sense, I was permitted to be "present at the creation" of the Hispanic community as a national political force.

The Congressional Hispanic Caucus now has 20 members, a number that I believe will only continually grow in the coming years as the average age of our overall population is still very young. While Hispanics remain under-represented in Congress, we are headed strongly in the right direction. Predictions today state that Hispanics will be the largest minority in the United States by the year 2010. We are now a force to be reckoned with, both politically and economically. Although the Hispanic giant is not fully awake quite yet, it will be soon, and this nation will be the better for it.

Chapter 4

A Republican Hawk
Takes on the Pentagon

Denny Smith (R-Oregon)

A \$4.5 billion antiaircraft system with radar that identified an outhouse as a threatening target: *Project canceled.*

A \$90 billion armada of fleet defense ships whose missiles couldn't hit target planes: *Project halted for further testing.*

There should be a sense of accomplishment for a newly-elected congressman who forced the Pentagon to reverse decisions on ineffective billion dollar weapon systems. Instead, even a decade later, the frustrations I encountered then seem to overshadow the victorious moments.

The word "frustration" surfaces repeatedly when I reflect on all aspects of the first of five terms I served in Congress. I was not completely naive to the ways of Washington or the Pentagon when I arrived as a newly-elected congressman, and when I returned to private life, there were several battle scars replacing any hint of naivety. So I can't use that as an explanation of why my mind often dwells on the frustrations, not the accomplishments, of public service.

Added to the frustrations of the system were the rigors of more than 300 coast-to-coast flights in ten years to stay in touch with the Oregonians I represented, the lack of time for my family and business, the constant pressure of maintaining a vigorous re-election campaign organization.

So why did I take on the Pentagon, too? Good question.

A bit of history first . . .

It had been my first run for public office and I arrived in Washington on the eve of the Reagan Revolution eager to apply my proven business skills to put sense back in the business of government. As a Vietnam combat veteran who stood for a strong national defense, I was quickly labeled a Hawk. The Cheap Hawk label was yet to come.

There were many challenges greeting all of us participating in the December 1980 GOP congressional orientation sessions, held for the first time in years in something larger than a phone booth. We came away from these meetings determined to "make a difference," just as we had pledged on the campaign trail, only to have our determination met by road blocks inherent in the way Washington works.

Undaunted, a few found ways to express themselves outside the "go-along-to-get-along" boys made up of our senior colleagues, the bureaucracy, the Beltway bandits, the media . . . even in some cases the friendly administration.

Mavericks in the minority, often lonely on the losing side of a vote, we weren't there to get accolades from the club or earn tenure. There's no doubt we were fueled to some extent by just coming off high-profile, hard-fought campaigns that unseated powerful, long-entrenched incumbents—in my case, Ways and Means Chairman Al Ullman, a 20-year veteran.

Confronting the Pentagon was almost a natural progression of events after my warm-up period in a committee where the legislative process bucked our efforts to balance the scales.

My appointment to the Interior and Insular Affairs Committee was not inappropriate for a representative from a state with significant environmental concerns producing equally significant economic conflicts. Oregon's leading industries were the result of rich farm and timber lands, and nearly three-quarters of the land mass is in public hands. Sincere, organized, vocal, well-financed environmental activists were pitted against the Oregonians who felt their livelihoods were threatened and sent me to Congress.

Working "within the process" in a Democrat-controlled House with a committee ratio so stacked against us proved to be the ultimate in frustration until I met the granddaddy of them all, dealing with the Pentagon. Many of my old military buddies now were well-connected brass who told me about inadequate testing hidden failures of weapons systems on which billions were being spent.

One was the first Aegis guided-missile, the *Ticonderoga*, whose test claims of hitting 13 out of 13 target planes were suspicious. Unlike most challenges to Pentagon programs, this one was not about the cost–$90 billion earmarked for an armada of radar ships to protect the fleet. I just wanted to be assured they worked as advertised. It took nearly a year–during which the Navy practiced stonewalling to perfection–but our suspicions proved true enough that they ordered the *Ticonderoga* home from the Mediterranean for further testing, putting a restraint on construction of dozens more Aegis cruisers and destroyers.

More dramatic was the Pentagon's final decision on a less costly program–a mere $7.8 billion for 618 antiaircraft guns. In an almost unprecedented action, the Secretary of Defense canceled a weapon program while it was in production–a contract for 276 of the guns had been signed. The good news is we saved $6 billion. The bad news is we'd spent $1.8 billion before the plug was pulled.

DIVAD, an acronym for Division Air Defense, was developed for antiaircraft protection for Army tank divisions against Soviet fighters and helicopters. The

$6.3 million per gun was three times the cost of the M-1 tank it was designed to protect.

Both the Aegis cruiser and DIVAD could provide case studies of dealing with the Iron Triangle–the military services, defense contractors, and members of Congress representing areas where military spending plays an important economic role. A congressman whose political ideology nearly mirrored mine tried to dampen my persistence on the *Ticonderoga*. As I stepped up the pressure for the Navy to release testing details, my friend, the House Republican whip, pointed out that killing the program would affect 16,000 jobs at a shipyard in his district. My justification remained that I wasn't trying to ax the program, I was simply trying to get the Navy to be honest and if there were flaws in that ship, fix em before building the others.

I had political allies and strange bedfellows in the Military Reform Caucus, which I co-chaired, by the time we were trying to halt progress on DIVAD until tests proved whether it should be fielded. This bipartisan group of 50 or more members of the House and Senate representing the extreme left and the extreme right had a common goal of seeking military efficiency and more accountability. We weren't anti-defense–far from it. DIVAD and the *Ticonderoga* are just two examples of the programs we used to correct what I saw as bad business decisions–and damn poor public relations.

Accountability in the case of the *Ticonderoga* was a classic. If, as the Navy reported, it had hit 13 out of 13 target planes in the simulated test attack, why be tight-fisted with the reports?

During the five months it took the Navy to deliver the report for me, my Pentagon moles came up with enough confirmation that the press had reported the *Ticonderoga* had hit only 5 of 21 targets. Finally, the Navy agreed to let me look at the full report. If we had not been talking about billions of dollars and protection for our men and women in combat, the meeting in my office would have been humorous.

Glancing through the huge secret document under the gaze of six Navy representatives who intended to take it back with them, I discovered the copy in my hands was missing the most significant page summarizing test results in my own secretly obtained copy. My question "Where's page A-29?" was met with look of embarrassment on a captain's face, an explanation from another that it must have been a Xeroxing error. I wondered what was in their minds next when a civilian engineer fessed up that it was in his copy and handed it to me. No one asked for it later when they walked out, no doubt heading for the nearest Officer's Club to regroup and count their losses.

Four months later, the *Ticonderoga* was on its way home from the Mediterranean for further testing and, sadly, further conflicting testing reports and stonewalling.

Sadistic humor was a part also in the DIVAD episode. By mid-1984, the antiaircraft gun had stalwart supporters in the Army top brass and the Secretary of Defense, in spite of technical problems, some high-level opposition within the Pentagon, and news leaks of rigged tests and embarrassing failures.

The $6.3 million radar-guided gun relies on a computer to focus on targets. During one test for American and British Army brass, DIVAD's turret swerved away from a target drone back toward the reviewing stand sending the brass ducking for cover. When the first full-fledged production model debuted, it focused on a rotating latrine fan in a nearby building which the computer had singled out as the closest threatening target. To pass cold-weather tests, the gun required heating for six hours with the field equivalent of a hair dryer before it was ready to fire. In another test, an old helicopter drone was decorated with four large metal reflectors to help DIVAD's radar find the target.

The ineffective DIVAD, conceived at a time the Soviet threat was very real in most minds, was an expensive response to the need for more modern air protection for Army tank divisions against Soviet fighters and helicopters. But, in addition to the price tag and the poor test results, this old fighter pilot had reservations about its necessity. In the cockpit, I would have a greater fear of traditional antiaircraft batteries which are harder to evade. As a businessman, I had trouble understanding the Army's policy of building and producing DIVAD while it was being tested. It seemed incredulous that just three months after DIVAD's computer zeroed in on the brass in the reviewing stand as threatening targets, the Defense Department signed a $1.5 billion contract to buy 276 guns.

Testing first would have interrupted the natural flow of money . . . and the equally indigenous bureaucratic momentum. Once the system buys onto the program, there's almost no way you can stop it.

It's not just the military and the contractors. An attempt to kill DIVAD on the House floor drew the eloquent ire of five defenders: a California Republican and member of the House Armed Services Committee from the district where DIVAD was assembled; another committee member whose Maryland district is where Westinghouse Electric built DIVAD's radar; an Alabama Democrat from where DIVAD's chassis was made; a Texas Democrat whose district includes the Army base where DIVAD was conceived and tested; and, a New York Democrat, chairman of the Armed Services Subcommittee on Procurement.

No wonder even my Republican friends were not supportive when I sought appointment to the Armed Services Committee. There was little in my district to feed any pork out of the barrel.

After live fire tests in May 1985, the director of the Office of Operational Testing and Analysis called me with glowing reports that DIVAD had hit and destroyed its targets. But that wasn't the report from my next caller, a military officer. Asking to remain anonymous, he identified himself as range safety personnel and thought I should know that DIVAD had scored zip, zero lethal hits. All drones were destroyed by the range safety officer.

The Army brass recommended the Secretary of Defense move ahead. An Undersecretary, who helped launch the DIVAD program when he was a vice president at Ford Aerospace, called to assure me he felt DIVAD was a big leap forward, a 10 to 20 percent improvement on existing antiaircraft.

My network of the moles in the Pentagon, who had been arming me with under-the-table documents, gave me the other side of the story. The tests were conducted in a shooting gallery. The target fighter planes were patsies, flown at a suicide elevation with no evasive maneuvers. Even under those conditions there may have been *no* lethal hits.

Expecting more stonewalling, I was surprised to find my request for video tapes of the test responded to quickly. No wonder. The tapes showed DIVAD firing and target drones exploding almost immediately. Almost too immediately.

The reports and conjectures varied, but there was no doubt the range-safety officer had a fast trigger finger . . . faster than the DIVAD. He had been unusually quick to detonate safety charges on the target planes which had destroyed most, if not all, of them before DIVAD's shot hit neared its mark.

My protest letters to the Pentagon were countered by strong defenses of their weapon. The media picked up on our conflicting versions, while two versions of the internal final test evaluations were being debated within the Pentagon walls. Copies of one, a blistering and fatal indictment of DIVAD, were made for nine Pentagon officials. The next day, the top echelon attempted to squelch the evidence by issuing orders to retrieve every one of the nine copies. Thirteen copies came back.

In a letter and subsequent phone call to the Secretary of Defense, I urged him to read that report before making his decision. The day after our phone conversation, the Secretary announced he was canceling DIVAD. The Army three-star who lied to me was asked to retire.

Part Two

Getting Elected and Settling In

Running for Congress is a terribly demanding proposition, requiring a great deal of money and placing severe strains on family life. Why does anyone do it? How do people arrive at the decision to make the race when most of us would balk at the financial and personal obstacles? The first three selections in this section address these questions. Both James Symington and Jay Rhodes came from political families, and the decision to run for Congress came naturally to them. However, Don Sundquist (now Governor of Tennessee) did not have such a background; he became involved in politics via the more conventional path of membership in Young Republicans and subsequent activity on behalf of another candidate for office (Senator Howard Baker).

Tom Downey describes the sense of awe felt by many new members when they first arrive at the Capitol. He also reviews some of the ways in which life in Congress is not so very different from life in a normal high school. Finally, he provides a humorous account of the very real importance of the House Gymnasium in the socialization of new members.

How much can a newly-elected member expect to achieve in Congress—particularly one who serves as a member of the minority party? Pete McCloskey addresses this question in his chapter. While there are very real limits to what new members can accomplish most of the time, McCloskey describes the little-known role of the House Republicans in prodding House Democrats to end the system of selecting committee chairs on the basis of seniority. This episode, spearheaded by junior members in the middle 1970s, suggests that newly-elected members—for all their very real weaknesses—can sometimes accomplish important changes.

Eugene McCarthy prepares newly-elected members for the advice they will get on every side when they arrive in Washington—particularly from party leaders, think tanks, and the press. He goes on to offer some "old advice for new members" that is characteristically both insightful and humorous.

Finally, Carlton Sickles tells what it was like to be the only at-large member in the U.S. House, representing the entire state of Maryland in the 1960s. As suggested by Romano Mazzoli in Chapter 1, every member of Congress wears many "hats," performing a wide variety of tasks as legislator, caseworker, teacher, and politician. Representative Sickles tells us what it was like to wear all these hats while representing a large and heterogeneous constituency that spanned his entire state.

Chapter 5

The Lure of Politics

James W. Symington (D-Missouri)

The idea of running for Congress had been in my mind since boyhood. My Granddad, James W. Wadsworth, Republican, of Geneseo, New York, after six years in the New York State Legislature (where he became Speaker at the age of 27) served two terms in the U.S. Senate (1914-27) and nine subsequent terms in the House (1933-51). His father had served eight terms in the House. His granddad, General James Samuel Wadsworth, served at Gettysburg, and was killed the following year (1864) in the battle of the Wilderness. A 56 year old soldier in the field, he had run, in absentia, for Governor of New York in 1862. Losing to New York Mayor Horatio Seymour, he philosophized, "The Republicans went South to fight and the Democrats stayed North to vote." These and other ancestral memories absorbed over many a working summer on the Wadsworth farm land instilled the idea that public service was more or less expected of us, together with a little humility concerning one's importance to the big picture. One person can indeed make a difference, but that fact shouldn't go to his (or her) head.

During the summer of 1940, my grandfather Jim Wadsworth, a stickler for military preparedness, successfully shepherded a draft bill through the Congress. Congress was understandably loathe to renew a draft within a generation of the Great War, so it put the government on a short tether, providing that the new draft would expire in October of the following year. "OHIO" was the cry this provision inspired in the troops (Over the Hill in October). Accordingly, opposition in the Congress was instant and overwhelming when, the following summer, President Roosevelt asked it to extend the draft. The Republicans, particularly, were outraged by what they saw as "a broken promise and a betrayal our young men." Wadsworth, however, breaking ranks with his party colleagues, supported the draft extension. He argued that with Hitler, Mussolini, and Tojo carrying the ball, calling the plays, and refereeing the game it would be dangerous to the point of folly to prevent America from taking the field. He explained that a ready army consisted of teams of men who have learned to work together in their several areas of responsibility. To break up these teams could render the country helpless to respond in a timely fashion should the danger touch our own national security. He already had successfully fought to approve Lend Lease, and the speech was entirely consistent with his known views. Having chaired the Military Affairs Committee of the Senate during the First World War, these views commanded respect. The House was packed. When the question was called, the draft extension was passed by a margin of one vote. The Aye votes included 18 Republicans and an unknown number of faltering Democrats. FDR sent him the pen with which he signed the bill. Wadsworth, believing the president had known all along we would be drawn into the war, broke it and threw it away.

If I may move the film up to 1960 and the Democratic Convention in Los Angeles, I would invite the reader to join my brother Stuart and me in the courtesy call we made along with our father, who was a presidential candidate, to the suite of Convention Chairman Sam Rayburn. "Mr. Sam" took us aside and said, "Boys, I've heard a few speeches in my life that changed votes one way or the other. But I've only heard one such speech that changed the *result* of the vote. That was your granddad's speech on the draft extension Bill. It was powerful and completely persuasive." Indeed, we had been told by our grandmother, Alice Hay Wadsworth, that a day or so after Pearl Harbor, a mere four months after the Bill's passage, George Marshall, a close friend of my grandfather's, called him up and said, "Jim, you have saved two million American lives, and shortened the war we are about to enter by two years." Thus did the calculating mind of our great chief of staff range over the dim future to confer such a compliment.

Now for the humility. During that contentious summer of 1941, my brother and I accompanied our grandfather on his daily rounds of his farmland in Geneseo, New York. There was a bushel basket filled with letters on his front porch. His staff was under instructions to insure that only "hate mail" be included in the pile; that is to say only severely critical letters–many of which would begin, "murderer, warmonger," etc. and be signed, as a rule, by sundry mothers and fathers of draft age sons. Every day, Grandpa would lean over, fetch up a handful, read them slowly and carefully, and return them to the heap. When our curiosity finally got the best of us, we asked, "Grandpa, why do you do that?" His unforgettable response: "keeps me from getting a big head."

The war we could not avoid lasted through many millions of drafts and enlistments, including my brother's in the Army in 1943 and my own in the Marines in 1945. So, by 1952, when my own father, Stuart Symington, an industrialist and Democrat who had been unanimously confirmed for six successive posts under President Truman, decided to run for the Senate from his chosen State of Missouri, I was already hooked.

Taking a year out of Columbia Law School to help in my father's campaign, I, along with my brother Stuart, a third-year Harvard law student, drove the old family Pontiac and a vintage sound truck some 30,000 Missouri miles, and wore out some shoe-leather, taking President Truman's advice to "shake a lot of hands." I took my guitar and folksongs to barbeques, church suppers, political rallies, county fairs, and roadside inns. It was total immersion in the life and times of a vibrant and fairly cantankerous state. The result was a victory over an incumbent Republican, James Kem of Macon, Missouri, despite an Eisenhower landslide which engulfed the nation, and Missouri as well.

My father's subsequent Senate service was marked by Cold War national security issues that he had earlier addressed as our First Secretary of Air, and Chairman of the National Security Resources Board. The only senator to serve on both Foreign Relations and Defense committees, he could measure threats and opportunities from both perspectives. His greatest challenge, however, came upon him early in the form of Joe McCarthy and the "ism" to which he gave his name. More than uncomfortable with Senator McCarthy's cavalier methods and insensitivity, he became an active opponent when Senator Joe singled out the Army as a haven for the disloyal.

I was taking my finals in law at Columbia during the heat of the hearings. That was May 1954. My studies suffered from an attention span broken daily by the gavel of counsel Ray Jenkins calling the hearings to order with such diverse participants as McCarthy, his counsel, Roy Cohn, Army Secretary Stevens, and Senators Mundt, McClelland, Jackson, and, of course, the deceptively whimsical but razor sharp Boston lawyer, Joe Welch. My most vivid recollection of the various exchanges however, is that of McCarthy's muttered comment about Symington being "afraid." My father leaned over, looked him in the eye, and said, "Senator, you said something about being afraid. I want you to know I am not afraid of you, or anything you have to say. I will meet you any time, any place, any where." McCarthy shuffled and changed the subject. Moments later when they shared an elevator for the lunch break, McCarthy said, "Hi, Stu!" as if no such exchange had occurred. But it had been a pivotal moment in a drama which held the nation spellbound.

The streets along Morningside Heights were bare with the populace glued to its TV sets. There were few in America who could honestly say they were not afraid of Joe McCarthy. The hearings went their course, and, shortly afterwards, the Senate voted to censure him. A couple of weeks later at a hearing my father was chairing, Mrs. McCarthy appeared. He instructed a page to find her a chair. That evening, he received a call from McCarthy who invited him and my mother to join the McCarthys for dinner. A previous engagement prevented the event, but my father was glad for the opportunity to put the personal bitterness aside. In an interview following McCarthy's death, he dwelt only on the latter's positive contributions to his state and country. Criticized by an unforgiving journal for such a mild response, he quoted the old Latin expression "speak nothing but good of the dead." Folks have enough grief and other burdens to bear through life without adding unnecessary grudges to the pile.

It was a valuable lesson to observe a Democrat father and Republican grandfather as they shared confidences, insights, and initiatives bearing on the nation's welfare (and issues of scope and dimension which render the recent all-consuming congressional contretemps pale by comparison). I think that is why I felt perfectly comfortable as a member of Congress wandering across the aisle from time to time to chat with Republican friends. Indeed one of them, Pete DuPont of Delaware, would ask me to address his high school delegations because he knew I wouldn't shock them in some fashion. I returned the compliment and for years we traded "bi-partisan" commentary. But my plunge into those waters did not occur until 16 years after my father's first Senate race.

Those years (1952-1968) were spent first prosecuting in police court, then lawyering, politicking (in my father's senatorial and presidential campaigns), and serving in various federal posts, including Deputy Director of Food For Peace, Administrative Assistant to Attorney General Robert Kennedy, Director of the President's Committee on Juvenile Delinquency, and U.S. Chief of Protocol for President Johnson. As was the case of my father, preparing to address domestic and international issues in Congress and getting elected were two entirely distinct, though not unrelated, enterprises.

In spite of some 30 years of exposure to the "realities" of politics, I felt at the outset of my first campaign that the process could be refreshed, nourished by first principles, and, in effect, "born again." Thus, I stocked my campaign headquarters with biographies of founding fathers, treatises on the Constitution, and essays on history for my own inspiration and that of my young volunteers. Campaign "tricks" were discouraged. A young supporter who proudly boasted he had made off with a thousand of an opponent's flyers was ordered to take them back. In my first Democratic primary (1968), a resourceful township committeewoman who supported an opponent somehow secured permission to cast ballots for all 150 housebound residents of an old folks home in my district, and did so, unsurprisingly, for her candidate, not even giving me one for good luck. Recalling the warm and happy visit I had made to that institution and the tearful pledges of support it occasioned, I realized that the process of securing votes was more complicated than I had thought.

In any event, I would never have won that first primary, or the general election that followed it, plus three additional congressional terms, without campaign managers, treasurers, supporters, and volunteers who could overcome such tactics without engaging in them. The lady committeewoman who had absconded with the old folks' votes during the primary became one of my staunchest supporters in the general election, a point not to miss.

I recall my father's observation that the greatest thrill in politics was to make a friend of an enemy. This point was reinforced on another occasion. After a pleasant coffee klatch with about 20 ladies, I sent them each a letter of thanks. Unaccountably, that letter also went to a lady who had not attended. I learned this directly from her in a scolding and scalding letter informing me that, as a lifelong Republican, she did not and would never attend any function on my behalf. As my philosophic Missouri colleague Bill Hungate would have said, "I put her down as 'doubtful'." In any case, a month or so later while driving through this lady's neighborhood, I gave in to an impulse born of residual chagrin and curiosity. So I shortly appeared at her doorstep with a dozen roses. She answered the door with her hair in curlers and a vacuum sweeper in her hand. The expression on her face transformed from irritation to astonishment and then dawning recognition. Before she could speak, I told her that I certainly had been at fault to not have been more careful in getting out letters of thanks, and I wanted her to know how sorry I was to have given her grief. She immediately invited me in, sat me down, and over a cup of coffee, apologized for the tone of her letter, and then told me a good bit about her life, her divorce, and her job search. With pledges of mutual support, we parted. I left refreshed and exhilarated, and the day was beautiful.

Although my grandfather Wadsworth would jokingly refer to "The House of Reprehensibles," his love and respect for the Congress were contagious. Arriving at the House floor as a new member in January 1969, tingling with anticipation at the prospect of contributing ideas and sweat equity to its deliberations, I stopped at the threshold as one might at the entrance to a great cathedral, humbled by the thought of those who had gone before and what they had built. In the ensuing rush of handshakes, backslapping, and laughter, I was reassured that the other 434 members were mortals too. One of these with a happy countenance and easy affability took a seat with me to await instructions from the Speaker. After a few moments of pleasant conversation, he was accosted by a nervous page of some 16 years of age and told that, as a Republican, he was supposed to sit on the other side of the chamber until the formal organization matters were concluded. This blunt instruction from a beardless youth confirmed our own mortality, and the gentleman and I have enjoyed many a laugh over it since. His name? Manuel Lujan of New Mexico, subsequently Secretary of the Interior.

Floor debates, committee wrangles, indiscreet or hasty public commentary, tend to define the Congress for a citizenry that depends for its understanding on a media addicted to "sound bites" and driven by the profit motive that sensationalism gratifies. What the citizen does not see are the countless human kindnesses that characterize life in any institution of intelligent, sensitive, hard-working people. Like the people they represent, members of Congress engage in prayer, sport, the arts, music, bull sessions, and joint endeavors for good causes other than their respective re-elections. Their regular returns to their districts keep them mindful of constituent needs, apprehensions, and national and world views. Their spouses are another dependable source of objectivity as well as much-needed reinforcement. The Congress, by its nature, cannot and does not operate in some kind of lofty isolation. The best guarantee that this will always be so is a vigilant, participatory, and judgmental electorate, the ultimate and only dependable monitor of congressional performance. It is the role of every center of learning, from cradle to grave, and of every citizen personally, to prevent such public watchfulness from being terminally infected with cynicism. The faith and hope that built our country are more than sufficient to sustain it.

Chapter 6

Mr. Sundquist Goes to Washington

Don Sundquist (R-Tennessee)

I've been involved in politics as an avocation going back to the mid-1960s, when I got involved in the Young Republicans and in the campaign of a young Senate candidate named Howard Baker. I found that I loved politics, and I thought it would be appropriate to return something to the system by serving in office myself, but with a young family and a new business, running for office was something I put off until 1982. That year, the incumbent congressman, Robin Beard, decided to run for the U.S. Senate, leaving an open seat in the seventh district.

Nobody gave us a chance in 1982. For one thing, it was the mid-term election of President Reagan's first term, and the president's party usually suffers losses in the mid-term elections. In addition, there was a recession that affected most of the counties in the district, especially the rural, Democratic-leaning counties between Memphis and Nashville.

On top of that, redistricting had made the district more Democratic: the legislature took out Williamson County, one of the most Republican counties in Tennessee. Of the 16 counties left in the district, only three were Republican. Fortunately for me, one of those areas was the eastern portion of Shelby County—the heavily-Republican suburbs near my home in Memphis remained in the district. These communities represented a third of the entire district's population and cast close to 40 percent of its votes.

The heavy favorite to win the seventh district seat was Bob Clement, a member of one of Tennessee's leading political families. His father, Frank Clement, had dominated Tennessee politics for almost two decades, serving as Governor during the 1950s and again in the early 1960s. Bob Clement had been elected statewide in 1972 as a Public Service Commissioner, was appointed by President Carter to serve as a director of the Tennessee Valley Authority, and had run for Governor in 1978. (He lost in the primary, narrowly, to Jake Butcher.) The first poll we ran in February 1982 put Clement's name identification at 79 percent, mine at 4 percent -

and the poll had a 5 percent margin of error.

What encouraged us, though, was another finding in that poll: I won a majority of those voters who were familiar with both candidates. Our challenge was to become as well-known in the district as Clement was. We felt we could do that, and we believed we could win the election.

We were behind the entire campaign. We were close, but the only poll that showed us winning was the one that counted, the one on election day. We made an important decision in October to preempt our opponent's attack ads on Social Security. Democratic campaigns all across the country charged that Republicans intended to do away with Social Security. It was not a fair attack, but it proved to be very effective for the Democrats that year.

We were told by my friend, the consultant Charlie Black, that these kinds of attacks were going to be used against us late in the campaign, and so we beat them to the punch by airing some very good ads featuring seniors who vouched for me on Social Security issues. Those ads immunized us on the Social Security issue, and when the attacks came in the campaign's last week, they had no affect on our momentum. Beginning on the Wednesday before the election, we were gaining about a half-percentage point daily on Clement. On election day, I won by 1,400 votes out of 155,000.

It was a big upset as far as most of the media were concerned. A lot of the early returns came in from smaller, strongly Democratic counties near Nashville, and Clement won them handily. Most of the Nashville television stations declared him the winner. The early returns worried us some, because we weren't doing as well as we needed to do in the two rural Republican counties (Wayne and Henderson). As the evening went on, though, we were doing better than expected in the Democratic counties, and suburban Shelby County gave us 76 percent of the vote to put us ahead. I'm fairly sure ours was the closest congressional race in the country that year, and the only open seat race won by a Republican. It took time to recheck the returns, and I didn't accept the victory until after all of the machines had been audited. Three weeks later it was final, and I was headed to Congress.

Chapter 7

Settling Into Washington as a First-Term Representative

John J. "Jay" Rhodes, III (R-Arizona)

Coming to Washington as a newly-elected representative from the first district of Arizona was, in many ways, a homecoming. My father had represented the same area for 30 years, from 1953 until his retirement in 1983. Along the way, he had moved through the challenges of those times, emerging as the leader of the Republicans in the House in 1973, just in time to deal with the possibility of the impeachment of a president, and to help guide the party and the country through those amazing years.

When he first came to Washington, all of us came with him, which was the norm in pre-jet plane times. In those days, Congress adjourned in June, and left town, not to re-appear until January. Our family would pack up and go home to Arizona; we would attend school for the first semester, then pack up and return to Washington for the congressional session and, incidentally, the second semester of school.

As time went on, this arrangement became increasingly unsatisfactory. Congressional sessions started to lengthen, and school got harder. By the time I was ready to go into high school, the split school year was no longer working, and my brothers and sister and I became full-time school-year residents of Washington (still going home—to Arizona—for the summer).

I went to college in 1961, and to law school in 1965, and into the Army in 1968, but was still here frequently during school vacations, worked here a few summers, and didn't really get into a life-mode when I wasn't in Washington on a regular basis until about 1970.

Even then, I was back frequently, and more importantly, never lost my fascination with the place and with the Congress.

When Dad announced that he was going to retire, with no advance notice to any of his children, my wife, Annie, and I seriously thought about running, but ultimately determined that it was not our time nor our place. With that decision, we basically put the entire idea of being in Congress out of our minds.

When the seat came open again in 1986, Annie and I re-examined our circumstances, and determined that it was now our time, our place; we ran; we were elected.

We wondered what to do next.

Winning that election was an incredibly wonderful highlight of our lives. We can both remember flying in to Washington for our orientation session early in December 1986. We came in at night, flew down the river, and past the Lincoln Memorial and the Washington Monument, fully lit, with the magnificent Capitol dome in the background, and we hugged each other and cried a bit.

The next day, we met the other members of our class—the 100th Congress—the *historic* 100th Congress—for the first time. There were about 50 of us in total, roughly evenly divided between the parties. There were three who were already well known for other accomplishments (Jim Bunning, Fred Grandy, and Joe Kennedy). Only two (Jon Kyl and I) had never held office before. Two (Buz Lukens and Jamie Dark) had been in the House before. Almost all were male, white, and over 40.

We went through a fairly rigorous orientation session. Orientation begins with all of the in-coming members of each party meeting together for the generic information about staff limits, salaries, and ethics— the things that apply to all members. After those sessions, the parties take over. For we Republicans, there were some spectacular social events, including dinner in Statuary Hall in the Capitol, and a dinner put on by the campaign committee where each of us showed our best commercial, came to the podium, and introduced ourselves to our classmates.

Since I was from the first district of Arizona, I was first to make a presentation that night, and I chose to bring Annie with me to the podium, because I felt and still feel that politics is a family affair, and if it had not been for her, I would not have been there that night.

I advised my classmates that I had seniority, because in 1953, when my Dad had been sworn in, I was with him on the floor, and when Speaker Martin (Republican) roared "raise your right hands and repeat after me," I wasn't going to disobey.

After the official orientation in Washington, most of the Republicans went to Williamsburg, Virginia for a three-day issues seminar. Most of the Democrats went to a similar event in Boston at the Kennedy School at Harvard.

The Williamsburg meeting was valuable both from the standpoint of us having a chance to get to know each other better and to explore in some depth the issues which we were facing. It was, frankly, a very sobering experience. I think that many of us were forced to face, for the first time, the magnitude of the debt, the deficit, Social Security and Medicare, and the then-problem of the threat from the then-Soviet Union.

We also discovered that we were a pretty homogeneous group, that we liked each other, and that there probably was some merit in sticking together for awhile, for each other's mutual benefit. We decided to try to meet once a week for an hour or so, until everybody got sorted out and squared away, to share experiences and advice, and to help each other.

Twelve years later, the class still meets, Wednesday afternoon at 4:00 p.m. in one of the member's offices. Those who have gone to the Senate still come over. Those who are out are welcome back. It is a remarkable group of people, and good friends.

Incidentally, the class hasn't done badly. A few of us have gone, but five are in the Senate, and Denny Hastert is Speaker of the House.

A first-termer's biggest task is establishing an office. There are more templates for the "right" way to accomplish this job than there have ever been members. My personal bias is that a new member should never hire anybody whom he has known before. A new member should not bring to Washington his campaign manager to be his chief-of-staff.

A new member needs people in the three top positions (administrative assistant, executive assistant, and legislative director) who know the Hill and the House. They can learn the district, and they will. But those three people are the ones who keep the congressman running on time, and that's what gets the congressman re-elected.

For Annie and me, the first hard decision was whether or not she and our son, Arthur, should stay in Arizona, or move to Washington. Unlike my parents' time, when virtually all of the non-east coast members moved to Washington, in our class, virtually none did. After several months of commuting to and from Arizona every weekend, we decided to swim against the tide, and moved to Washington. Finding a school for Arthur was an adventure, but we were able to overcome that, and quite successfully.

We think that being in Congress is, aside from an honor, a life experience, and it should be enjoyed and shared by the family. That is not possible if the spouse and children are in the district and the member is only home from late Thursday or early Friday until Sunday night or Monday morning.

There really is no set answer to the where-to-live question, and each family has to decide on its own. We happen to think that, in most cases, the decision to leave the family at home and have the member commute is more political than anything else, and, from the family's standpoint, is probably wrong. But, honestly, there are 540 different answers to this question. (See Chapter 12 in this volume for more on this point–ed.)

Certainly, our being in Washington provided many opportunities we would not have had otherwise. Annie was active in the Congressional Club, chaired the First Lady's luncheon in 1992, and edited the Club's latest edition of its cookbook. We were able to make friends among members who do have their families here, and, while maintaining our ties at home, to have experiences connected to Congress that would have not otherwise been possible. It was, indeed, a pleasure.

Chapter 8

Tales from the House Gymnasium

Tom Downey (D-New York)

I had visited the chamber of the House of Representatives as a seven-year-old boy. The marvel of men and women hurrying in and out of the hall, the shouting of *yeas* and *nays*–I was a witness to history that day.

And how I loved history. Dates and places, the facts of the founding fathers - it rivaled my love of Willie Mays and the New York Giants. It was more real than baseball and more permanent than the Giants. When my family moved to Long Island, I began to learn about my congressman, the Great Otis Pike. A witty, wise, handsome, bow-tie wearing, aristocratic Democrat in a sea of Republicans. A champion of the Party turning back each electoral challenger with a quip and a song. (He played the ukulele.)

This was the Congress in my mind and I wanted to be part of it. To my utter amazement and delight, 18 years later I was.

There were 95 of us in 1975, mostly unseasoned by prior political office and all convinced we were elected to make a difference. A revolutionary class. "To get along, you had to go along" was the old saying about the Congress. This group was not going to wait; we were going to be seen and heard. No ritual of seniority or respect for "leadership" would endure our withering ambition. We were senators, governors, and presidents in waiting.

The first thing to know about the House of Representatives is that it is just like a large suburban high school. It has a principal (the Speaker), teachers who run the classrooms (committee chairmen), upperclassmen and women (senior members), bells that tell you to go from class to class (or when to vote). It even has its own cafeteria and gymnasium. But most importantly, the tools that made you popular, smart, and successful in high school apply in the Congress. A willingness to volunteer for tough yet tedious assignments - like canvassing your colleagues to determine their positions on an upcoming vote (a whip count), takes time and skill in reading and understanding people; raising money for the junior or senior class, in this case the party or for a friend in political trouble - will separate you from the pack of other freshmen. Superior performance in class, perfect attendance, and being well groomed and courteous may make you "the most likely to succeed" in your senior class. They also will get you noticed in Congress.

Of course there are differences between high school and the House of Representatives. The media did not cover your English class, everyone is much older, you get paid a lot of money, you have a staff of 18 to help you with your political homework, people laugh at your jokes, and they stop traffic for you when you cross the street to vote.

My best, friends in the Congress came not from the great ideological battles of the '70s and '80s over the nuclear freeze, the energy crises, Nicaragua, or the issue of race, but from the House gym. Every day at about 4 o'clock in the afternoon between votes and office appointments, a group of about 20-30 guys (female members of Congress used the gym, but did not play basketball) would make our way down to the gym and play a full court game. It was the one completely nonpartisan activity we engaged in during the day. There was no ideology down in the gym, just basketball and sports talk. The gym, like much of the rest of the Congress, had its rituals and characters, as I was to learn.

The characters of the House left the biggest impression on me. These were members elected before the age of television homogenized the House. "You guys all look blow-dried to me," Dan Rostenkowski once told a group of us. The city machines of Chicago, Jersey City, and St. Louis once produced congressmen who could easily pass for a family member everyone referred to as "colorful" — men who ate without utensils or knew how to place a bet from the cloakroom and got the racing form delivered to the House floor. There was a lot of "winking" in the old days during a conversation. Now it means your contact lens is itching. I had no idea who these members were when I arrived. To me, they were all Otis Pike.

"Let me tell ya one simple ting," Representative James Burke of Massachusetts intoned, "in orda to come back here, ya gotta get reelected." I started out listening carefully to my elders. Despite my anti-Vietnam protest background, I'd been elected and reelected to the Suffolk County Legislature all before the age of 24. My parents made me say "Yes, sir and ma'am" to people growing up in suburban Long Island and it didn't take me long to realize that it disarmed the large number of my constituents who were my senior and set the right example for the few who weren't. It worked wonders in the House of Representatives. "Why, call me John, son," said Representative John McFall, the Democratic Whip from California who seemed especially friendly to the freshmen he encountered. In fact, all this talk about how the committee chairmen were unapproachable and haughty seemed like nonsense. Could it be that our "reform" effort to reelect these guys (it was only guys then) in the Democratic Caucus with a secret ballot had transformed them into anxious supplicants? Hardly, but we did have their attention. "Now, what I do to get reelected is not have opponents." I began to wonder, coming as I did from a very Republican district, whether Jamie, as I now called the 75 year old Mr. Burke, had key insights into how I might get reelected.

The House Gymnasium was the sanctum sanctorum of the House of Representatives. "Your staff can't come here," I was formally told by Herb Botts who had run the gym for 25 years. "We used to be in the Longworth building and the AA's had gym privileges and a 'member' couldn't get on a paddleball court." He sneered at me, "How old are you, Congressman?" He was having trouble believing I was to be in the members' gym. "Twenty-five," I replied in my best "don't even start with me" voice. "Gonna be down here a lot?" There was real apprehension in this query. "I hope so. By the way, could we move the basketball backboard from the corner of the wall?" The gym, located in the sub-basement of the Rayburn building, was about 100 feet by 40 feet, and the "half moon" backboard was in the extreme corner of the long wall. It was a serious afterthought. "It's a little hard to play a game with it two feet from the wall." Now the look was real sadness. Herb was a big man and his historic DNA told him that fawning respect for members was an absolute requirement, but members were older men who didn't make demands about the gym before being given a locker. "Well, I'll have to ask the Committee. The members like to play paddleball and no one really plays basketball." I was, at heart, a wise ass, "There are a lot of younger guys in our class who will probably want to play basketball. Who is the Chairman of the Gym Committee?" [You, pops, are not going to make this call.]

Herb had been around too long not to recognize that he worked for the members, even the ones young enough to be his grandsons. "Mr. Boland is chairman. Mr. Natcher and Mr. Myers are the rest of the committee." "Thanks, Herb, I'll see ya soon." I've been told by the other guys who work in the gym that it took Herb several weeks to get over our first encounter.

"Move the backboard?" Representative Edward Boland, elected in 1952 with majority leader Tip O'Neill, was a subcommittee chairman of the House Appropriations Committee, one of the College of Cardinals. Our new reforms would require each one of them to be elected by the whole Democratic Caucus. He made my request seem as though I wanted to relocate the Hoover Dam to Long Island. "Yes sir, it is at the corner of the wall and you can't play a game with it located there." Eddie didn't use the gym much except to take an occasional shower and probably hadn't noticed the backboard originally. "I'll ask the committee." This, I would learn later, meant that he would think about it. I organized sympathetic older members to explain that it was not an unreasonable request and then, during some recess when we were in our districts, the Architect of the Capitol, directly under his supervision, would detail part of the "craft" army at his disposal to accomplish the deed. Since "Eddie" was running for reelection, I got some of my Freshmen colleagues to ask him the same question. They moved the backboard the next weekend. This job was going to be fun.

Otis Pike was Mickey Mantle to me. Elected in 1960 in the First District of New York (also an overwhelmingly Republican area), he wore a bow tie, wrote the wittiest newsletter of any member of Congress to his constituents, played the banjo, had a wonderfully self-deprecating sense of humor, was tall and handsome, and everything about him said *congressman*. He was my congressman as I grew up and now I was in the same outfield with my hero. I sat next to him in the caucus meetings and when he spoke to me I hung on every word. "I learned more on the back of a bus than I did in school," I heard him tell an angry group of constituents once about why he was opposed to a constitutional amendment to ban busing to achieve racial balance. They all laughed and he went on to discuss the really important questions of whether to dredge the Fire Island Inlet again or let nature take its course and close the waterway to recreational boats. Humor and humility.

I was the youngest member of Congress and Ray Madden of Indiana, chairman of the powerful Rules Committee, was the oldest. He was 81. Every time we were together at some party function or reception, someone would cleverly want us to be photographed together. This happened about eight times. Old Ray and I were getting to be quite an item. It was our ninth meeting that was the most memorable for me.

In the gym, there was a steam room adjacent to the showers. Most steam rooms are very hot; this one was volcanic. I walked in when Ray was whistling the Battle Hymn of the Republic. We were both in the "all together." "Mister Chairman," I said in my most respectful tone, nodding my head in his general direction.

There are three levels in the steam room, each about two feet above the other. They are marble slabs. I took a seat on the first level. My butt is still scarred from this encounter. He peered down through the rising steam at me, perched on the top level, where it was 40 degrees warmer. There was that glow of recognition; after all, this was our ninth meeting. "Ya look like one of those new members," he said wistfully. I was confused. Surely he knew me. "Whood ya beat?" Initially, the older members only know you by your predecessor, a humbling though understandable reality.

"I beat James Grover."

He paused a second, "Howda ya like it here Grover?"

I stifled a short laugh because a larger one would entail a deep breath, possibly searing my lungs. "No, Mister Chairman, I beat James Grover. My name is Tom Downey."

"Downey, Downey" He was searching for something. "Whood ya beat?"

It was getting very hot in the steam room, very hot. "I beat *JAMES GR-OV-ER.*"

He was, frighteningly, just warming up. "Grover, I'm gonna give ya some advice." This 81-year-old man, impervious to heat, was the chairman of the Rules Committee, a power in the House. Notwithstanding my previous inability to completely identify myself, I now needed to heed every steam-drenched word from his thin white lips. *THE HEAT.* I was having trouble breathing. I tried to remember a yoga class, "let the heat pass through you." I was becoming one with the marble. "I'm gonna tell ya how I got elected." The Chairman sat up a little straighter, I craned my neck to look back at him. He was only a few feet above me, but the steam made his white wrinkled skin appear as the "ghost of Christmas past."

I did not know that "Ray" was a thorough man. He started telling me about every election he had ever been in. "I started in 1912 with Woodrow Wilson. I ran for clerk in my county back home." The heat and the steam were making me delirious. He got really excited in 1924. "Ya remember that one?"

I was fading, but rallied with, "Wasn't that the Democratic Convention in New York? Didn't we nominate someone named Cox?"

"Hell, that was the year of *RADIO*."

The year of radio? "Yes Mister Chairman, I have one, we advertised on it during the campaign."

"I loved *RADIO*," again wistfully. He plunged on through the years - 1926, '28, '30, '32, '34, '36 '38, '40, '42, '44, '46. I passed out in 1948. Well, not exactly, but I had lost 40 percent of my body weight and was near whatever the reverse of hypothermia is. I somehow made it to the shower and waited to resume my conversation with my new best buddy, the Chairman of the Rules Committee.

We never had a long conversation after that day. He always called me Grover and felt snubbed by my hasty exit from the steam room. I never did hear about the '50s, '60s, or the '70s.

Chapter 9

What Can a New Member Accomplish?

Paul N. "Pete" McCloskey (R-California)

I left Congress in 1982, 18 years ago. The rapid changes in every field of human endeavor during the past 18 years have been paralleled in the United States House of Representatives. It is possible that many of the processes of the Congress of the late 1960s and 1970s are now as obsolescent as the dial telephone and the typewriter. Thus, the observations and experiences stemming from my own service in the House, from 1967 to 1983, may be little more than an interesting bit of history of a bygone era. There has been a Republican Speaker and a Republican majority only since 1994, the first in 40 years. Nevertheless, I offer the following anecdotes with the humble thought that they may add a bit of humorous perspective on a brief period in the history of a great institution, one which most of us recognize as much greater than the sum of the individual participants briefly privileged to serve there.

THE NEWEST MEMBER

When an ordinary citizen is sworn in as a member of the House, his or her first conception is generally one of privilege, that he or she has been granted a tremendous honor in being allowed to serve the country in that historic institution.

Regrettably, that sense of privilege is soon diffused, if not forgotten completely. The hours are long, much of the work inconsequential and boring, and the necessary efforts to raise money and obtain reelection not only exhausting, but often demeaning. At the end of a typical legislative day, commencing with a 7:30 a.m. breakfast with one group of constituents and ending with an 8:00 p.m. dinner with another, rushing around seemingly helter skelter from one subcommittee meeting to another, the mandatory photographs on the Capitol steps with two to ten groups during the day, responding to press inquiries, editing as many as 50 different letter replies to mail from home, I can remember only a few days out of each year when I could say with satisfaction that I had gotten something done that day rather than simply wash back and forth in the ebb and flow of the waves of legislation crashing to the House floor. Worse, of perhaps 400 issues coming to a vote in any given year, I was often sure of which way to vote on less than a quarter of them.

On a majority of issues coming out of the 19 committees other than my own (and more than a few of those *from* my two committees), I would check the electronic roster on the wall of the chamber during the 15 minute voting period and vote as a trusted colleague did, believing that he or she, unlike me, must have seriously weighed the issue and reached a sound judgment. When they were in the House, I relied on Peter Diester of Bucks County, Pennsylvania, George Bush of Houston, Texas, Gil Gude of Maryland, Chuck Wiggins and Bill Mailliard of California, Chuck Whalen and Charlie Mosher of Ohio, and Phil Ruppe of Michigan as my bell-weathers. Later on in the 1970s and early 1980s, I came to rely on Joel Pritchard of Washington, Jim Johnson of Colorado, Barber Conable of New York, Ralph Regula of Ohio, Jim Leach of Iowa, and John Erlenborn of Illinois. I knew they were honest men of great wisdom and judgment with thought processes similar to my own.

Years may pass before a new member of the minority party has any opportunity to feel confident that he or she is effective in the work of the House.

For a freshman congressman, particularly a Republican in the minority during the 40 years between 1954 and 1994, there was a golden rule of expected silence.

For example: Jerry Pettis, first elected to Congress in 1966, and a very able, quiet decent human being, after five years was nominated by his California colleagues to fill a suddenly-vacant "California seat" on the prestigious Ways and Means Committee. The Constitution gives a special power to the House alone: the initiation of all tax legislation. This awesome power is assigned to the Ways and Means Committee. Since there were then ten Republican members on Ways and Means, and California had ten percent of the Republicans in the House, it was generally accepted that California was entitled to one of the ten seats. Of elderly House members, it was often said: "Few die and none retire," and its former occupant, Jimmy Utt, had passed away at an advanced age.

The process for selection for committee membership, on the Republican side, was through the Republican "committee on committees," a group of perhaps 35 members, but five of whom, from the five biggest Republican states, each cast a vote measured by the number of Republicans from their respective states. The five biggest Republican states in the 1970s were New York, Illinois, Pennsylvania, California, and Ohio. For one, therefore, to aspire to those holiest of holies, the Ways and Means, Rules, or Appropriations Committees, he would need the support of all five of the senior members representing the 80 to 85 votes of those five states. These were men generally in their late 60s or 70s and often in their 80s.

Jerry dutifully went, hat in hand, to solicit the support of each of these worthies. He was successful with the first four, and finally, with some trepidation, approached crusty old Frank Bow of Ohio for his approval.

Frank Bow grunted: "Pettis, how long have you been in the House?"

"Five years, sir."

"I don't believe I've ever heard you speak on the floor, Pettis."

"That's right, sir."

"I like that, Pettis. You'll have my vote."

THE DEMISE OF THE SENIORITY SYSTEM

There were only a few things a junior Republican member could do in the late 1960s.

Like a Marine Pfc., one could gripe about the leadership, but do little about it. One such gripe, commonly shared by anyone under age 50, was the seniority system.

The seniority system had been a hallowed tradition of the House since the dominance of Speaker "Uncle Joe" Cannon in the early 1900s. The system was simple: the member of the majority party with the longest continuous service on a committee automatically became its chairman. If you could breathe, you were entitled to be chairman. The minority member with the longest service became the "ranking minority member."

My first committee chairman, the venerable (in his 80s and senile) Bill Dawson of Illinois, chaired House Government Operations between 1967 and 1970. Each year, there was an annual meeting of the committee, at which time he was helped into his chair, banged the gavel twice, to open and adjourn the meeting, after which he was assisted back out of the chair to await the next annual meeting. Thus, the committee with jurisdiction over the economy and efficiency of every executive branch agency was virtually immobilized for three years. I once asked the man second to the chairman in seniority, Chet Holifield, how he could accept the system. Chet simply repeated former Speaker Sam Rayburn's famous admonition to new House Democrats: "Go along and get along."

The 11 southern states, following a disastrous period of reconstruction following the Civil War, perceived early on that as a minority, they could still enjoy great legislative power in the Congress if their representatives could obtain seniority. Consequently, if the state of Mississippi could elect a congressman at age 25 and a senator at age 30, the minimum ages specified by the constitution, and if they were thereafter reelected, it was only a matter of time before they reached that pinnacle of power–chairmanship of a major committee. Until the late 1960s, the South had been pretty much a Democrat enclave for 80 years. To win the Democrat nomination was tantamount to assured election. Once elected, the southern political powers rarely permitted challenge to an incumbent. They could be reelected until overtaken by death or infirmity.

Without question, on a scale of 1 to 1,000, a committee chairman of a powerful committee such as Rules, Ways and Means, Appropriations, or Armed Services would rate 1,000 (equal to the Speaker). The chairman of a minor committee such as Government Operations, Veterans, or the District of Columbia, might rate only 300 on the Power Scale. By comparison, a freshman member of the minority party would rate a one. A freshman of the majority party might be a two, based on the expectancy of a subcommittee chairmanship after two or three terms.

In December 1967, when I was first elected, the 21 committee chairmanships were in the hands of elderly members, five from Texas alone. The four most powerful chairmen were Bill Colmer (Mississippi) of Rules, Wilbur Mills (Arkansas) of Ways and Means, George Mahon (Texas) of Appropriations, and Mendel Rivers (South Carolina) of Armed Services. Note the southern dominance.

The Speaker was John McCormack of Massachusetts. Mr. McCormack was in his 80s and looked it. He was so old and his approaching senility so apparent that it inspired George Bush and me, each in our second terms in 1969, to approach our Minority Leader, Gerry Ford. We asked permission to initiate an effort to promote the Republican cause by publicly pledging to end the seniority system if we could obtain a Republican majority in the 1970 elections, thereby making the healthy and vigorous Ford Speaker in place of McCormack.

Gerry had no difficulty in seeing the merits of the proposal, although he could foresee some problems with his own ranking members, most of whom were over 70. He diplomatically appointed a 19 man task force, six freshman or sophomores, six ranking Republicans (understandably skeptical of any proposal that could curtail their power after spending so many years to achieve it), and seven members in the five to ten term "middle" category. George Bush, the first Republican elected to Congress from Houston, Texas since Reconstruction, was our chairman.

George was a born leader. As chairman of the 19 member seniority investigation committee, 13 of whom were his seniors, George took his only real task in the Congress in 1969 very seriously indeed. He sought and received the solemn and scholarly testimony of a number of the leading Political Science professors in American academia on how seniority affected the legislative process. We learned to our dismay that the professors had very little understanding of how the House really worked. H. L. Mencken's comment, "Every profession is a conspiracy against the public," is especially true of members of the House, as well as lawyers, doctors, and newspaper publishers. Only a House member knows the real story, and he generally discusses it only with other House members.

By early 1970, we had the votes on the committee to urge upon the Republican Conference (all Republican members of the House) and have passed a solemn pledge that, if elected to a majority in 1970, we Republicans would end the seniority system and elect our chairmen by secret ballot. We called for a secret ballot because we knew that retribution against dissenters by an outraged chairman who was reelected would be swift and terrible. The bravest people in America today may be those eight Republican House members who unsuccessfully voted on the record against the election of Newt Gingrich as Speaker in early 1997, following the finding that he had violated House ethics standards.

The Democrat Caucus was forced by this brash flippancy to adopt an identical resolution. If reelected, they too would abandon that butt of recurring Washingtonian jokes, the obsolete seniority system, and elect their chairmen by secret ballot.

There is no indication that this great leap forward affected the voters in the 1970 elections, nor did it really change the seniority system. When Congress convened in 1971, both parties *elected* the most senior members as chairmen and ranking members. This occurred again in 1972, but the 1974 elections saw a different result. Over 70 freshman Democrats were elected, largely because of the disasters of Richard Nixon and Watergate. They promptly proceeded to eject three elderly power-abusing chairmen, Eddie Hebert (Louisiana) of Armed Services, Wright Patman (Texas) of Banking, and Bob Poage (Texas) of Agriculture.

A great blow had been struck.

The work of five years earlier had borne fruit. To George Bush's greatest accomplishments–Desert Storm, the Thousand Points of Light, and getting Israel to initiate the Mid-East Peace Process–should be added the end of the seniority system.

Chapter 10

Old Advice for
New Members of Congress

Eugene J. McCarthy (D-Minnesota)

Between the time they are elected and the date of their swearing in, new members of Congress live precariously—in a condition not very different from that of newly hatched green turtles on the shores of Tortuga as they make their run for the safety of the sea. The young turtles are beset by attackers from the air, by land animals, and even by fish waiting for them in the shallow waters offshore.

Waiting for new members of Congress is a variety of predators: various committees of their own parties, numerous foundations, think tanks, "public interest" groups, and special interests. Some of these are concerned about policy, some about procedures. Some are concerned about morals and deep ethical concerns. Lobbyists lurk in the shadows or hover in the air.

The press, especially the columnists, gives advice—solicited or unsolicited.

The John F. Kennedy School of Harvard—somewhat in the way of Mohammad inviting the mountain—hosts and instructs new members, telling new congressmen how to be congressmen.

The Brookings Institution stands ready, not so much to advise as to pronounce. Note that Brookings is an institution, not an institute, like Carnegie. Members of Brookings do not say that they are with or from the organization but of it, just as members of separate choirs of angels do not say they are with or from the cherubim but of it.

The Heritage Foundation will be waiting for conservatives in need of help. Common Cause will be present, insisting that it is, possibly, the only pure, uncontaminated public interest lobby. The Americans for Democratic Action, which originated in order to protect liberals from communist influence and now includes as one of its purposes protecting little liberals from toys that are dangerous, physically or psychologically, is still around. (The ADA is strong on maintaining attendance records of members of Congress.)

Newly-elected members, of whatever class, will be asked by one or more of these organizations or people to support reorganizations or reforms of various kinds. They will be told that it is essential to their success to have a dedicated, hardworking staff; that it is vital that they know the rules of procedure of the body to which they have been elected; that they should maintain a near-perfect, if not perfect, attendance record; that national politics is very complicated, or that it is simple, if one only follows the principles of the organization applying the pressure.

Some of these counselors will condemn the seniority system.

Party spokesmen will emphasize the importance of party loyalty. Democratic Party spokesmen undoubtedly will quote remarks long attributed to Speaker Sam Rayburn that "those who go along get along." Others will praise "the middle way," the vital center, and the art of compromise. A few will explain how important it is to have good relationships with the press.

Most of this advice is questionable. Some of it is very bad. Every two years, I offer a set of ten countercommandments, which, if observed by members of Congress, will save them much time and save them from making many mistakes.

1. Do not have a perfect or near-perfect attendance record. Watch ADA on this. If a new member has an attendance record that is better than 80 percent, there is reason to believe that he or she has been wasting time. A member who has been in office for several terms should work his attendance record down to 65 percent to 75 percent.

Note that this will not be well understood by the press.

2. Do not worry too much about rules of procedure or spend too much time trying to learn them. The Senate rules are simple enough to learn, but they are seldom honored in practice. House rules are too complicated. Use the parliamentarian. (My own rule in the House of Representatives was not to trust a member who quoted the Bible, chapter and verse; the Internal Revenue Code, section and subsection; or the Rules of the House.)

3. Beware of a staff that is too efficient. My old administrative assistant, Jerome Eller, advised that a member of Congress should never trust a staffer who regularly got to the office before the member did. Or who stayed later.

4. Don't worry too much about understanding the issues or being a "policy wonk." Remember that politics is much like professional football. Those who are most successful are, as the dean of my college said, smart enough to understand the game but not smart enough to lose interest.

5. Don't knock seniority. You may have it sooner than you anticipate. And remember what Gilbert Chesterton said: that it makes no sense to have the oldest son of a king succeed his father, but it saves a lot of trouble. (Alexis de Tocqueville held that in a democracy, seniority is a last defense against anarchy.)

6. Unless the issue is of overwhelming importance, don't be the only one or one of a few who are right. It is difficult to say to one's colleagues in Congress, "I am sorry I was right. Please forgive me." They won't. It is easier to say, "I was wrong." Forgiveness is almost immediate.

7. Remember that the worst accidents occur in or near the middle of the road. Bipartisanship and balance are usually stressed by the League of Women Voters. Be wary of all three.

8. Do not respond to the appeal of "party loyalty." This can be the last defense of rascals.

9. Abide by the advice given to young members of Congress 40 years ago by a leftover New Dealer: "Vote against anything introduced that begins with the syllable *re.*" Reorganizations, recodifications, reform, and especially resolutions. The puritans really do slay St. George and feed the dragon.

10. Perhaps most important: the advice of Ed Leahy, noted reporter for the *Chicago Daily News*—"Never trust the press."

Chapter 11

Congressman-At-Large: Representing the State of Maryland

Carlton R. Sickles (D-Maryland)

It is a privilege and an honor to serve as a member of the U. S. Congress. I had that privilege for two sessions of Congress, as a congressman-at-large from the state of Maryland in the 88th and the 89th Congresses. It gave me the opportunity to share the feelings of pride and responsibility with my colleagues. It provided me with the ability to actively participate in the process of addressing the national needs of the country.

HOW I BECAME INVOLVED IN POLITICS

I became a politician of sorts because of community needs, not because of any political ambition. My family and I moved from Northern Virginia to Langley Park, Maryland in the early 1950s. (I had been recalled to active duty with the Air Force Office of Special Investigations during the Korean Incident and was serving at Bolling Air Force Base.) In this new development, there was a need for local government attention to our community needs (streets and traffic lights in particular) and so, a civic association was formed. I attended the first meeting, and, since I was in uniform, was elected as president.

We were not successful in receiving the services we requested, so someone, not me, suggested we start a political club. We formed the "Langley Park Democratic Club." It changed the attitudes of the county government officials. I was elected president of the Democratic Club because most of the members were federal government employees and, under the Hatch Act, could not hold an office in the club, and I was a civilian again by that time. Subsequently, I also became the precinct chairman.

At the next political election (1954), the Democratic organization fielded its usual slate of candidates for the entire county. The gentleman whom the party selected to run for the State House of Delegates chose to run for the State Senate, leaving a vacancy on the ticket which I was asked to fill. At that time, I had lived in the state of Maryland for less than four years. I ran and was elected, and served for eight years.

My experience in the state legislature turned out to be very interesting and challenging. The Maryland State Legislature was a part-time commitment. The sessions were held in the early months of each year. In addition to this political function in my life, I was also very busy with my law practice in the District of Columbia and with my business which involved servicing employee benefit plans resulting from negotiations between labor unions and their employers. I did realize that, as time passed, I became actively involved in more and more significant issues and constituent services which took more time.

I served in the state legislature for two terms (eight years total). When I first went to the state legislature, I was disappointed to find that it was not adequately staffed. A few of the major committees had secretaries, but individual members did not. In my last four years, I did have a secretary for the labor committee which I chaired. There was a legislative research section which was very helpful in preparing legislation, but each member had to rely upon personal background and experiences in performing the legislative functions.

Since I was a new Marylander, I sought out delegates from other parts of a very complex state to get some background on their community needs and concerns which helped me to perform my legislative duties. These contacts were invaluable in subsequent elections.

I spent the first four years in the state legislature on the Judiciary Committee, which I found interesting and challenging. I spent the last four years on the Ways and Means Committee, which I found boring and frustrating because, under the Maryland Constitution, the Governor's budget could not be increased by the legislature, even though Maryland, like many other States, was not addressing their major needs.

However, during my service in the legislature, I worked for civil rights legislation, Chesapeake Bay cleanup, library support, prevailing wages on state projects, and a host of other issues, many involving local matters in my own Prince George's County. The list grew as time went on. I finally realized that I should either be a full-time or a no-time legislator.

THE OPPORTUNITY TO RUN FOR CONGRESS

The congressman who served the fifth congressional district decided, prior to the 1962 election, that he would not run for reelection. He said that I should know early that he was not going to run again, in case I wanted to run for the office. He had had my support in his previous election, and I appreciated his advice, which whet my interest.

I tried to assess my possibilities for success. I'd been active in the Young Democrats organization and had traveled around the state and met many people.

In my personal business, I had contacts with people throughout the state and was able to develop some strong support, particularly from the industrial city of Baltimore. I also finally realized that I was, in fact, a politician.

As a result of the 1960 census, Maryland became entitled to one additional congressman. This new seat became a "congressman-at-large" serving the entire state, instead of a small district. The action of the Maryland legislature in creating the new boundaries for the new eighth congressional district was removed from the books by citizen action, pursuant to a constitutional procedure, because the eight districts created by the legislature were not approximately equal in population.

During the process of establishing the seat as an at-large seat, a "Draft Sickles for Congress" movement emerged, mostly by people from other parts of the state. It was at that time I decided to be a "full-time" politician rather than a "no-time" politician, so I decided to run for the office.

It was a busy campaign. I was invited to, and did, join the anti-organization slate of candidates in the primary. We crisscrossed the state nonstop and, when it was over, I had won the primary. I then joined all the victorious candidates on the party slate and thereby was elected the congressman-at-large.

After the swearing-in ceremony, my new key staff members, whom I had selected, set out to locate our new offices and start to work.

CONGRESSMAN-AT-LARGE

The fact that I represented the whole state, and its impact on our office operation and my performance, now came home to all of us.

Instead of having no staff in the state legislature, I expected that I was going to have a full staff. I soon found out that, even though I had a larger constituency than any other Maryland congressman, I would have the same staff authorization as they and all members of Congress, no matter the population (unlike the Senate, which provided staff based upon population).

The attention paid to a state legislator pales in comparison to that paid to a congressman. There was a feeling among many constituents that a congressman can do anything if he wants to. Many of the requests involved the concern that the constituent had not been treated fairly by a federal agency. The agencies were very cooperative in reviewing these matters for we congressmen so that we could respond to the constituent.

We did the best we could. In order to provide adequate salaries with the money available, it became necessary for many employees to work full time for part-time salaries. (Cheerfully??)

No matter how much we tried, there was not adequate paid staff to perform the service functions. We relied upon many volunteers. We had a district office in Prince George's County, Maryland. We also had one in the city of Baltimore. We didn't have any paid personnel to run that office in Baltimore, so a group of volunteers was formed called the "Sickles Score." There were 20 members of the group who volunteered a day a month and followed some general instructions in the office so that the people in Baltimore City would feel they could make some direct contact by phone with their congressman. Within the office in Washington, we also had to rely heavily upon volunteers who came in to handle our correspondence. We spent a great deal of time and effort on these constituent services, and I remember, at one point, it was suggested that about 85 percent of our office operation was constituent service, and actually my role was pretty close to that. The district was not only an at-large district, but it abutted the national capital and, therefore, we were close to our constituency, and we were required to travel all over the state on a constant basis in order to satisfy the needs and requests of our local citizens.

Many people learned they had a second congressman, so if they had something that they needed in a way of a constituent service or legislative action, they would write one letter to their local congressman and one, of course, to me.

I can't say too much in praise of my staff and volunteers in meeting the needs of our citizens.

I should point out that members of the state legislature had not been very partisan. Democrats, and the few Republicans we had, worked together. I soon learned the increase in partisanship at the federal level, but at least congeniality and respect were the rules at that time in the House.

I had learned of the "praise" and "abuse" of public officials over the years. I believe I was lucky to have been in office at a time when politicians were generally respected by the community at large. I was further blessed to have felt very little "abuse" during my career. My conclusion, both in Congress and in the state legislature, was that each of my colleagues was highly motivated and worked hard. The fact that we disagreed on an issue didn't make either one of us wrong. Only time would tell that.

The most significant result of being the congressman-at-large rather than representing only one particular area of the state is that I was very busy trying to sort out the conflicting views among my constituents. I often recalled my days in political science class at Georgetown College, reading about the noted English politician, Sir Edmund Burke, who averred that we are not merely delegates, but rather representatives, to exercise our best judgment. Of course, this is easier said then done. If one doesn't care about local concerns, one's service may be limited. All in Congress wrestle with this challenge.

As congressman-at-large, I had to represent the interests of all the citizens of the state of Maryland, which is sometimes called "America in Miniature." It meant that one had to be aware of the industrial area of Baltimore City, the Eastern shore abutting the ocean on one side and the Chesapeake Bay on the other side, the tobacco growers of southern Maryland, the horse country of northern Maryland, the suburban counties abutting the nation's capital, the mountainous area of western Maryland, and on and on. And I heard from all of them, it seemed, at once. I loved every minute of it. I had a warm, wanted feeling 24 hours a day. I hope I served them well.

Part Three

The Personal Side of
Life in the House

The selections in Part Three focus on what it is really like to serve in the House of Representatives--the stresses and strains, the impact on family life, the idealism associated with public service, and the sense of awe commonly experienced at finding oneself a part of this hallowed institution.

Drawing on interviews with 60 congressional spouses, Christine LaRocco provides a fascinating survey of the various ways congressional service affects family life. Each congressional couple must decide what the role of the spouse should be in the campaign, whether to move to Washington or live in the district, what the spouse's role should be after the election, and how to carve out some time for family life.

George J. Hochbrueckner provides an in-depth account of how one couple made these choices, conceiving of congressional service as a husband-wife team. Representative Hochbrueckner and his wife Carol Ann operated as a team in every aspect of their political lives, getting started at the township level, winning election to the New York State Assembly, and eventually serving in the U.S. House of Representatives.

Former Speaker Jim Wright describes the stresses and strains congressional service puts on any member who comes to Congress driven, in whole or in part, by religious idealism. He reviews the seductive aspects of life in Congress and offers some practical advice to idealists of all stripes, reminding any who might need reminding that men of good will often disagree. He also cautions new members of Congress to be realistic about what they can contribute.

Finally, Joe Bartlett, who served as Chief of Pages, Reading Clerk, and Minority Clerk of the U.S. House of Representatives, recounts the challenges and frustrations awaiting anyone who aspires to work as a member of a legislator's staff, a committee staff, or an Officer of the House.

Chapter 12

Family Life in Washington:
The Spouse's Perspective

Christine Bideganeta LaRocco

The evening news draws a glamourous picture of senators and representatives in the seat of power making heady decisions, microphones thrust in their faces. Yet the real story that often goes untold is about average men and women who set out to make a difference by running for elective office. Most are part of Middle America, hard workers, risk takers. They come from towns across this country where their grandparents may have homesteaded or cities where economic opportunities and an enhanced quality of life have led them. They have spouses, babies, school children, and grown children, each with different needs for affection and attention.

At that first swearing-in ceremony in January, none truly knows the chaotic waters into which the member and the families have been swept. The term in office is short, and there is much to accomplish. Excited families watch the members with pride from the galleries. Television cameras capture the auspicious occasion for audiences around the world.

For the spouses and children, this is a banner day and life-altering event. These families sacrifice their privacy and their precious time together so one of them may serve. They are the congressional team, the mates, coaches, and supporters. They send a senator or representative out the door in the morning and welcome home a Mom or Dad at night.

From the recollections of spouses of senators and representatives who served from the 1940s through the 1990s come snapshots of that experience, both stimulating and poignant. (See the chart at the end of the chapter for names and terms in office.)

Whether the negative is forgotten or overshadowed as time passes is not clear, but their comments repeatedly echo a strong sense of mission, honor, tradition, sacrifice, and support. These reflections suggest the success of the senator or representative is somehow linked with family unity, strength, and harmony. Without a doubt, no book about life in Congress is complete without the voice of the spouse.

THE SPOUSE AS CAMPAIGNER AND ADVISOR

In an elegant ballroom before thousands of energetic supporters, a member of Congress rises to address the crowd. Proudly, he introduces his spouse, seated at his side. "I reminded my wife one day that her former boyfriend digs ditches for a living. I said, 'Honey, if you had married him, you'd be the wife of a ditch digger.' She glared at me and replied, 'No, darling, if I had married him, *he*'d be the congressman.' "

Most congressional spouses are politically astute, well-informed, and deeply interested in the political process. During a campaign that can last more than a year, not only is the spouse a primary supporter and hand-holder of the harried and over-scheduled candidate, but he or she often serves as political strategist, campaign consultant, staffer, speaker, scheduler, fundraiser, driver, and volunteer organizer.

Over kitchen tables and in quiet conversations, husbands and wives decide to run for political office and open their lives to public scrutiny. Because the switch to public life will test a marriage to its limits, the two partners must carefully weigh the decision about the role the spouse will play. During the next weeks and months, households will be turned upside down.

On election night, the viewing public sees the proud spouse with arms waving alongside the beaming candidate. Whether the election is won or lost, the spouse truly earns that moment at the podium.

Supportive Role

In the past, accompanying the candidate was likely the only role of the spouse. Betty Rhodes remembers, "In the early years of my husband's congressional career, the spouse's role was, like the mother of the groom, to be seen but not heard. I attended functions, smiled a lot, and remembered names."

Nearly all spouses serve in the traditional supportive role. Constituents expect to meet both husband and wife, and many join the media in discreetly scrutinizing their relationship. A loving couple with complementary strengths is a strong component of a winning campaign.

Millie Grisham was more comfortable greeting people and mingling, than any other task. It was the same for Virginia Lipscomb whose husband was elected in California in 1953 where there were so many volunteers that she was not needed in the campaign office. So she found her niche attending functions along with her husband. Opal Karsten had a special role helping the candidate remember names of those rude voters who asked, "Do you remember me? What is my name?"

Not all spouses are free to participate because they have other duties at home or work. Some, like Hazel Avery, had young children who needed their mother's attention at home. They became her primary responsibility, freeing their father to campaign day and night.

Members of Congress agree that any campaign is enhanced by a supportive, team-playing spouse beside them. It can make all the difference in having a great experience, whether winning or losing.

Volunteer Role

Now in her 90s, Agnes Deane remembers organizing "folding parties" for her husband's campaigns in the mid-'40s, along with working in their insurance office. "I typed and typed personal letters to lists of people, and later, when we lost the first go round by so few votes, I said, 'Oh, if I had just typed a few more letters!' "

Spouses who love the action of politics participate directly as volunteers. They often are called on for help in the early stages when the activities may be conducted out of the candidate's own home. But as the campaign progresses, they may find their role broadens. They work in the campaign office, conduct polls, or go door-to-door in neighborhoods. Spouses write widely-circulated letters extolling the candidates' record and vouching for them as upstanding citizens, husbands, wives, mothers, or fathers. They push strollers filled with brochures tucked in beside the baby, take polls, make phone calls, drop leaflets, lick stamps, and stuff envelopes.

The role of a volunteer often assumes an importance that goes beyond contributing to the immediate task at hand. Working alongside other volunteers, spouses can encourage the troops, detect problems, and offer suggestions to make the campaign run smoothly. They become the "eyes and ears" of the candidate, especially when personalities clash or morale is low.

They also can become specialists. Jane Broomfield remembers how the latest 1950s technology affected their campaigns tremendously. "What a boon an addressograph machine was! I worked on mailings in every job, addressing or stuffing," she says. Today, the need for someone who has mastered the latest computer software for databases and electronic mail or Web sites to promote the candidate's message can create a similar niche for a spouse.

And it's not just the spouses. Even the children, relatives, and family dog swing into action as "volunteers" sometimes. Dorothy Hungate remembers when she, her parents, and numerous friends were all in different locations campaigning. "Our 13-year-old daughter took care of the home phone calls, and our 15-year-old son recruited older friends to drive while he delivered campaign materials," she says. June Bingham's family dog, a small poodle, wore a sandwich-board that read, "underdogs for Bingham."

Surrogate Candidate

Claire Schweiker was an effective young campaigner for her husband's initial race for the House. "I was expecting our second child during that first primary and general election, but I campaigned with my husband and also did my own campaigning with women's groups." The strong positive impact of her efforts as a young wife and expectant mother championing her husband's causes contributed to a victory on election night.

Like Claire, more gregarious spouses attend events in the candidate's place. When the calendar is booked, they speak before groups in another part of the district and participate in special events. Spouses appear in campaign ads on television, speak on talk shows, and agree to interviews. The obvious advantage is that the candidate can be two places at once. Filling in for a candidate, spouses can actually double the number of events where their side of the story is personally represented. The courage and strength of spouses, especially in the heat, or even hostility, of the campaign, is a testimony to their firm belief in the cause and their devotion to the candidate.

Elizabeth Mayne participated in Wiley's Iowa campaigns by speaking at retirement homes and small-group coffees. She remembers the difficulty of adjusting to the lack of privacy and to seeing their names on everything from billboards to bumper stickers.

Like many others, Lana Bethune kept a separate schedule of events and speaking engagements on her husband's behalf. "I did radio, newspaper, and TV interviews because I could say positive things about him that he could not say about himself." She advises, "A spouse needs comfortable shoes, a big smile, and a thick skin."

Participating in events that her husband could not attend because of other commitments, Marjorie Fithian often spoke on his behalf. In North Carolina, Louise Broyhill even narrated slide shows on the nation's capital for schools, retirement homes, and various clubs.

Side-by-side Campaigning

A campaigning spouse will use any excuse to speak with constituents. Agnes Deane says, "I would go in to a store and just buy a spool of thread or something, introduce myself and talk a bit."

Animated and outgoing spouses are effective crusaders bringing a personal touch to the campaign trail. At community events, the public meets a friendly couple. While candidates talk national business and political issues, the spouses can engage people in personal conversations that reach beyond the issues. Most spouses agree that rewards are reaped in long-lasting friendships.

While attending county fairs, walking the towns' streets, and joining campaign caravans are time consuming and tiring, spouses are a "secret weapon" in swaying many voters. This role cannot be filled by staff members or other volunteers. The public appreciates and sometimes *insists* on the personal approach.

Sylvia Symington says, "The thing I liked the most were conversations with people. They told us so many things about their lives we could never have learned any other way." Marian Adair agrees. "It is fortunate that we worked together as a team. I loved meeting the people," she says.

Gretchen Quie participated in campaign caravans covering the district. "I went business to business on the other side of the street. I also greeted people at luncheons, breakfasts, or dinners with him."

Another spouse who participated in caravans was Barbara-Ann Hanrahan, who campaigned out of an old school bus that tilted to the right after being used as a worker bus on a construction site.

Dorothy Runnels remembers, "Coming from a small area and a small state, I found the people were thrilled to have a spouse come back and bring them first-hand news. The women thought I did more, knew more, went more, and was better informed than I really was!"

Being involved in the campaign allows the spouse to serve as advisor and motivator. On days when candidates are barraged with criticism, questions, and negative feedback, the spouse can be a sounding board. Some seasoned spouses call this "cooling the horse before sending it back to the barn." In a strong relationship, the spouse can be trusted to tell the truth without hurting and to help re-energize the candidate before the next event begins.

Justine Prokop describes her role "to provide a sense of support for Stan during these tiring trips and keep him motivated throughout the campaign." Because she wanted to be there for him, she accompanied him on all campaign visits throughout the counties in his Pennsylvania district.

Candidates can rely on their spouses, who hear the same speech over and over, to effectively critique its delivery. Opal Karsten's husband was elected in 1947. She remembers, "When Frank was out pleading for votes, I was usually with him to tell him if he needed to speak louder or tell more jokes." Keeping the campaign manager from over-scheduling the "utterly exhausted" candidate was June Bingham's job, along with conferring with her husband on which issues to emphasize.

Spouses buffer the candidate from an over-zealous staff as tension mounts. From their insider's position, they not only realize the diverse pressures of the campaign, but also have the inside track on personal finances and family matters unknown to the staff. A quiet evening debriefing with a supportive and under-standing spouse takes the edge off a distressing day, allowing a candidate to unwind, regroup, and analyze strategies.

Major Campaign Positions

Often, spouses manage the campaigns. "My role included working with staff, writing a column for Wisconsin newspapers, campaign organization, and fund-raising," says Ellen Proxmire. She served as manager of the 1957, 1958, and 1964 campaigns for her husband, Senator William Proxmire.

Marlene Howard-Lazzaro was another full-time campaign manager. After her husband James Howard became chairman of the Public Works and Transportation Committee, she also represented him back in the New Jersey district.

The professional and multi-talented spouse sometimes assumes full responsibility for some aspect of the campaign, especially in the first race. During the incumbent's subsequent campaigns, the spouse's role may not be as extensive because staff members and supporters fill the position. However, many spouses raise funds, oversee the finances, coordinate volunteers, or manage the campaign office during each cycle.

Because these specific tasks demand full-time attention, spouses with greater responsibilities are major political strategists who devote themselves wholly to the cause and work tirelessly for a seat in the House or Senate.

Cathy Long, who was elected to her husband's seat upon his death in office, recalls, "When Gillis ran the first time, he had difficulty getting a script he liked for his first TV appearance, and so in desperation, I sat down at my dining room table and wrote one. I wrote many of his speeches after that." Her experience with his campaigns prepared her for her own campaign for the same congressional district after his death.

Another spouse taking on a major role was Nancy Hutto, whose husband Earl entrusted in her the weighty responsibilities of campaign treasurer for his congressional races in Florida.

Spouses bring warmth and personal talents to a campaign, a special touch that makes a difference. The unique and winning personalities of spouses provide subtle differences that help win elections and strengthen the relationship. Having a partner in the struggle gives the candidate added vigor and renews his or her spirits during the long months before election night.

Jean Grotberg, an accomplished pianist, added a musical touch to campaigning. "Both of us had been professional musicians in our earlier years. Many times, John would be asked to lead the National Anthem or a sing-a-long, and I was the piano accompanist."

After the polls closed on election night, Claire Gallagher opened the family home to thousands of people who stayed until the wee hours of the morning. "It was our way of saying 'thank you' to all the people."

Most importantly, spouses can encourage laughter in campaigns. Dwight Patterson, who worked evenings for his wife Liz's campaigns in South Carolina while practicing law during her six years in office, remembers a situation where humor helped ease the stress. As one of the growing group of male spouses of women in Congress, he recalls a particularly humorous incident at a White House dinner where he and his wife were being lined up for the president's receiving line by a young female Naval officer. He correctly stood behind his wife, but was told to move in front of her because "Principals go first." His wife, the congress-woman, turned to the officer, smiled brightly and said, "Young lady, *I* am the principal."

MOVING TO WASHINGTON

Heated campaigns and boisterous victory parties soon cool with the realities of what follows. An early challenge to the elected senator or representative is the demanding lifestyle on both the home front and in Washington. Constituents hound elected officials to attend banquets, benefits, state fairs, and local meetings, while the rigors of legislation and appointments keep them double and triple booked on Capitol Hill.

Marguerite Lichtenwalter remembers how she and her husband Franklin felt in 1947 when they arrived. "During those times, a new member of the House was not supposed to address the House or submit any bills. That was a 'hard pill to swallow' for the Speaker of the Pennsylvania legislature to become 'low man on the totem pole' in the U.S. House," she says.

After a successful campaign and election, the spouse becomes a major support for a senator or representative whose attention is almost totally absorbed by legislation, constituents, staff, lobbyists, party politics, and the press. Thus, traditionally shared responsibilities like running a household and caring for children – virtually all family life – become by default almost the sole territory of the spouse.

As the legislator has little time for a private life, the immediate question of where to live is a tough one. The problem centers around the family's needs and the family members' willingness to make major lifestyle changes. Where will the children thrive best and see their parents most? The complicated formula in the decision on whether to move the family full time to Washington or to continue to live at home has several components.

The Distance Factor

The most obvious element is distance. How many hours does it take to travel home at the end of the week? Pennsylvania and West Virginia residents might have only a two-hour drive door-to-door. New England, the midwest, and the southeast are a short flight away. However, for those living in the west, as many as seven hours of connecting flights and possibly a few hours driving from the airport take their toll.

Congressman Paul Fino's spouse Esther and the family stayed in New York because the children were 12 and 9 years old, and the parents felt no need to uproot them. With only an hour flight, the children saw their father every weekend. Freda Solomon also stayed in their upstate New York district. The flight to the Albany airport and subsequent drive home were a manageable commute, allowing her to attend events in Washington with her husband several times a month. One New York City representative even managed to commute almost daily to Washington, leaving early each morning and arriving home at night in time to tuck his children into bed.

Family Considerations

Closely related to the distance of the home district are family considerations and the children's ages. Elementary school children are easier to move than teenagers who are gaining credits for graduation, involved in sports, and more active with friends. Some families with smaller children spend the first half of the school year in Washington and the second half in their home state. To accommodate the family's needs, some House and Senate members may share an apartment, lease a small efficiency, or even sleep on a couch in the office during the week.

Kati Machtley's husband took an apartment with another Congressman to avoid the expense of maintaining two homes and moving two young children. Many such arrangements are made in apartments on Capitol Hill, where members bunk together three nights a week, keeping expenses low.

To avoid interrupting the children's school year, Dorothy Hungate's husband Bill rented an apartment near his office. He commuted almost every weekend until the family moved to a Virginia suburb of D.C. his second term.

The family of John Lindsay also stayed home in New York in the beginning, but the arrangement proved unsatisfactory for the family. So, although Mary Lindsay had to commute back to New York for her work, she eventually found a move to Washington was a better choice. Conversely, Zoe Mikva moved with her children to Washington from 1969 to 1972, but returned to Illinois because the family was happier back home.

Some compromise. Families remain at home as they adjust to this new rigorous life, or they split the time between the district and Washington. After the dust settles and the next election is won, a major move is less risky because the seat is more secure.

This response is more pronounced on the House side where the two-year term sends members scrambling back home to campaign almost immediately after their swearing-in ceremony. Since the move to Washington is disruptive and chaotic, House members and their families must think twice before making such a major decision. With the longer term, Senate families have six years to settle in, find schools and jobs, and adjust to the new life.

Frances Hagan and her children moved back and forth from Georgia, dividing the year for the children. They enjoyed friendships in both places but were always happy to return to Georgia for the summers. Bea Smith's family also split the year, six months in Iowa and six in Washington. Summers and first semester were spent at home so their son could continue his 4-H activities. Marlene Howard-Lazzaro moved the children to Washington only for the school terms, then returned to New Jersey during the summers and long holidays.

For successful congressional families, state-of-mind and maintaining a positive attitude are all-important in this yo-yo life. Nancy Hutto learned early on that "when we locked one door, that was behind us. Upon opening another door, that was the 'present.' Family togetherness was of great importance to us." Whether staying home or moving to Washington, families must adjust to the commuter lifestyle of the member, meaning Mom or Dad is away for half the week. Most agree there is no perfect solution.

The Economics of Moving

The bottom line frequently plays a major role in the decision to move the family. Real estate "sticker-shock" is a common memory among spouses. Purchasing a home in the area may cost three times the price of the family home in the district.

For those who decide to buy a home in Maryland, the District, or northern Virginia, the investment can be a struggle financially, but it may become an anchor later. Often former members stay in the area after leaving Congress, becoming longtime residents. Jackie Lloyd and her husband Jim commuted from California during his six years in office, purchasing a condominium in Washington. "Twenty years later we still have both places, and we use both in our on-going bi-coastal life," Jackie says.

Two homes can be a burden financially, yet congressional pay raises are rare. The stress of paying bills and saving for children's college expenses weighs heavily on families and is often a major factor in decisions to leave office.

An important element in the equation is the spouse's employment and two incomes. The move to Washington, D.C. involves the risk that a comparable job will be difficult to find or that a continuing career will be impossible. Some families maintain the status quo in the home state so the spouse can work, simply to stay afloat financially.

Living on a $12,000-a-year congressional salary in 1947 kept Agnes Deane in North Carolina the first term to run the family insurance office for an additional income. From then until 1968, when Tom and Lou Bevill moved the family from Alabama, congressional salaries had risen to only $22,500. Lou remembers how difficult it was to "make ends meet with two houses and three children who would be entering college soon."

However, for other couples, the move to Washington provides a little breathing room financially. Evelyn Burnside's husband Maurice, who won a seat in West Virginia in 1948, had been a college professor with a very low salary. The congressional salary was much better, and as he had a Ph.D. in government, he was "much at home" in the House.

While constituents resent pay raise proposals for legislators, maintaining two residences and raising and educating children are challenges facing congressional families that they cannot discuss with voters. The pressure, however, is significant and often even the thriftiest of couples leave office with increased personal debt.

The Logistics of Moving

The move itself can be an expensive, difficult, harrowing, and even humorous experience. Surprised after winning an election with the little-known fact that there is no allowance nor reimbursement for the cost of moving to the nation's capital, elected officials must pay movers to transport household furnishings across country, and this occurs one month after a long, expensive campaign. To save money, congressional families pack up the silverware, dishes, television, blankets, and family dog to drive mid-winter to Washington. Then, on several weekend flights to and from the district, many stuff their extra bags with additional household items.

One representative tells the story of the weekend his wife stuffed cookie sheets and pots and pans into his luggage for their apartment in Washington. To his embarrassment, the bag popped open upon arrival, causing great commotion in the airport's baggage area. Congressman Larry LaRocco once dutifully toted his wife's sewing machine across country from Idaho, hand carrying it to prevent damage.

Moves can be not only disrupting but also downright dangerous. Lucy Carter recalls the family drive of 1,200 miles from Iowa the day after Christmas. "Along the way we encountered rain, snow, ice, and a blizzard with high winds that gripped us on the Indiana turnpike. Somehow, we crept along and our cars stayed upright."

Humbled by the imposing sight of the Capitol and its awe-inspiring surroundings, many spouses share the sentiments of Claire Gallagher who "felt like Alice stepping through the looking glass whenever I entered this magic place." Amidst all the trauma of winning an elected seat in the House or Senate and moving to new surroundings, congressional families learn to be flexible, resourceful, adventuresome, and fearless.

CAREERS

A spouse's professional career or beloved job sometimes falls victim to the move to Washington. To leave a teaching position, abandon a law-practice, or drop out of a master's program is a difficult decision with both financial and personal considerations.

Positions are sometimes difficult to find in Washington for a spouse of an elected candidate with only a short term. Businesses are reluctant to hire someone who may not be around in two years. In addition, conflicts of interest must be considered. For a spouse with a law degree, a position with a firm in Washington means possible involvement in lobbying Congress. Most spouses are very cautious about putting their husbands' or wives' political careers in jeopardy, for while there is no restriction against taking a job in advocacy, a snoopy reporter may find an angle that warrants unfavorable press. As one savvy congressional spouse puts it, "It's not the legality of the matter that counts; it's the headlines."

An experienced attorney, James Schroeder moved the family to Washington when his wife Pat won her first election. Jim closed his law practice in Denver and joined a D.C. firm. "Your actions and career can positively support your spouse, to some extent, but they can easily have a very negative effect," he says, explaining that in his new practice he had to be very careful to avoid any lobbying or conflicts of interest. "Or even the appearance of conflicts of interest," he says.

Many of today's congressional spouses enjoy energizing, stimulating careers in Washington and the surrounding areas. Well-educated and highly competent, they are respected professionals in their diverse fields, playing major roles in the corporate world, promoting social issues and special causes, and participating in international affairs.

Spouses who give up careers in the home district to move to Washington must weigh the advantages over the disadvantages. Congressional couples are expected at banquets and receptions sponsored by constituents, advocacy groups, and the international community. To participate in all the activities and opportunities of congressional life as well as raise a family involves time both during the day and most evenings. Some choose not to continue their professional careers to ease the pressure.

Bea Smith had professional degrees when she arrived in Washington. "I am a social worker and graduated from law school," she says. After the election, she gave up the law to stay home and care for the children. "It was a joint decision. It was important with Neal gone so much and busier each year, that one of us should always be there for them."

Nancy Hamilton from Indiana remembers, "There were times in Washington social life that I felt a bit uncomfortable because I had no 'title.' That is probably one of the advantages my painting eventually gave me. I could use the title, 'artist'." Another artist, Peggy Fisher, recalls, "My profession as artist and art teacher was greatly enhanced. My classes were full. My paintings hung in Joe's office and in many public exhibits and continue to sell widely."

Claire Schweiker gave up her career conducting a daily, hour-long children's television program. "Raising five children and campaigning were most satisfying, stimulating, and rewarding for me."

Doris McClory left a promising job in New York. "I married Bob when he was a widower and a sitting member. But I had been working in television production in New York."

The musical Lou Bevill gave up her career as an instructor in piano, organ, and Spanish at a local junior college when they began campaigning and moved to the D.C. area. "I was also working toward a Master's degree; there was no question of my continuing any of this in Washington."

Time is a factor, and spouses are expected to attend events with the elected officials. A teacher at home in the district, Dorothy Hungate remembers that when she discussed taking a teaching position in Washington after their move, "The Congressman vetoed that suggestion!"

While many spouses decide to discontinue their careers, still the move offers new and rewarding opportunities that may not be available back home. The Washington area presents a wide range of possibilities for part-time or full-time employment in exciting and interesting fields. Among congressional spouses, the poster that advises, "Bloom Where You Are Planted" is particularly significant

Lola Pierotti Aiken had an interesting position in Washington from 1941 to 1967 as administrative assistant to Senator George Aiken of Vermont. After they married in 1967, she continued the job, although it entailed many more hours on Capitol Hill as she accompanied her husband to receptions, dinners, and special events. She considers it an exceptional experience all around.

Barbara Wortley's job was important to her, but keeping it meant she was often alone. "Since the district was only one hour away by plane, all local organizers thought my husband should be present for their events. He was expected to be in the district each weekend, so I would be either alone in the district during the week or alone in D.C. on the weekends."

June Hansen acted in British theater before marrying Orval and moving to Idaho. Then, after their move to Northern Virginia, the chance to return to theatrical life in Washington lured her back to the bright lights. "Perhaps the reason I enjoyed campaigning so much was the challenge of communicating with people—often total strangers—a similar challenge to when one is on stage in a play." June continues to perform and has won several awards in her field.

Becoming a business owner was new for Alta Leath when her husband was elected. She opened a jewelry store in Washington "to supplement our income. I had never been in business before and had not worked outside the home after our children came. Opening the store was a tremendous challenge. When I look back on the 18 years of owning the store, I'm amazed at what I was able to accomplish."

Alice Lancaster continued her career as a community college instructor when the family moved from North Carolina. Many weekends they drove home for events in the district. "The chief negative was fatigue, especially when I would make the trip to North Carolina and back after work on one day and be back in class in Virginia the next morning."

"My own career was probably helped by the move to Washington," recalls Evelyn Cohelan, a nurse and professor. "I do not know of another congressional wife who had a full-time job during the years 1959-1971. How rapidly things have changed."

During the 1980s, for Emily Scheuer "the transition never presented a problem. I had a full-time job and was used to juggling family needs and career pressure. I had to be in New York on weekdays and Jim there on weekends. However, after seven years of this, I was able to transfer jobs and work in Washington, which made our life much happier."

The decisions on where and how to live are as numerous and unique as the 535 members of the House and Senate. No two are alike, but all agree that family life in Congress becomes what the family members make of it. Resiliency and a positive outlook are cornerstones of successful transitions.

CHILDREN

For congressional children, activities on Capitol Hill offer opportunities to observe the government at close range. At times, history is made in their own living rooms. A carefree fourth grader answers the phone, listens, then gasps, "Oh gosh, Dad, it's the White House!"

But ball games are missed, piano recitals become disappointments, and Sunday family dinners disappear when Dad or Mom is attending an event back in the home state. Adjustments in home life are significant. Families try to make the advantages outweigh the disadvantages, yet the struggles of the children are sometimes the most poignant.

Congressional children benefit from the richness and excitement of life in the center of the nation's capital. They grow personally from adapting to new environments, make friends from all around the world, shake hands with celebrities, and attend exciting political and international events. The transformation to life in Washington can be especially productive for congressional children's development.

Moving children from California to Washington, although difficult, proved memorable for the Cohelan family. Evelyn remembers, "Our children were frequent visitors to the Capitol. They roamed freely throughout the office building and gave their friends tours of 'Daddy's Office'."

The transition for the family of Gretchen and Albert Quie was definitely positive. "The children were amazed at having friends across the street or just next door. Back on the farm, they played mostly with each other. At first, though, our son wished he had an 'electric friend-maker.' We all learned what it is like to mix with other religions and races." Barbara Foreman "showed the children that they should enjoy life no matter where they lived, and they learned that lesson well. They are very adaptable now as adults."

When the move takes children away from extended families at home, their parents sometimes find substitute relatives for them. Chris and Tom Downey's children were raised "with fellow members as aunts and uncles, and they saw them weekly. Our home was always open to members, and we had many dinners where our family hosted," she says. These relationships are still strong.

Joanne Kemp's previous role as spouse of a pro-football player was just as demanding as Congress, for her husband was away often at six-week training camp and every other weekend at an away-game. So the children could see more of their father while he was in Congress, she recalls, " Rather than going out to dinner with adults, we invited them home for dinner with our family. This exposed the children to many interesting people from all over the world."

Liz McEwen preferred her husband's schedule when he stayed in town on weekends. "Often, he would be in D.C. on weekends and would fly out late on Sunday, schedule meetings in Ohio all day Monday, and return Tuesday a.m." The arrangement allowed more time for the children with their father.

The Statons decided to move their two children to the Washington area, and it worked well, according to Lynn Staton. "Moving here was better for them as they were relatively anonymous as opposed to living back home in the district as children of the Republican congressman in a Democratic district."

The daughters of Michaelene and Jim Bilbray took part in the social life in Washington. "We gave the girls each the opportunity to take a turn at the various events, whether it was filling in for me once as a hostess on a congressional trip, attending a White House function, or serving as Cherry Blossom princess."

One special and highly-coveted invitation is the White House holiday party held every December. Many teens take turns accompanying a parent to this glittery event. The picture with the president and his wife is among the most coveted souvenirs of these exciting years.

The long and distinguished careers of Albert Gore, John "Jay" Rhodes, Compton White, John Dingell, and Clarence J. "Bud" Brown are testimony that the gene for serving in office may be transmitted to the next generation. They all were raised in Washington while their fathers held seats in the House and Senate, then followed in their footsteps. Perhaps family pride, loyalty, and strong modeling erase memory of times when their fathers were absent or distracted by the many responsibilities of the office.

Off-the-record comments by spouses about life in Congress reveal a negative side to raising children while a parent serves. One spouse remembers, "Congress was very unfriendly to families. The schedule was very difficult. It was difficult to go back and forth, hard to make friends. We suffered financial sacrifices and gave up our privacy."

An overworked and often "missing" father, torn from the family by public duties, is the focus of another spouse's comments. "There was no family life. The children were raised by their mother alone for 25 years of public life. It was the most difficult time of our teenagers' lives."

With any situation in life, the effort to maintain balance is critical, and the disadvantages of family life while a parent serves in Congress are not always forgotten.

The family of James Corman moved from California. His wife Nancy Malone says, "The older kids resented the intrusion, phone calls at dinner time, Daddy often gone, feeling used by family photos on Christmas cards – it was hard to be compared to 'Father Knows Best'. "

For Frances Hagan, the years spent in Washington were exhilarating but hard on the family. "The greatest sacrifice was leaving home and seeing our children so unhappy. They were pulled out of familiar and happy surroundings to go to a place where they knew no one. We had to do this to back up my husband." Sarah McDade also remembers sacrifices. "We had no privacy from TV and newspaper crews who would show up at our doors."

Even adult children are affected by a parent's years in public service. New Hampshire inn owners Sydna and Bill Zeliff came to Congress in 1991, where he served three terms. "Our youngest son, the only one left in New Hampshire, was in a fish bowl. As a new husband, father, and also businessman, this was difficult."

Some families leave children at home with relatives. The oldest daughter of Martha Shriver "didn't want to finish her last semester in high school in Virginia, so she stayed with an aunt and uncle. She missed a lot and now regrets it. The other two enjoyed the activities and friendships they made while they were here," she says.

With not enough hours in a congressional day, the family life suffers. Alta Leath says, "Serving as a member of Congress often seems to become all-encompassing, and the wife and children can become less significant than before. I don't believe this is intentional; it just happens as the nature of the job becomes more and more demanding, and there isn't enough time to go around."

Congressional spouses agree that the personal lives of national office-holders are not ideal. Members of Congress and their spouses continually search for better ways to handle the overwhelming pressures and still share the joys of raising children together.

MAKING A DIFFERENCE

A decision to run for national public office will, in the best case scenario, present a whole new set of challenges for the spouse and other family members. Few outsiders ever fully comprehend the demands on those whose every day lives are spent under such intense public scrutiny.

Yet women and men continue to seek a coveted seat in the U.S. Congress for a unique opportunity to make a difference in the history of the nation and the lives of all Americans. With patience, perseverance, understanding, and devotion to one another, congressional spouses and children play a significant role in the daily events that make the pages of history turn.

List of Contributors

Name	Spouse	State	Terms
Marian Adair	Congressman E. Ross Adair	IN	1951-71
Lola Aiken	Senator George D. Aiken	VT	1941-75
Hazel Avery	Congressman William H. Avery	KS	1955-65
Lana Bethune	Congressman Ed Bethune	AR	1979-85
Lou Bevill	Congressman Tom Bevill	AL	1967-97
Michaelene Bilbray	Congressman James H. Bilbray	NV	1987-95
June Bingham	Congressman Jonathan Bingham	NY	1965-83
Jane Broomfield	Congressman William S. Broomfield	MI	1957-93
Louise Broyhill	Congressman/Senator James Broyhill	NC	1963-86
Evelyn Burnside	Congressman Maurice Burnside	WV	1949-57
Lucy Carter	Congressman Steven V. Carter	IA	1959
Evelyn Cohelan	Congressman Jeffery Cohelan	CA	1959-71
Agnes Deane	Congressman Charles B. Deane	NC	1947-57
Chris Downey	Congressman Thomas J. Downey	NY	1975-93
Esther Fino	Congressman Paul A. Fino	NY	1953-69
Peggy Fisher	Congressman Joe Fisher	VA	1975-81
Marjorie Fithian	Congressman Floyd Fithian	IN	1975-83
Barbara Foreman	Congressman Ed Foreman	TX, NM	1963-71
Claire Gallagher	Congressman Cornelius E. Gallagher	NJ	1959-73
Millie Grisham	Congressman Wayne Grisham	CA	1979-83
Jean Grotberg	Congressman John E. Grotberg	IL	1985-86
Frances Hagan	Congressman G. Elliott Hagan	GA	1961-73
Nancy Hamilton	Congressman Lee H. Hamilton	IN	1965-99
Barbara-Ann Hanrahan	Congressman Robert P. Hanrahan	IL	1973-75
June Hansen	Congressman Orval Hansen	ID	1969-75
Marlene Howard-Lazzaro	Congressman James Howard	NJ	1965-88
Dorothy Hungate	Congressman William Hungate	MO	1964-77
Nancy Hutto	Congressman Earl Hutto	FL	1979-95
Opal Karsten	Congressman Frank M. Karsten	MO	1947-69
Joanne Kemp	Congressman Jack Kemp	NY	1971-89
Alice Lancaster	Congressman Martin Lancaster	NC	1987-95
Alta Leath	Congressman Marvin Leath	TX	1979-91
Marguerite Lichtenwalter	Congressman Franklin Lichtenwalter	PA	1947-51
Mary Lindsay	Congressman John Lindsay	NY	1959-65
Virginia Lipscomb	Congressman Glenard P. Lipscomb	CA	1953-70
Jackie Lloyd	Congressman Jim Lloyd	CA	1975-81
Cathy Long	Congressman Gillis W. Long	LA	1963-85
Kati Machtley	Congressman Ronald Machtley	RI	1989-95
Nancy Malone	Congressman James C. Corman	CA	1961-81
Elizabeth D. Mayne	Congressman Wiley Mayne	IA	1967-75
Doris McClory	Congressman Robert McClory	IL	1963-83
Sarah McDade	Congressman Joseph McDade	PA	1963-99
Liz McEwen	Congressman Bob McEwen	OH	1981-93
Zoe Mikva	Congressman Abner Mikva	IL	1969-79
Dwight Patterson	Congresswoman Elizabeth Patterson	SC	1987-93
Justine Prokop	Congressman Stanley A. Prokop	PA	1959-61
Ellen Proxmire	Senator William Proxmire	WI	1957-89
Gretchen Quie	Congressman Albert H. Quie	MN	1959-79
Betty Rhodes	Congressman John Rhodes	AZ	1953-83
Dorothy Runnels	Congressman Harold Runnels	NM	1971-80
Emily Scheuer	Congressman James Scheuer	NY	1965-93
James Schroeder	Congresswoman Patricia Schroeder	CO	1979-97

Claire Schweiker	Congressman/Senator Richard Schweiker	PA	1961-81
Martha Shriver	Congressman Garner E. Shriver	KS	1961-77
Bea Smith	Congressman Neal Smith	IA	1959-95
Freda Solomon	Congressman Gerald Solomon	NY	1979-99
Lynn Staton	Congressman Mick Staton	WV	1981-83
Sylvia Symington	Congressman James W. Symington	MO	1969-77
Barbara Wortley	Congressman George Wortley	NY	1981-89
Sydna Zeliff	Congressman Bill Zeliff	NH	1991-97

Christine LaRocco, educational consultant and textbook author, is the spouse of Congressman Larry LaRocco of Idaho, 1991-1995. She compiled the responses from a June 1999 survey of spouses of former members of Congress.

Chapter 13

Dynamic Duo:
A Marriage Devoted to Public Service

George J. Hochbrueckner (D-New York)

Most Americans assume that one is born to, or early in life programs oneself to, a career in political service. Clearly, that is the path for many in elective office. However, for countless others the path is less direct. In my own case, nothing in my background or that of my wife, Carol Ann's, could have predicted a political future. At the onset, I must reveal that the political career that I relished over 18 years of my life I consider to be "our" career. From the very start, it was Carol Ann's initial inquisitiveness and ultimately her strong suggestion that I run for elective office. As I have repeatedly said in countless speeches, it was she who took this conservative engineer and made me into the "flaming moderate" I am today. And, as Carol Ann always says, "She's not done yet."

I met my future wife, Carol Ann Seifert, upon my honorable discharge from Navy service when I returned to New York and began attendance at the State University College on Long Island at Oyster Bay, N.Y. (now the State University of New York at Stony Brook). Carol Ann was a sophomore and I a lowly freshman. She was involved in everything on campus including being Editor-in-Chief of the college newspaper. She was very popular and social; I was older, wiser, and motivated to capture her heart. We met at an after school dance and the sparks flew - mainly because she thought I was "different." One month later, I finally got her to say yes to our first date. And what a date it was–more like a marathon–and that has been the profile of our life ever since. She is my best friend, my key advisor, my soul mate, and the love of my life.

GETTING INVOLVED IN POLITICS

We were married a year and a half later in 1961, and I accepted an engineering job opportunity in California. Our life revolved about work, two little boys, George and Michael (and a daughter on the way), and a liberal Catholic Church group known as the Christian Family Movement (CFM). It was this unique organization and the people we met through it that convinced us that our moral and religious responsibilities included knowing about and participating in our government. Through the CFM, we worked for an equal rights in housing proposition, voter registration, and a variety of good government issues. We also worked for various candidates, local and national.

In 1968, our opinions were divided. Carol Ann chose to work for Eugene McCarthy for President and I for Robert Kennedy. Robert Kennedy's assassination coming on the heels of Martin Luther King's crystalized in our minds that one day we would run for elective office.

I worked in southern California with brief field engineering assignments to New York and Connecticut during the years 1961-68. During that period, our political involvement grew. We worked locally to get people registered to vote and to help turn out the vote for our candidates in the November elections. Occasionally, our candidates actually won and we found that while one could not easily influence voters with regard to their vote for president or governor, people would be willing to accept recommendations for almost every other elected office.

In 1968, we moved back to where we began, Long Island, New York. My engineering role as field engineer and site manager on the Grumman F-14 "Tomcat" aircraft was challenging and exciting. During this time, we continued our involvement in local church, community, and political activities. The area in which we lived was heavily Republican and so the Democratic Party was happy to welcome us and appoint us as committee members. Our role was to encourage people in our Long Island Election District to register and vote. We shared a great enthusiasm for this grassroots activity.

In 1972, I took the lead in spearheading a move to place a proposition on the ballot to bring councilmanic districts to my local township. This would have replaced the at-large system, in which every one of the 360,000 people in Brookhaven Township votes for all council members, with a new process where each of the six districts elects their own town council representative. The petition drive was successful and in 1972, the people of Brookhaven Town approved councilmanic districts. However, the Town Board took successful legal action to set aside the vote because the town clerk had failed to legally advertise the vote as was required in the state law. The following year, 1973, I cajoled the Town Board to submit the question of councilmanic districts to the voters.

It was also in 1973 that Carol Ann convinced me that I should run for one of those town council seats. Fortunately, my activities regarding the councilmanic districts had provided much positive name recognition. The Republican leadership with great effort prevented the councilmanic district proposition from passing, and in my view was so distracted by this effort that on election night I was declared the only winner from my party in any of the town races. Being an engineer, I decided to visit the Board of Elections at 3:00 a.m. following the election in order to "see the numbers." It was indeed delightful to be greeted by the commissioner of elections and congratulated heartily for my victory. Upon my review of the election results, I stunned Carol Ann and my supporters by announcing that, according to my calculations, I had not won. A math error had been made.

This outcome was actually quite serendipitous in a positive way, since this positioned me as a potential candidate for the State Assembly race in 1974. Initially, Carol Ann and I had committed to support a friend for the position. But after Carol Ann pointed out to him that I had actually won a plurality of the votes that were cast in 1973 in the Assembly district, our friend removed himself from contention and endorsed my candidacy.

Although we had worked on various campaigns, we had no idea as to how one got elected. Our assumption was that first you had to have a huge bundle of money (even in those days) and then you put forth your candidacy. However, that is not how it worked for us.

I remember in my first Assembly race when my opponent, the incumbent Peter Costigan, welcomed me to the "hustings." We hadn't a clue that the word meant the route followed by a campaigner for political office. We also didn't have a clue about the mechanics of fundraising or staffing a viable campaign office. My initial foray into the world of elective office (Town Council) had been operated from the dining room table of our best friends, Carol and Jack Corrigan. Again, this dynamic duo volunteered to run the operation in tandem with Carol Ann and me: four political novices - Carol, a former teacher; Jack, a banker; Carol Ann; and me. We rented an H&R Block office space adjacent to a Chicken Delight with its range of odors. Our workers, all unpaid, were made up of our friends from church, a few Democratic Committee people, and lots of kids of all ages. In fact, our first few campaign offices required equipment such as playpens, baby swings, toys, and books. In those days, we did a lot of "lit dropping." We didn't have the money to mail campaign literature, but did have "kid power." The best ages for great runners with boundless enthusiasm were six to eleven, both boys and girls. After 12 years of age, they slowed down and wanted more indoor work, such as stuffing and sealing envelopes. Give me an army of elementary age kids and I'd match any mail house. We'd blanket all the important swing districts with my pamphlets by going door to door with the material–and I do mean door to door. Postal Authorities wouldn't allow anything in or on mailboxes.

The money we raised in that first Assembly and subsequent races as well was generated by a simple philosophy. "Give people a good time and value for their money and they will come and give." We held pool parties, garage sales, spaghetti dinners, and probably most unusual of all, Carol Ann, a former lifeguard, gave swimming lessons. (This mini-career would later help put our children through college.) The last four weeks of the race, we supplied our army with thousands of flyers and sent them to the dozens of supermarkets in the district. We were thrilled when, after the first weekend of this activity, it was reported back that other candidates' literature was tossed or left in shopping carts. Ours was kept. We were on to something! Could it be the fact that only one side had campaign information about me while the other side had great recipes from Carol Ann and our friends? Each week the campaign message as well as the recipes were changed.

In November 1974, I was elected to the New York State Assembly having defeated a nine-year incumbent in this three-to-two Republican dominated district. I served for five two-year terms before deciding to run for Congress in 1984. In my ten years in the State Assembly, I served on a variety of committees. Included among them were Education, Environmental Conservation, and Real Property Taxation, of which I became chairman. As chairman of the Real Property Taxation Committee, I successfully worked to improve the grievance system in the New York State law. The net effect of my grievance system improvements was that 15,000 homes in my Assembly district received approximately 25 percent reductions in their property taxes, including my own community where it all began.

Part of my success as a chairman had to do with good food. I often found that it was difficult to bring all of the committee members to the weekly meetings on time. Carol Ann provided the solution. Each week, she would package homemade cakes and cookies. Needless to say, this got my colleagues to meetings on time and in a supportive frame of mind.

I also enjoyed my time on the Education Committee where, based on my technical background, I studied the complex field of state aid to education. New York state government distributes billions of dollars each year to the over 600 school districts around the state. Using my knowledge of the formulas, I was delighted when I was able to converge on a formula change that not only placed those funds into the poorest districts on Long Island that year, but also had the effect of continuing that more equitable distribution of school aid into future years.

RUNNING FOR CONGRESS

In 1984, in spite of the fact that we anticipated a landslide by President Reagan on Long Island, which historically delivers large pluralities for Republican candidates, Carol Ann and I decided it was time to move to the national level. Consequently, I gave up what many considered a "safe" Assembly seat for me in order to take a chance and run in the 1st congressional district of New York state. Fortunately, my Assembly district represented about one-third of the congressional district and my ten years of Assembly service had given me the opportunity to "show my stuff" to people of all political persuasions. One of the reasons we decided to take this risk, even with the impending Reagan sweep, was that the voter turnout in a Presidential year is substantially higher than any other election year, and we had a local history of ticket-splitting. President Reagan did receive his landslide; I received 47 percent of the vote and returned to my engineering career for the next two years.

In those two years, I devoted much of my time to writing letters to the editor and staying involved politically. There has been a history in my county of

Democrats, including myself, losing the first time around and winning the second time. In 1986, I ran again and due to odd circumstances, the incumbent member of Congress, Bill Carney, who defeated me in 1984, did not run. Consequently, I ran for and won the open seat with 50.3 percent of the vote. The moral to that story is, "be prepared, be persistent, and have the breaks go your way."

We continued the highly successful fundraising practices that had served us well in our Assembly races throughout my entire political career. We've been told that there are a few collectors out there who have the complete set of our recipes from 1974 to 1994. Later on in the congressional races, when the bake sale approach to fundraising was a thing of the past, we still tried to provide fun events, activities, and good food as an incentive for all our supporters to participate in the process. The events covered the gamut and ranged from the guest appearances of Billy Joel, Christie Brinkley, actor Peter Boyle, and politicians Bill Bradley, Daniel Patrick Moynihan, Mario Cuomo, and Al Gore at fancy Hampton digs to casual back yard cookouts. But perhaps the most successful on-going fundraising event was our International Brunch. Here we involved representatives from our district's international quilt of people. The event was a celebration of diversity and starred people, food, and ethnic dance. The food was lovingly prepared by a dozen or more international home cooks and the glorious entertainment provided by young performers in the dress of their heritage. Hundreds of people attended these events with their children of all ages. What a joy to look across a room of Americans with such close ties to their international backgrounds.

When it came to our Washington, D.C. fundraising, Carol Ann decided that the best way to encourage large attendance was through great food. Consequently, all of those events featured the "bounty of Long Island's farms, waters, and vineyards." Our guests feasted on Long Island seafood, wine, duck, great vegetables, and, of course, Carol Ann's famous pies.

SETTLING INTO WASHINGTON

In January 1987, Carol Ann and I traveled to Washington for our initial look at our new life. Although we would have loved to move part-time to Washington, D.C., we just couldn't manage it either financially or politically. Financially, we had three kids in college. Politically, in a two-to-one Republican district, I had to maintain a very visible presence in the district. Fortunately, Carol Ann's sister, Linda, and husband, Ken Joy, lived nearby in Maryland and offered their hospitality and guest room. They were pleased when occasionally I could "pay the rent" by doing some household repairs. During my eight years in Congress, we maintained our home on Long Island with me commuting as required and Carol Ann visiting Washington, D.C. for special occasions.

My first encounter with the Washington "system" was when I sought committee assignments. I felt that, having worked for over 20 years in the aerospace-electronics field, the highest use of my experience would be an assignment on the

House Armed Services Committee. That committee was regarded as the third most important committee in the House. Consequently, a seat on that committee was highly prized. As one might expect, I was told there were no seats available since more senior members received higher priority in committee assignments and the available seats had already been taken.

It is always important to know the rules. I had studied the rules of the House and knew that the ratio of majority-to-minority members on the committees was supposed to reflect the same ratio that existed in the entire House. The Democrats had picked up additional seats in 1986; so I calculated the number of Democrats that should be on each of the committees based on the existing number of Republicans on those committees. On our first night in Washington, D.C., I calculated the proper number of Democrats that should be on each committee. To my delight, I found that the Democrats were entitled to at least one and in some cases two additional seats on several of the committees. I was especially pleased to find that the Democrats were entitled to two additional seats on the House Armed Services Committee (HASC).

I believe that a picture or chart is worth a thousand words, so I drew up a chart presenting my findings on the 22 committees and took it to the leadership with an appeal that they claim the additional seats to which they were entitled. The leadership listened and acted. The first of the two new seats on the HASC was given to now Senator Barbara Boxer of California; and the second, to me. The moral of this story is, "it pays to do your homework."

SERVING MY DISTRICT

One of my predecessors, former Congressman Otis G. Pike, told me many years ago that good constituent service was the key to longevity in our congressional district. He was absolutely right. I attribute my survival in the State Assembly and Congress for those 18 years to the service my office has been able to provide to my people. Usually, when people resort finally to calling their elected officials, it is because they have reached a high level of frustration with government bureaucracy and have no other place to turn.

My philosophy is that constituent service is helping people get the government benefit or service that they were entitled to receive in the first place. Over my almost two decades in elected office, I have been blessed with excellent staff, whose good work solved thousands of constituent problems. Many of our key leadership staff were our old friends from my pre-election era. Because of the efforts of Ann Marie Coleman, Pat Howley, and Ellen Joyce, my right-hand man Bill Schumacher, and many other highly competent individuals, my district offices achieved a marvelous reputation and countless people benefitted by having their governmental problems resolved.

I also worked to serve my district through the legislative domain. On Long Island, we have six inlets along the south shore. They connect the ocean to the bays. The easternmost tip of the Island, Montauk Point, is slowly being eroded with the sand flowing westward nourishing the beaches all the way to Brooklyn at the extreme west end of Long Island. At each of the inlets, shoals tend to form and make passage difficult and dangerous. From time to time, dredging is done to remove the shoals and allow safe passage of our recreational and commercial boaters. The Shinnecock Inlet is the easternmost and is in the 1st congressional district. Coincidentally, the inlet was created by a hurricane in 1938. One of the issues in my 1986 campaign had been to have that inlet dredged. Three people had drowned trying to pass through the inlet. This was an important issue for me, and we were hopeful that President Reagan's budget request would include funds for the dredging of this inlet.

Unfortunately, the president's request contained no funds for the Army Corps of Engineers to dredge the inlet. Consequently, it was essential that I work in the Congress to secure the funds. My new staff advised me that I needed to have the Energy and Water Development Subcommittee of the House Appropriations Committee add the funds. They also indicated that I already had cast several votes in opposition to positions taken by the chairman of that Subcommittee, Tom Bevill. That weekend, I explained my dilemma to Carol Ann; she suggested that I ask for a meeting with the chairman and take him one of her homemade strawberry-rhubarb pies. The pie and I were well received. I explained my problem and he advised me that he would look into the matter, assess the condition of the inlet, and call with his decision. One week later, he called and said the $3.6 million would be in the budget.

After the money was released and the dredging done, we had a celebration at the inlet where several of Carol Ann's strawberry-rhubarb pies were shared with the celebrants. The moral here is that "a little sweetness, straight-talk, and a good cause can be combined to produce success."

One of the more serious health problems that faced the people of the 1st congressional district was lyme disease; my district had the highest incidence of it in the country. In 1987, very little was known about this disease. The carrier of lyme disease is the deer tick. Once bitten by this tiny insect, victims develop symptoms mimicking other ailments. These symptoms range from flu-like conditions to potentially serious nerve damage and, in rare cases, death. One of the individuals who raised my consciousness on this issue was Richard Bond, advisor to President Bush and soon to become head of the National Republican Committee. Richard and his family lived in my district. He offered to work for the president's support for any program that I could move through the Congress. I assigned my staffer, Kim Bryant, who already had become my lyme disease expert, to investigate any and all possible solutions to reduce the incidence of this disease. One interesting suggestion involved the use of guinea hens. These fowl have keen eyesight and an appetite for insects.

It just so happened that two of our more famous constituents, Billy Joel and Christie Brinkley, were concerned about lyme disease and kept a flock of guinea fowl on their East Hampton property. When our office contacted them and explained our mission, they generously agreed to let us, along with some scientists, conduct experiments on their property and in the lab. The results of the study were conclusive–the guinea hens were amazingly effective in controlling the tick population. While this was by no means the solution, the publicity associated with these celebrities, along with the bipartisan support of my colleagues and the White House, helped me obtain substantial funding for ongoing lyme disease research, control, and efforts to find a cure.

Another Long Island concern that was resolved through bipartisan action was associated with Peconic Bay, which lies between the North Fork and South Forks at the eastern end of Long Island. Many were concerned about its environmental condition. Also, major algae blooms had occurred, resulting in the dramatic reduction of Peconic Bay scallops. The condition of the bay was of great concern to everyone but especially environmentalists, fishermen, and those involved in the tourism industry. After researching the problem, it was clear that the best long-term solution for cleaning up and maintaining Peconic Bay water quality was to place it into the National Estuary Program. Under that program, the bay would be entitled to special consideration for federal funding. I embarked on a bipartisan effort to accomplish that goal. My Long Island Republican colleague, Norman Lent, played a key role in our successful effort, along with many other local elected officials and performer Billy Joel.

Although my departure from Congress was involuntary, it came at a good time. Just as I had the good fortune to have a life and a career before government service, now I have the time and enthusiasm for a life and a career of business consulting after politics. Life and its magnificent timing have been very good to me. I feel very philosophical about my entrance into and departure from elective office. The Bible says it best, "There is a time for every purpose under heaven." I am and have been a very blessed man. I am very thankful for all the treasures in my life, my incredible wife Carol Ann, our wonderful children George, Michael, Elizabeth, Matthew, my special daughter-in-law, Nicole, and my precious grandchildren, Kate and Kyle. The unique opportunity and privilege of serving my country has been a delight and a joy that I never could have anticipated in my wildest dreams. Best of all, it was an experience shared by my best friend.

Chapter 14

Religious Idealism and Reality in Congressional Politics

Jim Wright (D-Texas)

In September 1964, the House was debating the first appropriation of money for the antipoverty program. Advocates recited the stark statistics of grisly want in the midst of affluence. Democratic spokesmen rhapsodized on our unrivaled opportunity to "banish poverty from our land." Some of us were thinking, "What a chance to carry out the Scriptural mandate to feed the hungry and clothe the naked! To visit widows and the fatherless in their affliction! Could anyone doubt we were doing the right thing?"

Then Joel Broyhill, Republican congressman from Virginia's tenth district, entered the debate. Joel is a decent guy–friendly, energetic, hard-working, popular with both constituents and colleagues. But his speech ripped into some of my most cherished assumptions. Broyhill denounced the antipoverty program as the "most flagrant, unabashed vote-buying scheme I have seen in all my years in Congress." He scorned the idea that the Federal government is capable of eliminating poverty. He quoted Scripture:

> The Bible says, "For ye have the poor always with you" and while I do not wish to make an odious or offensive comparison, I have a good deal more faith in the Bible than I have in some politicians' promises!

Others in the House elaborated the Broyhill theme. Some expressed deep concern over the increasingly popular fallacy that "the world owes me a living." One voiced the view that anyone who really wants to work can find a job, and another hinted darkly that too easy access to goods without work was "destroying the moral fibre" of the American people. Someone charged that multiple welfare payments were encouraging illegitimate births. A southern Democrat, leaning on the back railing of the House chamber, peered over his glasses and grunted to a colleague: "The Bible says if you don't work, you don't eat!"

MEN OF GOODWILL OFTEN DISAGREE

We can derive three important lessons from the little story I've just recited. The first is that men of goodwill and sincere purpose often disagree. And this can happen without either antagonist being a sycophant, a demagogue, or a rascal. Or even stupid, for that matter. None of us is given an exclusive franchise on God's truth, and we indulge a powerful presumption when we try to create God in our own images.

The idea of revelation is deeply imbedded in Christianity. If the Creator is omnipotent, as we say he is, then the source of infallible judgments must be right here somewhere for us to tap. There has to be a socket into which we can screw our bulbs and show forth the light of perfect truth. Yet for most of us imperfect creatures, it isn't quite that simple.

Is it possible that the Creator in His infinite wisdom makes internationalists and isolationists, liberals, conservatives, and moderates in the precise electoral proportion to accomplish His will? Could it be that He shows to each of us a part of the truth and then "stacks the deck," so to speak, so as to achieve the result He foreordains in some mysterious and inexplicable way and on a timetable beyond our mortal comprehension?

Somehow I can't quite think it works just that way. For one thing, I just don't believe that God intended for people to hate and kill each other. I don't think He ordained for some to live in misery and pain and want, or for any to die of starvation. I can't conceive that He purposes some to be hounded and persecuted by others. These things just do not square with my conception of a loving Creator.

I believe He intends His creatures to work for peace among men, for a just and compassionate social order, for reconciliation of differences between people of different races, different nations, different religions, different social strata, even between men of different generations. "Blessed are the peacemakers" may apply with particular force to members of Congress.

None of this has come to me in a blinding flash of light as to Saint Paul on the road to Damascus or as to Moses in a voice from a burning bush. It just happens to be the only logical set of assumptions I can equate with the great commandment to love the Lord your God and love your neighbor as yourself.

But how do we go about achieving this perfect state of things with laws which must of necessity bear the frailties and imperfections of their authors? I have some personal ideas about that from time to time, but so do my equally conscientious colleagues. Sometimes our ideas differ. When I start delineating all the specifics of how to achieve these divine ends, I begin to get into trouble.

Compromise—not necessarily a dirty word—is the very essence of the legislative process. Those who scorn the art of conciliation and consider it somehow lacking in principle simply do not understand the business of lawmaking.

How do we reconcile this necessity with the idea of profound moral conviction? Certainly not by abandoning our convictions. Each of us must work as hard as he can and argue as persuasively as he can for the positions he believes to be right.

But he must not play God. He must not arrogate to himself the presumption of almighty wisdom. He must be very slow to pass harsh moral judgment upon those whose convictions disagree with his. He must proceed from an assumption that his antagonist is as sincere as he and may indeed have a thought worth considering.

ORDINARY AMERICANS AND EXTRAORDINARY PROBLEMS

The second lesson we can draw from the incident with which I began this chapter is that members of Congress are, after all, just people. The Congress is *of* the people. It is in one sense their mirror, and it reflects the aggregate strengths and weaknesses of the electorate. Its membership might include just about the same percentage of saints and sinners, fools and geniuses, rogues and heroes as does the general populace. The typical legislator is a fairly average American–a bit better educated, a little more gregarious, and considerably harder working than the norm, but still rather generally "representative."

In sum, Congress is a collection of ordinary Americans grappling with extraordinary problems. These problems will not yield to simple, one-sentence solutions. Where are the clear moral absolutes, and how do they apply? Often there is truth on both sides. We can't just ponder and pontificate; we must vote! Often we'd like more time, more information. Sometimes we wish that we might answer, "Yes, but..." or "No, if..." But as the roll is called, each individual Congressman's individual response must come as one unequivocal monosyllable. It is either "Yea" or "Nay," and that's that. Afterward, we hope that we were right.

What I'm saying is that if any group of people ever stood in *need* of the superhuman insights of divine revelation, it is we.

IDEALISM OF MOST MEMBERS

The third lesson of our little story is that most congressmen earnestly *want* to do the right thing. Few are theologians and fewer still are mystics, but most do have religious conviction. Cartoonists and late-night talk show hosts to the contrary, a very appreciable number of legislators were inspired by idealism when they first decided to seek the office. It is a naive politician perhaps who thinks he can change the course of the world dramatically, but most members were convinced they could add something of value to the total political achievement of the nation. In my own case, I decided as a sophomore in high school that I wanted someday to serve in the Congress and to help create the foundations of a peaceful world.

Perhaps my case is revealing if not altogether typical. In my youth, I was very certain in my vision of the road to world peace and of what I conceived to be my "mission in life." Like Moses, I would lead people from the bondage of war and oppression into Isaiah's promised day when men would "beat their swords into plough-shares, and their spears into pruning-hooks" (Isaiah 2:4, King James Version). I'd fulfill Woodrow Wilson's Fourteen Points and Franklin Roosevelt's Four Freedoms. It was all extremely heady stuff. I was young.

I was, frankly, intolerant of conflicting views. Although I wouldn't have admitted it and was probably clever enough that it didn't surface too visibly, I had a sort of messiah complex which, if forgivable in youth, can be insufferably dangerous in a public official. I hadn't yet learned that other people too were smart, and could be equally sincere while seeing things another way. I hadn't learned to walk the tightrope between self-righteousness and cynicism.

SEDUCTIVE ASPECTS OF LIFE IN CONGRESS

Walking this tightrope is not easy to do. A political career in a way is like the medieval ordeals which once were supposed to test the inner worth of an individual. Elective officials are subjected to a long series of subtle trials which have the capacity to bend and change their very character and to reveal its imperfections.

Many people enter the legislative arena impelled by some basic conviction of service to fellow man. Whether the individual's vision of a better world be true or false is not the point here. The point is that he *has* such a vision, worthy in his own mind of the dedication of a major part of his life.

He wouldn't say this to you, but he sees himself as a potential servant of cosmic forces–at least as an instrument through which good may come to his fellow creatures, perhaps as a possible agent of deity. Our fledgling lawmaker dreams of reforms, laws of his authorship which bring strength, beneficence, and a better life to his land. Did he not so dream, why would he seek such an office? It would all be fatuous and empty, devoid of meaning.

Subtly and slowly, however, his dream of bringing off that reform begins to grow faint about the edges, dulled by reality, like the early-morning stars which fade as the gray light of dawn appears. Major legislation, the congressman discovers, is written by committee chairmen. And one gets to be a committee chairman by staying in Congress. But, as the star fades, something else takes its place.

People are constantly coming to our lawmaker for help, for advice, for intercession with administrative agencies of government. They keep telling him what a fine man he is, what a gracious fellow, what a real friend. While awaiting the opportunity to exercise important legislative craftsmanship, he *does* get some things done for his *district*, some local projects approved, some new jobs created. This is something. It is, after all, service of a sort. Sooner or later, they'll throw an Appreciation Dinner for him. They'll lionize him. And he'll discover, perhaps to his amazement, that he isn't embarrassed at all. He sort of *likes* it.

In the bright sunlight of personal acclaim, it's hard to keep the little stars of humility and altruistic service in one's vision. Nevertheless, our legislator rationalizes, if he can just hold on until he becomes a committee chairman, *then* he'll be able to make the great dreams come true. Therefore, naturally, it's important to be reelected.

I recall the first time a public official suggested to me what I might say in introducing him for a speech and my shock at his immodesty. All too soon, however, I found myself sending out mimeographed copies of a biographical summary to program chairmen where I was slated to give a speech. Although technically my staff sent them out, do you think I hadn't read the summary, or that they would send one of which I disapproved? I blush a little bit to tell you this. But not enough.

Press releases extolling a congressman's accomplishments become a way of life. Try keeping your humility as you edit a press release, written about yourself in the third person, careful to give yourself the credit due. The truth is that public office is just awfully hard on humility. We try to recapture it. We strike poses. We try to convince ourselves that we still possess it. We debate with the still, small voice and sometimes shout it down. Finally convinced that we're humble, we grow very *proud* of our humility. But feigned humility is worse than none at all. For it isn't only others but ourselves that we deceive.

A member of Congress who has reached this point–and it's easy to do–begins to believe his own propaganda and to invest his private judgments and opinions with a sort of divine infallibility–and his reelection and advancement with the broader public interest.

BE REALISTIC ABOUT WHAT YOU CAN CONTRIBUTE

Clearly, it is critically important to understand and keep a firm grip on the very real limits of what an individual lawmaker can realistically expect to accomplish in a career. There was a time when I felt at one with Saint Paul's assertion, "I can do *all* things through Christ which strengtheneth me!" (Philippians 4:13, King James Version). You know, I still accept that as a sort of philosophical abstraction; I wish I could still feel it as an absolute spiritual truth.

Actually, about the best that a good Congressman can reasonably hope for is to leave a decent footprint on the sands of progress. If he has done a good job, he will know, when he leaves Washington, that he has helped thousands of constituents with their individual problems. He will have the satisfaction of realizing that he has accomplished some worthwhile things for his district. Perhaps he will rejoice in the fact that some of his ideas become a permanent part of a major piece of legislation, even though someone senior to him (or perhaps of the opposite party) has been given the credit.

When the average Congressman completes his tenure of service, he will not really have changed the world much, but he will have seen important changes and will have participated to one extent or another in many of them. Remembering the thousands of individual services he has performed for people, the world leaders he has met, a few really good speeches he may have made on important issues, the hundreds of votes he has cast, the slice of history he personally has witnessed, he certainly will have the feeling that he made some contributions to the democratic process and to the shaping of his time.

Chapter 15

The Impeachment of Richard Nixon: A Personal Recollection

Lawrence J. Hogan (R-Maryland)

On June 17, 1972, burglars entered the headquarters of the Democratic National Committee at the Watergate office building in Washington, D.C. That event profoundly changed the life of Richard M. Nixon. And mine.

An unrelenting drumbeat of news coverage aimed at discrediting President Nixon began. Since I knew that the news media, led by the *Washington Post*, had harbored a long-standing animus against President Nixon, I tended to tune out much of the anti-Nixon news coverage on Watergate. I felt it was decidedly biased against him.

IMPEACHMENT BEGINS AS A PARTISAN INQUIRY

Later, to my surprise and outrage, the House Judiciary Committee, chaired by Democrat Peter Rodino of New Jersey and on which I served, began an investigation of impeachment against President Nixon. The media consistently praised Rodino for his handling of the inquiry in a fair and objective manner. I did not share this assessment. Nixon and Rodino were freshmen congressmen together and I don't think Rodino liked Nixon. I had the distinct feeling that he and several other liberals on the committee had their minds made up to vote for impeachment from the beginning. Prior to the impeachment inquiry, I had a very cordial relationship with Peter Rodino. Before he had become chairman of the full committee, I had served under him on a subcommittee. I was very fond of him and I still am.

However, I got involved in several controversies with Rodino in committee and on the House floor over what I perceived to be unfair handling of the impeachment inquiry. I objected to the committee's refusal to allow the president to put on a defense, or have his lawyer present during our deliberations, to have the right to cross-examine witnesses against him, and to offer witnesses in his defense. Eventually, the committee did relent and grant these rights to the president. During one of my rather heated exchanges with Chairman Rodino, he cut me off and snapped that he had not recognized me for one of my "usual harangues." There was an audible gasp from other members of the committee for this breach of the usual civility toward colleagues.

I also created controversy among my fellow Republicans on the Judiciary Committee when I strenuously objected to the bias of our own Republican counsel against our Republican president. Unfortunately, my fellow Republicans ignored my entreaties and refused to fire him. Late in the impeachment inquiry, when it was too late to prevent the incalculable harm he had done in collusion with the Democrats' counsel, they finally came to the conclusion that I had been right and fired him.

A TREMENDOUS RESPONSIBILITY

Hundreds of media representatives from all over the world covered every minute of the Judiciary Committee's deliberations. Whenever one of us would leave the committee room or our office, they would swarm about us asking questions and probing for our leanings or assessments of the evidence. I told one and all that I had no comments to make, that I would make up my mind after I had heard all the evidence from both sides, and then I would tell them my decision. In retrospect, this pledge was a mistake.

As a member of the committee, I felt a great burden. We were closeted in the committee room day and night and yet we also had to keep up with our office and constituent work, and our votes on the House floor as well as our work on the other committees on which we served. It was the most trying and agonizing ordeal of my life. The pressure was intense and unrelenting. The responsibility was awesome and weighed heavily on me and other members of the committee. A sense of being unable to escape history remained with us throughout the proceedings.

I empathized with U.S. Senator Edmond Ross of Kansas who, in 1868, was called upon to cast his vote in the Senate impeachment trial of President Andrew Johnson. As the fateful hour approached, only Senator Ross' vote was needed to make the required number of votes to convict the President. Senator Ross later described the experience:

> It was a tremendous responsibility, and it was not strange that he upon whom it had been imposed by a fateful combination of conditions should have sought to avoid it, to put it away from him as one shuns, or tries to fight off, a nightmare...I almost literally looked down into my open grave. Friendships, position, fortune, everything that makes life desirable to an ambitious man were about to be swept away by the breath of my mouth, perhaps forever.[1]

I knew exactly how Senator Ross had felt. Feeling many of Senator Ross's emotions and misgivings myself, I decided early on in the impeachment inquiry that my decision would be made only on the basis on the evidence presented to the committee and the dictates of my own conscience regarding the interpretation of the evidence.

MY DECISION PROCESS

Despite the inherently political nature of the impeachment process, I chose to approach the entire matter, as best I could, from a purely legal standpoint. To my chagrin, I soon found that the keystone of the lawyer's trade–legal precedent–was virtually useless in the area of impeachment law. The impeachment power rarely has been invoked and, when it has been, the precedents established thereby stand alone in each case.

Question 1: What Is an Impeachable Offense?

Some cases held that an impeachable offense must be an indictable offense while other cases suggested that an impeachable offense is just about anything the Congress wants it to be. In the area of presidential impeachment, the precedents were even more restricted. Prior to the Watergate case, only President Andrew Johnson had been impeached by the House of Representatives, and he avoided conviction in the Senate by only one vote–that of Senator Edmund Ross.

The precedent established by that House impeachment process leaves much to be desired, however. The original resolution recommending impeachment was debated in the House of Representatives on December 5-6, 1867, but the only point debated was whether the commission of a crime was an essential element of impeachable conduct by the president. The impeachment resolution was defeated on December 7th by a vote of 108-57, short of the necessary two-thirds.

Less than three months later, on February 25, 1868, President Johnson was impeached by a House of Representatives vote of 126-47. The House had adopted 11 articles of impeachment against Johnson: nine related to his removal of Secretary of War Edwin M. Stanton, allegedly in deliberate violation of the Tenure of Office Act which had been passed by the same Congress in 1867, and the tenth and eleventh articles charged that Johnson impugned the authority of Congress in several speeches. There was a dramatic reversal within a three-month period. In December 1867, the House failed to impeach because there was no evidence of commission of a crime, but in February 1868, the House impeached notwithstanding the lack of evidence of the commission of a crime. This attests to the fundamentally political nature of the Johnson impeachment. Unfortunately as well, it provided virtually no useful precedent for the impeachment process of 1974.

Therefore, my 37 colleagues on the House Judiciary Committee and I faced the task of determining in our own minds and in accordance with our own interpretation of the U.S. Constitution what constitutes an impeachable offense, what standard of proof should be applied, and finally, how the evidence should be measured against those standards.

Impeachment itself is a political remedy for serious abuses that disqualify an incumbent officeholder or threaten our constitutional system of government. James Madison's notes show that the impeachment provision was written into the Constitution to provide some means for removal of any civil officer who abused his power and whose continuation in office would not be in the best interests of the country. It does not substitute for the normal processes of justice, or preclude later indictment and trial for criminal offenses or barring from future positions of political trust.

The framers of the Constitution, fearing an executive too strong to be constrained, gave the Congress the power to remove, for acts of "Treason, Bribery, or other Crimes and Misdemeanors" in Article II, Section 4. We were faced with the responsibility for defining an impeachable offense, which the Constitution does not do. We know what "Treason" and "Bribery" are, but what are "other Crimes and Misdemeanors?" They are undefined, indefinite, and vague.

Because the language of the Constitution is so vague, and because the precedents are so sparse and contradictory, each of us on the committee had to decide for him or herself what constitutes an impeachable offense. Obviously, it had to be something so grievous that it would warrant the removal of the president of the United States from office. I did not agree with those who said an impeachable offense is anything that Congress wants it to be and I did not agree with those who said that it must be an indictable criminal offense. I felt that somewhere in between these two positions is the standard against which the president's conduct should be measured. In my mind, the president's conduct had to have at least some aspects of criminality, and it had to be so grievous that it would make the president unsuitable for continuing in office.

Question 2: What Should Be the Burden of Proof?

Some members argued that we were not required to pass judgment on the guilt or innocence of the president, that this should be the function of the trial of the impeachment in the Senate. I disagreed. This matter was so important and the consequences so far-reaching that I felt we should decide in our own minds whether we believed the president was guilty of committing offenses so grave that he should be removed from office. Others said that the president should be impeached for the wrongdoing of his aides and associates. I could not concur in that contention either. I felt that we had to find personal wrongdoing on the president's part if we were to justify his impeachment.

After a member decided what, in his or her mind, constituted an impeachable offense, he or she then had to decide what standard of proof should be used to determine whether or not the president had committed an impeachable offense. Some said that the House Judiciary Committee was analogous to a grand jury and a grand jury need only find probable cause that a criminal defendant had committed an offense in order to send the matter to trial. But, because of the vast ramifications of this impeachment and its quasi-criminal nature, I thought we needed to insist on a much higher standard. Committee counsel recommended "clear and convincing proof." "Clear and convincing" and "preponderance of the evidence" are the standards for civil liability. I thought we needed a higher standard of proof. I came to the conclusion that we could have no less a standard of proof than the standard we use in a criminal trial–"beyond a reasonable doubt." I felt that we could insist on no less a standard in a matter of such overriding importance as impeachment of the president.

Question 3: Was the President Guilty? Evaluating the Evidence

Being guided by these criteria which I had established for my consideration of the evidence, I carefully scrutinized the material which came before the Judiciary Committee. After all of the evidence had been heard, I began the agonizing process of recapitulation of all that we had seen and heard. I weighed exculpatory evidence against each charge and sifted the bits of evidence back and forth for many hours. I then re-assessed the voluminous material which had been presented to us in 30 thick, black, loose-leaf notebooks containing "statements of information," three large notebooks summarizing the material in all the volumes, and numerous tape transcripts.

Finally, I came to the inescapable, but extremely painful conclusion, that my president was guilty of impeachable offenses and, regardless of my personal feelings, I was compelled by the dictates of my conscience to vote for his impeachment. While I felt great relief that my decision had been made, I was overcome with great sadness and foreboding. I had given the president every benefit of the doubt, but that did not make me feel any better. I knew we were creating a crisis for the country and personal agony for Richard M. Nixon and his family, for all of whom I felt deep affection and admiration.

There was no single dramatic revelation or "moment of truth" in the impeachment inquiry that made it obvious to me that Mr. Nixon was guilty. The body of evidence fell into place one piece after another, finally demolishing the presumption of innocence that I had given him gladly.

A CRITICAL PRESS CONFERENCE

I had promised the news media representatives who had hounded us every day throughout the impeachment inquiry that, after I had heard all the evidence and had made up my mind, I would let them know how I was going to vote. Consequently, I scheduled a press conference for July 23, 1974 to announce my decision. In retrospect, I should have waited until the televised proceedings to announce my vote, because my action was misunderstood and misinterpreted. Having made my agonizing decision, I suppose I wanted the catharsis of getting it out of my system.

That morning, Vice President Gerald Ford telephoned me and said he did not question what I was going to do, but only my timing. I said, "Jerry, I have given the president every benefit of the doubt." And I had.

I faced hundreds of media people and announced that I had decided to vote for impeachment. To my amazement, it became front page news throughout the world. Because I had apparently been considered one of Nixon's staunchest defenders, my announcement received more attention than it otherwise would have warranted.

I am sure my announcement came as a shock to President Nixon because I had been one of the most steadfast opponents of what I considered unfair treatment of him by the Judiciary Committee. This might have been misinterpreted as an indication that I would not vote for impeachment under any circumstances. Later, Mr. Nixon said in his memoirs that he resigned the presidency for three reasons: because he learned the southern Democrats would not vote with him, because the Supreme Court had decided against him on release of tape recordings, and because of my vote.

THE PRESIDENT'S POSITION DETERIORATES

The following day, on July 24, 1974, the day of reckoning arrived for members of the committee to announce their votes. Each member of the committee was given 15 minutes to announce his or her position on impeachment. I was extremely nervous when it came my turn to speak.

I discussed how I came to define what an impeachable offense was to me and what standard of proof I had used to assess the evidence. I traced the constitutional history of impeachment and then pointed out that Mr. Nixon had overwhelmingly been the people's choice for president. I concluded:

> ...The thing that is so appalling to me is that the president, when this idea was suggested to him, didn't rise up in righteous indignation and say, "Get out of here. You are in the office of the president of the United States. How can you talk about blackmail, bribery, and keeping witnesses silent? This is the presidency of the United States...." [I thought he should] throw them out of his office and pick up the phone and call the Department of Justice and tell them there is obstruction of justice going on. Someone is trying to buy the silence of a witness.

> But my president didn't do that. He sat there and he worked and worked to try to cover this thing up so it wouldn't come to light....

> The president...consistently tried to cover up the evidence and obstruct justice. As much as it pains me to say it, he should be impeached and removed from office.

The vote for impeachment on various articles was approved with only ten Republicans voting "no." However, on August 5th, the final blow came: devastating evidence that the president had personally approved the cover-up six days after the burglary of the Democratic National Committee headquarters at the Watergate. This was the long-sought "smoking gun," incontrovertible proof of the president's obstruction of justice. One by one, all ten of the Republicans who had voted against impeachment announced that they would support impeachment. The House Judiciary Committee then stood 38 to 0 in favor of impeachment. Three days later, on August 8, 1974, President Nixon avoided near-certain impeachment by resigning the presidency.

ADVERSE REACTION TO MY DECISION

Because of his vote of conscience to acquit President Andrew Johnson, Senator Ross for the remainder of his life was looked upon as the greatest of scoundrels. He voted his conscience rather than his politics and he was vilified for it. (I endured somewhat similar treatment for own vote of conscience.) Any objective observer will, I believe, concur that the impeachment of President Johnson was politically motivated and completely unjustified. Senator Ross was most certainly right. I had hoped my vote would eventually be judged the same way.

I received approximately 15,000 letters from all over the country, about evenly divided between pro- and anti-Nixon. Most people on both sides of the issue made up their minds about impeachment on an emotional basis rather than on the basis of the evidence. Some of those who wrote vilified me viciously. I was sent packages of human excrement, and two sent me 30 dimes, alluding to the 30 pieces of silver for which Judas Iscariot betrayed Jesus. One of my staff members said that, after reading these letters, she did not think I would ever want to run for public office again. People came up to me on the campaign trail and asked me what I did with the 30 pieces of silver. Some of my good friends and staunch political supporters called and wrote to withdraw their support and to cancel their financial pledges. Many of my House colleagues shunned me and many of my friends in and outside of politics did the same. To this day, some of them have not forgiven me. Not all, however. About 15 years after my impeachment vote, one of my former political backers called to tell me that at the time of my vote for impeachment he had been furious with me, but now he realized that I had been right and he had been wrong. He called up to tell me that and to apologize for the way he had felt. I thanked him for his kindness in calling.

Notwithstanding comments by President Nixon and his aides about my "faltering" or "flagging" campaign for governor, it had actually been going very well up to the time of my announcement that I would vote for impeachment. After my press conference, I sensed the impending doom. I telephoned my campaign manager and told him that I thought I should withdraw from the gubernatorial race. (There were only a few more days left within which I could withdraw.) I asked him to poll my key campaign aides for their opinion. He called back later to say that they felt that I should stay in the race.

I had an opponent in the Republican primary but, prior to my announcement, the polls had consistently shown that I would win the primary election overwhelmingly. After my announcement, my Republican support plummeted. On primary election day, Maryland Republicans went to the polls in droves, not to vote for my opponent, but to vote *against* me. I lost the primary election, which the prior polls had shown I could not possibly lose, and the Republican victor went on to lose in a landslide to the Democratic candidate in the general election.

As a defeated gubernatorial candidate whose term in Congress was ending, I began the task of trying to find a job. I would have liked to stay in governmental service, but I was rejected for several jobs in the new administration of Gerald Ford who took over the presidency when Richard Nixon resigned. Through friends, I learned that I would never receive a job in the Ford administration. (In the subsequent administrations of Presidents Reagan and Bush, the results were the same.) I had interviews with several law firms and one large national public relations firm, but when they learned what a pariah I was among Republicans in Congress and in the administration, no job offers were forthcoming.

While my vote for impeachment haunted me for years after that fateful day in 1974, most Maryland Republicans finally forgave me. In 1978, I was elected the County Executive of Prince Georges County, and in 1982, I was the Republican nominee for the U.S. Senate.

EPILOGUE

While it saddens me when I think of the pain endured by Mr. Nixon and his family through the impeachment inquiry, I believe Watergate was a tragedy not just for the president and his family, but for the whole nation. I greatly admired Richard M. Nixon. I worked in all three of his presidential campaigns and was a Nixon delegate to the 1968 and 1972 Republican National Conventions, which nominated him for president. I supported him politically and ideologically. He, his daughters, and a son-in-law campaigned for and with me. As a Congressman, I supported most of the programs he proposed as president. To me, Richard Nixon was a great man and a great president. If it had not been for Watergate, I believe history would have honored him as one of our nation's greatest presidents.

Ultimately, however there was no evading the responsibilities that flowed out of my position on the House Judiciary Committee. I was forced by circumstances to weigh the evidence meticulously and objectively and vote my conscience. I know that I had no choice but to vote the way I did.

Notes:

1.John F. Kennedy, *Profiles in Courage* (New York: Harper & Brothers, 1956), p. 139.

Chapter 16

Never Quite Over the Hill:
Working as a Congressional Staffer

Joe Bartlett
Chief of Pages, Reading Clerk, and Minority Clerk
U.S. House of Representatives

Many a young American studying government, or simply watching a television broadcast of a session of Congress, or an inauguration ceremony, fantasizes how great it would be to be a part of that premier panoply of democracy in action. If not as an official, at least as a part of the support staff.

I certainly can relate to such an ambition, because similar circumstances sparked my interest in the Congress about a half-century ago.

If you harbor such an ambition in your heart, I would tell you, "go for it!" Ours is a government "of the people," and you have a right to aspire to participate in any way that you can. Congress is the epitome of government-by-the-people, and provides some of the ultimate opportunities for public service.

A word of caution, however: It is not likely that a job in Congress will prove to be as glamorous as you might have imagined, and it is quite certain you will not be given the authority to have an immediate impact on "changing the world," as you might hope. Now, if you can live with that, you may find the opportunities for employment in Congress very fulfilling.

During my years as a "hired hand" of the House of Representatives, I can tell you, there was never a day that I did not look forward to going to work, and I cannot recall ever having a "boring" day. The hours were longer than anybody knew, the work was exacting, but I went 30 years without taking a day's "sick leave," which should be some indication as to job satisfaction!

Were there challenges? Sometimes insurmountable.

Were there frustrations? Of course.

But the privilege of confronting those challenges, in association with some of the finest and most dedicated people you would find anywhere, was the opportunity of a lifetime! And in the end, I had the gratification of feeling that, in numerous instances, I had made a difference.

Had I accomplished everything I had hoped to achieve? Does anyone ever?

There is quite a variety of occupations in the various staff positions. Mine may not have been typical, but they are all there for the single purpose of facilitating the federal legislative process. The role of the staff is not to make policy, but to make it easier for those who were elected to make policy on behalf of the American people.

Congressional staffers come to this employment by many ways. My own interest was inspired by a very misleadingly glamorous Hollywood movie about congressional pages. For a boy of my humble beginnings, such an ambition was altogether unreasonable. But fate can make even unreasonable things real. Being singled out from a Washington parade of youngsters, and dubbed "America's Typical Schoolboy Patrolman," brought this West Virginia farm boy to the attention of a congressman who had been a World War I buddy of my sponsor. Their wives got together and cooked up a 30-day page appointment for me. And, at the age of 14, by this strange happenstance, my congressional career began.

I am sure there are a host of interesting accounts about the funny things that have happened to others on the way to employment in this forum, but it is likely that most of *them* have something to do with a congressman.

The pages I went to work with got their appointments in many ways. One of them, John Dingle, was appointed by his father, a Michigan congressman. Now John, having succeeded his father, is dean of all the members of the House, and was recently seen performing the duty of administering the oath of office to the Speaker at the beginning of the new Congress.

Currently, they have refined the process of selecting pages, somewhat. Now only juniors in high school, with good academic standing, are considered. Even so, you had best begin by writing to your congressman. Unlike in my day, when all the pages were boys, presently about half of them are girls.

THE CONGRESSMAN'S OFFICE

The largest number of congressional employees are those on the staffs of the individual congressmen. Members are authorized some 20 employees for their offices, and they may have additional staff in connection with a committee assignment.

Frequently, new members seek some experienced congressional staff members to augment and initiate their home-grown staff, and help them get off to a good start. This has become increasingly popular, and "lateral mobility" is quite common on Capitol Hill today. A congressional staff member who has some experience, and a reasonable reputation, finds it rather easy to move from one office to another, and may have served several members.

Most members prefer staff who come from their home district. However, at least one member never hires from his district because, as he said, if they prove not to perform satisfactorily, he wants to be able to terminate their services without concern they might go back home disgruntled! So you may find that not being from a particular district is not necessarily disqualifying.

The House does have an employment office, and they do accept applications and maintain a file of employment possibilities. If a member has a vacancy, he or she may call on the employment office for a list of qualified prospects, and arrange interviews. I am assured they do place people, but I have not personally known many who arrived in this way. Formerly called the "House Placement Office," it is now known as the "Office of Human Resources"–an unmitigated misnomer, because you cannot get a human being to receive or return phone calls. However, if you would like to appeal to one of their many recorded messages, the number is (202) 226-6731. I would strongly recommend you make your application through your member of Congress.

I am sure you have been counseled many times about the importance of a well prepared resume. I would only add that, in this field, do not fail to list community services performed, and any special experience you have had that would serve the interests and purposes of a congressional office. Among applicants, most will have good academic records. The reviewer will be looking for unusual qualifications that would make you an especially useful addition to the staff. Good luck!

Within the office of a member of Congress, the job assignments are several and various. The person best known to the visiting public is, of course, the receptionist. That person has a tremendous responsibility for making that "first impression" as favorable as possible. A pleasing personality is essential, but knowledge and diplomacy are no less important. A receptionist needs to know who the congressman would want to see promptly, and to whom different subject matter should be referred for action. The performance in this position can make, or break, an office.

The receptionist, in most instances, has to cover other assignments as well. Because of the complexity and heavy demands on the work of a congressional office, most of the staff have to "double in brass" whenever the occasion requires.

Coordinating all of this is the administrative assistant (A.A.), the office manager, or the "chief of staff," as some now choose to be called. This person must have the confidence of the member of Congress, who delegates these managerial duties. This is a very personal relationship, and usually comes from extensive experience learning the ways and the wishes of the congressman.

The business of the Congress is legislating, so the legislative assistant is a key member of the staff. The "L.A." keeps track of the progress of all legislation, and alerts the congressman to the status of matters of special interest to that constituency. The member may want to initiate a bill, and there are professional offices to assist in the drafting of legislation, but it is the duty of the "L.A." to follow through on this kind of thing.

The largest number of any staff are those described as "case workers." To them are referred the voluminous communications coming into the office seeking help of some nature. They acknowledge the correspondence, and try to determine what the congressman's office might be able to do to satisfy the particular request. They then pursue the appropriate possibilities for resolving the matter.

An effective case worker is worth his or her weight in gold in any office! An effective case worker needs to possess intelligence, an uncompromising commitment to the interests of the congressman, knowledge of how the agencies function, imagination and creative resourcefulness, and untiring tenacity to cut through red tape and bring matters to a happy conclusion! A big order, but we have just such extraordinary people in many offices on Capitol Hill, and to watch them work their special magic is a marvel in human endeavor! We can always use another!

Members usually have a public relations assistant, by that name or some other. This assistant takes care of press inquiries, writes press releases, often composes newsletters, schedules and coordinates public appearances, and handles related matters. To be able to speak on behalf of the congressman requires a very special relationship, and talent. Often these are people who are media trained or experienced, and have been with the congressman for a while. There are other assignments in many offices that may be unique to that congressional district. A dominate industry, or a troubled product, a tourist attraction, a coming convention, or any matter that puts an unusual demand on the office, may cause the congressman to designate an assistant to handle matters relating to that subject. Long or short-term, this situation sometimes provides an opportunity for someone with special qualifications in that subject.

Again, if these jobs sound glamorous–and in many ways they are–I must caution you that the working conditions can be anything but glamorous. Most offices have divided up the limited space into little cubicles that are so confining they probably would be unacceptable in any other agency of government, or in private enterprise. Within these cramped quarters, each has to make room for a computer terminal. Few enjoy a window or direct overhead lighting. It is amazing how well they perform in spite of these cooped up conditions. You seldom hear a complaint from the staff. They count themselves lucky to have this coveted job. Morale is high.

Depending upon the district, a member may have one or more offices located back home in the district, and will have a number of employees staffing those offices. Their work is similar to the work of the Washington office, and in case work, for example, a great deal of liaison takes place between the two offices. Citizens have walk-in access to the congressman's home office, and can usually get prompt attention to their petitions. I must say that most staffers envy the better working conditions in the home office, but few would give up their Washington assignment, and their nearness to the action.

COMMITTEES

Every member of Congress is assigned to at least one committee. This becomes the focus of his or her legislative activity, and defines, to some extent, the primary attention of the legislative assistant. Committee assignments frequently gain for the member additional staff, for the specific purpose of assisting with the committee work. These assistants have their workplace near the main committee room, and while they work for the congressman, they are under the general supervision of the chief clerk of the committee. For young people whose interests lie in a particular area, whether it might be taxes, the environment, science, or whatever, they may find it more fulfilling to seek an opportunity with a congressman who serves on the committee that considers that subject. However, it would be only fair for me to emphasize again that rarely do staff employees have an opportunity to influence the course of legislative considerations. That is not their role. They are there to assist the representatives *who* were elected to make the laws. It is, however, a marvelous opportunity for learning.

However, senior committee staff members with long experience in the work of their committees are among the most prominent and respected members of the congressional community. Some become the resident experts, vastly knowledgeable in their chosen fields, so it is not surprising to see former clerks of the Ways & Means Committee, for example, being nominated to be judges of the various tax courts, and such. It is safe to say they learned a great many things as committee staffers, not the least of which were the limitations of their respective roles.

PAGE TO PAGE

When I first came to the House (August 1, 1941), the Minority Clerk of the House was a man named William Tyler Page. Most of you would recognize his name even now, as the author of The American's Creed. His creed was selected from a national competition back in 1918. For decades after that, every school child received a copy of that creed, and most learned to recite this very inspiring patriotic affirmation.

With pride, I claim the friendship of the late William Tyler Page. He was the very personification of dignity: gray claw-tail coat, wing collar, cravat, and all. He was the soul of integrity. He was a kind man who took an interest in a young page who wanted to learn about the Congress. William Tyler Page was a product of the congressional staff system. The very best. I was deeply mindful of that history when, some 30 years later, I was elected to the post of Minority Clerk.

Years ago, when Congress met for only part of the year, the elected officers of the House literally ran this institution while the Congress was not sitting, and ran it responsibly and well. I revere the memory of some of those good men, and their exemplary service in behalf of the Congress.

Because of some of the untoward events, to which I referred earlier, the status of the elected staff Officers of the House is in a state of uncertainty. Few are there today who have an historical perspective on these matters, or care to. I fervently hope they will not fail to preserve institutional faculties that have contributed so much to the greatness of our beloved Congress.

The senior officer of the House is the Clerk of the House. You may have seen the clerk, the Honorable Robin Carle, presiding over the House at the organization of the 105th Congress. That was not an easy task, but she received the deserved congratulations of the members for her outstanding conduct.

THE MINORITY OFFICERS

The minority, through its caucus, nominates staff officers to compete in the election of officers of the House. The outcome is never in doubt, and when they have lost, they are chosen by resolution to be officers of the minority. Having been chosen that way myself, six times, I have a healthy respect for that procedure, and a warm regard for the privilege it afforded me. There is a distinction that needs to be drawn between these minority staff officers, and other congressional staff. The staff officers perform their duties, serving the members, on the floor of the House. They facilitate the legislative work of the members in a myriad of ways. In doing this, there is no substitute for experience, and no greater requirement than an energetic desire to be helpful.

THE ROSTRUM

The focal point of the House Chamber is the rostrum, and those who are employed there are among the most visable. With the Speaker seated at the top of the rostrum, to his far left is a desk where two pages, who want to be called "documentarians," sit and dispense the documents under consideration.

To the Speaker's immediate left is the timekeeper. All debate in the House is had under a time limitation–no filibusters here–so the timekeeper keeps the Speaker advised as time expires, and performs other duties.

To the Speaker's right is truly his "right hand man," the Parliamentarian of the House, who is unquestionably the chair's most indispensable assistant. The presiding officer, whoever that may be, is utterly dependent upon the knowledge and skills of the excellent parliamentarian and his staff.

Further to the Speaker's right, you would note a desk where is seated an assistant sergeant at arms in charge of the mace. The mace is a handsome instrument of decorum, 13 rods of ebony, bound with silver strappings, and topped by a globe and eagle. In the event of disorder, the Speaker would direct the sergeant at arms to present the mace. It has a colorful history, but in my half-century, I have never seen it actually brought into play. While a chairman is presiding over a "committee of the whole House," the mace is placed in a stand just a bit lower. Nonetheless, the mace always retains its awesome symbolism.

Immediately in front of the Speaker is the Reading Clerk's stand. It is from this familiar dais that the president addresses joint sessions of the Congress (at which time the vice president joins the Speaker at the top of the rostrum), and it is from this stand that many of the world's most illustrious personages have addressed the Congress over the years.

During normal legislating, two reading clerks sit to the viewer's right of that stand. They are the voices of the legislative process, and they have very exacting and demanding responsibilities. However, the Reading Clerk's role affords a marvelous position from which to witness democracy in action, as I can attest from 17 great years in that post.

On the other side of this central dais is the position of the Tally Clerk. He tabulates the call of members on the official tally sheet, and he presents to the Speaker the summary of the vote to be announced.

To his right sits the Journal Clerk, who keeps the minutes of transactions, and prepares the daily Journal (not the *Record*!).

Hovering in that area, particularly at the time of convening, is the Bill Clerk, who receives bills being introduced, and in consultation with the Parliamentarian and the Speaker, assigns numbers to the bills, and refers them to an appropriate committee. This assignment can be of the utmost importance to the fate of a piece of legislation. The attention and sympathies a measure may receive can vary a great deal from one committee to another. Sent to one committee, the proposal may well be on the fast track to becoming law, while if it were sent to another committee, it might never be heard from again.

Just to the viewer's left of the Journal Clerk, on the lower tier, a small mahogany box is attached to the end of that podium. This is the famous "hopper." All legislation in the House has its beginning by being dropped in the hopper while the House is in session. This can be done only by a member of the House (although, in reality, a page may deliver the document), but it cannot be done by the president, a member of the cabinet, or any other official, except through the aegis of a member of Congress.

Completing this account of staff activities at the rostrum, the front tier is where the official reporters of debate and their clerks function. They transcribe and assemble the proceedings of the House. Their accumulated copy is sent to the Government Printing Office where, overnight, it is printed, and it reappears the next morning as the daily edition of the *Congressional Record.*

PERSPECTIVE AND PROMISE

I am frequently asked what is the biggest change I have seen in Congress in the last half-century. In a word, there is a dramatic difference in the *access* the people have to their elected representatives.

There are a number of reasons, but that remoteness is being greatly exacerbated by the proliferation of technology. Personal contact is being replaced by electronic communication that is growing faster than we mere mortals can comprehend. It has been said that we have taken the heart out of politics, and replaced it with a computer chip.

One thing is certain, technology is not going to go away. The challenge to this republic, at this millennium, is to assimilate these wondrous things our God has wrought, to the greater good of mankind. Democracy need not be diminished.

My commentary has concentrated on the House of Representatives, and I must confess a bit of a bias. A description of the legislative process in the United States Senate would be quite similar in almost every aspect. Membership in the Senate numbers less than a fourth of the House, but senator's staffs are about four times as large, so there are opportunities there, as well.

There is a friendly, competitive spirit between the two bodies. I wonder if I could be forgiven for repeating an old story–apocryphal, I am sure–about the congressman's wife who was awakened in the night by what she feared was an intruder, so she tried to stir her husband with: "Wake up! Wake up! I think there is a burglar in the house." To which her husband rolled over and replied: "Oh, no, Honey. There may be one or two in the Senate, but there are none in the House!"

During many years of acting as liaison with the Senate, I did not find any there, either. In truth, I treasure my association with splendid friends at the north end of the Capitol.

Now, if you are thinking about a government job as a place to grow rich, better you should be a burglar! When I went to work at the Capitol, the pay was four dollars a day, and the pay of the most senior staff was only five thousand dollars a year, tops!

Pay is a great deal better than that today, but so are the costs of living in the nation's capital. While most employers in the Congress pay their staff members a reasonable compensation, and while it may sound like an awful lot of money to the folks back home, believe me, it is extremely unlikely you will ever get rich in the public service. And isn't that the way it ought to be?

Public service should be its own reward, and for those who are altruistically motivated, it will be. If I had it to do over again, there is nowhere I would rather spend my productive years, than in the service of the members of the House of Representatives. My life has been enriched beyond measure by this fabulous experience.

The Hill presents a fascinating kaleidoscope of characters, among whom are some of the most magnificent human beings you could ever hope to meet. I shall never cease being grateful for the privilege of passing a part of this fateful pilgrimage in such good company.

More, I could not wish you.

THE WRITER gratefully acknowledges valued consultations with Virginia Bartlett, Linda Hobgood, Laura Perkins, Virginia Gano, and Edith and Betty Gail Elliott.

Part Four

Political Parties and the Life of the House

The chapters in this section all focus on the role of political parties in structuring the work of legislative bodies. Political scientists have long been attracted to the responsible parties model, with its vision of ideological parties that offer voters a clear-cut choice on the issues and then keep their promises once elected. The late Eugene A. Forsey, a member of the Canadian Senate and noted expert on the Canadian constitution, gives us a vision of how parties operate within a parliamentary system. While the parliamentary system lacks the checks-and-balances that protect intense minorities—and foster deliberation—within the American system, parliamentary parties offer voters a mechanism for holding officials accountable for performance in office that our system cannot match.

For better or for worse, political parties in the United States do not operate in this way. They do not run as teams committed to a political platform. The Contract for America is an exception that proves the rule here. In a move that is almost surely without precedent in the American experience, almost all the Republican candidates for the U.S. House in 1994 pledged themselves to a ten-point program, to be taken up within the first 100 days of the new Congress. However, Republican Senate candidates did not pledge themselves to enact the Contract, and many of its provisions died or were modified when they reached the Other Body. William Cramer provides an overview of the critical role played by the congressional parties in structuring lawmaking in the House, with a particular focus on the power of the majority party to control committee agendas and the rules under which bills are considered on the floor.

The leaders of the majority party exercise much more control over the business of the House than is true for their Senate counterparts because the much larger membership of the House precludes the kind of individualism and unlimited debate that characterizes the Senate. Former Speaker Jim Wright identifies the awesome responsibilities and challenges facing every House Speaker, while John J. Rhodes describes how a clever minority leader can devise ways to influence the work of an institution that is, of necessity, dominated by the majority party leadership.

In Chapter 21, Peter Peyser explains how and why he started out his political life as a Republican (running against the party establishment) and ended up as a Democrat—all without appreciably changing his positions on issues.

Part Four concludes with Sonny Montgomery's account of how he wielded influence as a conservative Democrat within a liberal party.

Chapter 17

Party Government in Canada

The Late Eugene A. Forsey
Member, Canadian Senate, 1970-79 [1]

Canada and the United States are both democracies. But there are important differences in the way Canadians and Americans govern themselves. We are a constitutional monarchy while the United States is a republic. That looks like only a formal difference. It is very much more, for we have parliamentary-cabinet government, while the Americans have presidential-congressional.

ELEMENTS OF THE PARLIAMENTARY SYSTEM

Parliament consists of the Queen, the Senate, and the House of Commons.

The Queen is the formal head of the Canadian state. She is represented federally by the Governor General, and provincially by the lieutenant-governors. Federal acts begin: "Her majesty, by and with the advice and consent of the Senate and the House of Commons, enacts as follows"; acts in most provinces begin with similar words. Parliament (or the provincial legislature) meets only at the royal summons; no House of Parliament (or legislature) is equipped with a self-starter. No federal or provincial bill becomes law without the Royal Assent. The monarch has, on occasion, given the assent personally to federal acts, but the assent is usually given by the Governor General or a deputy, and to provincial acts by the Lieutenant Governor or an administrator.

The Governor General and the lieutenant-governors have the right to be consulted by their ministers, and the right to encourage or warn them. But they almost invariably must act on their ministers' advice, though there may be very rare occasions when they must, or may, act without advice or even against the advice of the ministers in office.

Canadian senators are appointed by the Governor General on the recommendation of the Prime Minister. Where U.S. Senators must run for reelection every six years, Canadian senators hold office until age 75 unless they miss two consecutive sessions of Parliament. Until 1965, they held office for life, and the few remaining senators appointed before that date retain their seats. Senators must be at least 30 years old, and must have real estate worth $4,000 net, and total net assets of at least $4,000. They must reside in the province or territory for which they are appointed.

The Senate can initiate any bills except bills providing for the expenditure of public money or imposing taxes. It can amend, or reject, any bill whatsoever. It can reject any bill as often as it sees fit. No bill can become law unless it has been passed by the Senate.

In theory, these powers are formidable. But for over 40 years, the Senate has not rejected a bill passed by the House of Commons, and very rarely insisted on an amendment that the House of Commons rejected. Then, in 1988, it refused to pass the Free Trade Agreement until it had been submitted to the people in a general election; and in 1989-90, it insisted on amendments to the Unemployment Insurance Bill, amendments the Commons rejected. The Senate eventually passed the bill as submitted by the House. And in 1991, the Senate simply defeated a Commons bill respecting abortion. In other cases, the Senate has not adopted bills before the end of a session, thereby effectively stopping them from becoming law.

Most of the amendments the Senate makes to bills passed by the Commons are clarifying or simplifying amendments, and are almost always accepted by the House of Commons. The Senate's main work is done in committees, where it goes over bills clause by clause, and hears evidence, often voluminous, from groups or individuals who would be affected by the particular bill under review. This committee work is especially effective because the Senate has many members with specialized knowledge and long years of legal, business, or administrative experience. Their ranks include ex-ministers, ex-premiers of provinces, ex-mayors, eminent lawyers, and experienced farmers.

In recent decades, the Senate has taken on a new job: investigating important public problems such as poverty, unemployment, inflation, the aged, land use, science policy, Aboriginal affairs, relations with the United States, and the efficiency (or lack of it) of government departments. These investigations have produced valuable reports, which often have led to changes in legislation or government policy. The Senate usually does this kind of work far more cheaply than royal commissions or task forces, because its members are paid already and it has a permanent staff at its disposal.

The House of Commons in Canada is the major law-making body. It has 301 members, one each from each of the 301 constituencies. In each constituency, or riding, the candidate who receives the largest number of votes is elected, even if his or her vote total is less than half the total.[2]

POLITICAL PARTIES

Our system could not work without political parties. Our major and minor federal parties were not created by any law, although they now are recognized by the law. We, the people, have created them ourselves. They are voluntary associations of people who hold broadly similar opinions on public questions.

The party that wins the largest number of seats in a general election ordinarily forms the government. Its leader is asked by the Governor General to become Prime Minister. If the government in office before an election comes out of the election without a clear majority, it has the right to meet the new House of Commons and see whether it can get enough support from the minor parties to give it a majority. This happened in 1925-26, 1962, and 1972.

The second largest party (or, in the circumstances just described, the largest) becomes the Official Opposition, and its leader becomes the person holding the recognized position of Leader of the Opposition. The Leader of the Opposition gets the same salary as a minister. The leader of any party which has at least 12 seats also gets a higher salary than an ordinary MP. These parties also get public money for research.

Why? Because we want criticism, we want watchfulness, we want the possibility of an effective alternative government if we are displeased with the one we have. The party system reflects the waves of opinion as they rise and wash through the country. There is much froth, but deep swells move beneath them, and they set the course of the ship.

CABINET GOVERNMENT

In the United States, the head of state and the head of the government are one and the same. The president is both at once. In Canada, the Queen, ordinarily represented by the Governor General, is the head of state, and the Prime Minister is the head of the government.

Does that make any difference? Yes; in Canada, the head of state can, in exceptional circumstances, protect Parliament and the people against a Prime Minister and ministers who may forget that "minister" means "servant," and may try to make themselves masters. For example, the head of state could refuse to let a Cabinet dissolve a newly-elected House of Commons before it could even meet, or could refuse to let ministers bludgeon the people into submission by a continuous series of general elections. The American head of state cannot restrain the American head of government because they are the same person.

The Governor General governs through a Cabinet, headed by a Prime Minister. The Cabinet consists of a varying number of ministers. The national Cabinet now usually has 30 or more, and provincial Cabinets vary from about 10 to 22. Most of the ministers have "portfolios" (that is, they are in charge of particular departments—Finance, External Affairs, Environment, Health and Welfare, etc.), and are responsible, answerable, and accountable to the House of Commons or the legislature for their particular departments. Sometimes, there are also ministers without portfolio, who are not in charge of any department; or ministers of state, who may be in charge of a particular section of a department, or of a "ministry," which is not a full-fledged department (for example, the Ministry of State for Fitness and Amateur Sport).

The ministers collectively are answerable to the House of Commons or the legislature for the policy and conduct of the Cabinet as a whole. If a minister does not agree with a particular policy or action of the government, he (she) must either accept the policy or action and, if necessary, defend it, or resign from the Cabinet. This is known as "the collective responsibility of the Cabinet," and is a fundamental principle of our form of government.

The Cabinet is responsible for most legislation. It has the sole power to prepare and introduce bills providing for the expenditure of public money or imposing taxes. These bills must be introduced first in the House of Commons, and the House cannot *initiate* them, or *increase* either the tax or expenditure without a royal recommendation in the form of a message from the Governor General. The Senate cannot increase either a tax or an expenditure. However, any member of either House can move a motion to decrease a tax or an expenditure, and the House concerned can pass it, although this hardly ever happens.

FORMING A GOVERNMENT

If a national election gives a party opposed to the cabinet in office a clear majority (that is, more than half the seats) in the House of Commons, the Cabinet resigns and the Governor General calls on the leader of the victorious party to become Prime Minister and form a new Cabinet. The Prime Minister chooses the other ministers, who are then formally appointed by the Governor General.

If no party gets a clear majority, the Cabinet that was in office before and during the election has two choices. It can resign, in which case the Governor General will call on the leader of the largest opposition party to form a Cabinet. Or the Cabinet already in office can choose to stay in office and meet the newly-elected House which, however, it must do promptly. In either case, it is the people's representatives in the newly-elected House who will decide whether the "minority" government (one whose own party has less than half the seats) shall stay in office or be thrown out.

If a Cabinet is defeated in the House of Commons on a motion of censure or want of confidence, the Cabinet must either resign (the Governor General will ask the Leader of the Opposition to form a new Cabinet), or ask for a dissolution of Parliament and a fresh election.

In very exceptional circumstances, the Governor General could refuse a request for a fresh election. For instance, if an election gave no party a clear majority and the Prime Minister asked for a fresh election without even allowing the new Parliament to meet, the Governor General would have to say no. This is because, if "parliamentary government" is to mean anything, a newly-elected Parliament must at least be allowed to meet and see whether it can transact public business. Also, if a minority government is defeated on a motion of want of confidence very early in the first session of a new Parliament, and there is a reasonable possibility that a government of another party can be formed and get the support of the House of Commons, then the Governor General could refuse the request for a fresh election.[3]

No elected person in Canada above the rank of mayor has a "term of office." Members of Parliament or of a provincial legislature normally are elected for not more than five years, but there can be, and have been, Parliaments and legislatures that have lasted less than a year. The Prime Minister can ask for a fresh election at any time but, as already stated, there may be circumstances in which he (she) would not get it.

The Cabinet has no "term." Every Cabinet lasts from the moment the Prime Minister is sworn in until he or she resigns or dies. If a Prime Minister dies or resigns, the Cabinet comes to an end. If this Prime Minister's party still has a majority of the Commons, then the Governor General must find a new Prime Minister at once. A Prime Minister who resigns has no right to advise the Governor as to a successor unless asked; even then, the advice need not be followed. If he (she) resigns because of defeat, the Governor must call on the Leader of the Opposition to form a government. If the Prime Minister dies, or resigns for personal reasons, then the Governor consults leading members of the majority party as to who will most likely be able to form a government that can command a majority of the House. The Governor then calls on the person he (she) has decided has the best chance. This new Prime Minister will, of course, hold office only until the majority party has chosen a new leader in a national convention. This leader will then be called upon to form a government.

VIRTUES OF THE CANADIAN SYSTEM

Parliamentary-cabinet government is based on a concentration of powers.[4] The Prime Minister and every other minister must by custom (though not by law) be a member of one House or the other, or get a seat in one House or the other within a short time of appointment. All government bills must be introduced by a minister or someone speaking on his or her behalf, and ministers must appear in Parliament to defend government bills, answer daily questions on government actions or policies, and rebut attacks on such actions or policies.

In the United States, the president and every member of both houses are elected for a fixed term: the president for four years, the senators for six (one-third up for election every two years), the members of the House of Representatives for two. The only way to get rid of a president before the end of the four-year term is to impeach him (her), which is very hard to do. As the president, the senators, and the representatives are elected for different periods, it can happen, and often does, that the president belongs to one party while the opposing party has a majority in either the Senate, or the House of Representatives, or both. So for years on end, the president may find his (her) legislation and policies blocked by an adverse majority in both houses. The president cannot appeal to the people by dissolving either house, or both; he (she) has no such power, and the two houses are there for their fixed terms, come what may, until the constitutionally fixed hour strikes.

And even when the elections for the presidency, the House of Representatives, and one-third of the Senate take place on the same day (as they do every four years), the result may be a Republican president, a Democratic Senate, and a Republican House of Representatives, or various other mixtures.

A president, accordingly, may have a coherent program to present to Congress, and may get senators and representatives to introduce the bills he (she) wants passed. But each house can add to each of the bills, or take things out of them, or reject them outright, and what emerges from the tussle may bear little or no resemblance to what the president wanted. The majority in either house may have a coherent program on this or that subject; but the other house can add to it, or take things out of it, or throw the whole thing out; and again, what (if anything) emerges may bear little or no resemblance to the original. Even if the two houses agree on something, the president can, and often does, veto the bill. The veto can be overridden only by a two-thirds majority in both houses.

So it ends up that nobody—not the president, not the senators, not the representatives—can be held really responsible for anything being done or not done. Everybody concerned can honestly and legitimately say, "Don't blame me!"

True, a dissatisfied voter can vote against a president, a representative, or a senator. But no matter what the voters do, the situation remains essentially the same. The president is there for four years and remains there no matter how often either house produces an adverse majority. If, halfway through the president's four-year term, the elections for the House and Senate return adverse majorities, the president still stays in office for the remaining two years with enormous powers. And he (she) cannot get rid of an adverse House of Representatives or Senate by holding a new election.

The adverse majority in one or both houses can block many things the president may want to do, but it cannot force him (her) out of office. The president can veto bills passed by both houses. But Congress can override this veto by a two-thirds majority in both houses. The House of Representatives can impeach the President, and the Senate then tries him (her), and, if it so decides, by a two-thirds majority, removes him (her). No president has ever been removed, and there have been only three attempts to do it. In two, the Senate majority was too small; in the third, the president resigned before any vote on impeachment took place in the House of Representatives.

Our Canadian system is very different. Nobody is elected for a fixed term. All important legislation is introduced by the government, and all bills to spend public funds or impose taxes *must* be introduced by the government and neither House can raise the amounts of money involved. As long as the government can keep the support of a majority in the House of Commons, it can pass any legislation it sees fit unless an adverse majority in the Senate refuses to pass the bill (which very rarely happens nowadays). If it loses its majority support in the House of Commons, it must either make way for a government of the opposite party or call a fresh election. If it simply makes way for a government of the opposite party, then that government, as long as it holds its majority in the House of Commons, can pass any legislation it sees fit, and if it loses that majority, then it, in its turn, must either make way for a new government or call a fresh election. In the United States, the president and Congress can be locked in fruitless combat for years on end. In Canada, the government and the House of Commons cannot be at odds for more than a few weeks at a time. If they differ on any matter of importance, then, promptly, there is either a new government or a new House of Commons.

Presidential-congressional government is neither responsible nor responsive. Parliamentary-cabinet government, by contrast, is both responsible and responsive. If the House of Commons votes want of confidence in a Cabinet, that Cabinet must step down and make way for a new government formed by the official opposition party, or call an election right away so the people can decide which party will govern.

An American president can be blocked by one house or both for years on end. A Canadian Prime Minister, blocked by the House of Commons, must either make way for a new Prime Minister, or allow the people to elect a new House of Commons that will settle the matter, one way or another, within two or three months. That is real responsibility.

Notes:

1. This chapter was adapted from a substantially longer work by the late Eugene Forsey, *How Canadians Govern Themselves*, 3d ed. (Ottawa, Ont.: Public Information Office, House of Commons, Canada, 1991). In so doing, the editor also has benefitted from comments by Mr. Forsey's daughter, Helen Forsey.

2. The number of constituencies may be changed after every general census, pursuant to the Constitution and the *Electoral Boundaries Readjustment Act* that allot parliamentary seats roughly on the basis of population. Every province must have at least as many members in the Commons as it had in the Senate before 1982. The constituencies vary somewhat in size, within prescribed limits.

3. Provincial governments in Canada are formed, dissolved, and reformed in precisely the same manner—e.g., the provincial lieutenant governor calls on the leader of the party that was victorious in the provincial general election to form a Cabinet, and so on. (At the provincial level, first ministers are called "premiers.") The provincial lieutenant governor plays all the same roles in this process that the governor general performs at the national level.

4. Presidential-congressional government is based on a separation of powers. The American president cannot be a member of either house of Congress. Neither can any of the members of his (her) Cabinet. Neither the president nor any member of the Cabinet can appear in Congress to introduce a bill, or defend it, or answer questions, or rebut attacks on policies. No member of either house can be president or a member of the Cabinet.

Chapter 18

How Political Parties Shape
the Policy Decisions of Congress

William C. Cramer (R-Florida)

Most people do not realize that Congress often acts and reacts to the policies, ideologies, and pressures of political parties. This was not envisioned by the framers of the Constitution in that political parties were neither mentioned in it nor prohibited by it. They have come into existence through the window of opportunity resulting from this silence on the subject of political parties in the Nation's basic foundational document.

POLITICAL PARTIES AND
THE ORGANIZATION OF CONGRESS

The Constitution provides in Article I for the vice president to preside over the Senate and for the election of a president pro tempore, a temporary president, to preside in the absence of the vice president. It also provides for the presiding officer of the House to be the Speaker elected by the entire membership. The Constitution further provides for the election of other officers and specifies that "each House shall determine the rules of its proceedings."

Accordingly, under the presently prevailing two party system, the Democrats in their caucus and the Republicans in their conference, made up of all the members of their parties elected in the preceding even year elections, meet in advance of the new session. In these meetings, the party members decide the nominees for House and Senate Leadership positions, the rules to be proposed for the conduct of the business, and sometimes some of the top priority policy matters to be scheduled for the early agenda of the ensuing session of Congress.

Majority party status allows that party's members in the House to choose the

Speaker, majority leader, majority whip, and the administrative officers, such as the parliamentarian, Senate secretary and House clerk, sergeant-at-arms, and chief administrative officer. The minority chooses their minority leader and whip, and party members unite in party line voting in selecting their leaders and parallel minority administrative officers. This is one of the relatively few party line votes during the session in which party members vote 100 percent with their party. Independents, who seldom are elected, choose a side they wish to join and are adopted by that side and that party.

MAJORITY PARTY DOMINANCE OVER COMMITTEES

All members are assigned to one or more standing legislative committees, with the majority having the greater number of members on each committee in order to ensure a possible majority vote and to control the committee legislative activities. The exception is the Committee on Official Conduct, which is not a legislative committee, on which an equal number of Democrats and Republicans serve in determining members non-compliance with ethics rules.

The Democrats set up a Steering and Policy Committee to handle committee assignments and the Republicans set up a Committee on Committees. On the Republican side, the ranking (in-time-served) members from their states and their party serve on these committees and have a vote equal to their state's number of members belonging to their party in voting on assignments to committees. On the Democratic side, the leadership and 25 members of their Steering and Policy Committee and their Caucus make final decisions on recommendations for committee membership and chairmanships.

The most important work of the Congress is done in committee and subcommittee. Committees hold life and death power over bills assigned to them. When it is realized that most of the policy making and agenda setting on legislation is under committee control, in that nearly all bills must go through the committee incubation and gestation process before they are ready to reach the full chamber for consideration and vote, then the significance of the party dominance becomes apparent.

All public bills are referred to the committee that has subject matter jurisdiction after the first reading. Such bills are thereafter under control of the committee until reported out, and thus put on the action agenda called the calendar (with the exception of discharge or calendar Wednesday or bills having passed the other body). Bills not reported are buried in committees. Committees have the power to subpoena witnesses and compel testimony, to oversee the executive branches in the administration of the laws passed by Congress, and to explore the need for revision, curtailment of activities, or elimination thereof. Again, this delegation of life and death power over legislation to the committees under the rules of the House and Senate demonstrates the significance of committees and their powers and the importance of party control over them.

The chairmen of the committees–always members of the majority party–decide, often upon consultation with the leadership, what bills to process, when to put them on the agenda for consideration, what hearings are to be held, how proposed bills are to be worded, and the nature of the reports which explain the proposals approved by the committees. The chairman assigns committee members from his party to subcommittees and designates a chairman for each.

The chair also controls the administrative offices and staff on the majority side. The ranking minority member acts similarly relating to minority committee members and their offices and staff. For many years, through limiting minority staff personnel, the majority made it difficult for the minority to be effective in preparing for and participating in hearings, bill and report drafting, and research. In the early 1950s, for instance, the minority on many committees had only one staff member, while the majority had dozens of such staff members. The Committee on Public Works, on which I served, is one example. This disparity has been somewhat relieved in that the rules now provide for approximately one-third minority membership on committee staffs in most committees.

When the Republicans took control of the House for the first time in 40 years in the 104th Congress, they reduced the number of committees from 22 to 19 by eliminating the Post Office and Civil Service, District of Columbia, and Merchant Marine and Fisheries Committees, assigning their subject matters to other standing committees. Committee staff and other personnel were reduced by about one-third. The number of subcommittees was reduced also. This movement was propelled by the Republicans' conviction that, under the Democrats, the number of committees and subcommittees had grown too large and too powerful, resulting in a diffusion of responsibility.

The committee meetings were opened to the press and the public, voting by proxy of the members was eliminated, chairmen of committees were limited to a six year tenure, and the number of subcommittees were decreased. These drastic changes reflected the pent up 40 years of often frustrated minority domination by the majority that had muted their ever-present cry for a change.

These major changes in the rules of the House, followed by changes in the Senate, were of historical significance. They indicate the import of a change in party control of a legislative body, particularly after being long out of power.

MAJORITY PARTY CONTROL OF THE RULES COMMITTEE

Once a bill is reported to the calendar with its accompanying report by the committee, it is ready for Rules Committee action in the House and in the Senate for majority leadership assignment for floor action. In the House, traditionally, equal time is allocated to majority and minority members for floor debate and the minority rights are further protected by the power to offer a motion to send the bill back to committee, with or without instructions to incorporate the minority provisions, by use of a motion to recommit. Thus, the minority is guaranteed the right to be heard despite being outnumbered.

The Rules Committee in the House epitomizes the power of the majority party. Since the mid-1970s, the Rules Committee has been firmly under the control of the majority party whose members are appointed by the Speaker This committee decides when and if a bill goes to the House floor, the length of debate, whether amendments are allowed by an open rule or not allowed by a closed rule. The minority party generally favors open rules and consultation as to scheduling and debate so that its point will be fully considered.

The Democrat-controlled House used the powers of the majority for 40 years (1955-1995) to dominate proceedings and policy decisions. The Republicans in the 104th Congress adopted similar tactics to enact the Contract With America during its first 100 days.

In the Senate, a smaller body with 100 members, compared to 435 members in the House, most bills are open to amendment and debate is unlimited. In the place of the Rules Committee, the majority leader, in consultation with the minority leader, determines the rules for consideration of legislation. However, a debate can be terminated by 60 votes for cloture.

During debate in both bodies, the chairman of the committee that reported the bill has the power to manage and control the debate for the majority while the ranking minority member controls the debate on the other side of the aisle. The decisions relating to a bill voted out of the committee is accompanied by a written report explaining the bill and its background, provisions, justification, and cost. The report contains the views of the majority supporting the measure and those opposing it or desiring modification of it. Thus, the right to express the minority view, which is often a party position unless members splinter off from that position, further protects against total majority party domination of the committee process.

In the House, committee chairmen have lost some of their power through party procedural changes since 1977, particularly changes on the Democratic side in the 1970s that called for the election of committee chairmen and the assignment of committee positions by the party caucus as well as for greater autonomy of subcommittee chairmen and staffing. Subcommittee chairmen now are voted on by the party members of the committee rather than by being chosen by the chairman and not necessarily by seniority.

On the Republican side, the seniority system was generally the basis for the appointment of committee chairmen and subcommittee chairmen until the 104th Congress. When the Republicans elected Newt Gingrich, he became the first Republican Speaker in 40 years and, interestingly, the only one re-elected in over 65 years with the election of a Republican majority in 1996. Upon his election, Speaker Gingrich personally selected key chairmen and stacked some committee memberships–particularly the Rules Committee–to assure favorable consideration of the Contract With America. The party membership in conference supported their newly-elected Speaker and also elected choices to the leadership positions.

POLITICAL PARTIES AND CONGRESS:
GRIDLOCK OR DELIBERATION?

This chapter attempts to encourage a better understanding of the fact that Congress often acts and reacts to the policies, ideologies, and pressures of political parties. Both political parties exercise their right to fully express their views and to support their party's policies at every step of the legislative process. I have explored that process in this chapter, illustrating the many procedural opportunities for pursuing their legislative goals such as introducing bills, committee activities, and floor debate. These exhaustive and time consuming legislative procedures give the impression to the public of excessive arguments, differing opinions, and gridlock.

This gives rise to the questions: Is there a better system? Does our system really work? Does lengthy debate impede necessary action, or does it give greater assurance of adequate consideration of proposals resulting in a better final product?

Our constitutional system of checks and balances, along with the development of a two-party system, guarantees many opposing policies and necessitates lengthy consideration, debate, and often compromise to mold an idea into law. Consensus on a party line basis is often difficult, if not impossible, to attain. In Congress, the 435 members of the House are elected by the people in 435 Congressional districts and the 100 members of the Senate by people in the 50 states. They are expected primarily to represent the views of their constituents in our republican, representative form of government. The president, being the only nationally elected official, can enunciate national party positions, but to accomplish his goals, he must rely on the co-equal independent legislative, as well as the judicial, branches. Thus, party policies, whether they are initiated by the president, or by party leaders in Congress, result in a consensus party position only when that policy is consistent with that of often widely varying local constituency desires expressed through the ballot box. While this unique system of government makes it difficult to develop a consensus on issues and usually takes a substantial amount of time to reach an agreement, it also has the advantage of making sure that a policy affecting all the people of America is subject to adequate debate and consideration before it is enacted.

No nation has yet devised a better system, although ours can be improved and we should pursue such improvements constantly. Lengthy debate and distillation of legislative proposals is our best guarantee of results that serve the public good. Moreover, our two-party system both encourages alternative solutions to pressing problems and assures that the people will be given a choice of leaders. After all, the essence of our democracy is the right of the people to be able to make a choice by supporting the party and the candidates that reflect their concerns and aspirations.

Chapter 19

Challenges That Speakers Face

Jim Wright (D-Texas)

The speakership provides fully as much challenge as any Speaker is prepared to accept. Ordained by the Constitution as presiding judge and chief voice of the legislative branch of government and third in line in succession to the presidency, the office of Speaker has been what changing times and individual occupants have made of it. Some, such as Henry Clay and Sam Rayburn, have been catalysts of major change. A few, such as Joseph Cannon and Thomas Reed, have thoroughly dominated the House. Others have seen their functions essentially as presiding with fairness and decorum while maintaining as much harmony as possible.

Rayburn was Speaker when I entered the House in 1955. He impressed me enormously. Quite probably I formed my basic concept of a Speaker's function from his example. Rayburn was an effective leader. He saw national needs and made things happen. Under his guidance, the legislative branch fulfilled a role more creative than passive, initiating much of the domestic agenda during the Eisenhower presidency, when one party held the White House and the other led in Congress.

It is possible that from this, and from my personal friendships with Speakers McCormack, Albert, and O'Neill, I had developed an exalted view of the Speaker's role, perhaps even an impossibly demanding conception of what a Speaker should be able to achieve for the country. On the occasion of my swearing in, set by my wish on January 6, 1987, the 105th anniversary of Speaker Sam Rayburn's birth, I called the office "a treasure more precious than any material possession and an honor more sublime than royalty." To be Speaker, I said, was "the highest responsibility that can come to a lawmaker anywhere in the world."

THE SPEAKER'S ROLE

The challenges that beset a Speaker include both obstacles and opportunities. Some are endemic, embedded in the very nature of our system of government. Others are ephemeral, arising from the times. A Speaker's first responsibility, as with that of any other public official, is to the nation. After that responsibility is fulfilled, he has a specific obligation to uphold the position of the legislative branch in our constitutional balance of powers, to defend the rights and prerogatives of the House in relation to the Senate, and to maintain the authority of the office entrusted to him so that it is passed on to successors with its inherent powers intact.

Beyond all of this, speakers assume a peculiar responsibility for the well-being of their colleagues, and owe a certain degree of fealty to the political party that elected them Speaker. Against this latter loyalty, every Speaker must balance the overriding duty to promote an atmosphere of peace, comity, and mutual respect among the members. The Speaker must protect the minority from intolerance or abuse by the majority while protecting the majority from the obstructive actions of a minority.

STANDING UP FOR NATION: IRAN-CONTRA

The Iran-Contra scandal and the bitterly divisive issue of our covert involvement in Central American wars posed a constitutional crisis. No controversy since the Vietnam War had rent the country so painfully or produced such sharp polarization among lawmakers. The issue of whether to continue funding military efforts to overthrow the leftist government of Nicaragua was provoking angry confrontations in Congress and between the legislative and executive branches. On three occasions, Congress had voted to discontinue all military assistance to the Contras.

In November 1986, the nation was traumatized by the discovery that a secret group operating out of the White House had contrived, contrary to law, to sell U.S. weapons to Iran. Without notifying anyone in Congress, perpetrators had turned over the proceeds to the military forces trying to overthrow Nicaragua's government. President Reagan vowed that he personally had not known of this, and I wanted desperately to believe him.

This was the most shocking revelation since the Watergate burglary and cover-up. At least four laws—the National Security Act, the Arms Export Control Act, the Department of Defense Appropriations Act, and the Anti-Terrorism Act—had been violated blatantly. These laws specifically forbade undertaking any such covert effort without giving official notice to the intelligence committees or the House and Senate leadership, and these laws prohibited the sale of arms to any terrorist country, specifically naming Iran.

So flagrant was the flouting of law that a hot volcanic lava of anger began boiling inside the Congress. First whispers, then audible demands, for impeachment proceedings growled in private conversations wherever Democratic members met. Fortunately, Congress was out of session when the shocking news broke. But activities in the White House did little to abate the outrage. Soon it was known that Lieutenant Colonel Oliver North was systematically shredding all written evidence relating to the illicit adventure before Congress could reconvene and subpoena the documents. This fanned the flames to a higher intensity.

This situation had explosive potential. Several House committee and subcommittee chairs contacted me during December, each wanting to schedule hearings on some separate facet of the big story that dominated Washington news that month. Without a clear sense of direction, the new Congress could degenerate into a nine-ring circus as committees vied with one another for sensational confrontations with various officials of the executive branch.

The last thing our country needed was an impeachment outcry or a frontal challenge to the president's personal integrity. Like other members of Congress and millions of private citizens, I had agonized through long weeks in 1973 that led to and included the impeachment hearing on President Nixon and culminated in his resignation. I wanted no repeat of that scenario. The country could ill afford it. Determined that all of the pertinent facts must be disclosed in a dignified way, preserving the congressional authority without precipitating a full-scale constitutional crisis, I met with Senate Majority Leader Byrd. He felt exactly as I did.

Together we announced that there would be one congressional hearing on the subject, not several. It would be a joint meeting of select House and Senate committees. Byrd and I would appoint Democratic members; Minority Leaders Michel and Dole would select Republican panelists. Eager to protect the credibility and prestige of the special select committees, I very carefully chose the most respected authorities I could find: Chairs Peter Rodino of Judiciary, Jack Brooks of Government Operations, Dante Fascell of Foreign Affairs, Les Aspin of Armed Services, and Louis Stokes of Intelligence. To signal the importance I attached to this mission, I asked House Majority Leader Foley to serve as my personal representative and appointed Edward P. Boland, principal author of several of the laws that had been violated.

I thought a long while before choosing a chair for the whole group and finally settled on Lee Hamilton of Indiana, ranking member of the Foreign Affairs Committee and former chair of the House Intelligence Committee. I picked Hamilton because of his reputation for objectivity and his judicious, noninflammatory manner. I did not want the hearing to be, or even seem to be, a witch hunt. As much as I disagreed with Reagan on domestic priorities, I did not want anyone on the committee with the private agenda of personally embarrassing the president. To complete my list of appointees, I named Ed Jenkins of Georgia, a good country lawyer. I was not trying to prejudge the committee's findings, but merely trying to moderate their explosive potential for splitting the country apart.

Senator Byrd also chose a responsible panel. He and I agreed that, to the extent of our ability to influence it, the hearing must not smack of partisanship. It would be open to the media and nationally televised. Byrd's chair, Sen. Daniel Inouye (D-Hawaii), was ideally suited by temperament and conviction for his role. His demeanor was calm and rational. He and Hamilton did their best to be impartial and scrupulously fair to Republican colleagues appointed by Dole and Michel and to hold down temptations to inflammatory rhetoric.

Hamilton wanted to agree in advance to an arbitrary date to terminate the proceedings. Otherwise, he argued, they could go indefinitely to the detriment of other business. He also proposed giving limited immunity from prosecution to induce testimony from Colonel North, the individual most involved in handling a number of the details of the covert transaction. At least two of the House panelists privately protested, but a majority agreed to back the chair's decision. As it turns out, this may have compromised the efforts of the special prosecutor, Lawrence E. Walsh. But our overriding objective in the congressional leadership, frankly, was not to embarrass the administration or send people to jail but to get at the truth, maintain the nation's equilibrium, emphasize the rule of law, and avoid a bloody constitutional confrontation.

In addition, I felt that we had to heal the lingering wound that had festered for five years over our country's secret, and sometimes illegal, sponsorship of the gory attempts to overthrow the Nicaraguan government by force of arms. Some 30,000 people had died in Nicaragua along with some 70,000 in El Salvador. Congress itself had been closely divided, vacillating between funding and rebuffing President Reagan's demands for military aid to the Contras.

In July 1987, a Republican former colleague, Tom Loeffler, came by my office to inform me that he had been appointed by the president to help round up votes to revive military funding of the Nicaraguan war. I told Loeffler that, in my opinion, Congress would again reject that demand. The Iran-Contra revelations had damaged his cause.

Acknowledging that possibility, Loeffler suggested that as Speaker I should join President Reagan in a bipartisan initiative for peace. We would call jointly on the Central American nations to negotiate settlements in Nicaragua and El Salvador based on a cease-fire, political amnesty for those who had been in revolt, and free elections to resolve the issues in dispute by popular will. In other words, ballots instead of bullets, with assurances of U.S. support.

That idea appealed to me. After talking with the White House, Republican House leaders and the bipartisan Senate leadership, I was encouraged. Some of my fellow Democrats were skeptical of the president's intentions, but most felt I should take the risk if there was a chance it could lead to peace. I talked also with Secretary of State Shultz, who was instructed by President Reagan to work with me in the preparation of a joint statement.

Before formally agreeing, however, I wanted to test the waters in Central America. I had personal conversations with Presidents Jose Napoleon Duarte of El Salvador and Oscar Arias of Costa Rica. Both of them rejoiced at the prospect. They believed a united pro-peace front in Washington could lead to a series of negotiated settlements throughout Central America and stop the bloodshed.

Michel and I asked Nicaraguan Ambassador Carlos Tunnermann to meet with us in the Capitol to probe the Nicaraguan government's probable response to an initiative such as we had in mind. "What would it take," I asked "for your country to get rid of Cuban and Russian military advisors, live in peace with your neighbors, cut off any aid to those who want to overthrow the government of El Salvador, and restore the constitutional freedoms of your people that were suspended in the emergency law?" Tunnermann denied that his country was doing anything to interfere in El Salvador. As for the rest, he vowed that his government would be quite willing to do each of the things I asked if we would simply "stop financing the invasion" of Nicaragua.

The presidents of the five Central American republics would be meeting on August 7 in Guatemala. It was important that President Reagan and I agree on the contents of our statement and issue it before that date. I dictated the first draft. Secretary Shultz suggested minor alterations, which I accepted. The president and I jointly issued the call for a regional cease-fire and peaceful negotiation on August 5, two days before the Guatemala conference.

The result was better than I had dared hope. The Costa Rican ambassador called me from the conference site to report the happy news that all five presidents had entered a formal agreement embodying almost all the elements of the Wright-Reagan plan. The principal architect of the Esquipulas Accords, as the agreement would be known, was President Arias of Costa Rica. For this work, he was awarded the Nobel Peace Prize.

At my initiative, we invited Arias to stop off on his way through Washington in September and address the House. Meanwhile, the Nicaraguan government appointed a peace commission, opened newspapers and radio stations that had been shut down, offered amnesty to those who had made war against the government, and invited them to participate in the political process including free elections, which ultimately would be held in 1990. The same amnesty procedure was going on under Duarte's direction in El Salvador.

At about this point, I discovered that the White House was far from happy with the turn events had taken. While I fully expected our joint statement to stimulate the movement toward peace, President Reagan's advisors apparently anticipated refusal of the Nicaraguan government to comply. From negative comments emanating from the White House, it slowly became clear to me that highly placed people in the administration did not *want* a peaceful settlement in Nicaragua. They actually wanted the talks to break down so they could use the "failure" of the peace efforts as an excuse for renewing the war.

This confronted me with a moral dilemma. At the urging of the administration, I had joined in a bipartisan call for peace. Overjoyed at the initial success of our efforts, I had met at the White House's request with leaders of the Contra Directorate. Most of them, I saw, had faith in the peace effort. I was convinced that most Nicaraguans on both sides were eager for peace. But some bitterness lingered. Someone had to be a go-between, an honest broker who could bring the two sides together.

The only Nicaraguan fully trusted by both sides, I had learned, was Catholic Cardinal Miguel Obando y Bravo. Responsible people in both camps agreed that he was the one to monitor the cease-fire and help arbitrate the differences. As Speaker and co-author of the call for peace, I met with the cardinal, whom I knew personally, on November 13, 1987, and encouraged him to undertake that critical role. He agreed, and Nicaraguan President Daniel Ortega at my personal urging agreed to give the cardinal a free hand. The White House, bitterly resentful of my efforts in helping to keep the peace process on track, began attacking me angrily in the press. The president and Assistant Secretary of State Elliott Abrams considered my endeavors intrusive and presumptuous. Perhaps they were. But having committed myself in good faith to the effort to make peace, I was unwilling to be a party to its deliberate unraveling or to allow that result if I could prevent it.

On two occasions–in December 1987 and February 1988–the president's forces tried to forsake the peace process altogether and revive the war by renewing military aid for the Contras. On both occasions, a majority in Congress voted down the request. At my personal urging. Congress did appropriate funds for humanitarian assistance–food, clothing, shelter, and medical needs–for the Contra forces during the ceasefire.

As a consequence of my unwillingness to abandon the effort I had helped set in motion, I became a target for many personal attacks, both in the conservative press and from some Republican members of Congress. It is ironic that, in bringing peace to Central America, I unconsciously drove a wedge between myself and the congressional minority that ultimately inhibited my capacity to promote consensus on other issues. In retrospect, I firmly believe I did the right thing. One of the unavoidable challenges of the speakership is determining when the end result is worth risking one's own popularity, perhaps even one's moral authority, with a segment of the membership. I do regret my inability to make peace between Democrats and Republicans over the issue.

It was in March 1989, with George Bush now serving as president, that Secretary of State Baker and I, along with others in the congressional leadership, issued a second statement that clearly disavowed the use of force and put all the influence of the United States behind the peace negotiation. This culminated in the free and fair election from which Violetta Chamorro emerged as president of Nicaragua on February 25, 1990. In a broad sense, the fourth goal of my speakership was attained, but its attainment used up almost all that remained of my political capital.

STANDING UP FOR THE HOUSE: THE PAY RAISE ISSUE

The Speaker has an obligation to uphold the public reputation of the House. Thus, one of the most difficult challenges all modern Speakers have faced is posed by the news media. All Speakers want their colleagues collectively to get credit for their hard work and the institution for its achievements. These wishes frequently are dashed by reporters, editorialists, pundits, and commentators. Their apparent thirst for scandal, their seeming eagerness to debunk, and their slowness to give credit, their frequent fixation with the trivial and tawdry, their boredom with legislative substance, and their ready assumption of an adversarial relationship against public authority in general and Congress in particular may only seem to be getting worse.

The problem is not new. Contempt for Congress is a well-rehearsed habit. Mark Twain once quipped that America has no native criminal class "except of course, for Congress." And Speaker Nicholas Longworth ruefully concluded in 1925 that "from the beginning of the Republic, it has been the duty of every freeborn voter to look down upon us and the duty of every freeborn humorist to make jokes about us."

Congress is, after all, an easy target, an amorphous and heterogeneous collection of opinionated mortals grappling with extraordinary, and sometimes intractable, problems. When one of its members does something foolish or says something stupid, the world is told gleefully and the whole institution suffers public disfavor.

Throughout my 34 years in the House, it was common for public opinion polls to reveal that most Americans give a low performance rating to the institution as a whole while evaluating the local representative highly. Few citizens and hardly any journalists speak up to defend Congress. Most members feel Congress gets a bum rap, but there is little personal profit with the voters in correcting the negative misimpressions of the institution. It is easier to separate oneself from Congress in the public view. Some members of Congress even seek to aggrandize their own popularity by cynically joining the chorus of critics. Still, most want the Speaker to stand in the breach.

It has been the goal of every Speaker to improve the public image of Congress. To the degree that any one individual can break through the cacophony of strident attack to speak up for the legislative body, the Speaker has that responsibility. Every Speaker I have known has tried to do this, and each has been repeatedly disappointed. From time to time, waves of public displeasure wash over the Congress, driven by high-profile, sometimes grotesquely over-hyped, criticism.

In the past 40 years, the institution of Congress has been battered from pillar to post by sensational media attacks. Since the 1950s, Congress has been successively whipsawed for nepotism, absenteeism, taking "junkets," Koreagate, and more recently, in 1992, for the highly publicized House banking "scandal" in which members were loosely characterized as "bouncing" checks and even "kiting" checks. The terms were misleading. No check bounced and there was no indication of kiting. Nothing dishonest occurred. Nobody lost any money, least of all the taxpayers. The little private bank was not even federally insured. Nobody got hurt except members themselves, whose collective honor was held up for public scorn.

Perhaps it has always been this way. During one week about 30 years ago, Congress was characterized in various newspaper editorials as "slothful," "incompetent," "congenitally slow," "lobby-ridden," "structurally incapable of leadership," and as a collection of "jet-set goof-offs." The truth is that Congress is neither much more nor much less than the sum of its 535 parts. It is, as the title implies, *representative* of the public. Composed of mortals, it is fallible. But it can rise on occasion to heights of statesmanship usually unnoted. "Face it, Mr.

Speaker," a reporter once insisted, "the praiseworthy is not newsworthy." Congress can and often does behave responsibly. The institution deserves a better perception than it usually enjoys. If that were not so, this experiment in self-government would have perished long ago among the shoals of democracy, as Alexis de Tocqueville prophesied.

As Speaker, I tried every stratagem I could imagine to prevail on news people to see and report the positive side of Congress. I held daily news conferences. I invited media representatives to join me at working luncheons. I held dinners at my home in McLean, Virginia, where newspeople could visit socially with key House members. I conducted public bill-signing ceremonies. I accepted every request to appear on a radio or television talk show. I took press telephone calls at home, on weekends, and late at night. I wrote courteous personal letters to those whose writings or broadcasts contained factual errors detrimental to the Congress. Once when a staff assistant, without my knowledge, wrote a sarcastic letter to the publisher of the *Los Angeles Times* complaining of inaccuracies in a news story, I even invited the two offended reporters to lunch in the Speaker's private dining room; when the waiter brought out prime steaks for the reporters, he set before me, by my prearrangement with him, a plate of baked crow!

Maybe some of this worked to one degree or another. Frankly, I never felt that any of it did much good in cultivating a favorable public image for the institution I loved and served. A hundred evidences of good work and entreaties of good will could be undone by one thoughtless deed of a colleague magnified by one headline-hungry journalist. I might as well have been trying to teach cats to respect birds.

One incident stands out. It was in January 1989, before the 101st Congress convened. The presidentially appointed pay commission reported a recommendation that federal judges and members of Congress receive cost-of-living salary adjustments. The methodology had been created years before as a "reform" to separate Congress from the task of setting its own pay. After all, it was argued, nobody else in government did so. Congress determined the pay scale of others; why not let others determine theirs?

This made sense superficially, but did not work out so well in practice. The reason it did not work, ironically, is that some lawmaker, eager to make points with folks at home, would offer a motion to delete any pay benefit for members of Congress. Some such motions were offered by lawmakers of independent wealth; others by members who secretly hoped colleagues would vote their amendments down. No such luck. Usually a majority, confronted with voting on their own pay and not wanting to appear self-serving, would vote to decline any increase in salary for themselves.

The irony of this was that the public hardly ever knew of their lawmakers' self-abnegating gesture. It would receive scant, if any, publicity, and the membership generally never got any public credit for turning down their own pay raises. In 11 of the previous 18 years, members had voted in open session to deny themselves the automatic cost-of-living adjustments that Congress was authorizing for practically everyone else in government. (Federal judges, on the identical pay track with members of Congress, had to suffer the same decline in buying power to pay for the purity of their legislative peers. Some judges were retiring prematurely because of this, and many highly qualified lawyers were refusing to accept judicial appointments.)

The presidential pay commission reported that, in terms of constant dollar value, Congress had forced its own members and the judiciary to lose slightly more than one-third the buying power they had enjoyed in 1970. Attempting to rectify the disparity between these two classes and most others in government and business, the commission recommended a 51 percent increase for national lawmakers and judges. Congress had absolutely nothing to do with the commission's decision. I even told members of that panel after their formal proposal was announced that I thought it represented too big a jump at one time. I felt sure the public would have a hard time understanding the commission's reasoning, and experience had taught me not to expect much help from the media in explaining it. But even I was unprepared for the vicious onslaught that ensued.

On the Sunday after the proposal was announced, Senate Majority Leader Mitchell and Minority Leader Dole, answering questions on national television, announced that the Senate would summarily vote down the proposed increase. I made no such announcement. Feeling that my colleagues and the judges deserved some reasonable increase, but aware that a 51 percent boost would not fly, I privately polled every Democratic and Republican member of the House, assuring each that his or her individual response would be held in my confidence. I wanted to learn what amount of raise, if any, the majority actually thought fair, and what a majority would be willing to support in a public vote.

Meanwhile, the media lambasted Congress mercilessly for three weeks, accusing members of plotting to avoid a vote on the issue. Several headlines referred to it as an effort to "steal." Since House Republican leader Michel and I had not hastened to denounce the proposed raise publicly, we were singled out and bombarded daily with demands that we promise to kill the "greedy pay grab."

For much of this time, Congress was out of session. While I was trying to make personal contact with every member and get a reading on whether we could piece together some fair and reasonable compromise, radio call-in and talk show hosts throughout America importuned their listeners to "contact the Speaker of the House," demanding an end to this "cowardly money grab!" Some broadcasted my home telephone number, and at least one encouraged his listeners to jam my facsimile machine with messages of bitter outrage so that my office had trouble conducting other legitimate business.

Analysis of my private poll showed that most members felt some upward adjustment was fair and needed, but they thought the 51 percent figure excessive. A majority would vote for a 30 percent increase accompanied by the abolition of all speaking and lecture fees. (Members at that time were allowed legally to accept as much as 30 percent of their salary in fees of no more than $2,000 each for public appearances they might make outside their districts.)

But most members, it was clear, would be forced by media hype and resultant public disfavor to reject any increase whatsoever if that vote should arise. Under the rules, there would have been no way to prevent a member from offering such a motion. That, of course, is what happened. Elements in the media enjoyed a brief feeding frenzy at the expense of Congress. Members received nothing whatever at the time except accusations of stealthily plotting to enrich themselves. As Speaker, I was powerless under the circumstances to protect my colleagues and my institution from the largely unjustified criticism.

Up to that point, the Congress had been gaining steadily in public esteem. The fact that we were producing a positive agenda of legislative accomplishments had lifted approval ratings for the institution from about 45 percent to about 68 percent over a three-year period. In the final analysis, the public will support its legislative branch when it perceives that Congress is doing its work, making good on its promises, and seriously addressing the nation's problems. No amount of cleverness or legislative legerdemain on the part of any Speaker can change that. To expect fair treatment from the media is folly. When all is said and done, two things matter: substance and self-respect. Everything else is window dressing.

PROMOTING MUTUAL RESPECT: RELATIONS WITH THE MINORITY

In dealing with the major policy challenges facing the country, Speakers will at times encounter critical situations in the legislative process that challenge their judgment and test their resolve. On one occasion, a miscount of vote commitments on a crucial bill precipitated a parliamentary crisis, confronting me with a series of critical decisions. Pressured by circumstance, I pursued a forceful course that seriously damaged my relationship with the Republican minority in the House.

The date was October 29, 1987. The issue was the reconciliation bill, embodying hard-won cuts in the deficit. Exactly ten days earlier, the stock market had suddenly plummeted by 508 points, or 22.6 percent—a greater comparative drop than the one in 1929 that had sparked the Great Depression. Economists and market analysts were blaming the deficit. I thought it important to show the American public, and quickly, that Congress was capable of making the tough, controversial choices necessary to reduce the deficit. For this reason, I was determined to pass the reconciliation bill without delay.

There was one hitch. Chairman Rostenkowski and other members of the Ways and Means Committee had worked hard to hammer together a welfare reform bill, itself an object of controversy. They wanted to incorporate the text of that reform into the reconciliation bill to avoid the need for a separate vote. My instinct argued that we could be taking on too big a challenge by wedding the two and inviting a united opposition from the enemies of both. But Majority Whip Coelho and the vote-counting task force insisted, after polling the members, that we had enough solidly committed votes to pass the reconciliation bill with the welfare reform engrafted onto it. Since both were important parts of the leadership agenda, I assented to this strategy.

But the vote count was wrong. Support for joint consideration was softer than we thought. Prominent members of the minority argued persuasively that we were stuffing our welfare reform down the members' throats without any chance to debate—and perhaps amend it—and then vote on it as an important separate issue. When the rule combining the two came to a vote, it was rejected by a tally of 203 to 217. This unexpected event threw matters into sudden disarray. At the worst possible time, Congress was demonstrating what would be interpreted as an inability to come to grips with the deficit. That message, I knew, would be trumpeted to the nation by evening telecasts and morning newspapers. I was unwilling to let matters rest there. We needed to reverse the vote, to demonstrate resolve on the budget issue.

No sooner was the vote announced than Republican leader Michel took the floor to propose that we scrap the reconciliation bill and start anew. He wanted to abandon the long summer's work, go back to the beginning, and try to piece together an entirely different "bipartisan" substitute. Without questioning Michel's sincerity, I knew that such a course, with its attendant delays and uncertainties, would be degenerative of public confidence and disruptive of the legislative agenda. There would have been no way to recoup before mid- November, holding everything else at standstill. I was determined to salvage the reconciliation bill, that very day if at all possible. I thought I saw a way to do it.

We had lost 48 Democrats on the vote, most of them over the welfare reform issue. It was obvious that the House wanted to vote separately on the two questions and would support a rule bringing up the deficit-reducing reconciliation bill alone. There was one problem, however. House rules prohibit reconsidering a rule on the same day it is defeated. The only way around that would be to adjourn the House and reconvene for a second legislative day later in the same afternoon, with a new rule to present. This had been done before, but only rarely and in cases of unusual urgency. I thought that the circumstances justified doing so in this instance, and I announced my intention of following that course.

As we reconvened for a second "legislative day" that Thursday, I knew that many Republicans would regard my action as highhanded. The new rule, to consider the revised reconciliation bill with the welfare language deleted, passed by a safe vote of 238 to 182. I thought we were over the hump. What I failed to consider was the disappointment of some who had wanted welfare reform to ride piggyback on the deficit-reduction bill, and the disapproval of others who apparently considered my decision to convene a second legislative day arbitrary.

When it came to a vote, the big measure teetered between passage and failure. At the expiration of the allotted time, members crowded into the well below the Speaker's rostrum. Some had entered the chamber late and had to be recorded by voice vote. When it appeared that everyone had voted, the count stood at 205 to 205. We were down by one. As was the custom, I asked if any members desired to change their votes.

Someone told me that George Miller of California and Marty Russo of Illinois, having voted no, had changed their minds and were on their way back from the

House office building to change their votes. This, as it turned out, was false. But I held the vote open awaiting their return to the chamber. Minutes went by, finally ten minutes, not unprecedented but certainly longer than usual to accommodate members desiring to reverse their votes. Miller and Russo did not return, but Jim Chapman of Texas reentered the chamber and asked to change his vote from "no" to "aye." This reversal flipped the balance and the bill passed by one vote.

Republicans were furious. They felt, and perhaps with justification, that I had stretched the powers of the Speaker to the limit. Almost six years later, on August 5, 1993, another Thursday, I watched the late change of a vote by Rep. Marjorie Margolies-Mezvinsky (D-Penn.) create a dramatic come-from-behind win for President Bill Clinton's deficit-reduction bill. Without her switch it would have gone down, and much of President Clinton's program with it. Déjà vu. I knew the minority would be angry–I hoped not as angry as on that Thursday in 1987.

What does a Speaker owe to the minority? Courtesy, consideration, fair play—certainly all of these. I know that some in the minority felt quite strongly that I strained the rules of comity that day and abused the powers of the majority. I did what I thought was right. In the process, unfortunately, probably hardened the opposition and made future consensus more difficult.

On other occasions, I went out of my way to cultivate a relationship of mutual respect and trust. Throughout my years on the Public Works Committee and my early years as majority leader, I had worked often with members of the other party to find common ground. On matters such as foreign affairs, national defense, trade reform, environmental concerns, public works, and antidrug legislation, I often joined in bipartisan coalitions and sometimes led them. At times, I intervened with the Rules Committee on behalf of Republican requests. At the beginning of each Congress, to satisfy requests of new Republican members, I made a point of accommodating the wishes of Republican leader Michel with regard to committee numbers he needed.

All Speakers face an occasional dilemma in their dual roles as activist and presiding judge. It is the duty of the Speaker to use the rules to get things done. Never, however, should any Speaker deny access and equal protection to the minority party or any of its members. My former colleague, Richard Cheney, later Secretary of Defense in the Bush administration, once joined his wife Lynne in writing a fascinating book titled *Kings of the Hill*. It is about the use and abuse of power in the House of Representatives. From any modern perspective, Republican Speakers Joseph Cannon and Thomas Brackett Reed blatantly denied rights to their political opposition. Reed once said that the only purpose of minority members was to make a quorum and their only right was to draw their pay. While deploring these excesses of power, the Cheneys' book also deplored the failure of timid leaders to use the authority inherent in their positions to break deadlocks, dissolve obstructions, and carry out the programs they were elected to fulfill. How to reconcile the two—legislative effectiveness and fairness to the minority—is a challenge no Speaker escapes.

THE SPEAKER: PRIEST, EVANGELIST, AND PROPHET

I once defined the ideal House leader as a tripartite personality: "part parish priest, part evangelist, and part prophet." The Speaker's pastoral function challenges him or her to nurture and console, to be a sort of confessor to the flock, helping other members with committee assignments, legislative projects, and, where appropriate, with their reelection efforts.

Like an evangelist, the Speaker must use the pulpit to promote Congress and its role to the public and the members. By open advocacy and vocal defense of the institution, the Speaker sometimes can make doing the right thing more palatable for the members by making it more generally understood and publicly acceptable.

Above all, I feel that a Speaker worthy of the title must look ahead and see the needs of the future. As with the captain of a ship, the Speaker is responsible; the eyes of one so entrusted must watch both the compass and the waters ahead. Like a sentry on the wall, the Speaker sometimes must sound alarms, calling on the membership to summon vision and courage to act, in the words of the well-known aphorism, not just for the *next election* but for the *next generation*.

Chapter 20

The Job of the Minority Leader

John J. Rhodes, II (R-Arizona)

A person is elected minority leader for various reasons. Members of the minority party have ambitions to be part of a new majority. They realize that their selected leader will be in a position to get recognition from both the press and the public. The person selected must be able to communicate well, and put forth ideas and party positions which make sense and which impress the public and the news media.

The selectee could come from the party leadership (the whip, the Conference chairman, or the Policy Committee chairman). Perhaps he would come from the "back benches"–a person whose work in committee or on the House floor got favorable attention from his colleagues. He must be a person who, for some cogent reason, has convinced a majority of his colleagues that he possesses the qualities which can enhance the position of his party, and therefore can make the ever present dream of a majority position and power come true.

I became minority leader for the Republicans after serving as Policy Committee chairman. As chair of that committee, I called frequent meetings on subjects which were either ripe for consideration by the House or had attracted national attention without recognition by the majority. My staff would have prepared a proposed statement setting forth the party position. After lively discussion and usually some amendment, the committee would vote either to adopt the statement or to remain silent on the subject. The amended statement usually was adopted.

The House Republican leadership had the reputation of being "stand-offish" from the press. So, after a policy statement was adopted, Jerry Ford, our leader, and I would go unannounced to the press gallery. I would read the policy statement and invite questions. Soon, the questions would become general, directed mainly to Jerry as minority leader. We got some press we didn't particularly enjoy, but the result was that our press corps suddenly became aware that the Republican leadership had ideas which we were not afraid to express.

Jerry and I had often regretted the fact that House committees were actually fiefdoms, with little communication even between Republican members of the various committees. So, Jerry and I hosted a breakfast once a month to which we invited Republican members of committees and their staff directors. I acted as chairman, and each ranking member reported on the business of the committee and the attitude of the Republican members. The results were little short of spectacular in developing relationships among the members of this important group and the spirit of teamwork which made the House minority cohesive beyond expectation. Later, when Jerry Ford became president and called upon his troops to sustain his vetoes, it was this cohesion which provided the almost unanimous Republican votes which did the job.

When Jerry Ford became vice-president, I became Republican leader by unanimous vote of the Conference. When I became leader, Barber Conable became Policy Committee chairman, and we continued the breakfasts and regular exposure to the press. I always made myself available to the Sunday talk shows to try to make the American public aware of the congressional Republicans and the fact that the Congress they abhorred was run by Democrats.

At the beginning of each Congress, I appointed a Platform Committee. Its job was to develop a complete statement outlining what Americans could expect from a Republican majority in Congress. The press would give these statements a lot of attention, right? Wrong. They all but ignored them, whispering, "This is just politics. They don't have the votes and never will." Nevertheless, we kept producing our "GOP platforms."

Unlike the leaders of the majority, the minority leader has few goodies to hand out. He needs to work hard to retain a loyal band which will usually "follow the leader." Listening to the ideas of various groups of members is vital. Some of them know that they will probably not agree with the leader and a majority of their party on certain matters, but if they have had an audience, they will be more likely to vote with the party, maintaining the Republican cohesion which is so important.

I would gladly have "mortgaged the farm" to have had even one term as Speaker of the House. We had the talent to have legislated wisely and well, and to put into place reforms in the House structure which were badly needed. For example, on important aspects of democratic government, the Democratic Caucus lagged far behind the organization of Republican members of the House, which we call the Conference. In contrast to the Democrats, the Republican Conference did not bind its members' votes. Also in contrast to the other side, our Conference meetings were open to the public and the press.

Moreover, the Republican Conference took the lead in challenging the seniority system, an archaic method of selecting committee chairs clung to tenaciously by the Democratic Caucus. There is something to be said for long experience as a factor in the selection of committee chairs and ranking minority members. It takes years to learn thoroughly the ins and outs of the legislative process, as well as to gain the confidence needed to maintain an adequate grip on headstrong and independent members. But a strict seniority system, in which length of service is the *only* determinant of power and responsibility, is not conducive to quality leadership. For while length of service is an important factor, the individual who has served the longest is not necessarily the one best qualified to lead.

In recognition of the shortcomings of the seniority system, the House Republican Conference in 1970 appointed a special task force to study it and possibly recommend an alternative. Placed in charge of the task force was one of the most intelligent and capable members of the House, Congressman Barber Conable of New York, who was to succeed me as chairman of the Republican Policy Committee when I was elected minority leader in 1973.

After many long months of hard work, the Conable task force came up with a remarkable answer to the problems posed by the seniority system. It proposed that all ranking Republican members on the committees be recommended at the start of each new Congress by the Republican Committee on Committees, but that each of these recommendations be either ratified or rejected by a mandatory secret ballot of the Republican Conference. Were it the prevailing view of a majority of House Republicans that a given ranking member was not best qualified, he could easily be replaced by someone else. Even if a ranking member was not replaced, an inordinate number of no votes would cause him to mend his fences with his own colleagues.

After our progressive reform, the Democratic Caucus changed its method of selecting committee chairmen too. But once again, the Caucus was only prepared to go so far. The Democrats provided that a vote by secret ballot on the fitness of a chairman could occur, *providing* that ten Democrats (it was later changed to four) were willing to stand for the purpose of demanding that such a vote take place. Obviously, those members were not going to stand unless they were fairly certain that their challenge would prevail. For if the chairman in question survived the vote, he could make life miserable in a number of ways for those who dared challenge his authority.

Congress cannot really be changed until the people at the top, the people who make up the majority leadership, are changed. When I served in the House, the Democratic leadership presided over a majority that had controlled Congress for an unhealthy period of time. The Democratic majority was largely oblivious to the pressing need for congressional reform. People in power are reluctant to tamper with a system that has served them and their predecessors well over the years.

However, I was very proud of the fact that I could say, and prove, that during my time as minority leader, the House Republicans were the "largest cohesive force on Capitol Hill." I gladly pass the torch to Speaker Hastert and his Republican majority. Our country needs them!

Chapter 21

Crossing the Party Line:
My Life as a Republican...
And a Democrat

Peter A. Peyser (D-New York)
as told to Joseph Naar

Why do otherwise sensible human beings go into politics? There are a thousand reasons, some noble, some misguided, a few even venal. In my case, I got involved because I just plain got mad. That's certainly not unique. What makes me unusual is that, after a successful career as a Republican congressman, I left office, switched parties, sat on the sidelines for two years, then returned to my congressional seat as a Democrat. That switch proved to be a fateful turning point, but more about that later. Let's begin at the beginning.

In 1962, I was your typical middle income, middle-aged, career-oriented WASP. I was 40 years old, had a thriving insurance agency in New York City, a house in an upscale Hudson River suburb, a wife, five children, and assorted pets. The closest I'd come to politics was to head the local PTA. I'd been a staff sergeant with the 99th Infantry Division in World War II, and some say that war is just an extension of diplomacy. But in nine months of combat, from the Battle of the Bulge to Remagen Bridge, my thoughts were not on the politics that had caught me up in mud, blood, and misery, but on surviving one hour to the next.

What lured me from my cozy 1962 suburban commuter life to the rough and tumble political stage was, of all things, a recreation program. My little village of Irvington on the Hudson had none, so for some years, a good friend and I had been raising money from our acquaintances and hiring a small staff to run a summer program for village children. The uncertainty of funding was making staffing increasingly difficult, and finally I went to the Village Board to suggest that it was time for a tax-supported recreation program. I told the members what my friend and I had been doing and, frankly, I expected them to thank us. Instead, the mayor, a former high school shop teacher, lambasted me. "We're not going to waste taxpayer money on entertaining kids. When I grew up in this village, we had a bat and a ball. That was good enough then and it's good enough now."

Well, I went home in a rage, blew steam at my poor wife, Marguerite, and decided to run for mayor. The great adventure had begun!

Like most Hudson River bedroom communities, Irvington was divided between those who lived and worked there, commonly referred to as "Main Street," and those like me who lived there but worked in New York, sometimes known as "carpetbaggers." "Main Street" was mostly Democrat, and on local matters, the political thinking had long been "let Main Street run the village." The Republicans had elected one mayor in 20 years and most trustees were Democrats.

Having impetuously made my decision to run, I met with local Republican leaders to share the good news. They looked at me as if I were crazy. "You can't run for mayor," they snapped, "we've promised someone else and it's his turn." My argument that they needed new blood because they hadn't elected anyone to village office in years was a waste of breath; they had made their choice and I wasn't it. So I said "Fine, I'm gonna run anyway." That rattled them, and one said in horror "there'll be a primary," an exercise in democracy that Irvington had never tried. "So be it," said I, and left.

To my surprise, I learned that I had a secret supporter, Jack Irwin, a village Republican leader who had been at the meeting. Jack wanted to talk, and we met in his car the next night, parked outside the elementary school so that no one would see us. I said: "Jack, those people are off the wall. I'm going to run." He said: "I'm for you. This candidate of theirs has run for trustee three times and never won, so now, since he's had so much campaign experience, they think he should run for mayor. Let me talk to them." Jack talked and eventually I got a call from one of the GOP leaders who told me, "Okay, you can run, but we're not going to do anything for you." I said, "Fine. We'll do it that way."

We put on a real campaign and it was a lot of fun. A friend introduced me to John Roosevelt, FDR's Republican son, and he came to Irvington to speak in my support. We had a big rally near village hall and got a lot of publicity. After our speeches, John and I mingled with the crowd and were approached by an old-time Irvington policeman named Peter Gorey. Gorey said to Roosevelt, "You probably won't remember this, but I arrested you." I was stunned. "Pete, what are you talking about?" "Well," said Gorey, " He (John Roosevelt) was speeding through the village and I didn't know whether he'd been drinking, so I arrested him. Do you remember that, Mr. Roosevelt?" Mr. Roosevelt did not remember that, nor did Mr. Roosevelt care to remember that, but he allowed to me later with a chuckle that it had been quite a welcome to Irvington.

A few months later, I was installed as mayor of a village ripe for improvement. The roads were in disrepair, the water system was falling apart, we had no firehouse and, of course, no recreation program. We solved the latter problem by turning a former Methodist church into a rec center, which function it serves to this day. For the record, I raised taxes every one of my eight years in office, and was reelected three times, each time by a larger plurality.

I loved the job. It paid $100 a month and was taking 75 percent of my time, but I really felt that I was doing something constructive, something that touched people's lives. I'd not just been bitten by the political bug; I'd been thoroughly infected. After eight years in office, the next logical step was to go full-time and shoot for a larger stage. So in 1970, I turned my insurance agency back to the parent company and prepared to challenge the popular incumbent congressman, Democrat Richard Ottinger.

Once again, the first hurdle was the Republican organization. The county leader said the party wouldn't support me; that the Republican mayor of Yonkers was going to make the race and was the only one who had a chance to beat Ottinger. In truth, I now admit that he was probably correct. Ottinger had been in office several terms and had gained national attention, especially for his shrill attacks on New York's Republican governor, Nelson Rockefeller, concerning the governor's proposal to build a highway down a section of the Hudson River. But my mind was made up, and I made my pitch one-on-one to every Republican leader in the county. Not one of them bought it.

My last hope was the governor himself, with whom I had a quasi-friendly relationship. I'd met him when I was mayor, campaigned for him in '68, called him Nelson and he called me Peter. He agreed to see me at his Manhattan office and after hearing me out, he sent me downstairs to talk to Jim Cannon, his chief of staff. Jim heard my story and told me to wait while he talked with the governor. In due time, I was summoned back to Rockefeller's office and he said, "Peter, Jim thinks that you really should not make the race at this time, that you don't have any support and can't win." I said "Well, Governor, what inspired me to make this race is the way that Ottinger has been attacking you for the past three years. I want to get him out of there."

Rockefeller lit up like a Christmas tree. He turned to Cannon and said: "I don't think you understood Peter. He wants to run, and run against Ottinger, and we're going to support him." Cannon said: "Yes, of course, that's what I thought all along." The governor asked me what he could do to help, and I told him all I needed was a letter from him saying he was going to support me. "Done," he said, and I had it the next day. I personally delivered copies to every one of the party leaders I had talked with earlier.

I also paid a call on the party's chosen candidate, the mayor of Yonkers, who turned out to be a very nice guy. He said he appreciated my coming in but didn't think I had much support. "You're right," I said, "but I do have some," and I showed him the governor's letter. He was stunned and wanted to know how I'd gotten it. "I asked for it," I replied. "Well, we're going to have a race anyway," he said, but three weeks later, he announced that he was dropping out.

Then Ottinger took himself out of it to run against Conservative James Buckley for the Senate, and suddenly Republican Congressional hopefuls were crawling out of the woodwork. So we had a primary—three other unknowns and me. "Remember folks," I told Republican supporters, "I was the only one willing to take on Ottinger." It was also a plus that I was the only one of the four who had held elective office, and with a lot of help from my many Irvington supporters, I won the primary and went on to the general election. That was a four-way race–a Republican, Democrat, Conservative, and Liberal–and when the dust had settled, I was a Congressman.

Meanwhile, Ottinger had lost to Buckley, and two years later we finally squared off when he tried to recapture his House seat. That was one tough race. Rockefeller commissioned a poll which showed me trailing by 30 points two months before election day. The pollster told me there was no way I would win; most people in the district thought Ottinger was still their congressman. He was almost right, but when the ballots were tallied, I had won reelection by 1,425 votes.

I reported to Washington in 1970, a freshman Republican in a Democrat-controlled House. Minority Leader Gerald Ford seemed pleased when I asked for assignment to the Education and Labor Committee. The issues it dealt with did not coincide with the interests of most Republicans, but I was fascinated by those issues, and looking back, I would say that my most creative and constructive work was done on that committee. My crown jewel was my work on a piece of landmark legislation called the Pension Reform Act of 1974 (ERISA), which established new and more comprehensive pension safeguards nationwide. Jacob Javits had been working on pension reform in the Senate, but when the House took it up in an Education and Labor subcommittee, I found that having come from the insurance industry, I was one of the few committee members with any background in the subject. Consequently, I played a key role in formulating the legislation and moving it through the Congress. When President Ford signed ERISA, he invited me to the ceremony and gave me one of the pens he used plus a letter thanking me for my work.

Education and Labor deals with a wide variety of issues affecting the quality of American lives, and I was fortunate to be able to contribute to a number of them: the Museum Act, for example, that I worked on with Chairman John Brademas and that enabled smaller museums to exhibit valuable works by providing a federal guarantee for the expensive liability coverage such exhibits require.

John and I also traveled the country gathering information on child abuse. The bill that emerged from our efforts was the first to recognize this problem as a national issue. Among its many provisions, the law protects teachers and others who work with children from being sued after reporting their reasonable suspicions that children are being mistreated, and it established a national clearinghouse for information on missing children.

Often, my work on Education and Labor was to protect existing programs rather than propose new ones. Student aid, for one, was constantly under fire. When President Ronald Reagan took aim at the graduate loan program, I got more than 5,000 students to come to Washington from all over the country to talk to Congressmen, stage a demonstration outside the Capitol, and sign petitions. It worked. Reagan also wanted to cut the lunch program at senior citizen centers. I waged a one-man campaign in the House to save it and prevailed by being a royal pain in the neck. I had seniors contacting me from all over the country, and every day for almost three months I'd rise on the floor and relay their messages about how much they depended on the lunch program. After awhile, the members grew sick of listening to me and begged me to drop it. I'd say: "Fine, but when we bring this up, vote for continuance, not elimination." They did, and the program was saved.

As fulfilling as was my work on Education and Labor, I had more fun on the Agriculture Committee, although it seemed a strange assignment for a congressman whose district comprised the city of Yonkers, a large piece of the Bronx, and several well developed suburban townships. I got it after Shirley Chisholm flatly refused it; Shirley was a liberal black Democrat from Manhattan whose interests were far removed from the farm belt. House Speaker Carl Albert, a Democrat, was determined to have someone from New York on agriculture and embarrassed by having a freshman member of his own party refuse, so he asked me, a Republican. He said I'd only have to serve one term; he'd help me get any committee I wanted when it was over; and I could stay on Education and Labor, a big concession because you weren't supposed to serve on two major committees at once.

Like all committees of the House, Agriculture had both Republicans and Democrats, but except for food stamps, which the Republicans generally opposed, the members saw eye to eye on everything. Why shouldn't they? They had all come to Congress from farming and agribusiness. What an opportunity for a maverick from the urban east! I was in hog heaven.

The chairman was a tough old bird from the midwest, one of the last of a breed. Whenever I wanted to speak he would say, "And what does the gentleman from the Bronx who has so many farms want to talk about?" One day we were debating a bill of special interest to him when one of the Democrats said, "Mr. Chairman, there are a lot of good things in this, but I would like to amend one part of it." Undaunted by the roomful of reporters, the chairman replied, "You may offer your amendment, but thereafter there will be no need for you to come back to this committee because you will never again be recognized." The member said, "I withdraw my amendment," and sat down.

Basically, the Agriculture Committee represents the interests of the agriculture industry. I was one of the very few members who worried about the committee's effect on consumers and taxpayers, so rather than initiating legislation, I spent most of my time opposing it. The sugar bill was a prime example. It provided subsidies to domestic sugar growers and set import quotas on nations that could produce sugar cheaper, all supposedly to keep a lid on U.S. sugar prices. However, in 1974, sugar prices were going through the roof and sugar growers were reaping astronomical profits. So I mounted a campaign against the sugar bill, which traditionally reached the floor of the House as the congressional session's last item of business. I got my chance to speak around midnight and held up two five-pound bags of sugar, one marked with the average price of the year before and the other with the current price, which had trebled. I then offered a motion to kill the bill and lo and behold it carried.

"Tobacco for Peace" was another egregious farm support program that I managed to shoot down. At the very time that the surgeon general was telling Americans that tobacco was bad for their health, the U.S. government, meaning American taxpayers, was buying $40 million worth of the stuff and sending it to third world countries to keep them happy. Apparently, a majority of the House agreed that this was preposterous because my amendment to strike the program from the agriculture bill carried.

Then there was the peanut subsidy, near and dear to the heart of then Governor Jimmy Carter, whose family business was peanut warehousing. American farmers were growing a lot of peanuts, as were foreign farmers who were selling their crops in America for less than domestic producers would accept. So the U.S. government bought the peanuts that American farmers couldn't sell and shoveled them into warehouses. After a year or so, they'd rot and the putrid mess would be shoveled out and replaced with the next surplus crop. I repeatedly attacked the program and after a time I had a call from Governor Carter. He told me that the lives of many people depended on this subsidy and I told him that, in my opinion, a nation that had its share of poor people had no business buying surplus food and letting it rot. I was a Republican then, and Carter, of course, was a Democrat, but nonetheless we had a very nice conversation.

There was an amusing sequel to this exchange when I returned to Congress as a Democrat in 1978. My wife, Marguerite, and I were invited to a dinner at the White House and were seated at a table adjacent to then President and Mrs. Carter. I walked to his table to say hello and he turned to his wife and said, "You know, I remember how concerned and frightened I was when I had to call this congressman about the peanut program." Then, turning to me with a twinkle in his eye, he said, "Peter, things certainly are different today, aren't they?"

Much has been written about the inability of the minority party to accomplish anything in Congress, but I think it's been overstated. In the first place, just being a congressman carries a lot of weight regardless of party affiliation. A congressman who wants a federal agency to do something because it's right, should be done, and will help the folks back home has a lot of power. No agency wants to challenge you because you can be a thorn in its side. You're the one who can speak on the floor of the House, not the agency, and you can carry your case to the public in a lot of different ways. Of course, you don't always get what you want, but you do have an extraordinary opportunity to influence affairs to the benefit of your constituents.

As for legislation, despite being in the minority party for six years, I had my share of accomplishments, ERISA being probably the most notable. On many domestic social issues, I was voting with the Democrats anyway, so I felt no frustration in that regard, although the Republican leaders weren't too pleased with me. Then, too, there are many, many occasions when members of Congress cross party lines to collaborate on critical issues. One such instance occurred for me in

1974 when Vietnam was winding down and military and national morale were at a low. The always controversial Defense Bill was coming up for a vote and it was especially acute that year because California Democrat Ron Dellums, supported by many of his party, had introduced an amendment to withdraw U.S. troops from NATO—pull them out of Europe completely. I thought this would be disastrous, as did most Republicans, the White House, and Democrat Dan Rostenkowski, who was in charge of the House on that bill. I was so concerned that I drafted an amendment of my own calling on Congress to appoint a committee to study the Dellums amendment, which in effect would kill it. I then let Republican leaders know that my amendment was ready if I could get a chance to introduce it. Shortly thereafter, a White House aide, Jack Marsh, who later became Secretary of the Army, called me off the floor and said, "We want you to offer that amendment." "I'd love to," I replied, "but as you know, I'm not on the Defense Committee and the rule is that no non-member of the committee may be recognized while a committee member is standing." "I'll work it out," he said. "You just be ready to jump up when everyone is seated."

As chairman, Dan Rostenkowski controlled the House debate on the bill from the Speaker's chair. I waited patiently until the last member of the committee sat down, then sprang to my feet. "For what purpose does the gentleman from New York rise?" said Rostenkowski. "I have an amendment," I declared, and Dellums and the Democrat side went ballistic. They were screaming, "You can't do that!" "Mr. Speaker!" "Point of order!" Rostenkowski said, "No one was on their feet. The gentleman from New York is recognized." So I offered my amendment, enough conservative Democrats joined the Republicans to carry it, and the Dellums amendment died aborning.

This is not to say that it was easy being a Republican in the early 1970s. Richard Nixon's management of the final years of Vietnam was a gut-wrenching time. I was very opposed to the war, but I believed Nixon's assertion that it was important we get out with honor, and I voted in support of that position and took a lot of heat from my family, my staff, and my district. Many Democrats tell me that they now regret having voted for the Gulf of Tonkin Resolution. I now regret many of my Vietnam votes, but at the time, I cast them in good conscience.

Watergate was another trauma that tested my Republican mettle. When the House Judiciary Committee began its hearings and Nixon's Oval Office tapes were being leaked to the press, a chorus arose on both sides of the aisle crying, "Impeach him, impeach him." I refused to sing along, on the grounds that the House's role was similar to that of a grand jury and that no action should be taken until Judiciary completed its hearings and released its findings. Despite a lot of unhappiness in the district, I held my ground until Judiciary permitted members of Congress to listen to the tapes. I was one of the very few who accepted that offer, and I listened to the whole sordid affair. The tapes were sickening. I couldn't believe that a president of the United States would say the things that I heard this man saying about women, various races, and you name it. When I emerged, the press asked what I'd do now and I told them I'd vote to impeach.

There was an interesting footnote to all of this. Vice President Ford was to award the Congressional Medal of Honor posthumously to a young man from my district killed in Vietnam, and he invited me to attend. He was just ready to begin when an aide dashed up with a message. Ford read it, said to me: "Peter, you're going to have to handle the presentation," and left. The message was that Nixon was resigning and Ford would be president.

On reflection, I'd say that I'd been a loyal moderate Republican during my first six years in the House and that despite having been a minority member, my work in the Congress had been rich and fulfilling. Why, then, did I become a Democrat? The reason lies not in my Congressional experience but in the attitude of the New York State Republican organization of that day.

In 1976, James Buckley, junior Senator from New York, was up for reelection and I decided to challenge him. Buckley was a Connecticut resident whose claim to hold office from New York rested on maintaining a Manhattan apartment. Furthermore, Buckley had won the Senate seat in 1970 as a Conservative, defeating a Republican and a Democrat. I'd watched his Senate votes closely and, in my opinion, he'd been on the wrong side of almost every issue affecting New York. I thought, as a lifelong Republican and New York resident, I could return the Senate seat to our party. But the state Republican organization, under the chairmanship of Richard Rosenbaum, seemed willing to hand the nomination to Buckley. Nonetheless, I pushed my case, determined to carry it even to a primary if necessary.

The GOP state convention was at the Waldorf Astoria in New York City, and despite the leadership's antipathy toward me, I showed up with Marguerite and our children, Peter, Jim, and Tom, who ranged in age from 22 to 13. The room was crowded, so I asked Chairman Rosenbaum where he'd like us to sit. "Peter," he said, "we don't have any place for you." Can you imagine telling a U.S. congressman that he's not welcome at his own party's convention? I said, "Dick, I'm here with my family," but he was adamant: "We know what you want to do and we don't want you to do it. There's no place for you!" So the family and I seated ourselves on the steps leading up to the dais, to the delight of the TV cameraman who caught it all for the evening news.

When the convention got underway, Rosenbaum didn't even want to recognize me, but I insisted and talked to the crowd about my qualifications and accomplishments and why New York deserved a Senator from New York. My talk was greeted with silence except for one upstate county chairperson who rose to say that she thought it would be good for the party to have a contest for the Senatorial nomination and that I seemed to be well qualified. I was shocked and saddened to learn later that within a week of the convention, she had been removed from both her county leadership position and her full-time county job.

As was preordained, Buckley got the nomination, so I forced the New York GOP to hold its first state-wide primary of this century. It was a very cumbersome and grueling process, requiring among other things that I gather signatures on nominating petitions from approximately 20,000 registered Republicans apportioned among all of the congressional districts in New York state. Few of the Republican committee people would even talk to me, so I put together a team of young people, leased four cars, and hit the road to pick up signatures at shopping centers and other public places. It took months to gather what we needed and weeks for the meticulous task of sorting it all out and filling in proper cover sheets. One error and an entire petition would be rejected.

On the morning of the last day for filing the petitions in Albany, we were still filling in cover sheets 150 miles to the south in Irvington. When we finished, we had one of the wildest rides of my life, but we made it. At two minutes before 5:00 p.m., we burst into the Board of Elections at the state capitol lugging boxes and boxes of paper. My press aide had alerted the media that we were running a breathless race to the finish and they were there to chronicle our arrival, providing a nice publicity boost for the campaign.

After weeks of review, the Board of Elections accepted the petitions, but the Buckley supporters weren't through. They challenged them in State Supreme Court, the Appellate Division, and U.S. District Court. I was upheld each time, but at the end of the process, I was flat broke. Gathering and defending petitions had been very costly, and during the prolonged review and adjudication, few would contribute to my campaign because of uncertainty that I'd even be on the ballot. Without funds, I had won the petition battle, but lost the primary war. The primary winner, Republican/Conservative Jim Buckley, went on to lose the general election to Democrat Daniel Patrick Moynihan, who subsequently served in the Senate for 24 years. I think I could have beaten him, but we'll never know. Pat has proved to be a great Senator and a real friend.

I'd been bruised by the Republican party organization before, but this time I'd really been mauled and had to do some painful soul-searching. For the first time in my life, I was out of a job and badly in need of money. I could seek work in the private sector, but I had loved the Congress and felt that I still had something to contribute. However, what were my chances of returning as a Republican after the party had soundly rejected me? For that matter, would I even want to?

From time to time, various Democrats, including John Brademas and Speaker of the House Tip O'Neill, had suggested that I consider coming over to their party, probably because I was voting with the Democrats so often on social issues. I concluded that the time had come to take their suggestions seriously, and in 1977, I held a press conference in my living room and announced that I was changing my party enrollment to Democrat. A little later, I decided that, in 1978, I would try to recapture my former seat in the House, now held by a Republican.

Once again, the party leaders blocked my path, but this time they were Democrats, who saw me as a turncoat and a wolf in sheep's clothing. Their chosen candidate for the congressional nomination was a three-term state assemblyman, so I had to hike the primary trail one more time. The leaders were certain their man would win and were shocked when he didn't.

The incumbent Republican congressman chose not to seek reelection, and my opponent in the general election was another popular Yonkers mayor. I not only won the district, but also beat him in his own city, which indicated to me that the people didn't much care what political party I belonged to.

Back in Washington, I found that my relationship with my former Republican colleagues was pretty much unchanged; those who had been my friends before were still my friends, while the leaders who had been unhappy with me were still unhappy. The Democrats, however, were delighted. I had returned a seat to their side of the aisle, a seat, incidentally, that I had taken from them ten years earlier. I was given the committee of my choice–Education and Labor–plus a bonus, now that I was a member of the majority, in the form of assignment to the Government Operations Committee. Government Operations is the investigative arm of the House and its work was fascinating. I took part in several NATO meetings and traveled to Europe and Israel on various fact-finding assignments.

Being one with the majority brought practical day-to-day advantages. As a minority member, I had been instrumental in drafting ERISA; now as a member of the majority, I was appointed chairman of a congressional task force to study problems and progress under this new law. When I wanted to introduce or amend legislation on Education and Labor, I could count on the committee to take it up; if I wanted to hold a hearing, Chairman Carl Perkins was almost certain to approve. Best of all, when I needed something special for my district, I could turn for help to my new party ally, House Speaker Tip O'Neill. All in all, as a member of the majority, I could get a lot more done while serving as a member of the United States Congress.

I was reelected handily in 1980, and had begun to think that my party change was no longer significant, when fate intervened and proved that old wounds do not heal quickly.

The 1980 census showed that New York state had lost population and would have to give up a congressional seat. That meant redistricting, a complicated task for the state legislature involving a lot of horse trading between the Democrat controlled Assembly and the Republican Senate. Who was to be the sacrificial lamb? The Republicans wanted their pound of flesh, of course, while the Democrats were not keen on giving up a party loyalist to save a Johnny-come-lately. I was odd man out.

When the plan was unveiled, the district that I would have to fight for in 1982 comprised my home township plus three very conservative rural counties that had been represented for some years by a well entrenched Republican. Both sides told me "Don't worry, Peter, it'll be a fair fight," and the Democrats added "you'll win." Students from all over the country volunteered to help us as did organized Labor. We waged a hard campaign in a new district where I was virtually unknown; still, I took 46 percent of the vote–respectable, but not enough. In 1983, I returned to private life for the final time.

Do I miss the Congress? You bet I do! I was privileged to have served this splendid institution for ten years, and I wish only the best to all those who serve it now and will do so in the future.

Chapter 22

Wielding Influence
as a Conservative Democrat

G. V. "Sonny" Montgomery (D-Mississippi)

In 1966, I was elected to the United States Congress from the third district of Mississippi. I ran as a Democrat and even though my vote for 30 years was conservative, I never considered becoming a Republican.

After the Civil War in Mississippi, the governor and other state officials were Republicans. During World War I and the Depression, the Republican Party in Mississippi was not active and the Democratic Party at that time was very conservative. There were no Republicans serving in Congress from Mississippi when I went to Washington. Prentiss Walker went to Congress on Barry Goldwater's coattails, ran for the Senate against Senator Jim Eastland after two years in the House, and got beat. I ran for the vacant congressional seat and won.

When I went to Congress, there were around 100 conservative Democrats in the House, mainly from the South. The number fell tremendously over the next 30 years, and when I left Congress, I would say only ten really conservative Democrats were still in the House. Those ten were more conservative than most of the Republicans. The Mississippi delegation now has one conservative Democrat in Congress and that is Gene Taylor of the Mississippi Coast. Out of the five Representatives from Mississippi, two are Republicans who vote conservative. The other two Democrats are classified as one liberal and one moderate. On military issues, all five vote for a strong defense.

In Congress, I voted mostly a conservative vote, but, like all members, you make certain votes that were not conservative but helped the people you represented.

My district was probably the most conservative of the five districts, and I was voting like the majority of my constituents wanted. I concentrated on veterans' and military issues. I never got heavily involved in areas like health, education, and transportation.

I really was part of the informal group called the "Boll Weevils," which was made up of moderately conservative and conservative members. We saved Ronald Reagan's programs his first four years. We were the swing vote that got his tax reduction through the first year of his administration.

The Boll Weevils met in my office about once a week. Texas Senator Phil Gramm was a House member and a Democrat and he was very good in drawing up budgets. He, along with Bob Stump of Arizona, Charlie Stenholm of Texas, Charles Whitley of North Carolina, and others, were all active in some of Reagan's programs. The Reagan Administration wanted to cut taxes 30 percent. We felt this was too much of a cut in revenues and the "Boll Weevils" insisted the last 5 percent be dropped.

Now, there is a group of moderate and conservative Democrats that we know as "Blue Dogs." They took the place of the Boll Weevils. Whereas most of the Boll Weevils were from the South, the Blue Dogs are from all over the country.

I became chairman of the House Veterans' Affairs Committee when Tip O'Neill was Speaker of the House. I was Chairman of the committee for 12 years, from 1981 to 1994.

I believe I was a good chairman for veterans and that is what the Veterans' Committee is about. I sponsored, along with Congressman Gerald Solomon of New York, the legislation that raised the Veterans Administration to the cabinet level Department of Veterans Affairs. I have worked hard for the individual service person for readjustment from active to civilian life. I also helped author the rewriting of the officers' promotion laws making officers time in grade and promotions be the same in all the services.

Of course, I am particularly proud of "The Montgomery G. I. Bill" that bears my name. It took about six years to get this legislation implemented. The G. I. Bill has become the best recruiting tool the military services have. It is also a great help in readjustment to civilian life when a college education is waiting for the serviceman or women. Over two million Americans are currently using "The Montgomery G. I. Bill" or have signed up for these benefits.

I was also very active on behalf of the National Guard and Reserve Forces. I believed I had to do something to bring about the Total Force concept, where you use Guard and Reserves in combat as well as peacetime. Years before, the Reserves were not given missions by the regulars and were not supplied equipment. That has changed now and the Guard and Reserves are front line forces.

So, I had a few achievements as a conservative Democrat. It has been a good ride for me!

Part Five

Serving on Committees
in Congress

As William Cramer observed in Chapter 18, the most important work of Congress is done in committees and subcommittees. The chapters in this section focus on various aspects of legislative life on committees of the U.S. House.

Barber Conable leads off with a discussion of the powerful Committee on Ways and Means, drawing on his 18 years on the committee (eight as ranking Republican). Conable identifies the sources of the committee's power and reviews the intricacies of tax reform. He also discusses how the personality of the committee's chair can affect the productivity of the committee

R. Lawrence Coughlin provides a similar account of life on the Appropriations Committee, reviewing the committee's role in the budget process, the relationship between the Appropriations Committee and the House Budget Committee (created by the budget reforms of 1974), the various devices available to the committee to effect policy change, and the ways in which the appropriations committees can be circumvented by "backdoor spending."

*For more than a decade, William Lehman served as chairman of the Transportation Subcommittee of the Appropriations Committee. He has recently published a diary of his service on that committee, **Mr. Chairman: Journal of a Congressional Appropriator** (Lanham, Maryland: University Press of America, 2000). Chapter 25, which is excerpted from that volume, gives us a glimpse of the hectic life of an Appropriations subcommittee chair, focusing on a representative 48 hour period in the 100th Congress.*

Given the vast powers of committee chairs, it is easy to overlook the critically important role played by the ranking minority member on congressional committees. John Erlenborn, who served for several years as ranking Republican on the House Education and Labor Committee, explains the role of congressional committees in the legislative process and the responsibilities of the ranking minority member on House committees.

Part Five concludes with Harry Johnston's discussion of two important transitions he had to go through in his career: moving from president of the Florida State Senate to member of the U.S. House of Representatives, and moving, late in his congressional career, from the majority to the minority. Johnston's account gives us a clear picture both of the impact of political parties in organizing the House and the importance of congressional committees to the work of the House.

Chapter 23

Congress and Ways & Means

Barber B. Conable, Jr. (R-New York)

Most members of Congress will tell you that circumstance and coincidence, not unusual virtue or ability, brought them to national office. To be a successful candidate you had to be in the right place at the right time, and to have some basis in your experience and character to give people a willingness to vote for you. Our system is not designed to bring philosopher-kings to public notice; one of the most important characteristics of democracy is that it gives ordinary people the chance to exercise extraordinary responsibility. Both sides of the electorate would do well to remember that, rather than believing that those elected have somehow assumed remarkable new capacity and wisdom. Given the intoxication that comes with public service, to keep my perspective, I constantly had to tell myself that there were probably at least 1,000 people in my district who could do as good a representative job as I if they had the same luck I did in being in the right place at the right time.

Much the same could be said about congressional careers, once achieved. I joined the House of Representatives as a Republican in 1964, not a vintage Republican year, and, as a result, after two years was senior to a large number of my colleagues, making me eligible in the view of my party for a senior committee far in advance of those first elected in more normal elections. The growth of my election plurality from the low 50 percentages to the high 60 percentages in two years also persuaded my political leaders that I would be a survivor, able to make tough decisions, and thus suitable for a hot seat on the difficult tax writing committee on Ways & Means. A chance light-hearted remark to one of my party leaders on the first day on the floor of the House led him to believe I had a good sense of humor, resulting in my selection from among the unknown newcomers to one of two seats in my class on the central Republican study group, from which good things continued to flow during my 20 years in Congress.

Ways & Means was a career in itself. There is no more central issue between the government and the people than taxation and its related programs. Again, I was fortunate to represent a fairly closely divided upstate New York district where no single economic interest dominated, and so I could stay in the real world of national politics, accessible to my colleagues, rather than being locked up in, for instance, Iowa corn land or central city ghetto.

Ways & Means of those days was a legislative pinnacle, even more than now. The majority Democrats were also their party's Committee on Committees, elected by the whole caucus and appointing other Democrats to their committee assignments. This critical political function assured them of "baron" status, and in the power framework of the House, gave strong presumptions to their legislative output, so that their bills were rarely challenged on the floor. In the early '70s, because the caucus had come to view Ways & Means as being too strong, unaccountable to the young liberals in the party, the political function of committee assignment was taken away. As a result, in the early '80s, a conservative Reagan floor coalition frequently challenged the work of the Ways & Means Democrats, and conservative Democrats could vote against Ways & Means without fear of direct retaliation in their committee assignments. During the '70s, the ratio of committee Democrats to Republicans was raised, reducing its bipartisanship and any sense of obligation by the Republicans to accept the work of the committee. The partisan committee staff during the same period grew from less than 30 to over 100, making it look more like a political operation than a legislative pinnacle. And, of course, taxes as an issue grew in sensitivity and controversy.

I would not want to imply that structure and function are the only conditions to affect legislative output: the personalities of the key people play an important role also. For instance, my first leader, Wilbur Mills, chairman of Ways & Means from 1958 to the early '70s, was not the autocrat of legend but a true legislative psychologist. He made a great effort to know the members of his committee and what was important to them. After a while, he knew what we thought better than we did, and could predict with frightening accuracy how we would feel about a pending issue. He almost never dictated, preferring to work for consensus. The committee consensus, once achieved (and he never failed to recognize it when it came) became the Mills bill, with broad committee support and therefore floor momentum. The liberal Democrats regretted this, because the committee consensus included conservative Republican votes, and that had something to do (along with Fannie Fox!) with Mr. Mills' leadership demise. His successor, Al Ullman, told by the Democratic Caucus to make the committee more politically accountable, found it hard because of his long schooling by Mills in the art of consensus. He was too nice to be autocratic. Dan Rostenkowski was not of the Mills school, and was perfectly willing to use his power and his leadership capacity to dominate the committee, once his elevation made it necessary for him to learn the intricacies of the tax law. Under his guidance, the committee became to some degree an arm of the caucus.

During my 18 years on the tax-writing committee, I participated in five major efforts to reform the income tax. Why so many? The income tax is the most painful and visible weapon in the government's tax arsenal. Everybody knows how much income tax he or she pays. Everybody thinks he or she pays more than his or her fair share. Everybody recoils from the accumulated complexities. Every one of the tax reform efforts in which I participated was preceded by clamor for "simplification" and every one sought to reduce the taxes of the poor or the middle class at the expense of the rich. What were the reasons for the dramatic failures of these efforts, at least in public perception?

Let's take complexity first. Two realities work against simplification: compromise and equity. A bi-polar Congress, a condition which the American people always resent, cannot pass a law without enough compromise to get a significant majority into the same tent. A group of strong minded people, even within a single party, have many different ideas about what makes sense in taxation. Important issues get bargained about, and compromised so that everybody can claim some credit. And with their six-year terms, senators look at politics differently from representatives, requiring comity (another word for compromise) between the Houses. Compromise is not a dirty word, but a legislative necessity. To achieve compromise, the necessary inclusion of elements from both sides of an argument, the softening of simple conflict through ambiguity, leave the ideology of tax philosophy less obvious than simplifiers would like.

As to equity, the other enemy of simplicity, any legislator can see with half an eye that people with comparable taxable incomes sometimes have to live quite differently because of family size, age, indebtedness, self-employment, capital needs, constructive life styles, etc. And there are lots of tax preferences (loopholes!) as American as apple pie, and generally viewed as fair: home mortgage deductions, charitable deductions, municipal bond interest exemptions, real estate tax deductions, business expense deductions, and others. If everybody worked for the same employer, had the same benefits, had only earned income, was protected against losses, and was the same age, equity would permit a simple tax law.

Another great unknown reality is the issue of who pays how much income tax now. As long as I can remember, 50 percent of the income taxes paid comes from the top 10 percent of the taxpayers, 40 percent from the next highest 40 percent, and 10 percent from the bottom 50 percent. Whether or not that's what people think, the income tax has a progressive profile, and you can't do much for poor people by cutting their income tax since they don't pay much to begin with. Note, I am not saying poor people don't pay taxes: they are particularly hard hit by sales taxes, and the social security tax reduces the first dollar they earn by as much as the last dollar they earn, thus impacting them in a regressive way on the major source of their income.

There's another factor. As F. Scott Fitzgerald said, "The very rich are very different from you and me." They have enough "cushion" of wealth to be able to make uneconomic decisions (long term growth instead of income, lower than average interest rates from tax exempt municipal bond returns, big gifts to the alma mater, etc) to avoid a tax rate which would otherwise take half their highest taxable investment income dollar. Some very wealthy people in some years have almost no taxable income, and yet, there they are, in your face. Trying to catch the big fish who would otherwise slip through the net has been one of the biggest causes of complexity in a tortured tax system.

What about the so-called flat tax? Despite its glittering appeal, I'm skeptical that it can ever happen, or if it happens that it will stay there for long. There's a remarkable lack of consensus about the details. How long will the majority enjoy the simplicity of the flat tax when they see that their taxes haven't gone down, but rich peoples' have? I know this all sounds very depressing. Tax legislating is not for sissies. To do a decent job, you've got to be prepared to live in the real world, and to carry a burden of explanation nobody wants to hear. As a matter of fact, those who advise you from outside, constituents and lobbyists, will give you only one message, "MY taxes should go down or you're not being fair. It isn't reform if my taxes stay the same or go up." For this reason, every tax reform is bought with a tax cut, and only the most devout supply-sider will deny that this is one reason our deficit is usually so high. It's also the reason Ways & Means members quickly become the toughest economic conservatives in Congress, because they know the price of every dollar spent. You can't pay for big government with pleasant theories, or tax cuts.

Good things can be said about other types of taxes than the unpopular income tax. A value-added (VAT) or other broad-based consumption tax has its advantages and its champions. It is the tax of preference in most of the rest of the world. It's a hidden tax of which nobody is aware as they pay it because it's built right into the price system, but it is regressive. A VAT costs about four times as much to administer as an income tax. Like any other hidden tax, it's a politician's dream in the amount of money it can raise painlessly. I personally like people to know how much tax they are paying –how much their government is costing them–so they won't think of government action as the easy solution to everything. In America, any form of federal sales tax is going to have to be bought from the states and municipalities with greatly increased federal aid, since by tradition they depend so heavily on their sales taxes.

What is the future of the tax code? I'm not foolish enough to predict, except to say that, in some ways, it's bound to become more complicated. One trend frightening to tax people is the globalization of our economy, for instance. With 60 percent of the world's multinational corporations investing like mad abroad, America must still decide what elements of foreign earnings it can most appropriately tax. Many countries don't tax foreign income of their taxpayers at all, giving them a competitive edge in the world market. The VAT countries, permitting rebates of local VAT taxes at the border on exports, give a competitive edge that corporate income tax countries cannot get. Massive international money flows occur totally outside the tax systems of the countries involved, and international agencies like the United Nations are eyeing these flows covetously, hoping to get their financing on a more stable basis than is possible with voluntary contributions. Some international thinkers are suggesting that we really need a General Agreement on Taxes and Investment, similar to our much debated General Agreement on Tariffs and Trade (GATT), to standardize tax treatment of international business, and make competition fairer. Look out, you tax sovereignty folks!

Taxes may be the center of Ways & Means daily grist, but there are some other modest opportunities for legislative service. Social security and medicare, for instance. Even welfare is part of the committee's jurisdiction, because President Roosevelt ordered the conjoining of welfare and social security in one bill back in the '30s for mutual support. Trade legislation, of late a hot button item, is also the responsibility of Ways & Means, because trade is normally regulated by a tax on imports known as a tariff. I won't dwell on these subjects, but each one is hardly less exciting than taxation itself, and many a career has foundered on imperfect political handling of any one of them.

A note of caution about Ways & Means. As John Byrnes of Green Bay, Wisconsin, one of the more brilliant recent members of the committee, told me when I joined Ways & Means, "If you want honorary degrees from prestigious universities, if you want to be loved, if you want to be an insider in the most comfortable sense of the word, set the Appropriations Committee as your goal. Spending the taxpayer's money is always easier than separating him from it."

But to those who enjoy pressure-cookers, Ways & Means has its satisfactions. People will care about what you think and do. You deal with real issues in a real world. Most people respect those who are willing to make tough decisions, rather than hiding in more comfortable places. The intellectual challenges are daunting, and so you're likely to be associating with bright people and to attract more than your share of media attention. I decided, in the final analysis, given all the garbage a congressman has to go through, there wasn't much point in staying unless I could work in an influential forum. I have never regretted it.

Chapter 24

The Appropriations Committee

R. Lawrence Coughlin (R-Pennsylvania)

The Constitution of the United States invested the "power of the purse" in the Congress. The nation's founders, who were rebelling against the King's taxes, wrote in Article I, Section 9 of the Constitution, "No money shall be drawn from the Treasury, but in Consequence of Appropriations made by Law." This "power of the purse" wrote James Madison in *Federalist Paper* number 58, was "the most complete and effectual weapon with which any constitution can arm the immediate representatives of the people..."

The "power of the purse" in Congress further devolved initially to the House Appropriations Committee. According to legendary Appropriations Committee Chairman, Clarence Cannon, (D-MO), who also became Speaker of the House, "The priority of the House in the initiation of appropriation bills is buttressed by the strongest and most impelling of all rules, the rule of immemorial usage."

House Appropriations is a fascinating committee. It has been called a mini-Congress, and indeed, it is a large committee with 60 members and subcommittees which correspond to the other full committees of the Congress. Because of the annual budget process, Appropriations has primary oversight of federal agencies and programs, all of which it funds, and agencies are likely to be particularly responsive to the subcommittee which provides their paychecks. Finally, Appropriations is the name of the game in terms of national priorities because where money is spent is where the priorities lie.

Understanding procedure and process is important to knowing how to get things done in the federal government. There is indeed much more routine, more hard work, more oversight, and fewer grand schemes than the public generally imagines. There is also, of course, partisan politics.

Early each year, the president submits to Congress a proposed budget. The budget contains the president's recommendation for levels of income (primarily taxes) and expenditures, in both cases line by line and item by item. It is a massive document prepared by the executive branch at the end of the preceding year. It also contains the president's suggestions for new programs as well as alterations to or elimination of existing programs.

The president's budget, as well as the congressional committees, talk in terms of budget authority, obligations, and outlays. Budget authority is what the Appropriations Committee creates. Budget authority allows the federal government bureaucracy to obligate federal funds, for example, to purchase equipment or pay personnel and contractors. These obligations, however, do not result in outlays until later, and it is the actual outlays that affect borrowing and the federal debt. The budget, therefore, must project spending and revenues to determine the debt or, hopefully, now the surplus.

When the president's budget is delivered to Congress, a two-track process commences. On one track, proposals for new programs and alterations of existing programs are assigned to the authorizing committees of appropriate jurisdiction. These committees may or may not hold hearings or act upon the president's proposals. They also may hold hearings, act upon, and bring before Congress proposals which they originate themselves.

On a parallel track, the president's budget goes to the Appropriations Committee which assigns portions to its appropriate subcommittees. The subcommittees commence hearings and review the budget requests of the federal agencies under their jurisdiction in the spring of each year. The president's cabinet secretaries and agency heads testify before their appropriating subcommittees each year to justify their budget requests and ask for their money. In some cases, the Office of Management and Budget, which prepares the president's budget, may have reduced (or increased) the original budget request of a department or agency, and the cabinet secretary or agency head may be in the difficult position of being a good soldier supporting a position with which he or she does not agree. Outside witnesses also appear at the subcommittee hearings to comment on agency funding or performance as will be more fully discussed.

Superimposed on this authorizing and appropriating process is the Budget Committee, created by the Congressional Budget Act of 1974. The House Budget Committee also receives the president's budget and recommends a fiscal year budget to the House which may or may not match the president's recommendations for revenues, outlays, and deficit/surplus. The Budget Committee also gives each of the authorizing committees targets for revenues or mandatory spending and suggests legislation which may "reconcile" the committee's agenda to those targets. Finally, the Budget Committee gives the Appropriations Committee a target for overall discretionary spending together with suggested spending, targets by function category. The macro figures for revenue, spending, and deficit/surplus become binding upon adoption of the budget, but each committee may determine how it will achieve its targets. The budget resolution adopted by Congress does not require the president's signature, so it is also not subject to the president's veto.

When the Appropriations Committee receives its discretionary spending allocation from the Budget Committee, it makes its own allocations of discretionary spending to its subcommittees. It does not necessarily regard the budget function categories or amounts recommended by the Budget Committee or the president's budget. It must, however, appropriate to already authorized programs or find its appropriations subject to a point of order for authorizing on an appropriations bill when the measure reaches the House floor.

The Appropriations Committee cannot create a new program–only an authorizing committee can create a B-l bomber or a welfare program eligible for funding. The Appropriations Committee can, however, decline to fund an authorized program. It also frequently continues to fund programs whose authorizations have expired and which time or controversy have precluded their reauthorization. It does this with the consent of the authorizing committee and/or a rule for consideration of the particular Appropriations Bill that waves the particular point of order.

Appropriation Bills are privileged legislation which can proceed directly to the House floor for consideration without going before the Rules Committee. Most legislation coming from authorizing committees goes to the Rules Committee which determines the length of debate, which amendments will be considered, and may waive points of order. Appropriations Bills generally go to Rules only if they need waiver of points of order against unauthorized appropriations.

Appropriation bills can become vehicles for policy changes in a number of ways. First, a bill may simply decline to fund a particular authorized program. Second, a limitation may be added to an appropriations bill to the affect that none of the funds will be used for a particular purpose. Hundreds of amendments regarding abortion have sought to use this limitations procedure to effect policy. Third, detailed legislative provisions can be added to an appropriations bill if it is possible to obtain a waiver of points of order from the Rules Committee, a majority vote on the floor of the House, and survive a potential or real presidential veto.

Appropriations is the name of the game in priorities for spending, but this does not mean that either the committee or the Congress itself has sole control of the "power of the purse." Appropriation bills must be signed by the president and are subject to presidential veto. This means they are the subject of negotiations.

Negotiations make strange bedfellows, and the president's budget may be low in funding for programs that he really wants but knows Congress will increase, and may be high in funding for programs the president knows Congress will reduce. The eventual result is that any appropriations bill must be one that can command a majority of Congress and not be vetoed by the president . The national priorities, then, are as true an amalgam of national opinion as possible.

Three additional aspects of the Appropriations process are important:

1) *Continuing Resolutions* (CRs). In the relatively frequent event that an Appropriations bill has not passed before the end of the fiscal year on September

30, a CR may be necessary to continue the funding of the agencies and programs within the jurisdiction of the particular funding Committee. The failure to pass an appropriation on time may result from inability to provide a majority vote in the House or Senate, or funding levels or riders that are unsatisfactory to the president, and insufficient votes for the two- thirds majority required to override a veto.

In 1995, Congress confronted the president with appropriations bills that contained insufficient funds for programs the president wanted or riders unacceptable to the president. There were insufficient votes to override the president's vetoes, which were supported by the public, and Congress had to back down. However, in Fiscal Year 1988, the entire budget was included in a massive continuing resolution which was passed by Congress and signed by the president.

A continuing resolution can make fundamental changes to the law without being subject to points of order for authorizing on an appropriations bill. A CR is not an appropriations bill. In October 1984, an entire revision of the Federal Criminal Code was included in a CR.

2) *Supplemental Appropriations*. Often labeled "emergency supplementals," these bills can fall outside of the normal budget process. They are designed to deal with unexpected expenses facing the federal government. They are, however, the product of much negotiation because in addition to the emergency funds, they can carry other initiatives. The 1997 Emergency Supplemental was to provide disaster relief funds for floods in the Midwest. It also carried, however, $21 million for the repair of the solarium of the National Botanical Garden in Washington.

3) *Line Item Vetoes*. A recent development, line item vetoes, would allow the president to veto funds for specific line item projects with which he disagreed. The president would first be required to sign the appropriations bill, and there would follow a period during which he could veto specific items. These could be either items in the bill or earmarks in the committee reports. The president could also "look through" the appropriations bill to an authorizing bill to target a project he opposed. The line item veto itself is currently being challenged in court. Even if it is upheld, it would be subject to additional court challenges including a challenge based on the ability to veto what are essentially limitations of obligations.

There are three areas of spending which can circumvent the ability of the Appropriations Committee to exercise the "power of the purse." First are entitlement programs which entitle beneficiaries of the program to specific benefits. Social security is the classic example. Medicare, medicaid, food stamps, and student aid are others. All of these programs entitle individuals to specific monetary benefits over which the Appropriations Committee has no spending control. They are, in fact, the fastest growing part of the federal budget and the one most responsible for the federal deficit.

Second is contract authority which legislatively allows federal agencies to obligate funds which must then be paid. Spending of highway and transit trust funds by contract authority are examples. The Appropriations Committee has been able to limit obligations from the test funds to maintain the power of the purse, but there are continued ingenious new ways to get around the process.

Third is borrowing authority guaranteed by the federal government. While this does not create any immediate obligation or outlays, the federal guarantee has risk of default. Allowances for estimated defaults must be included in the budget process if the government is to be able to predict its deficit/surplus.

At the risk of suggesting that all things come in three's, any chair of the Appropriations Committee has at least three major sources of potential controversy.

1) The chair is subject to enormous pressure in terms of funding priorities and the contest of ideas. Each subcommittee chair thinks its programs are important, and the cumulative demands could be far over the budget for discretionary spending. The full committee chair must allocate and referee between subcommittees. The administration also may have different priorities for funding, and the president has the veto power. Finally, the chair must balance his and his party's spending priorities against the need to produce a bill and to govern.

2) The chair and subcommittee chairs are always under pressure to include unauthorized projects. Sometimes, this is at the urging and with the complicity of the authorizing committees and/or the leadership itself. School voucher proposals, an article of faith for Republicans, have constantly appeared in appropriations bills for the District of Columbia. They did not survive, but anything can be done in an appropriations bill or a CR if you have the votes. Often, appropriations bills are the only vehicle readily available for significant initiatives.

3) The bane of the chair's existence can be riders to appropriations bills which seek to limit spending in a way that affects national policy. The riders may have little to do with conclusion of a budget as such. Major efforts to terminate the war in Vietnam occurred through riders prohibiting spending for that purpose.

Over the years, the power and authority of the Appropriations Committee has changed. There was a time when it would have been unthinkable for a freshman member to serve on the Committee and when the Committee operated behind closed doors. It now operates with freshmen and in the sunlight. The "power of the purse," however, always will attract attention and attach significance to this fascinating committee of the Congress of the United States.

Chapter 25

Forty-Eight Hours in the Life of a Congressional Appropriator

William M. Lehman (D-Florida)

MARCH 11, 1987 - WEDNESDAY

This morning, our subcommittee marked up the supplemental appropriations on the section dealing with transportation appropriations. The markup sessions are for the committee's preparation of a bill for Floor action by editing, amending, and drafting language. The draft of the bill is literally "marked up." On my suggestion, the markup on our transportation function of the bill was closed to the public, including lobbyists. We appropriated $5 million of new money into the FAA Air Traffic Controllers Academy in Oklahoma City to build simulated air towers in which to train radar operators for overcrowded airports, as in Los Angeles and Cleveland; the trainees now will have firsthand supervision and the capability to practice their skills right at the academy. One million dollars of new money was also marked for the National Highway Traffic Safety Administration, of which $150 thousand will go to Dade County, which needs this financial shot-in-the-arm for Metro-Dade's trauma network, my pet project and the main reason I included funds for the National Highway Traffic Safety Administration. The balance of the money went to the Center for Disease Control in Atlanta for the study of trauma research.

The Amtrak hearing followed the markup, and we talked about the ridiculousness of Amtrak having to deal each year with a nonfunding request from the administration. There were two witnesses: John Riley, Federal Railroad Administrator, and Graham Claytor, president of Amtrak. In John's opening remarks, he said that despite improvements, Amtrak still projects an operating loss in excess of $600 million in the next fiscal year. The administration's position was that with the present budget deficit, the country could not afford to continue subsidizing Amtrak.

I knew Riley from when he was administrative assistant to Senator Dave Durenberger (R-MN), Chair of the Senate Public Works Committee. During a break in the hearing, Riley took me aside and told me that as FRA Administrator, he had to go through the motions of supporting the administration's position even though he did not believe in it. Riley believes that the administration should support Amtrak and provide federal funding, but he could not voice that opinion in a public hearing. The FRA Administrator is an appointed position, and as such, Riley has no choice but to support the administration or lose his job.

Our committee did do some tough questioning on the recent Amtrak/Conrail accident that happened this past January 4, in Chevy Chase, Maryland - one of the worst accidents in Amtrak's history. (Of the 600 people aboard the Amtrak train, 15 died and about 350 were injured.) I found interesting and alarming Riley's comments regarding the accident. He said that both Conrail employees came on duty and were "eyeballed" and talked with by a supervisor who had undergone a special training program in recognizing drug symptoms. In this case, the supervisor did not recognize the symptoms and cleared both employees for duty. They tested positive several hours later, but it was not established that the men were impaired at the time of the accident. This was yet another agency voicing the need for mandatory drug and alcohol testing of transportation employees. Substance abuse is a big issue this year.

Public transportation in our country should be the safest and most efficiently-run system in the world, and I reminded Riley that, "compared to the high-speed Japanese trains, or the high-speed French trains, Amtrak is not nearly as smooth a ride in the Northeast Corridor." I told Riley that I believed both the Amtrak and Conrail trains were exceeding the required speed limit when they collided, and asked him why the automatic brake did not work to slow down the train. Riley commented that the train actually was going at a slower speed than usual and if it had been going at the normal limit of 125 mph, the automatic brake would have kicked in. He went on to explain how they monitor for speed by using "speed guns," similar to what state troopers use, and the Amtrak trains have recorders that you can pull out to check if the engineer was speeding. He said occasionally you catch somebody, but it is not an endemic problem. We continued the hearing in early afternoon and finished all the Amtrak questions. Tomorrow, we will deal with the Federal Railroad Administration questions.

On the Floor today, we voted to eliminate aid to the Contras, which passed with a 230-196 margin, but not by enough to override a veto. Dan Mica, Buddy MacKay, and I were the only members from Florida who voted to cut off aid to the Contras. Most of the Florida members still vote the Cuban-American position on these issues. Prior to the vote, our Washington and Miami offices received hundreds of calls from mostly Latin Americans with such messages as, "if Congressman Lehman does not support aid to the Contras, we will see that he doesn't get reelected." The staff finally had to stop answering the phones until the rash of calls ceased. As always, though, I voted according to my convictions. Pragmatically, voting otherwise does not convince the other side, and only disillusions those who support my stand.

Late in the afternoon, I joined the Foreign Operations Subcommittee for the markup on the foreign operations portion of the supplemental bill. Chairman Dave Obey (D-WI) only has money for the Philippines and for the U.S. portion of U.N. aid to Angola. Other requests rightly will wait for the 1988 Appropriations Bill. Obey agreed that the $50 million to the Philippines were essential. Charlie Wilson (D-TX), a member on foreign ops, told an interesting story about his recent trip to Afghanistan where he spent time with the Afghan freedom fighters. When he was leaving Afghanistan, after being with them for several days, the freedom fighters asked Charlie if there was anything they could do, and Charlie said he would like to talk to some of their war prisoners. They brought him two Afghan pilots who had been trained in Russia and had been part of the Afghan government supported by the Soviets. Charlie spoke with the pilots and they gave him the usual answers and requested that he not make their position anymore untenable than it already was, presently held as "traitors" to their country. After the pilots left, Charlie asked the freedom fighters if he could speak to some of the captured Soviet prisoners. They replied: "There are none, but if we could know ahead of time, we will save you a few until you get here."

The Florida State Society had its reception this evening, and I attended even though I stayed only briefly. I feel I have to attend these kinds of events just to keep the Florida connection. I also had a few minutes, between a phone call and a vote, to attend the Association of American Vintage and Wine Institute reception. The food and wine were excellent, and I left wanting to stay longer. There are several things that I am scheduled to do today but cannot; I don't have time. I will miss the T.V. press conference on the Contra vote, and also my meeting with representatives from the United Nations Association. The staff will have to fill in for me, as I must chair the subcommittee. Even when I yield the questioning to Larry Coughlin, the ranking Republican on our subcommittee, I still remain. The other Democrats on our subcommittee really don't want to spend much time at the hearings unless they have particular questions to ask. They say they will help chair the hearings, but are not there when I really need them. Since their actions pretty much mirror my own under the preceding chairman, I may get annoyed at times, but it's usually seasoned with understanding.

MARCH 12 - THURSDAY

My morning started off with an interesting meeting with the Florida Sheriffs Association. Their biggest problem now is the Haitians who are dealing and using crack cocaine up and down the state. It is not just a Miami or South Dade problem, as these sheriffs are from central and northern Florida. When the Haitians are arrested, the counties do not have the space or cells to hold them, and the federal authorities won't take them. I told the group that the repeat offenders should be incarcerated in the Immigration & Naturalization Service (INS) facilities in Krome, and they are going to look into my suggestion as a possible solution.

Afterward, I met with representatives from the Joint American-Israel Committee, an organization comprised of well-to-do Jewish middle-aged women from all over the country. They wanted to know about the adverse effects of the Jonathan Pollack spy scandal, and how it would affect the funding for Israel this year. "So far," I said, "I have seen no signs that the scandal will affect funding for Israel." [And, this remained true.] Then, a reporter from *Roll Call,* a Capitol Hill newspaper, interviewed me on "my favorite restaurant" in Washington. They are doing a survey, the results of which will appear in Monday's issue, and I am curious as to what it has to say.

Our second day of hearings with the Federal Railroad Administration and John Riley as witness began at 10:00. Our subcommittee staff director, Tom Kingfield, is back at work almost completely recovered from a distressing back ailment. With Tom's return, we now will be running efficient hearings, and I am really glad to have him back. With the FRA, the questions continued on the influence of drugs and alcohol use of railroad workers, as well as safety devices and accident rates. Riley is a very good witness - open and forthright - and never more so than when speaking of Conrail's alcohol and drug program. He expressed his "unhappiness" with Conrail's program and said they had not executed the "Operation Red Block" agreement with labor - the voluntary prevention program developed by railroad labor and management. He then rated Conrail's program close to the bottom. (It is clear that the Chevy Chase, Maryland accident has had an impact on John and the agency, and Conrail's involvement in it.) It is almost a repeat of yesterday's hearing on Amtrak, except for the revelation of how extensive "equipment tampering" has become. John indicated that tampering with railroad safety equipment has reached epidemic proportion, and is a serious threat to the public safety. FRA had found 74 instances where essential safety devices were disabled in locomotive cabs, and this, apparently, was just the "tip of the iceberg." "It is so easy," he said, "to remove a tape from a whistle, to remove a block of wood from a dead man's control, to turn that switch that has been turned off and put it back in the 'on' position. It is so easy to drive a screwdriver through the circuit to short-circuit it and then pull it out."

They were finding employees that were not only irresponsible, but also careless, and not in insignificant numbers. He proposed that, as a deterrent, jurisdiction over the employees be given to the FRA. The agency does have enforcement jurisdiction over the railroad companies, but no enforcement jurisdiction over the employees who actually run the trains.

With my subcommittee hearing over, I went to the Foreign Operations markup where we reported out the foreign operations part of the half a billion dollars supplemental bill, most of which went to Central America and the Philippines. I spoke to Dave Obey about the possibility of Sam Nunn of Georgia, Chair of the Senate Armed Services Committee, and Rep. Bill Gray of Philadelphia, as a Democratic presidential ticket. "Not a bad idea," he said. In the afternoon, Majority Leader Richard Gephardt of Missouri came to see me, and I told him I would do what I could to help him in his presidential bid. Still hanging loose, I don't want to support anyone at this time. "If I decide to help anyone else," I said to Gephardt, "I will let you know at once." In the meantime, I will help him anyway I can in the Miami area.

Calling Bill Guralnik, Director of the American Jewish Committee in Miami, I wanted to know if the AJC would be funding some of Adele's trip expense to East Germany and also about agenda items for tomorrow with the condo leaders going into Liberty City to meet with the black leadership. Bill will be there, as his group actually is sponsoring the Black-Jewish relations meeting, and I feel good about my involvement in this effort.

My plane for Miami this evening is an hour late, par for Eastern. I seem to see the same people traveling back and forth like Leo Zeferetti, who goes to and from Washington every weekend. Leo is a former member who lives in Biscayne Park, and is now a lobbyist for the laborers union. Senator Claude Pepper is also on this flight. I arrived home about 9:00 p.m.

Chapter 26

A Ranking Member of a Committee of the U.S. Congress

John N. Erlenborn (R-Illinois)

One of the highest elected positions in the United States is election to the United States Congress. Only the president and vice president hold higher positions. Within the Congress, holding a position in the leadership of your party distinguishes one member from the rest. There are elected leadership positions such as Speaker, majority leader, minority leader, party whips and a number of others. In addition, each committee and subcommittee of the Congress has a chair (who is from the majority party) and a ranking minority member. The legislative process depends heavily on the activities of these individuals and that, in turn, depends on how they perceive and carry out their official duties.

Every member of Congress, including of course these leaders, brings with them the sum of their experiences. Where they lived, their education, job experience, political experience, prior government experience, and a host of other life experiences, all comprise the background from which they view the Congress and the issues with which it must deal.

My background included growing up in a Chicago suburb, a two-year stint in the U.S. Navy during World War II and a college and law school education. After law school, I worked for a law firm in a small Chicago suburb. After two years, I left to accept appointment as an assistant state's attorney. Working in the courthouse, I became acquainted with the elected officials, worked in their election campaigns, and soon became a candidate myself. My election to the Illinois General Assembly provided me with eight years of legislative experience. By then, I had married and begun raising a family, which included three children. While in the Illinois House of Representatives, I maintained a law practice in my hometown, learning what it meant to be a small businessman. Then, in 1964, I was elected to Congress, where I spent the next 20 years, retiring in 1985. For the last several years, I was the ranking Republican on the Education & Labor Committee of the House of Representatives.

COMMITTEE STRUCTURE

Both the Senate and the House of Representatives have large volumes of legislation to consider each year. Over the years, each body has established a system of committees and subcommittees designed to manage legislation. There are standing, select, special, conference, and other ad hoc committees. Of these, only the standing committees are considered permanent. Service on these committees allows a member to achieve an expertise in some aspect of the committee's jurisdiction.

Standing committees exercise jurisdiction over most legislative proposals. Select and special committees are not usually considered permanent, but may exist for a number of years. Conference committees are established to consider and resolve the differences in the Senate and House versions of a bill or resolution and are composed of both senators and representatives. Once the committee's purpose has been fulfilled, the committee is disbanded.

Although each member of Congress has a unique background, many are lawyers and a large percentage have some experience in their state legislature. Newly-elected members usually have personal, constituent, or other interests which lead them to seek appointment to one or more standing committees. Some may be fortunate enough to achieve membership to the committee they request, many are not. Committee assignments are very important to the career of a legislator. But whatever the assignment, members are well advised to accept it, at least for the time being, and immerse themselves in the work of the committee, becoming expert on some aspect of the committee's jurisdiction.

The ratio of the majority relative to the minority members of a committee usually approximates the ratio of majority to minority members in the body which has established it. The chair and ranking minority member of each committee are named by the party appointing them. Each is the acknowledged leader of his or her party members serving on the committee.

Subject to occasional variations, the chair and ranking minority member of a committee name the members of their party to serve on the subcommittees. Often, the most prestigious subcommittee will have the chair and ranking minority member of the full committee serving in those positions on the subcommittee. The subcommittee chair exercises rather broad authority to determine the schedule of the subcommittee, what bills or resolutions will be considered, and may or may not confer with the ranking minority member of that subcommittee. The personal relationship between the individuals often determines the degree of cooperation with one another. Good personal relations do not necessarily mean that either relinquishes their philosophical or political position, but rather that they agree that differences in positions on issues need not interfere with the legislative process or their personal relations.

THE LEGISLATIVE PROCESS

When we examine the normal legislative process, we can gain an appreciation of the role that the committees play. First, a member introduces a bill or resolution in the House or Senate. The proper officer in each body refers the legislation to a committee which has jurisdiction of the subject matter. Next, the chair of the committee refers it to the subcommittee which has jurisdiction. For much of the legislation introduced, this may be the end of the road. Often, bills are introduced merely for the sponsor to publicly note the sponsor's position on the issues involved. Only a small percentage of the thousands of bills introduced in each Congress is ever the subject of hearings.

In the event that the sponsor wishes to have a bill moved in the process, he or she will urge the subcommittee chair to set a hearing date when the subcommittee will hear testimony on the bill. The chair has authority to determine which witnesses will be heard and in what order. The ranking minority member of the subcommittee has the right to recommend witnesses that the minority would like to have heard. In most cases, the recommendation will be honored. If the bill is controversial, especially if there are party differences concerning it, the ranking member will urge his fellow party members to attend and to cast their votes to support the party position. In some cases, the subcommittee member may give his or her proxy to the ranking member or some other party member to cast the absent member's vote.

After witnesses have been heard, the subcommittee may be convened by the chair to consider amendments. This is referred to as "mark up" of the bill. The ranking member of the subcommittee will, if necessary, see that the proper amendments are prepared to reflect the minority's position. Again, the ranking member will urge attendance by his party members and will attempt to see that all of the amendments are presented by one or another of his members.

If the bill is favorably reported to the full committee, ordinarily there are no further witnesses heard, but the markup process is repeated with all of the members of the full committee taking part. The ranking member of the full committee may take the lead in full committee or the ranking member of the subcommittee may be allowed to lead, especially if that member has a special expertise or interest in the bill and its subject matter. As in the subcommittee, the ranking member will try to gain the attendance of party members or at least their proxies.

If the bill is favorably reported to the parent body (House or Senate), the majority party prepares a report explaining the issues and the arguments for the bill. The minority has the right to have printed, together with the majority report, the views and arguments of the minority. The ranking member will see that the minority staff prepares those views and includes all generally held views of the minority members. Other individual members of the majority and minority have the right to add their separate or additional views to the report.

FLOOR DEBATE

A bill which has been reported out of a House committee ordinarily will need to be considered by the Rules Committee. If a hearing on the bill is set by the chair of the Rules Committee, only other members of the House will be allowed to testify. Both proponents and opponents (if any) are permitted to present their arguments. After all have been heard, the Rules Committee may report the bill to the floor together with a special rule for its consideration. The rule will provide for the length of time that may be devoted to general debate and whether and to what extent the bill will be subject to amendment.

If the majority leadership decides to have the bill considered by the whole body, the rule will be scheduled for consideration. If the House adopts the rule, pursuant to that rule, the House will resolve itself into the "Committee of the Whole House on the State of the Union," or as it is commonly referred to, "the Committee of the Whole." In the Committee of the Whole, the chair and the ranking member of the committee originating the bill name which of their respective party members from the committee will manage the bill. Normally, each manager has one-half of the allotted time to yield to those of his or her party who wish to engage in general debate.

As in committee, the ranking member will organize the debate to see that the best arguments are made on the floor. Also, the strategy of how and when to offer amendments and motions to the best advantage of the minority will be determined by the ranking member. Under the traditions of the House, at the end of all the debate and the amendment process, the bill will be returned to the House and the Committee of the Whole will cease to exist. No further debate is allowed, and only one motion may be offered in the House just prior to the vote on the passage of the bill. This motion, to recommit the bill to the committee which had jurisdiction, is in the control of the minority if they wish to offer it. The decision to offer this motion to recommit is ordinarily made by the ranking member who managed the bill in debate and in consultation with party leadership.

A simple motion to recommit sends the bill back to the committee from which it emerged. This is tantamount to killing the bill since it has been rejected by a majority vote on the floor. However, the motion may be with instructions to adopt an amendment. The amendment may be simple, complex or even "in the nature of a substitute," i.e., a complete rewrite of the bill. The content of the motion will be part of the strategy that the ranking member will devise. If the motion to recommit with instructions carries, it has the effect of amending the bill which is then voted on for passage as amended.

CONFERENCE COMMITTEES

When a bill is passed by one body it is sent to the other. There, it will be subject to a process similar to that just described, i.e., committee, subcommittee, and floor consideration. If it is passed in a form differing from that which passed the other body, a motion may be offered to insist on the version as it first passed and to request a conference committee be appointed. If the other body agrees, a conference committee composed of a House delegation and a Senate delegation is appointed. These members meet to try to resolve the differences. If either delegation wishes to recede from their body's version and agree with the others, a majority of its delegation must agree. For example, before a Senate provision is removed or amended, a majority of the Senate conferees must agree.

In the conference committee, the chair of the committee which originated the bill will lead the majority members and the minority will be led by the ranking member. If the conference committee successfully completes its work, the result is compiled in a "Conference Report" which explains the result of the committee's deliberations. This report is sent first to one house and, if acted upon favorably, then to the other. The ranking member again controls the time for his party in debate and determines any strategy that may be needed. If both houses adopt the conference report, the bill is passed and sent to the president.

LEARN THE RULES

Being familiar with the rules and precedents of the body in which you serve is very helpful in achieving your goals. In addition, once you become known as a legislative strategist familiar with the rules, you will be consulted by other members and you will be rewarded with their trust and help when needed.

A case in point is the consideration of a bill to amend the Fair Labor Standards Act to increase the minimum wage in the early 1970s. This bill was considered in a subcommittee of the Education & Labor Committee. I was the ranking Republican of the subcommittee that had jurisdiction. The position of committee members was traditional, i.e., most Democrats favoring the bill and most Republicans in opposition. In fact, the Education & Labor Committee Democrats were to a great extent supported by organized labor and sought this committee assignment to aid their supporters. This had resulted in the committee being controlled by members who were more liberal and supportive of organized labor than the total membership of the House of Representatives.

The bill that was reported out of the committee not only raised the minimum wage but also provided automatic increases in the future pursuant to a formula. When the bill was considered by the House, I offered an amendment in the nature of a substitute. This amendment proposed to strike all after the title of the bill and substitute the bill that I had drafted. My proposal would have provided a more modest increase in the minimum wage and no automatic increases in the future. When the vote was tallied, my amendment was adopted and the bill was passed in that form. The Senate subsequently passed a bill similar to the Education & Labor Committee's bill that had been rejected by the House.

In the ordinary course, the bill would be returned to the House and the Chairman of the Education & Labor Committee would request unanimous consent to disagree with the Senate amendments and request a conference. Many of my supporters asked what our strategy would be. Most suggested that I offer a motion in the House to instruct the House conferees to insist on the House passed language. I was aware, however, that if the conferees were instructed, there was no sanction if they ignored the instructions and agreed to the Senate version. The conferees that the Speaker would appoint were certain to be supporters of the organized labor version of the bill and would cheerfully sell out the House passed version. Some other strategy had to be devised.

During my service in the House prior to that time, unanimous consent was always granted in agreeing to send a bill to conference. The very fact that unanimous consent was requested suggested that there could be opposition to sending the bill to conference. I studied the rules and precedents and discovered that if unanimous consent was not granted, the committee chairman would be required to obtain instructions from his committee to offer a motion in the House to send the bill to conference.

The then chairman of the committee was not known for fairness and was known to take advantage of opponents if he could. Therefore, I made it my business to always be on the floor at a time when he might ask for unanimous consent. When he did, I voiced my objection. It was the first time, as far as anyone could remember, that consent had not been granted. The chairman learned that the committee had to be called into session and adopt instructions for him to offer the motion on the floor of the House. Before he could accomplish this, I had sent a "Dear Colleague" letter to all House members voicing my belief that the House position would not be sustained by the conferees and that the motion to go to conference should not be adopted until the Speaker would agree to appoint a majority of conferees who had supported my version of the bill. When the chairman offered the motion, it was defeated. He tried again a week later and it was defeated again. That was the end of that legislation during that Congress.

The moral of the story is that knowing the rules is very important to your success. No one can fault you for citing the rules and precedents and they can be of inestimable value in achieving your goals.

THE RANKING MEMBER

Becoming the chair or ranking minority member of a committee of Congress is now a function of a party election process as established separately by the respective parties. With some exceptions, the process of selecting the chairs and ranking members by each party is substantially the same.

In my early days in Congress, beginning in 1965, the seniority system held sway. This was a system which elevated the committee member with the longest tenure on the committee to the top party position, chair or ranking member. This was described by many as a mindless, thoughtless system which rewarded longevity regardless of ability or even adherence to party position.

First the Republicans, and soon after the Democrats, amended their rules and procedures to provide for nomination by a committee or the party leadership and final election by the party membership. As a result, some who had held chair and ranking positions for a number of years were deposed and other members elected in their place. It was not always the next in order of seniority who was selected. I was one of the Republicans who had championed the change in my party. But the law of unintended consequences, I believe, has proven that the change was not without some adverse effects.

The election process meant that those who aspired to become chair or ranking minority member had to be popular enough among the general membership and especially the party members serving on the committee. This was recognized by the proponents of change. The result was to substitute democracy for seniority, not a bad result it would seem. But human nature being what it is, the search for votes among committee members at times resulted in the chair or ranking member devolving more and more authority over hiring of staff and the control of committee funds to the chairs and ranking members of the subcommittees. The coordinating function of the chair and ranking member suffered as they allowed more and more of the authority they used to exercise to be exercised by subcommittee members. Lines of authority, and therefore lines of responsibility, became blurred.

These changes took place in a time when many other changes were underway. Political action committees were becoming a prime source of funding of individual members' campaigns. Reliance on the party structure in a member's district was diminished commensurately. These and other factors led to conditions in which oftentimes the vote of a member could not be predicted by a political philosophy espoused by the member. Grassroots lobbying, not in itself bad, became of greater influence and was utilized most effectively by those with the financial means to use expensive new methods of mass communications.

DEVELOPING EXPERTISE

With 435 members of the U.S. House of Representatives and 100 senators, the Congress has been forced to devise rules to restrict the number and length of floor speeches. Each body has its set of rules and they differ as to approach. The Senate has fewer restrictions on debate. Agreed time limits are the principal restraint. When agreement cannot be reached, a vote to close debate, known as cloture, can be used. The House, as noted above, uses special rules to establish the restrictions on debate. General debate may be allowed for one hour on noncontroversial bills. For major and controversial legislation, general debate may extend for four, five, or more hours.

After general debate, the House rules allow amendments to be offered and any member may be recognized by the chair for five minutes to support or oppose the amendment. If a member requests unanimous consent to proceed for a longer period of time, and no objection is made, the time will be extended. Again, the Senate rules are more liberal and generally, the senator speaking will not be limited in time.

Most members learn that frequent or frivolous speeches tend to reduce a member's effectiveness. There are exceptions to the general rule, however. For example, when the Republican gentlewoman from New Jersey, Millicent Fenwick, first came to the House, she was a frequent speaker on many diverse topics of interest to her. A colleague approached her on the floor of the House right after one of these speeches and observed that most new members restricted their participation in debate until they had been in Congress for some period of time and had developed a recognized expertise. Millicent, who was in her late 60s at the time, replied, "My dear, at my age, I don't have the luxury of waiting."

It is wise, however, to choose some area of law and work at developing a knowledge that exceeds that of the other members. Usually, this will be done by seeking appointment to a committee that has jurisdiction over an area of law that is of interest to you. If you don't have a special interest, or are not successful in gaining appointment to the committee of your choice, there is an alternative. Sometimes this is exemplified by the exhortation: "If they hand you a lemon, you may as well make lemonade." In other words, it may well be much better for your congressional career to avoid complaining about your failure to obtain the committee of your choice and instead work within the committee and your subcommittees. Appointment to the committee of your choice may come later. In the meantime, you may find that the work of your committee is interesting.

As an example, I was asked in the later part of my first term to accept appointment to the Education & Labor Committee. Because of the controversial nature of labor legislation, many Republicans were reluctant to serve on the committee, and that was my reaction. In fact, when approached by Les Arends, the Republican Whip and a fellow Illinoisan, my reaction was to say: "Why are you doing this to me? I thought that we were friends." I accepted the appointment with a promise that Les would help me get a committee of my choice later. I never asked for another committee and served on Education & Labor for almost 19 years.

Within a few years, I became the ranking Republican on the General Labor subcommittee of Education & Labor. That committee was chaired by John Dent (D-PA), who enjoyed travel and arranged several trips which I joined. The subcommittee also soon began to consider pension law reform proposals. The topic was arcane and difficult. It required a commitment of time to attend many hearings and to study the subject so one could address the topic in a meaningful way. For at least five or six years, the committee spent part of its time on this subject. Although the initial proposals were controversial, as we progressed and the legislation was revised and expanded, a consensus was formed. Finally, the Employee Retirement Income Security Act of 1974 (ERISA) was enacted and signed into law. Because of my involvement over the years of its development, I was considered the House expert on the law. I continued my involvement with ERISA through oversight hearings. I was invited to speak to many groups with an interest in ERISA. When I retired from Congress in 1985, I joined the D.C. office of a national law firm and for almost ten years I practiced ERISA law and testified as an expert in litigation. Now in semi-retirement, I teach ERISA law at Georgetown University Law Center.

This may suffice to prove that if given a lemon, one can not only make lemonade but may learn to like it.

When I arrived in Congress in 1965, I was asked, along with the other Republicans, to state which committee assignments I would prefer. I identified the Judiciary and Interior committees. When the assignments were announced, I found myself on the House Administration and Government Operations committees. This was my introduction to the operation of the seniority system. Being one of the least senior members, my choices were not available to me. For a little over a year, I served on House Administration and learned much about the internal workings of the House. I left that committee to take the assignment to the Education & Labor Committee.

I had no idea what the Government Operations Committee jurisdiction might be. I learned that it was the principle oversight committee and also had jurisdiction over proposals to create new cabinet level departments. Soon after being appointed to the committee, I received an invitation to meet with Rep. Clarence Brown, Sr. (R-OH), who was the ranking Republican on the Government Operations Committee. Clarence advised me that he would like to appoint me to the Legislative and Executive Reorganization subcommittee. I accepted, not knowing one subcommittee from another. I suspected that it might be an important subcommittee when I discovered that the chairman and the ranking Republican of the committee were chair and ranking minority member on that subcommittee. There were only two Republicans on the subcommittee, Clarence and myself.

Soon after I joined the subcommittee, the Johnson administration proposed the creation of the Department of Housing and Urban Development (HUD). Before the bill to establish HUD was acted upon, Clarence was taken ill and died. Another Republican was appointed to the subcommittee. Although he had been in Congress and on the full committee longer than I, he was considered junior to me on the subcommittee. As a result, I became the ranking Republican on the subcommittee. When the bill was reported to the floor and debated, I was the manager of the bill for the Republicans. I also was the manager in the conference committee and on the floor for consideration of the conference report. Chance and the traditional authority of a ranking member combined to give me an opportunity to participate in the legislative process to a much greater extent than most other first term members. HUD was followed in short order by the Department of Transportation (DOT) and the Office of Management and Budget (OMB). I had the privilege of managing those bills as well.

HUMOR AS A LEAVENING

After my nomination to run for Congress, my law partner had an occasion to visit Washington. While there, he attended a committee meeting in the House. Upon his return, he told me of his impressions. One comment was about Rep. John Lindsay (R-NY). He noted that Lindsay had a good sense of humor. This surprised me, as I had thought of a committee meeting as a very serious undertaking.

During my service in Congress, I learned how important a sense of humor was. The nature of the legislative process is to be adversarial. It is all too easy to continue in that mode even after the need no longer exists. Even while being adversarial, one need not be antagonistic. It is altogether possible to disagree without being disagreeable. A sense of humor can make one easier to take while engaged in disagreement. Self deprecating humor is often the best. You don't have to take yourself too seriously.

In recent years, election campaigns have become more and more negative. Many members have been elected as a result of running down their opponent more than advertising their own good qualities. There is a tendency to carry over this attitude into the day-by-day relations with other members with whom one disagrees. It should not be necessary to accuse one of your colleagues of base motives just because he or she has taken a position opposite to yours. Especially in committee, but also on the floor, a little humor can defuse the emotions when the debate tends to become hot. My observation has been that other members appreciate those who can make us laugh or smile rather than grit our teeth. Leavening makes the bread rise and be light. Humor is the leavening that lightens the moment and helps the member rise in the estimation of his or her colleagues.

CONCLUSION

There are many things that go into the making of a successful legislator. The willingness to work hard, to play with the hand that is dealt to you without undue complaint, and to become an expert in the estimation of your colleagues are some of the most important. If you serve long enough, you may become a chair or ranking member of a committee or subcommittee. Seniority plays a very important part in reaching that level. But a title does not make one a leader. A ranking member must master the legislative process, have leadership qualities, and be respectful of his or her fellow members' viewpoints and needs. It helps as well to have good relations with the leadership on the other side of the political aisle. The ability to negotiate and compromise, while always keeping your core values intact, can lead to defusing an otherwise confrontational situation. I have noted that a person in leadership who could help other members avoid controversial votes which might come back to haunt them in the next election was admired. When all is taken into consideration, it becomes apparent that the qualities that make a good person and one who is admired are the same qualities that distinguish a good legislator.

Chapter 27

Power in the U.S. House and the Florida State Senate

Harry A. Johnston (D-Florida)

I have experienced two major changes in my career since I first became a legislator in 1974. The first was my voluntary move from the Florida State Senate, where I concluded service in 1986, to the United States Congress, which I entered in 1988; and the second was my involuntary move from the majority party to the minority party in the U.S. House of Representatives. Each of these changes exposed me to vastly different worlds in terms of power and responsibilities, and both reveal truths about these institutions and those who serve within them.

Clearly, the greatest power I have ever exercised was vested in me as president of the Florida Senate. I was essentially omnipotent. I commanded a staff of 200, selected all committee members and chairmen, hired all committee staff, assigned bills, and had final say over all questions of jurisdiction. While one might question any individual's wielding such authority in a democracy, I would make one observation: the trains ran on time.

It is custom in Florida that each Senate president serve only one two-year term. Clearly, this is a check on such broad authority; however, it is perceived by political scientists as both a strength and a weakness of the system.

The Florida State Senate is considered by many to be one of the most effective legislatures in the country. As presiding officer from 1984 to 1986, my mandate was simply to maintain substantive continuity and the spirit of bipartisanship that had always characterized the Senate, and to insure that the appropriations bill was passed in a timely manner. I was successful largely because of the Senate staff. They were at the heart of this uncommon efficiency.

The staff of the Florida Senate is non-partisan. There is no Democratic, nor Republican, staff. The workforce is highly professional and serves both parties equally, offering judgment and skills as objectively as possible. Political decisions are made by politicians, and the honest appraisals and technical expertise of staff are valued above party litmus tests. In short, like major league umpires, the staff calls them as they see them. The institution is strengthened by their neutrality.

This system could not contrast more sharply with the inner workings of the U.S. House of Representatives. In Florida, the staff are employed by the institution itself. In Washington, they are employed by individual members and serve at the member's will. In the Florida legislature, the staff is party-neutral. In Washington, committee staff is political in nature, and partisan loyalty is rewarded. Each committee and subcommittee has two completely separate and competing staffs, the larger and more powerful of which is hired by the majority. Every decision, large or small, is formulated in a political context.

Like the members of Congress who hired them, congressional staff are driven by the political process. To their credit, many remain committed to their issues, even in this politically charged environment. Often, they lead their respective members through the minefield of political ramifications toward constructive and healthy compromise.

One of the serious drawbacks to this system of maintaining separate majority and minority staffs is that these professionals are forever defined in terms of their party affiliation, rather than in qualitative terms. A good example of this phenomenon arose during my chairmanship of the Africa Subcommittee and my subsequent surrender of that position when the Democrats lost power in 1994.

When I first became chairman, I committed myself to assembling a world-class staff with extensive Africa experience, so that our work would be informed, effective, and valuable. I paid little attention to the political leanings of the tens of candidates whom I interviewed. This outstanding group developed a reputation for excellence and legislative accomplishment on the Hill, throughout Washington, and in the Africa-conscious international community.

Still, when we lost the elections and the House in 1994, the new Africa Subcommittee chairman immediately fired my entire staff—not because they had done a bad job, but because they were not Republicans. These professionals were a representation of the 2,500 individuals who lost their jobs within weeks after the House changed hands. I cannot be self-righteous about the partisan process here. Perhaps I would have done the same thing, since partisanship breeds more of the same. But I know from experience, there is a better way. I hope one day, Washington will rely more on merit and less on political and personal relationships.

This system of political connections transcending merit or experience was brought home to me in another context with my first committee assignments. When I arrived in Congress in 1989, I was hell-bent on serving on the Banking Committee. After all, I had chaired the committee handling banking legislation in the Senate, had represented a number of banks in my legal profession, sat on bank boards, and had even served as chairman of a state bank advisory board. But I did not have the political influence or regional support to gain the sought-after banking slot. So much for relevant experience.

The irony is that my failure to achieve that assignment was my first real lucky break in Congress. The Banking Committee became among the most fractious and beleaguered of assignments. The savings and loan crisis and the fiscal nightmares we experienced nationally were played out on the committee, and I was grateful every day that I had dodged that bullet.

Furthermore, my consolation prize was appointment to the Foreign Affairs Committee, and no other committee could have yielded me more challenging and satisfying work. Because of a confluence of events that saw a dozen members more senior than I leave the committee over the next four years, I became chairman of the Africa Subcommittee after only two terms. And my tenure as chairman was among the most exciting professional and personal experiences of my life.

Let me offer just one unique example of the raw opportunity—the reach and breadth—provided to an individual who assumes the role of chairman of a subcommittee of the United States Congress. As Africa chair, I became interested in the agonizing crisis in Sudan where an Islamic government encouraged terrorism throughout the world and subjugated its own people, particularly southern Christians. The south, led by an Iowa-educated self-styled leader named John Garang, fought back guerilla-style and had some success in rallying their people against the government, in winning sporadic battles, and in forcing the government to respond.

During my first several months as chairman, a rival rebel group had developed, and war between the government and the rebels was being upstaged by war among the southern rebel factions themselves. The loss of life was devastating, and the splintering of the opposition was demoralizing to the Christians and welcomed by the northern Islamic government. It was at this juncture that I became involved.

Our subcommittee held hearings on the crisis in Sudan, bringing national attention to the outlaw nature of the government itself and the exportation of terrorists to Egypt, Algeria, and other African and European nations. We called John Garang to Washington to testify to the deteriorating situation, and we became acquainted.

Months later, I called John Garang again, and invited him, as well as his rival rebel leader, Riak Machar, to come to Washington to meet face to face to negotiate a cease-fire. They each balked, but ultimately accepted our invitation, and each arrived with his entourage to my small personal office in the Cannon House Office Building. Among Garang's supporters that evening was Manure Bol, a 7'6" professional basketball player for the Washington Bullets, who stooped under my door frame to enter the office.

We had invited the very best negotiators from the State Department, and at 4:00 o'clock, we began our marathon session. At 9:00 o'clock, this group of warring Sudanese rebels, State Department mediators, one member of Congress, and committee staff sat together eating Domino's Pizza, hammering out the language to achieve an end to killing. When we seemed close to resolution, arguments would erupt, and our progress evaporate. Finally, at midnight, I intentionally left the meeting, warning that a cease-fire among the parties was the only civilized and rational option left to the opposition, and that if this attempt to stop the killing failed, these men were culpable.

The next morning, a cease-fire document was signed and released to the international press. It held for over a year. Today, the south is united behind John Garang, and the battle with the northern government continues.

It was this nature of work on the Foreign Affairs Committee that demonstrated to me how much more exciting it is to be a member of Congress—even a freshman—than a member of a state legislature—even Senate president. Washington is not just the capital of the United States; it is the capital of the world; and as a member of Congress, I was able to see and to participate in some of the great events of the day: the fall of the Berlin wall, the collapse of the Soviet Union and communism, the advancement of peace in the Middle East, a cease-fire in southern Sudan, to name just a few. Through my experiences on the Foreign Affairs Committee, I better understand the prominent role that the United States plays in the world and the tremendous capacity that we have for influencing the future—for ourselves and for humanity.

So, if Washington is an exceedingly political place, where does one go for objective information? The answer is to one of the finest institutions in the entire country—the Library of Congress and its research arm, the Congressional Research Service (CRS). Unlike the Florida State Senate, or any state legislature that I know of, the Congress has vast resources to investigate the smallest details of any issue. And by law, this staff must be non-partisan and objective. Each researcher is literally an expert in his or her field with years of experience. That is why I bristle when I hear that members of Congress are "out of touch" or "don't have all the information" to make judgments. With one critical exception, which I will explain later, we have abundant and accurate information, and if we don't have specific details, we can get them within a matter of minutes.

During my first term in Congress, I was expected to vote on issues relating to the Alaska National Wildlife Refuge. Obviously, coming from Florida, this was not a subject that I knew much about. So I arranged to be briefed by a researcher from the Congressional Research Service. I still remember his sketching out the migration patterns of caribou on a large map of the Arctic Preserve, explaining with great clarity how these animals would be affected by the bill under consideration. I knew then that there was nothing too esoteric or too exotic for the Congressional Research Service, and that I was on a learning curve that reached beyond my imagination.

The one exception to the rule of accessible resources relates to the financial implications of legislation. In the Florida Senate, a fiscal impact statement was stapled to the back of every piece of legislation. In Congress, no such analysis is required, and even more disturbing, it is difficult, if not impossible, for an individual voting member to calculate impact in real terms.

It is important to note that the fiscal impact of a bill and how much a bill costs are two very different questions. I can always find out how much revenue would be generated or lost with the passage of a certain piece of legislation. However, other effects, like the change in property values in an impacted area, are more difficult to find and would only be revealed in a responsible fiscal impact statement.

Another contrast between my state and federal experience relates to the daily structure and schedule. In Florida, committee meetings took place in the morning, with the legislature meeting in full in the afternoon. Because of the bifurcated schedule, all legislators were able to participate in committee meetings, as well as legislative debate, and voting took place rapidly.

Washington works much differently. Your average member of Congress is a member of two full committees and four subcommittees. At any time, the entire House could be in session voting on legislation while simultaneously all four of a member's subcommittees could be holding hearings and casting votes. What results is the member's running from hearing to hearing, then heading off at any point for a vote on the floor of the House of Representatives without even knowing what has been debated.

At times, this "system" can become truly ridiculous. I remember attending a hearing during Desert Storm with the Secretary of State as our primary witness. Suddenly and unexpectedly, a vote was called on the floor dealing with an arcane procedural matter. The hearing on American policy in the Gulf War was recessed for over half an hour, during which time this principal policy maker was forced to sit idly and waste precious time. This is hardly an efficient way to conduct a legislative schedule—or to direct our foreign policy.

On a personal level, this type of chaos can lead to exhaustion and confusion for many members of Congress. During the first 100 days of the 104th Congress, when the Republicans were attempting to push through the notorious Contract for America, the legislative calendar was merciless, with committee hearings and the full House in session some 12 to 16 hours a day. One of my colleagues, a former professional football player, visited the House doctor, complaining about a variety of aches and pains. The doctor determined that he was victim of fatigue, and he was not alone. In fact, the physician informed him that he was the 60th member who had come in suffering from total exhaustion since the session had begun.

The toll that the illogical legislative schedule takes in the House of Representatives is unquestionably a high one at times. Members of Congress simply do not know the issues as well as they should, not because there is a lack of information, but because there is a lack of time. What results is that members are forced to rely on their staff much more than any legislator must in any of the state legislatures around the country. Members of Congress frequently vote when they are less than fully informed.

Yet, the changes experienced when I moved from the ordered world of the Florida State Senate to the more chaotic world of the U.S. Congress pale in comparison to the changes I endured in shifting from majority to minority party status in the Congress after the 1994 elections: I left Washington as "Mr. Chairman" and came back as Harry. In Washington, that is a big change.

In the U.S. Congress, the minority party does not legislate—it is that simple. At best, the minority may fine-tune legislation; at times, it slows down legislation, but it never plays an activist role in shaping the laws of the country. Even further, minority members play only a minor role in the most basic aspects of the Congress. For example, the minority plays no part in devising the legislative calendar and rarely knows what the schedule will look like in a week's time. Even a matter as mundane as scheduling rooms for hearings and functions is the domain of the majority party, and as a member of the minority, I was at the mercy of the most lowly clerk when I needed a room.

For two successive Congresses, I chaired an annual U.S.-Canadian Inter-parliamentary meeting at which members of our respective legislative bodies discussed matters of mutual and historical concern to our two nations. When the Republicans gained control of the House in 1994, it became their prerogative to appoint whomever they wanted to attend this conference. Thus, although I expressed my desire to attend and was selected by my party leaders to represent them, and although I was the only candidate with the institutional and historical memory and substantive background to forward the U.S. goals, I was subject to the whim of the now dominant Republican majority. At the last minute, they allowed me to represent my colleagues, but not without my dangling in the wind for a while.

I should not complain. Democrats treated Republicans equally badly during their time in the majority. This is far from the bi-partisan atmosphere that I experienced in the Florida State Senate, where all voices were heard and everyone could play an active role in devising legislation.

Part Six

The Member's Environment: Interest Groups, Constituents, and the Media

Members of Congress do not operate in a vacuum. The chapters in this section focus on the forces outside the House that impinge on the life of a legislator: interest groups, constituents, and the representatives of the news media.

Lou Frey leads off this section by answering a series of questions young people have asked him over the years: Why are there typically so few members present on the floor of the House, and why are those on the floor not listening? Who are the members really speaking to? How do they decide how to vote? Do constituents really pay attention to how you voted? How do interest groups rate members, and has anyone ever tried to bribe you? These questions have a common denominator inasmuch as they all concern practical aspects of representation.

In the following chapter, Orval Hansen provides an enlightening treatment of how legislators interpret the mail they receive from constituents. Hansen discusses the members' attitudes and practices relating to constituent mail, the factors that affect its influence on legislative decisions, and the utility of organized mail campaigns sponsored by special interest groups.

G. William Whitehurst discusses the activities of lobbies and political action committees from the perspective of a former member of Congress. Whitehurst argues that, although lobbyists sometimes make clumsy attempts to pressure legislators, they nevertheless serve a useful purpose in the legislative process. He provides case studies of lobbying by the defense lobby, foreign lobbyists, and the National Rifle Association, concluding with a discussion of the rise of political action committees and the prospects for meaningful campaign finance reform.

Bert Levine, a former lobbyist for Johnson and Johnson, suggests that "what lobbyists do is not always what journalists and the public think that they do." In particular, Levine calls our attention to what he calls "soft behavior responses": requests by lobbyists for favors–short of overt support for legislation—that have an indirect, but nevertheless significant, effect on political and policy outcomes. Soft behavior responses have many advantages for lobbyists: they are legal, they typically require the cooperation of a small number of legislators or staff members, and they are often undisclosed to the public.

Finally, the dangers—and opportunities—posed for members by the news media are discussed in two chapters by Otis Pike and Lou Frey.

Chapter 28

Questions People Ask Me about Representation

Lou Frey, Jr. (R-Florida)

I had never run for political office when I was elected to Congress. I was a Republican, 33 years of age, running in an overwhelmingly Democratic district, with no name recognition and no money. I won by going door-to-door for 13 months, knocking on over 30,000 doors in my district. I was the fourth Republican elected to the United States Congress since reconstruction, and ended up the last time I ran carrying my district by close to 80 percent. I give you this brief background in order for you to understand that I never took being in Congress for granted and, although I reached the Republican leadership in Congress, I was always slightly in awe of the fact that I actually was a congressman. It was a privilege to serve in the Congress. I truly love the institution. It bothers me that so few people understand how it works or even care.

Because of my lack of knowledge about Washington, I started an intern program during my first year whereby seniors in a high school in my district would elect someone to come and stay with me for eight days in Washington. I also taught in every high school in my district. I had approximately 400 young people come during my ten years in Congress, and numerous other students and families visited my office. Since that time, I have taught in colleges and continue to teach in high schools and sometimes junior high schools. It is interesting to me that, over the years, many of the same questions are asked about the Congress by visitors to Washington, D.C. Let me share with you some of these questions and the answers that I have given over the years.

EXPLAINING WHAT YOU SEE FROM THE GALLERIES

When young people come to Washington and see the Congress in action, the first questions they ask are: "Why are there so few people?" and "Why are those on the floor not listening?" There are 100 senators, 435 members of the House, yet when visitors are in the gallery, on a normal day, there are very few senators on the floor of the Senate and not many more members on the floor of the House. They further observe many of the members on the floor talking to each other, apparently not listening to the debate and generally appearing uninterested in what's happening on the floor.

My answer to the young people follows. To begin with, most members have multiple committees, with the senators having more of a problem than House members. The committees usually meet in the mornings, but many times, when legislation is being debated, they will meet after lunch, if permission has been granted. Also, members have many duties to attend to in their office. They have to work with their staff to develop legislative proposals. They have to read and respond to letters and to telephone calls. They have constituents coming into town who want to see them and have the right to see them. They meet with lobbyists. They have to spend time meeting with other members trying to lobby them regarding their legislative proposals, or listening to someone else's proposals.

Floor attendance depends on the particular legislation being debated. When a bill comes to the floor of Congress, a committee report is printed, which comes out ahead of time and is available to every member. Someone on the legislative staff usually digests this for the member and gives him or her a summary. Each party puts out information on the bill. For instance, the Republican conference may take a position and send this to each Republican member. The Republican Research Committee, of which I was chairman, will take certain bills and send extensive information to members. Other members who are for or against the bill will circulate letters and information regarding the legislation. If it is an important bill, lobbyists on both sides of the issue will be in the member's office talking to staff and, whenever possible, the member, about the bill. Other times, members personally will lobby for or against the bill, catching you on the floor, in the hall, at lunch, or even working out in the gym. Most of the time, very little new is said on the floor about the legislation being debated. Most of the congressmen that are not there understand the issues because of all the information available. Also, members can watch the debate on C-SPAN from their office or committee room.

Usually, the people on the floor are the committee members who have handled the bill from its inception through the committee process and onto the floor. They have debated these issues and each other for the public, and for the press. They may not pay attention because they have heard the speech before, or they know the member and the member's philosophy and know what he or she is going to say. Most of the time, it is not a lack of interest, but the fact that they are otherwise occupied, have done their homework, and already have made up their mind as to how they are going to vote way before the debate on the floor.

Of course, there are exceptions to every rule, and when issues come up which are dramatic and important, the floor will be crowded. I have seen occasions where members have been swayed by the oratory on the floor, but that is happening less and less.

WHO ARE THE MEMBERS REALLY SPEAKING TO?

Another frequently asked question is, "If those present on the floor are not listening when members make speeches, who is their audience?" Their audience can range from a single individual to the United Nations. Sometimes, members are speaking to the whole Congress to stake out a position early and avoid unnecessary lobbying. Sometimes, they are speaking to members of their committee or subcommittee, to the administration, or to an independent agency. Sometimes, a member's real target is the people of his district or his state, or a constituent group within the district, such as senior citizens. In this regard, a member may aim remarks at a particular industry; for example, as a member of the space committee, I sometimes directed my remarks at those in the space industry. A member also may give a speech to establish legislative history on a bill. Finally, a member may want to send a message overseas, for example, a Florida member condemning Castro.

HOW DO YOU DECIDE HOW TO VOTE?

Another question frequently asked of me is, "How do you vote?" "As a member from Florida, must you vote as your district or state feels?" There is no one answer to this question, but here is my response.

The congressional system is built around two parties—today, the Republican and Democrat parties. There have been spasmodic attempts to form third parties, but they have not gotten very far. Some members have been elected as Independents, but they usually decide to work with one of the two main parties in order to get committee assignments. The recent public financing of presidential campaigns, coupled with the requirements of a certain vote total and dollar amounts to receive funding, makes it even tougher today to form a third party.

However, legislators do not always vote party lines. Unlike the British parliamentary system, which is built on strict party discipline, our system is much more freewheeling. In the parliamentary system, the majority either hang together or lose power. Here, by contrast, the government does not fall if a key issue is voted down. Furthermore, the executive branch is not composed of members of the Congress as in parliament.

Given this latitude, there are many reasons why a member may not vote with his or her party. One of the primary reasons is that a member may feel a greater allegiance to his or her district than to a national party. In many cases, individuals are elected who were not supported by the party machinery. Also, most members have strong egos and believe that they won the election despite the party and without much help from the party.

You also have various views on how a member should vote. Some would argue that a member should see what the people in the district want and vote that way, as the member is elected to represent the people. Others would argue that the voters expect the member to exercise judgment and to vote intelligently. The safeguard is that a House member must stand for reelection every two years, and thus can be replaced easily when he or she is out of line with the district.

There is no real answer to the above debate, which has gone on for years, and, of course, there are different degrees of "voting your district." Some people will argue that on issues that are minor and are not important to the member philosophically, the member will be more influenced by what the people in the district think. On major policy issues, however, which are basic to the member's reason for being in politics, the member will follow his or her conscience. Most members will agree that you can't "bleed on every issue" and that with close to 1,000 recorded votes a year, you have to pick and choose where you are willing to fight.

Once you get past the philosophical approach to problems, other factors enter in, such as geography, philosophy, sex, race, age, and interest groups. In numerous cases in the past 30 years, a majority of Republicans and southern Democrats have banded together to either pass a bill or sustain a veto, taking the more conservative position from the vast majority of Democrats in the House. You will find many issues that sometimes divide the sun belt from the rust belt, or in energy areas, the oil producing states from the oil consuming states. Most recently, we have had issues which have been defined as women's, environmental, or black issues. There are more and more caucus or issue groups in the Congress, where you may find the tourist caucus or the agricultural caucus working for a particular bill.

Personally, I believed that I was elected as a member of Congress to serve under the Constitution of the United States. My oath was not to a party, district, or state, but to the country. I tried to look at issues in a national light, but that national light was always filtered by who I was, my family background, where I lived, where I went to school, and how I made my living. You can't vote in isolation. You are a product of your background and your time.

For instance, I grew up in a geographic area where the space program was important; I had a background in navy aviation and a belief that science was an important part of our life. I supported the space program because I believed it was in the national interest. However, I can understand why someone from the inner city of Chicago, where poverty was the most important problem, could vote against the space program.

I remember a speech in which I said it is easy to vote right when you know what is right. It would be wonderful if there was a book where you could go down the list and see exactly how you should vote on every issue. But it does not work that way. There are many votes that I made that I know were right, some where I was wrong, and some where I'm still not sure. In conclusion, each member has an individual answer to this question of how to vote. If the member can look in the mirror and see someone who tried to do what was right, the system will function well.

DO CONSTITUENTS REALLY KNOW HOW YOU VOTED?

I was frequently asked whether people really knew or cared how I voted. The answer is generally no. There can be nearly 1,000 recorded votes per year in the House of Representatives, plus many more in the committees and subcommittees, many of which are not recorded and are probably the most important votes. Sometimes, on a major issue, your vote will hit the headline, especially if it is a close vote. Also, in a campaign, your opponent, who has researched your entire record, will bring up votes that you made if he thinks it can hurt you. Furthermore, various interest groups will rate you based on a very few votes to make you look either better or worse than you are, depending on their particular philosophy.

Unless you are totally out of touch with your district, your voting record will not stop you from being reelected. I found that the key to reelection was not my voting record, but the personal constituency services performed by my office or me. Most members have offices in the district, keyed to constituent services, such as helping with medicare, medicaid, veteran's benefits, social security, small business, passports, etc. We never turned a request away, even if it was about a local problem, such as zoning. My staff was conditioned to look at a request from a constituent as an opportunity to help. The better the job they did for the constituents, the better job security they had. This was the case of doing good while doing well.

The question of my voting record was driven home to me after my first campaign. I was an unknown, without money, and a Republican in a heavily Democratic district. I went door-to-door for 13 months and eventually ended up by winning with approximately 65 percent of the vote. It was my belief that I won basically on the issues, such as a strong national defense, cutting taxes, and help for our service people in Vietnam. However, a survey taken after the election found that many people voted for me simply because I knocked on their door. To some, I looked like their grandson. Others knew my wife from little league, did business with my dad, had kids that went to school or church with mine, or had served in the navy like I did. A few had played ball with or against me. Some merely saw that I was working hard and looked like I needed a job.

Over the years, I kept up these personal contacts, not just during campaign time, but all year long. In fact, the day after reelection, I was visible all over the district. This stood me in good stead when I was in the Republican leadership during the Watergate scandal. In the 1974 election, after Nixon resigned and was subsequently pardoned by Gerald Ford, my district had high unemployment and I still won more than 70 percent of the vote, not on my voting record, but rather on my personal relationship with the people in my district.

DID YOU EVER GET NASTY LETTERS?

Yes, of course. Letters pour into a congressional office. The amount can vary tremendously. If a particular issue is hot, such as Vietnam or health care, you can get hundreds of letters a day. All letters will be looked at by the office staff. Form letters or petitions were usually put into one stack and the handwritten or individual letters in another stack. I would read one of the form letters or petitions and glance at how many were sent. Normally, I would read all of the individually written letters and would write a response. We would write a form response to the form letters.

I asked my staff to pull out the most negative letters each day. I would try to make five calls a day, usually in the early evening hours. The idea was not to change the individuals' minds, but to let them know that I had read their letters, appreciated their opinion, but had legitimate reasons for disagreeing with them. When the calls were made, the first reaction was disbelief that I was calling—then surprise and pleasure. By the end of each conversation, I had neutralized the writer and often made a friend as well. The key was caring enough to take the time to discuss the issue.

It was tough to make these calls. Some days it was a lot tougher than others, and some days I was too tired and emotionally drained to make the calls. But when I did make the calls, they paid off. Not only did the calls establish a connection with the immediate family of the person I called, but those I spoke with would usually tell all their neighbors and fellow workers that their friend, Lou, had called and talked with them at home.

HOW DO INTEREST GROUPS RATE HOUSE MEMBERS?

Each session, a countless host of groups with confusing acronyms, such as the Americans for Constitutional Action (ACA), the Americans for Democratic Action (ADA), the League of Women Voters, and the American Association of Retired Persons (AARP), review the voting records and purport to give an unbiased analysis. A mixed bag of key votes are assembled and, presto, an instant analysis emerges. The media headlines the results and, in some cases, their impact on elections can be crucial.

Despite the media attention, the great majority of ratings are of minimal value. Some polls which masquerade under appealing labels are little more than shorthand efforts to elect or defeat a congressman over a particular viewpoint. Ratings focus on a minuscule portion of a member's voting record. Conclusions can be drawn which may, indeed, be overly favorable or unfavorable to a member's position. Moreover, ratings cast no light on a member's responsiveness to constituents, legislative ability, or integrity.

The most frustrating part of the entire "rating game" is that the media and the public often remain unaware of the issue preferences which underpin the various rating organizations. Rarely does the media focus any attention either on the structural validity of the rating in question or the ideological predisposition of the sponsoring organization. Widespread media coverage imparts an unwarranted legitimacy to rating results which reaffirms the public's view of ratings as somehow independently nonpolitical and impartial. I can remember being rated close to 100 percent by the National Alliance of Senior Citizens and given a very low rating (20 percent) by the National Council of Senior Citizens. How could this be? Very simply. The National Alliance of Senior Citizens was a Republican-oriented organization. Part of their votes at the time included a vote on common situs picketing, the Agency for Consumer Protection, and Aid to New York City, none of which directly affected the senior organizations. However, the National Council of Senior Citizens, Inc., was a Democrat-run organization; their ten votes included the emergency conservation and oil policy, community action programs, and the emergency job appropriations veto vote. My opponent trumpeted the fact that I had failed senior citizens, while I emphasized the fact that I had nearly a perfect voting record and had been voted into the Senior Citizens Hall of Fame. What this tells you is: Don't take as gospel what you read in the newspaper. See who the rating organization is, how many votes are involved, and what their particular bias happens to be. It would be nice if rating organizations were responsible; however, they are organizations pushing their own political philosophy. Fairness is not a key element of what they do.

HAS ANYBODY EVER TRIED TO BRIBE YOU?

It is somewhat a sad fact that most people feel that, being in Washington, you are going to be sitting in smoke-filled rooms where everybody is wearing dark glasses and flashing money around. My answer, in a semi-serious vein, was that I was never important enough to be offered a bribe. The fact is that in Washington, there are plenty of ways that members can be tempted. We have some obvious examples of outright criminal behavior, such as happened in Abscam or Koreagate, just to mention two. But there are many other ways people try to influence how a member votes, and many of these ways are legitimate.

The vast majority of the time, people in the district will write, call, or speak up at a meeting in the district, putting forth their particular viewpoints. This is much more effective than signing a petition. Also, lobbyists who represent different viewpoints will come by and brief you and your staff, both at home and in Washington. The good ones stick with the facts and outline their position clearly and concisely. However, there are many subtle and some not-so-subtle ways that a member can at least be softened up. In some cases, lobbyists will invite members to eat, to see sporting events, or even to travel. The rules regarding this have been tightened up recently, but somehow or other, members and the lobbyists turn up at the same functions. A lobbyist can help a member indirectly by contributing to his campaign, by contributing to his favorite charity, or by helping bring business to his district or state. Corporations even will go to the extent of finding old friends in the industry to come and present their position. In my case, when I introduced the bill that called for the divestiture of AT&T, one of my close friends (and a fraternity brother at Colgate University), who worked for AT&T, was asked to come from Long Island and present AT&T's case to me. At the same time, one of the officers of AT&T in the state of Florida stayed in Washington to monitor the legislation. In my office, he was called "the donut man," as usually once a week or so he stopped by and brought donuts for the staff. No matter what AT&T did, however, my position didn't change.

Washington is the toughest political league going. You have to set your own rules, which people learn about and respect. For instance, if you are one who likes to be entertained, go out and attend receptions, or go to the embassy parties, there will be plenty of opportunities available. If you happen to be someone who likes to play golf or tennis, somehow or other the word gets out and that also will be available. And I am sure if you like members of the opposite sex, somehow or other that could become part of the equation.

However, if you did not want to participate, that word also gets around. I had a rule that I would talk with anybody, but the timing was mine. When someone wanted to talk, I usually would suggest an early morning breakfast to see if they really were interested. About 75 percent of the time, people who allegedly wanted to meet decided that they had conflicts. Yet no one could say that I was avoiding them and was not available.

I had only one incident in my time in Congress that could have put me in a bad position; it involved a pastor of a church in my district. I had previously helped several denominations obtain federal funding to build senior citizen homes. A pastor from a Protestant Church came to my office to see me and said, "I understand you are the one to see about getting senior citizen housing built. We'll be glad to take care of you." I said, "Wait a minute, Pastor," and called my secretary, Ann Pickett, into my office. I said, "Ann, Pastor X probably did not exactly mean what he just said but, for the record, let me tell you what my reply is. My reply is that in my job, I don't want anything, I don't take anything, and hopefully there was a misunderstanding on his part, but that is not the way I work or the way things work in Washington."

Four years later, when I was thinking of running statewide in Florida, an FBI agent with whom I had worked regarding drug legislation came into my office. He was highly agitated and said that he had to talk to me, as a complaint had been filed that I was attempting to extort money from a church to build a senior citizen high-rise. My face turned white for about five seconds, and then I remembered the incident and the memo I dictated. I called Ann and asked her to bring in the memo that we had filed away four years before. We gave it to the FBI agent who said, "Boy, am I glad you have files. I'll take care of that blank, blank, blank." This illustrates two points: One, you have to be extra careful in politics, and two, you have to document what's going on.

In conclusion, a member is open to all kinds of pressures, some direct, some subtle, and some indirect. You must always be alert to what is going on around you. It truly is living in a glass bowl. Above all, you must remember that you have to deal not with what it is, but with what people think it is. Perception in politics equals reality.

Chapter 29

The Role of Mail in Decisions in Congress

Orval Hansen (R-Idaho)

Our constituents often ask whether writing to us serves any useful purpose. We respond reassuringly that it does. When they ask whether their letters have any influence on our votes on legislation our answer is a more qualified "yes." Some do and some don't. The next question is more difficult: What kinds of letters are more likely to influence votes? And why? We have learned that some do affect our votes while others are a waste of time and effort.

Finding the answers to these questions became the goal of my doctoral research. While still serving in the House of Representatives, I began my studies leading to a Ph.D. in political science at the George Washington University. I completed those studies and received my degree in 1986.

My dissertation research required a review of the published literature on the subject of mail to members of Congress and, more specifically, the role of the mail in their decisions on legislation. Much has been written about congressional mail, including its effect on specific votes. I was surprised, however, to learn that the published research did not include any in depth studies of the many factors and circumstances that affect the influence of mail on decisions in Congress. That became the central purpose of my doctoral research.

To learn how mail influenced their decisions, I talked to the members themselves. I conducted extensive interviews with a sample of 21 members of the House of Representatives from both parties and all regions of the country, including some of the most senior and the most junior members. These were supplemented by surveys of a large number of congressional offices to determine how they processed incoming and outgoing mail. At the time of this study, the mid-1980s, computers were being widely used to process incoming mail and to produce outgoing mail. Since that time, however, we have seen the rapid growth of the use of computer technology to send e-mail messages to members of Congress. The effect of this new form of communication with members is, therefore, not reflected in my study. It is an appropriate subject for future research. I would speculate, however, that the validity of the earlier findings has not been materially altered by the addition of e-mail to the other forms of mail to members of Congress. Its influence probably is affected by the same factors that determine the influence of other forms of mail.

This report will briefly summarize the findings in three major areas of the study: (a) the members' attitudes and practices relating to their mail; (b) the factors that affect its influence on legislative decisions; and (c) the utility of organized mail campaigns sponsored by interest groups.

HOW MEMBERS USE THEIR MAIL

Do members read their mail? Practices vary greatly from a lot to almost none. The study revealed a correlation between the length of service and the time spent reading the mail. One may speculate that more senior members with heavier responsibilities are able to devote less time to the mail than recently elected members. The reverse turned out to be the case. The most senior members gave more personal attention to the mail than their more junior colleagues. This could suggest that reading the mail enhances a member's reelection prospects. I believe that a better explanation for this disparity is that the mail reading practices of senior members were probably established at a time when there was less mail and most of it came from individuals rather than as part of an organized mail campaign. A less demanding schedule enabled members to devote more personal time to constituent concerns, including the mail.

While there were differences in the amount of mail they read, their attitudes toward the mail were remarkably uniform. They welcomed and often actively solicited mail from their constituents. They expressed keen interest in the mail and knew a great deal about what was in it.

Mail is valued by members for three main reasons. First, it helps them to be better representatives of their constituents. Second, it helps them get reelected. Third, in some cases, it is useful in reaching a decision on how to vote on a legislative issue.

Mail helps to reinforce the member's role as the representative of the constituency. It is the most important communications link with the constituency. As one member put it, mail helps him to "keep a finger on the pulse of the district." It provides useful guidance as they strive to speak and act for the people they represent. It alerts them to special problems and needs. One member cited the example of an elderly woman who wrote to him on the back of a church bulletin with no return address. She wrote that she was down to 70 pounds, that she had no food or fuel, and would commit suicide if she did not get help soon. The member tracked her down through the minister of the church, who was able to bring food and other assistance, and the congressman was able to help her with a social security problem.

Members said they often first become aware of an issue through the mail. Requests for assistance through the mail often lead to case work to help individuals who have become frustrated by their inability to get a response from the government. It enables them to serve the role of the ombudsman. Mail is also useful in planning communications to constituents and in setting the agenda for meetings in the district.

In addition, mail is valued as a powerful reelection tool. Those interviewed did not emphasize the political value of their mail, but their comments left no doubt of its usefulness in building support for reelection. Writing to a member enhances his name identification with the public. The greatest value of an incoming letter, however, is the opportunity it provides to send a response. When asked if he encourages constituents to write, one member said, "Oh, yes, it's nice to have 30,000 letters going out to them." Another described with pride his computerized system. He sends an initial response to a constituent letter and follow-up letters whenever there was some new development relating to the issue. He said this may result in eight or nine letters to the constituent by the time there was final action on the issue. Incoming mail is widely used to build mailing lists for future use.

Mail is valued less as a guide to voting decisions, but it can be useful in some situations. Among its limitations for this purpose is that it is not an accurate barometer of opinion in the district. Letter writers are often a biased sample of the constituency. The distortion occurs because a disproportionate amount comes from those at the higher socio-economic levels and an increasing amount is promoted by interest groups. The distortion increases with volume. One member said that a dozen letters from throughout the district that are not connected are probably a better barometer of opinion in the district than a thousand letters that are similar and are obviously motivated by a single source.

HOW DOES MAIL AFFECT DECISIONS IN CONGRESS?

Some decisions in Congress are influenced by the mail. All those interviewed said mail was among the sources of influence they weigh in deciding how to vote. All said they want to know about their mail on an issue before voting. Most identified specific votes which were either the direct result of the mail they received or that were strongly influenced by the mail. They were asked to describe the specific characteristics of the mail itself and other circumstances relating to the decision that increased or decreased the influence of the mail. Their responses identified and evaluated the following factors:

(a) *Source.* Where a letter comes from is important. There must be a constituency connection. Highest value is placed on mail from the member's district. Next is mail from outside the district but within the state. Such mail may reflect the views of the member's constituents on issues of statewide interest. One may speculate that members of the House of Representatives who are contemplating a future bid for statewide office such as governor or senator are more likely to welcome and pay attention to mail from throughout the state.

Another category of the mail from outside the district that often receives close attention is that from an organization whose members include some of the congressman's constituents. Such organizations often maintain voting records on issues of importance to them, which they publicize through magazines, bulletins, newsletters, and other means. Mail from recognized authorities on a subject outside the district is often valued by members who have developed a "national constituency" in a particular area.

(b) *Writer*. All letter writers are not equal. Greater weight is given to persons whose political support is important to the congressman and to those, as noted, who have recognized expertise on a subject. These include campaign supporters and contributors, public officials, and officials or organizations with members residing in the district that provide political support through active involvement in election campaigns or through political contributions. Mail from these sources is also more likely to come to the personal attention of the member.

(c) *Form*. Individual letters are clearly favored over form letters. Letters that were apparently composed by the sender carry much more weight than those which are identical or similar in form and were obviously promoted by an interest group. Whether it is handwritten or typed apparently makes little difference. One member described a mailing of individual letters that were similar in content which he discounted because all misspelled his name in exactly the same way.

(d) *Content*. The overwhelming preference is for a letter that states the writer's position, contains pertinent facts and analysis, and any relevant personal experiences. The nature of the writer's interest in the outcome of the issue is an important consideration, i.e., whether it reflects only a narrow personal interest or a broader public interest. Short letters confined to one subject are preferred. Those that reflect an obvious bias are discounted. A courteous and respectful letter is more likely to invoke a thoughtful response than one that is demanding or threatening. "Hate mail" and letters that impugn the integrity or motives of the member may be answered, but are almost always discounted in the congressman's decisions. A letter that reflects the informed views of one who appears to understand the issue is valued much more than one that echoes the views of those who are orchestrating the mail.

(e) *Issue*. The influence of the mail varies greatly with the issue. Greater weight is given to the mail that deals with "pocketbook" issues, i.e., those with economic consequences that have a direct effect on a large number of people, and to those that stir strong emotions, e.g., abortion, prayer in schools, and gun control. The consensus of those interviewed was voiced by one member who said that the letters on the issues he pays the most attention to are "...the ones that are gut issues, that you know the people are going to remember and, if they are mad at you, they're going to get back at you." The salience or visibility of the issue also affects the influence of the mail. A highly salient issue increases the probability that the member's votes will be known to and remembered by many of his constituents. A letter on an issue that touches the writer in a direct and personal way is more influential than one dealing with a more abstract issue that does not affect the writer personally. Letters on economic issues, for example, are generally given more weight than those dealing with foreign policy.

f) *Volume*. The influence of the mail is likely to increase with volume, but the relationship is not linear. If the mail consists entirely of form letters and printed postcards, a higher volume has little effect on its influence. However, the weight assigned to individual letters that appear to be spontaneous, reflect informed opinions, and come from all parts of the district increases greatly as the volume grows.

(g) *Past Votes and Expertise*. The member himself is a factor in the influence of the mail. He is less likely to be moved by his mail from a position on a recurring issue where he has a well established position than one on which he has not yet taken a position. Those voting on an issue for the first time are more likely to be influenced by the mail. Similarly, a member who has become an expert on certain issues is less likely to be influenced by the mail than those who have limited understanding or experience with the subject.

ORGANIZED MAIL CAMPAIGNS

Interest groups have been part of the political scene since the earliest days of the Republic. James Madison referred to them as "factions" working against the rights of others in *The Federalist Papers* in 1788. In recent years, the number of interest groups has mushroomed. Mail promoted by these groups to support grass roots lobbying is the largest and fastest growing fraction of the total volume of mail to members of Congress. The expanded use of mail as a lobbying tool has coincided with the growth in the number of organizations engaged in lobbying and the migration of many of these organizations to Washington, D.C.

There has been a shift in strategy to make greater use of constituency ties and the pressure of constituency opinion. Mail has become a key to interest group lobbying. Mail from this source may be distinguished from much of the other congressional mail in two respects. First, its purpose is clear and unambiguous – to influence specific decisions in Congress. Second, it is viewed as a pressure tactic rather than as a means for constituents to communicate their views, concerns, and attitudes which members welcome and find useful. Members show little enthusiasm for mail from organized campaigns, but its increased use as a lobbying tool suggests that its sponsors believe it can be effective in influencing decisions in Congress.

While all those interviewed said they encourage constituent mail, none expressed a desire to receive mass mailings from interest groups. The main value of such mail to them is the opportunity it provides to send letters in response and add the names to their mailing lists. They were generally critical of organized mail campaigns. They concede, however, that they are not without influence. They cited instances when they have changed individual votes and affected the outcome of decisions on legislation in Congress.

For the most part, the same factors that affect the influence of mail generally are applicable to organized mail campaigns. There are some differences, however, in the relative importance and the weight assigned to these factors. There must be a constituency connection. It must appear that there is a broad base of public support within the constituency or among members of particular groups within the constituency. A large volume is essential. Influence increases if it expresses the sentiments of the senders on salient issues that are important to them and if it is promoted by an organization that is active in election campaigns.

There are inherent limitations to the effectiveness of organized mail campaigns. They are seen to represent a biased sample of the constituency and as being motivated by the sponsoring organization rather than individuals. These limitations can be overcome if certain other factors are present. To borrow from a phenomenon in nuclear physics, a combination of these factors may create a "critical mass" which may be expressed in the following formula: Critical mass = volume plus one or more of the following: (a) issue salience; (b) emotional or "pocketbook" issue; (c) many individual letters in addition to form letters; and (d) an organization that is active in election campaigns.

The issue must be *salient* or highly visible to increase the probability that the public or the members of the group on whose behalf the mail is being sent are aware of the issue and will know how the congressman voted. The most effective mailings involve issues that affect the economic well being of the writer, e.g., Social Security, or that arouse an emotional response reflecting deeply felt religious or ideological convictions, e.g., right-to-life or school prayer.

If much of the mail is *individually composed* even though it was obviously inspired by the sponsoring organization, this shows that many constituents are aware of the issue, support the position of the sponsoring organization, and were motivated to write their own letters.

The sponsoring organization must be involved in *election campaigns* through endorsements and/or financial contributions or other campaign support. Single issue interest groups are often criticized by members, but the mail from these groups receives attention and influences votes to the extent that they are able to reward their friends and punish their enemies at the polls. The organization most frequently mentioned as being highly effective in the use of mail to promote its legislative agenda was the National Rifle Association. Others include "pro-life" groups, environmental organizations, and some business groups. They described specific lobbying efforts by these groups which had been effective in mobilizing congressional support for their positions through well planned and skillfully executed mail campaigns. However, they described with barely disguised contempt mailings that were a total waste of time and effort. These include printed postcards that are often sent from the organization's headquarters in the names of its members. They noted one potential benefit from organized mail campaigns. Efforts by interest groups to educate their members and the public may contribute to a better understanding of the issues.

Has the growth in the volume of mail from organized campaigns diminished the value of mail generally? Does the letter from the individual get lost in the shuffle and get overlooked? Apparently not. Members said quality still counts more than quantity and the individual letter still receives attention. The most effective organizations are those that are able to enlist the support of their members, provide them with relevant facts, and motivate them to write their own letters to their congressman. The effect of organized mail campaigns on the overall role of mail in decision making has been minimal.

Can money buy influence in Congress through mass mailings? Apparently not in most cases, but in a few instances, it can make a difference. Some organizations measure the success of their effort by the number of mailings delivered to congressional offices. Members reject this reasoning. Mass mailings are often a waste of money. In a few cases, however, votes may be changed if the issue is highly salient and members of a large or important segment of the electorate are motivated to write individual letters.

A few organizations are taking a more sophisticated approach to grass roots lobbying with some success. They have engaged the services of professionals who identify among the general public persons who support or are inclined to support their position. They provide them with relevant facts and analysis and motivate them to communicate their views to members of Congress.

CONCLUSIONS

Mail remains the most important communications link between members of Congress and their constituents. It continues to provide a channel for communications that is relatively open to all people. Despite the growing volume of mail promoted by interest groups, members are able to sift through and discount much of their mail because of the bias. One member said the mail can be very useful "if you know how to read it." While the growing flood of inspired mail has not significantly affected its utility to members of Congress, this could happen if this trend continues in the future. The possibility that the voice of the individual letter writer could be drowned out is real. Individuals may be discouraged from writing in the belief that their views will not come to the attention of a Congressman who is flooded with mass mailings.

The waste of resources in the production of mail to Congress and its processing in congressional offices is a matter of regret. Most of the form mail that floods Congress from time to time is of little or no value and is heavily discounted or ignored in the members' decisions. The demands on staff time and resources are heavy. If the volume of mail continues to rise in the future in the expectation that more mail means more influence, it may approach the limits of the system to respond and thereby diminish the utility of mail generally.

Much of the resources being applied to generate large volumes of mail could be more productively applied to informational and other educational activities that are designed to stimulate higher quality mail. Further research is needed to examine and evaluate various techniques and forms on decision-making in a variety of circumstances. This can help to demonstrate the futility of some kinds of mail and the utility of others. If a better understanding of the mail will serve to discourage quantity and to encourage quality, it can help to sustain and strengthen an important communications link between the people and their representatives in Congress.

Chapter 30

Lobbies and Political Action Committees:
A Congressman's Perspective

G. William Whitehurst (R-Virginia)

In the early 1980s, Congressman Mario Biaggi (D-NY), a former member of the New York City police force, introduced a bill that would have banned the commercial sale of ammunition that would penetrate a bullet-proof vest. Its purpose was obvious: police officers who occasionally found it necessary to wear a protective vest would not have their lives placed at risk by felons with armor-piercing bullets. When a member of Congress introduces legislation, he or she will often circulate among his House colleagues what we called a "Dear Colleague" letter, advising the recipient that such-and-such a bill was being introduced and inviting the member to become a cosponsor of the bill. So it was that when I received the Dear Colleague letter from Congressman Biaggi, I considered it to be wise legislation and told my legislative assistant to call his office and list me as a cosponsor. When I did so, I had no idea that I would set the wheels of a powerful lobby in motion and generate several dozen letters from constituents, all of whom objected to my cosponsorship on the Biaggi bill, and insisting that I withdraw.

Prior to this incident, I had not had much contact with the National Rifle Association. As a Republican congressman who was reasonably conservative and had a record that reflected it, I was not on their "hit list" nor can I recall receiving campaign contributions from the organization. I had never visited their headquarters near Scott Circle in Washington, nor did I know then about the bank of advanced computers that they had containing the names and addresses of their members who could instantly be alerted to their congressman's position on legislation that impacted upon gun control, or in the case of the Biaggi bill, ammunition sales.

The letters that I received were remarkably the same in content and style, an indication that they had been orchestrated elsewhere, but what puzzled me was their hostility. I had always thought that the NRA and its members stood behind the police in America, and as "law and order" adherents, would not want to see police officers placed at a disadvantage on the streets by allowing criminals to have legal access to bullets that could penetrate a Kevlar vest. When I replied to those who had written to me and asked them why they were opposed to this bill, their answer was, "This is the first step to take away our guns." I was mystified by what seemed to me to be a rank case of paranoia. I had never favored curtailing the right of law-abiding citizens to own a firearm, nor would I, but I drew the line on what I felt was an outrageous position. I did not yield to the NRA then, nor later when another more important bill affecting the sale of firearms was concerned, the McClure-Volkmer Bill, which I will discuss later in this chapter.

Lobbies have been part of the American political scene since the earliest days of the Republic. Indeed, the word "lobbyist" was initially coined in England, a reference to journalists who stood in the lobbies of the House of Commons, waiting to interview law makers. In the United States, the origin of the term was never identified with journalists, but from the outset with privilege seekers. First called "lobby agents" in the halls of the New York legislature in Albany, the term was soon shortened to "lobbyists" and they have been so ever since.

Practically all legislation that has had an impact upon an industry, a section of the nation, or any interest, has been tracked by a lobby or interest group, and more often than not, has been affected by that group's activity or efforts. As early as 1789, when the first tariff bill was enacted by the Congress, the Philadelphia Society for the Promotion of National Industry was formed to influence the legislators to protect certain American industries. Every piece of tariff legislation since then has come under the influence of multiple lobby organizations representing American industries and agriculture.

If there is a particular industry that dominates a congressional district, the representative himself will often be a watchdog and stand guard to protect it, not needing the prodding of a lobbyist. I recall in 1986, during my last year as a member of the House of Representatives, receiving a telephone call from a friend of mine in the German Bundestag. We had served together for ten years as delegates to the North Atlantic Assembly, the parliamentary representatives of NATO. He said that they were losing much of their forests from pollution and one of the worst offenders was the U.S. Army bases which were still burning anthracite coal for heating and generating power. He urged me to insert legislation in the defense authorization bill to have the military bases in Germany connect with the German energy grid system and cease relying upon anthracite coal imported from America.

The U.S. Army would probably have stopped using coal years before, but for the legislation that had been authored and preserved by the late Congressman, Dan Flood (D-PA). Flood represented a district in western Pennsylvania with extensive anthracite coal mines. Not only did he insist that anthracite coal be burned in the furnaces of the U.S. Army bases in Germany, but also he had the Defense Department stockpile it as a strategic energy source, this when America has a 500-year supply of coal!

It was calculated that, if the bases were integrated with the German energy grid, the savings to the American taxpayer would amount to $400 million over a five-year period. That, and the prospect of preserving good relations with a NATO ally, prompted me to introduce an amendment to plug into the German system and cease polluting German skies and forests. The reaction was immediate–not from Germany, but from colleagues from the coal mining regions of Virginia and Pennsylvania. One might say that it was a bipartisan effort, which I successfully fought off.

The district that I represented included Norfolk, Virginia, the largest coal-exporting port in the world. Most of the coal that we export, however, is soft coal, or steam coal. The amount of anthracite, or hard coal, exported was negligible. Nevertheless, my Democratic colleague, Rick Boucher, from Virginia's Ninth District, made every effort to get me to withdraw the amendment. In this, he was assisted by Republican colleagues of mine from Pennsylvania. They pleaded and threatened harsh words on the floor of the House, but I would not yield, and I successfully pushed it through in conference with the Senate. The coal industry, however, had every reason to be proud of their sponsors in the Congress. They went the extra mile.

Despite their subjective position, lobbies do serve a useful function in the legislative process. Simply because they are so knowledgeable about their industry or field, they are a source of considerable helpful information to a congressman or senator, or one of his or her aides. I recall many instances where I emerged from a meeting with an industry lobbyist better informed and therefore better prepared to vote on legislation that was pending.

THE DEFENSE LOBBY:
PERSONAL AND POLITICAL IMPLICATIONS

I served my entire 18 years in the House on the Armed Services Committee, which was charged with oversight and authorization of all funds for the military forces of the United States. During that period, I was a member of several subcommittees, including research and development, military readiness, and military installations and facilities. All of them were responsible for portions of the defense budget involving the expenditure of billions of dollars. Not surprising, there was fierce competition for them by various defense industries. This was especially true in the development of new weapons systems, where an appropriation was crucial to its ultimate adoption, and just as important in the eyes of the companies affected, who would get the contract.

For three years in the late 1970s, I was a member of the subcommittee on research and development. It was a time when the General Electric Company was in the process of developing a new jet engine for adoption by the Navy. The problem for GE was that the Navy was already being supplied by Pratt & Whitney with a jet engine for its new fighter, the F-14. However, there had been problems with the F-14 engine. The aircraft and its engine were overhauled at the Naval Air Rework Facility at the Naval Air Station in Norfolk. Twice a year, I made visits to all of the major installations in my district, and I had become familiar with some of the difficulties that the Navy was having with the Pratt & Whitney engine. The GE engine, it seemed to me, offered an alternative. Nevertheless, I talked to lobby representatives from both companies. Indeed, I had formed friendships with men from each company. My wife and I were entertained by both during that time when a congressman could accept a dinner or theater engagement and not be in violation of the rules of the House, as is now the case. In the end, however, I found the GE case more persuasive and offered an amendment in the subcommittee to add money to assist GE in the development of their engine. That engine, I might add, was subsequently adopted by the Navy with good results, but Pratt & Whitney is still in business as well.

There is certainly nothing wrong with having a lobbyist as a friend, so long as the relationship does not impinge on the judgment and ethical conduct of the legislator. Nevertheless, it carries a price. The day that I offered the amendment which would enable GE to continue with its engine development, representatives from both companies were in the room with their eyes focused on me. Among them was an officer with Pratt & Whitney who was a former Republican colleague of mine, Clark MacGregor, a thoroughly decent chap, whom I hated to disappoint. However, one does what one must. I would have felt far worse afterward had I failed to go with my best judgment.

The hiring of former members of Congress as lobbyists has obvious merit so far as a prospective employer is concerned. More than anything else, he has access, and he has it more effectively than anyone who has never been a member of the congressional fraternity. Former members have access to the House gymnasium, the Members' Dining Room in the Capitol, and the House chamber and cloakrooms, although they are not permitted to lobby in the House. But calling a former colleague and asking for a few minutes of his or her time will almost always be successful. A number of my former committee colleagues and staff members from the committee went on to serve as "consultants" for a myriad of defense contractors. Before I retired in January 1987, I was offered a similar opportunity by a former staff member of the Senate Armed Services Committee whom I had gotten to know and had occasionally seen socially. He assured me that I could make "well into six figures" in my first year with him, but I preferred to come home and resume teaching. I knew that it would be less stressful and neither my wife nor I ever had what is known as "Potomac Fever," an obsession with Washington and all that goes on there.

There is nothing inherently wrong with a former member of Congress going to work representing the business interests of a private concern, so long as the rules that govern all lobbying activities are observed. Some have been enormously successful, financially and otherwise, at it, and some have tried it for a few years and then left for home or other pursuits. Many senior military officers have followed the same path, taking executive positions with defense companies and making use of contacts in the Pentagon. Here one has to tread carefully, but the advantages to a contractor are apparent.

In some respects, the Defense Department is the shrewdest lobby of all. Major weapons systems, be they military aircraft or an aircraft carrier, are the work of multiple contractors located in a number of states. While it is true that the prime contractor may be situated in California, Texas, or Virginia, components of the airplane or ship are manufactured elsewhere as well. For example, toward the end of my congressional tenure, the Navy requested authorization for a new NIMITZ-class carrier. As I recall, the cost of this massive vessel at the time was about $5 billion, an enormous sum. The only shipyard in America that can build a nuclear-powered carrier is Newport News Shipbuilding in Newport News, Virginia, a neighboring community to my own congressional district. It has the largest employment of any company in Virginia, and many of my constituents worked there. The congressman for that district, Herbert Bateman, a fellow Republican, was obviously intent upon having the carrier included in the defense authorization bill, but so was I, as well as our Democratic colleague, Norman Sisisky, who represented the rest of the adjoining region of Hampton Roads.

This was no narrow provincial interest in the eyes of the Navy or the Department of Defense. They provided us with a detailed breakdown of what the industries in each state provided in the way of components of the carrier. Practically every state in the Union was represented. These were sent to members of the House and Senate to alert them to their *own* stake in the requested authorization. It was very effective and the authorization and subsequent appropriation for the ship were approved.

THE FOREIGN LOBBIES:
PRESSURE POLITICS AT WORK

In the course that I teach on lobbies and interest groups at Old Dominion University in Norfolk, I give several lectures on foreign lobbies, including a past look at the old China Lobby two generations ago that tied the foreign policy as well as the treasury of the United States to the corrupt and failed regime of Chiang Kai-Shek. Foreign governments have had unusual success in either shaping American foreign policy in their favor, or securing a pipeline to our treasury, or both. The two most successful nations in my experience in Washington were Greece and Israel. Why? Because they had substantial bases of support in the United States and a built-in lobby to work for them, with little orchestration on their own part.

In the 20th century, large numbers of Greeks and European Jews immigrated to the United States. In the case of the Greeks, they brought with them not only their rich culture, but the accumulation of generations of enmity toward Turkey, from whom they won their independence early in the last century, and with whom they have had friction and conflict off and on since. Very few Turks left their homeland for America, but the Greek-American population here grew and prospered. For the most part, they are seldom involved in the political issues that arouse and divide other Americans, but on one matter they are as one: any hostile action by Turkey against Greeks anywhere will rally them. This is what happened in July 1974, when Turkey invaded the island of Cyprus following a coup by a group of Cypriot Greek National Guard officers, who overthrew the government of Archbishop Makarios. It was done with the encouragement of the military junta which was ruling in Athens, who saw it as a popular move at home and one that would bring the island into a closer relationship with Greece. For the Greek-Cypriots, who comprised about 78 percent of the population of Cyprus, it was regarded as the first step toward *Enosis*, the union of Cyprus with Greece. The coup was foolish and dangerous, and also illegal. It was a violation of the agreement made when Cyprus became independent, whereby the rights of the Turkish minority on the island were to be protected and under no circumstances was union with Greece to be permitted. Turkey wasted little time in mounting a military invasion and ultimately occupying 40 percent of the island, driving from their homes thousands of Greek-Cypriots.

In no way was this a quarrel that concerned the United States, except that both powers were NATO partners, and with the potential threat of the Soviet Union to Western Europe at that time, any quarrel between Greece and Turkey was bound to be disruptive. Assigning blame for what happened was also difficult. Unquestionably, the Greek-Cypriots had acted in violation of an international agreement in overthrowing the legitimate government and threatening to jeopardize the rights of the Turkish minority. However, Turkey had used American-supplied weapons in carrying out the invasion and occupation. That was a specific violation of the terms under which we provided Turkey with modern aircraft, tanks, etc. Those weapons were only to be used in defense of Turkey from attack by Warsaw Pact forces, and not against anyone else.

Greek-Cypriot Americans wasted no time in beating a path to Washington and pleading their case before their congressional representatives. There was only one step that the Congress could take to pressure Turkey to withdraw its forces from Cyprus, and none of us had any confidence that it would achieve that. We were asked to cut off military aid to Turkey. I happened to have a rather large Greek-Cypriot American community in my district. Indeed, I had several close friends who had been strong supporters in my campaigns among them. Needless to say, I was attentive to their request. I was invited to and attended rallies at the social hall of the Greek Orthodox Church in Norfolk. Seldom have I seen such emotion on an issue as I experienced with these constituents. They took for granted my espousal of their cause, and I am frank to say that I engaged in a fair amount of demagoguery on their behalf. If there were any Turkish-Americans in my district, I never heard from them.

The Congress took up their cause and in time, both houses voted to cut off military aid to Turkey, despite the pleas and lobbying by the Ford administration. Not surprisingly, the Turkish government retaliated by closing American bases and intelligence surveillance sites in Turkey. In the election of 1976, the Greek-Americans came out in support of Jimmy Carter, who saw the Cypriot question as an issue on which he could capitalize at President Ford's expense, but once he became president, he pushed for the repeal of the arms embargo on Turkey and just as quickly lost the support of Greek-Americans.

Subsequently, military aid to Turkey was renewed, and the relationship between Washington and Ankara has entered a smoother period. On Cyprus, however, the status quo is unchanged. The Greek portion of Cyprus has prospered, but that has not caused the Greeks on Cyprus nor their American cousins to cease their demand that the Turks withdraw their forces. There has been no resolution of the dispute, despite efforts by the Secretary General of the United Nations to effect a settlement. The quarrel simmers, but the pressure on Congress to take further action has long since abated. Even the Greek lobby recognizes that there are limits to their efforts.

No foreign lobby has enjoyed so much favor as the Israeli, or Zionist, lobby in America. Its roots sprouted from the Zionist movement, the creation of a Jewish homeland in Palestine. That dream became a reality with the Balfour Declaration issued by the British government in 1917. Although the Declaration did not mandate the establishment of a Jewish state, the foundation for the modern state of Israel was laid in it. Between the two World Wars, Jewish immigration to Palestine swelled, and friction with the resident Arabs increased proportionately. Great Britain, which held the Palestine mandate following the First World War, found it difficult to keep peace between them. The Second World War proved to be the decisive factor in giving birth to Israel. The terrible ordeal of the Holocaust prompted a flood of European Jews to seek security in Palestine after 1945. In vain, the British endeavored to stop the influx of Jews, while simultaneously dealing with Jewish nationalism on the one hand in Palestine and Arab resistance to it on the other. Successive plans to divide the country between them failed and in May 1948, Britain washed its hands of the problem by withdrawing all of its forces and officials from the area. In that moment, the Jewish state was born and for the remainder of its history has confronted Arab hostility, either in war or terrorists. Not until the accession of Anwar Sadat to the presidency of Egypt and the resulting peace negotiations with Israel did the threat of perpetual conflict abate. Throughout most of the entire period, Israel has had the support of the United States, largely because of the effective lobbying of the Zionist organizations dedicated to that end.

When the first approaches were made to President Truman to secure financial aid for the struggling infant state in 1948, he told the Zionist representatives to go to the Congress. They did, and have ever since. In the years that followed, the most powerful and influential of all of the Zionist organizations, the American Israel Public Affairs Committee (AIPAC), became the Jewish voice for Israel in the United States. Under the leadership of Thomas Dine, a personable and energetic young man, AIPAC acquired more clout on Capitol Hill than any other lobby in the nation.

Several factors contributed to the success of the Zionist lobby. First, there was great sympathy across America at large for the plight of European Jews following the Holocaust. With Israel besieged in a hostile Arab sea, Americans were unwilling to stand aside and be a silent witness to a second Holocaust. Moreover, there was a natural American sympathy for the underdog, little Israel standing up to her far more numerous Arab foes. These elements alone, however, do not account for the incredible amount of American largesse showered on Israel. The presence of a large Jewish population gave Israel a solid base of unflinching support during its four wars with its Arab enemies, and between them. In fact, to this day, Israel is the largest recipient of foreign aid, even though it no longer confronts a military threat beyond occasional terrorist attacks. And just as the Turks never migrated to America in great numbers, neither have the Arabs. America's faithfulness to its little friend in the Middle East is without parallel. In spite of damaging and painful oil embargoes which the nation endured following two of the Arab-Israeli wars, America remained steadfast. Not once has there been a serious effort to cut off or even reduce aid to Israel. For this, the government in Jerusalem can thank its supporters in the United States.

Every congressman and senator was made aware of the political power of AIPAC when it targeted two members back in the 1980s. Senator Charles Percy lost his Senate seat to Congressman Paul Simon in an election that featured extensive hostile commercials that were financed either independently by a wealthy California Zionist, Michael Goland, who spent $1.6 million of his own money on advertising to tell the people of Illinois "to dump Percy," or by large contributions from pro-Israel activists. The irony of it is that Percy was not unfriendly to Israel, but he had warned that Israel could not expect to have a "blank check" in the future, and he had urged Israeli leaders to negotiate with Yasser Arafat and the PLO. AIPAC went beyond the rules of fair play by "cooking the data" on Percy's voting record. When the votes that they selected to rate senators on their support for Israel were tabulated, they showed that Percy had voted "right" 89 percent of the time. Simon had a 99 percent rating, but the difference was not that much, so AIPAC added some other votes, none of which were important, plus resolutions that Percy had failed to sign, and by combining these, dropped his rating to 51 percent. Percy lost the 1984 election by 89,000 votes, a narrow margin for a state like Illinois. Did AIPAC and the Zionist lobby make the difference? Listen to Thomas Dine's own words to a Canadian audience following the election: "All Jews in America, from coast to coast, gathered to oust Percy. And American politicians–those who hold public positions now, and those who aspire–got the message."[1]

The campaign of Congressman Paul Findley of Illinois followed a similar pattern. Findley, too, had called for negotiations between Israel and the PLO, and he held a personal meeting with Arafat. Now the target of AIPAC in the 1982 election, he lost his congressional seat to Richard Durbin, a strong Democratic opponent. The result was close, a margin of 1,407 votes. Following the election, Dine again took credit for the outcome. He spoke to a Jewish audience in Austin, Texas and crowed, "This is a case where the Jewish lobby made the difference. We beat the odds and defeated Findley." Dine estimated that $685,000 of the $750,000 that Durbin raised came from Jews.[2]

Thomas Dine was correct in his assessment of the importance that incumbent congressmen and senators attached to the power of AIPAC and associated lobbies. As a member of the Armed Services Committee, I visited Israel several times, meeting with political and military leaders there.   I was impressed by their character and ability, and also persuaded by their cause. In the Yom Kippur War of 1973, I did not hesitate to vote for emergency aid, but by 1986, after peace between Egypt and Israel had been signed, and after the Israeli incursion into Lebanon, I began to take a more balanced attitude. While I still regarded myself as a friend of Israel, my oath had been taken to the U.S. Constitution. The latent strength of the Israeli lobby was driven home to me in my last year in office. In 1986, a congressional resolution was brought to the House floor in opposition to an arms sale to Saudi Arabia.   In this instance, no aircraft or other offensive weapons of significance were involved. Indeed, the government of Israel raised no public objection, and even AIPAC was quiet. Nevertheless, the friends of Israel in the House brought the resolution out, pointing out that it was non-binding. It was simply another loyalty test for Israel. I made up my mind that I would not vote for it. Saudi Arabia was also a friend, and it was sitting on an ocean of oil that we relied upon. When I walked into the House chamber to vote that afternoon, I saw four of my Virginia Republican colleagues huddling and debating the merits of voting for or against the resolution. As I approached them, they asked me what I was going to do. I said that I had no intention of voting for it, that it was a mischievous piece of work, and I had no desire to offend the Saudis. "Well, you're retiring, so you don't have to worry about your Jewish vote," one of them said. "That may be true," I replied, "but none of them has called me or written to me about this." "What are you going to do?" I asked, and the one nearest me smiled and said, "Baby, I've got my yarmulke on right now," tapping his head where the Jewish skullcap is worn in temple by all males. My fellow Virginian, French Slaughter, said, "Come on, Bill, I'll vote with you." We were the only Virginians to vote against the resolution and we had precious little company from the rest of the House.

MANIPULATING THE SYSTEM:
THE NATIONAL RIFLE ASSOCIATION

Money and threatening tactics are not the sole province of foreign lobbies. A host of other domestic lobbies have employed them, too. The latent fear of the power of AIPAC reflected in the aforementioned vote was repeated in the vote on the McClure-Volkmer Bill, which was strongly supported by the National Rifle Association. Senator James McClure (R-ID) and Congressman Harold Volkmer (D-MO) collaborated to introduce this measure in their respective bodies of the Congress. Briefly, the bill rolled back key provisions of the 1968 Gun Control Act, which had been passed in the aftermath of the assassinations of Dr. Martin Luther

King, Jr. and Robert Kennedy. The background and legislative path of the McClure-Volkmer Bill are interesting in that they are a revealing commentary on human nature, particularly that of politicians.

Both Senator McClure and Congressman Volkmer came from states with a strong hunting constituency. The 1968 Gun Control Act placed certain restrictions on the purchase of weapons and was resented by many gun owners, who saw it as an infringement of their "right to bear arms." The NRA urged its repeal, or at least major revisions to weaken it. Jim McClure and Harold Volkmer became their standard bearers. McClure had little difficulty in getting the measure passed in the Senate, but Volkmer had to get over a formidable hurdle in the House. The chairman of the Judiciary Committee, to which the bill was referred, was opposed to any change in the 1968 law. Peter Rodino of New Jersey had made a name for himself as head of the Judiciary Committee during the Watergate hearings. Although he and Volkmer were both Democrats, Rodino held strong views on gun control and was determined to kill his colleague's bill by refusing to hold hearings on it. His position was supported by a fellow New Jersey Democrat, Bill Hughes, who chaired the relevant subcommittee to which the bill was referred.

The only avenue open to Volkmer, therefore, was to present a discharge petition to the House and seek the signatures of 218 of the House members on it to discharge the measure from the Judiciary Committee and bring it directly to the floor for debate and a vote. This legislative device is a useful safety valve for the House, employed when a recalcitrant committee chairman will try to block the will of the House when the members wish to consider a bill held back in committee. A discharge petition forced Congressman Emanuel Celler, a former chairman of the Judiciary Committee, to allow the Equal Rights Amendment to come to the floor. But discharge petitions rarely get the requisite number of signatures because most members prefer that proposed bills follow the normal legislative process.

Volkmer, however, had a powerful ally in the NRA. Its computers spat out thousands of letters to NRA members, urging them to write to their respective representatives requesting them to sign Volkmer's discharge petition and get his bill to the floor. Knowing that discharge petitions seldom get 218 signatures, many members decided that they would have their cake and eat it. They would sign the discharge petition, believing that it would suffer the fate of so many others and therefore not have to vote on Volkmer's bill, which was bottled up in the Judiciary Committee. They would then write to their NRA constituents and gratify them by declaring that they had signed the petition as requested. It seemed a clever political ploy, only the problem was that too many of their colleagues decided to do the same thing and Volkmer quickly got within reach of the magic 218 signatures. At that point, Rodino and Hughes belatedly put together an alternate bill of their own, which made some cosmetic changes in the 1968 Gun Control Law, but did not go nearly as far as McClure-Volkmer. It was too late. Volkmer had planned his campaign with skill and now was able to have his bill considered. Moreover, he had commitments from all of those members who had signed his discharge petition, even if they had done so for political reasons.

The bill was opposed by law enforcement officers over much of the country. Indeed, the day that the vote was taken on the measure, police officers in uniform from departments in cities along the East Coast formed lines outside the doors leading into the House chamber, begging the members going in not to vote for the bill. I was already on record opposing it, but when I walked into the Republican lounge just off the House floor, I found a dozen of my colleagues stewing about their vote, moaning aloud that they wished that they had not signed Volkmer's discharge petition. The police officers outside had nicked their conscience. I stood it as long as I could, and then said, "Well, why don't you go back in the House and change your vote? It's not too late." At this, one of them spoke for all when he replied, "I can't. I signed that damned discharge petition, and I'm afraid to have the NRA on my back. It isn't so much that I worry that they won't give money to my campaign, it's that they'll contribute to my opponent." The bill passed, of course. Harold Volkmer and the NRA had scored a brilliant legislative coup. Riding back to the Rayburn House Office Building in the subway car that connects the Capitol and the Rayburn Building, I was a witness to a scene that said it all. Sitting across from me were Rodino and Hughes, looking for all the world as though they had just left a wake. In the compartment behind them sat Volkmer with the satisfied expression of one who knows that he has beaten the system.

PACS AND MONEY: POLITICS WITH A $ SIGN

It is impossible in a single chapter to cover all of the principal lobbies with whom I have dealt in my nine terms in the House, but the incidents that I have set down here give an accurate picture of what my colleagues and I confronted. Of course, no discussion of them would be complete without some comments on the relatively new American political phenomenon, the political action committee, or PAC. I say relatively new, because in 1974, there were only 608 of them in existence. Within 20 years, there were 4,000. This explosion in growth is matched by a concomitant rise in campaign contributions and spending.

Let me give a personal example. In 1976, I faced my last Democratic opponent for my congressional seat in the Second District of Virginia. I won decisively and thereafter I was unopposed, which I am frank to say was a rare and marvelous experience. In that 1976 campaign, I was opposed by a former Delegate to the Virginia General Assembly. It was a spirited contest, in the course of which my campaign treasury spent $130,000, the largest sum of any of my contested races. Ten years later, I announced that I would not run again. The Republicans in my district nominated an attorney named A. Joseph Canada, who sat in the State Senate. He raised and spent $600,000. His Democratic opponent was Owen B. Pickett, also a member of the General Assembly, a Delegate. He raised about $600,000 and spent all but $100,000 of it. There was an independent candidate in the race, who raised and spent far less. The election was a close one. Canada narrowly carried Virginia Beach, but Pickett's margin in Norfolk offset his loss of Virginia Beach. The presence of the independent gave Pickett a plurality, but it was enough to send him to Washington where he represented the Second District until 2001, when he retired. The point that I wish to make is this: where did the two principal candidates raise over a million dollars between them? They certainly did not get most of it from contributors in the Second District. If they did, I certainly failed in my own fundraising efforts in the previous 18 years. They got those dollars from PACs, which by 1986, were providing enormous sums to congressional campaigns across the country.

What do these large contributions by PACs buy? They buy access. Access is everything to the industry or interest that creates a PAC. It ensures that they will have the congressman's or senator's ear to promote a weapons buy, a change in the tax code, or some other federal regulation, or any of a host of provisions in a bill that has an impact upon that industry or interest.

Not all PACs make campaign contributions. In the 1992 elections, 35 percent of them gave nothing, and 23 percent gave $5,000 or less to candidates. Only 43 gave between $500,000 and one million dollars, but nevertheless, they placed their money carefully. PACs do not bear total responsibility for all of the massive contributions made to campaigns in recent years. In industry, corporate officers "bundle" their contributions to a particular candidate that they favor. Labor unions disguise their support for a pro-labor candidate by spending money on "Get-Out-the-Vote" literature. There are dozens of ways to manipulate the system, and the courts themselves have struck down some of the regulatory rules as unconstitutional, opening the doors further.

For incumbents, particularly majority incumbents, campaign reform is a little like the weather. Everyone talks about it, but nobody does anything about it. When the Republicans were in the minority in the Congress, they called for campaign reform. As soon as they became the majority party, their record began to look like that of their Democratic predecessors. PACs almost always support the incumbent in a campaign, if they become involved at all. The record of PAC contributions to challengers is negligible. Only when the congressional or senatorial seat is open is the playing field generally even.

There has been one reform that is noteworthy. Prior to the last congressional pay raise, House members were lobbied both in kind and with cash. A ceiling was placed on honoraria earnings, but it was a comfortable one, close to $20,000 when I was in office. The honorarium for a single speech could not exceed $2,000, but it was easy to arrange ten such speeches if one was a member of the Ways and Means Committee, which is responsible for tax legislation, or the Appropriations Committee. Even those of us on the Armed Services Committee did not fare badly, especially if we had seniority. Like Maria Theresa in the partition of Poland, "She wept, but she took." I did not feel at ease about receiving $2,000 for a speech to an industry organization, but I must confess to making several such addresses. I tried to draw the line between what I regarded as outright influence peddling and sharing my views at a podium before a trade organization or one of industry representatives. One of the more outrageous ones occurred in my last term.

One afternoon, my receptionist, Judy Butler, informed me that she had just received a call from a representative of The Tobacco Institute, inviting me to attend a breakfast the following week at which there was to be a discussion of tobacco legislation. There was $1,000 in it for me if I attended, and as the caller said, "He doesn't have to say anything, just sit and listen." I told her that this was the closest to being offered a bribe since I had come to Washington, even though it wasn't illegal. I asked her to call back and decline the invitation, but to spare them my reasons. They would have been superfluous. The following week, however, on the day that the breakfast was held, I attended a meeting of the Armed Services Committee when one of my Republican colleagues came in to take a seat several places from me. I suspected that this member had been to the breakfast and I asked with a trace of sarcasm, "Did you go to The Tobacco Institute breakfast this morning?" My colleague looked a little surprised, but nodded. "Did you get your money?" I asked. The reply came back with a grin, "In an envelope on the way out."

Golf outings, vacations in the islands with honoraria-attached speeches, dinners at Washington's best restaurants, and entertainment at the Kennedy Center are all part of the past now. Honoraria for speeches ended with the last large congressional pay raise for House members. They can still be paid, but must donate the money to a charity. More recently, the House became totally spooked by adverse publicity regarding influence peddling and cut off accepting lunches and dinners. That, it seems to me, is foolish. No one ever sold his vote for a free meal or allowed a decent dinner to influence a legislative position. I suspect that in time these rules will be relaxed.

In spite of the fact that true campaign reform has so far failed to gain ground in either a Democratic-controlled Congress or a Republican-controlled one, there is a growing bipartisan chorus of current and former members of Congress insisting that campaign finance restrictions be enacted into law. In the Senate, John McCain, a Republican from Arizona, and Russell Feingold, a Democrat from Wisconsin, along with nearly 20 of their colleagues, have declared their support for legislation that would bring major changes to campaign financing. The proposed bill contains a ban on PAC contributions, or should that be ruled unconstitutional, to place a limit of $1,000 on them. Currently, PACs are allowed to contribute up to $5,000 per federal candidate per election. "Bundling" would be prohibited. "Soft money," a dodge currently in vogue, which allows contributions to parties in unlimited amounts, ostensibly for party building activities but which is routed to individual campaigns, also would be banned. Other features would affect independent expenditures and incentives to limit campaign spending. Senate Republicans opposed the measure in the 104th Congress, mounting a filibuster against it, chiefly because of the ban on soft money from which they have profited more than the Democrats.

In the House of Representatives, a companion bill to McCain-Feingold was introduced by Sam Farr (D-CA) and a number of Democrats have gotten behind it, but there is little hope that the measure will have better luck there than it had in the Senate.   Two Republican members, Linda Smith of Washington, and Christopher Shays of Connecticut, also have sponsored campaign finance reform legislation, but to date there has been little movement.

Not surprisingly, each party is subjective in what it is willing to support in the way of campaign finance reform.   The Democrats would ban or limit PAC donations as well as "soft money."   They favor more public financing and putting limits on campaigns in exchange for free or low-priced advertising.   Most Republicans would end the practice of labor unions spending compulsory union dues on political activities.   They are still angry about the $35 million that labor spent to try to unseat Republican incumbents in the 1996 congressional elections. Republicans also would raise the limits on individual contributions while restricting the donations from PACs.   Whatever their positions, neither side seems willing to yield, and the impasse continues to serve them both.

Outside the Congress, there are a number of organizations pushing hard for campaign reform.   The most prominent are Common Cause, which supports the McCain-Feingold Bill, the Center for Responsive Politics, which monitors campaign spending and disclosure reports, and the Center for Public Integrity, which is also a watchdog organization.   On the other side, there is the National Association of Business PACs, which opposes PAC donation limits.

More recently, a new group, which I have joined in the company of some of my former congressional colleagues, is Public Campaign: Clean Money, Clean Elections.   It is a bipartisan organization and proposes a formula to which any candidate could subscribe and qualify as a Clean Money Campaign Reformed candidate.   Unlike other reform minded groups, this one provides a Clean Money fund that would be made available to candidates who signed on.   They would, of course, take no money from PACs or other special interest groups.   Free and discounted television time would be provided.   The program is an ambitious one, but it is novel, and if it is successful in its adoption in any future elections, it may well find favor with the voters, the ultimate arbiters in choosing office holders.

Over a decade has passed since I retired from the Congress. Surveying the political scene today, I am glad that I left Washington when I did.   There is a penchant for people who are in the autumn of their lives as I am to recall their earlier years as the best and to be overly judgmental about the present. In truth, the Congress was a more congenial place then than it is now. In my first year in 1969, we would have thought it ludicrous to go on a retreat for a weekend, as many House members did in 1997 to learn how to behave more harmoniously toward one another. We would have been shocked at the cost of campaigning today. In fact, I suspect that I would have been discouraged from running in 1968 if I had been faced with raising the amount of dollars that are now required.

Lobbies alone cannot be blamed for these developments. They have been with us throughout the history of the Congress, and their role today is a mirror of our times.   The public has become infinitely more single-issue oriented. If Greek-Americans care only about the fate of Cyprus, there are millions of other un-hyphenated Americans who are wedded to a lone cause or issue, be it abortion, the environment, or a myriad of others ranging from prayer-in-school to animal rights. Many of them are shrill and uncompromising, so it is not surprising that PACs have mushroomed from just over 600 to 4,000. Each of these organizations or groups demands a separate voice, and the result is a cacophony that leads to an unstable legislative arena, where calm, dispassionate, and reasonable discussion is made more difficult. The House has always had its share of demagoguery, but the present condition only encourages more of it to placate the multi-faceted constituency outside. Moreover, increasing numbers of the members themselves have become converted to single causes and positions, ideologues, who in many cases find it impossible to seek the common ground so vital to the success of any legislature. To compound this, throw in immense sums of money that can determine the political fate of an incumbent and the result is clear for all to see.

When will the nation and its national legislature come back to their senses? That is impossible to say until the sane voices crying out to break the chain of self-interest that shackles the political system are heeded. When that happens, lobbies and interest groups will not disappear, nor should they, but their role will once more reflect an America more tolerant and less divided.

Notes:

1 . Paul Findley, *They Dare to Speak Out* (Westport, CT: Lawrence Hill, 1985), pp. 111-13.

2 . *Ibid.*, p. 11

Chapter 31

Soft Behavior Responses: How Legislators Serve Lobbyists in the Shadows of Capitol Hill

Bert Levine
Former Lobbyist, Johnson and Johnson

What lobbyists do is not always what journalists and the public think that they do. Certainly, pressing lawmakers to vote the "right way" in committee or on the floor, asking them to cosponsor bills and write amendments, and delivering up political contributions are a big chunk of what most lobbyists, especially business lobbyists, do for their clients. They well know that, at some point, and in some way, what policies legislators agree upon and what presidents sign into law affect the interests that they are paid to represent. Lobbyists are acutely aware of this and deploy their resources accordingly.

But votes, bills, and contributions are only a part of the lobbying business. And while, for most lobbyists most of the time, they are the biggest and most high profile piece of the business, there is another less easily seen, less well documented level of activity that can pay off handsomely for lobbyists and clients alike. This is an activity that is never reflected on a tote board and that often requires the cooperation of not more than one or a few lawmakers. In fact, sometimes it requires little more than the support of an energetic senior staff person.

These activities are, in many ways, to public policy what soft money is to political contributions: they are legal; only the more sophisticated lobby groups tend to use and benefit from them; they *may* have an indirect, but not insignificant, effect on political and policy outcomes; and they are often undisclosed to the public.[1] Much as party building contributions are "soft" in a stealth-like sense, lobbyists and legislators pursue these activities precisely because they are completely–or largely–off the record. For legislators who are responding to interest group requests for favors, they may be termed "*Soft Behavior Responses*" (*SBRs*).

What is important to understand about SBRs is that they can and do take many different forms–many more forms than exist for on-the-record responses. While some forms are relatively common–arranging for witnesses to appear at hearings, setting up meetings with congressional offices, asking questions of federal regulators, intervening at an early stage in bill and amendment drafting, and, importantly, inserting language (often drafted by an interest group) for inclusion in committee reports–SBRs can be unique, one-of-a-kind.

One example will serve to illustrate a relatively creative SBR, one which provided significant benefits to an important lobbying organization and may have had an indirect effect on the policy making process.

Nearly two decades ago, the pharmaceutical industry was rocked by a series of congressional allegations that aimed at the heart of the industry's credibility as the developer and producer of safe and effective medications. A senate committee had amassed overwhelming evidence that some clinical investigators—physicians who play a key role in administering the studies that determine the safety and efficacy of new drugs and are thus pivotal figures in the FDA's drug approval process—had falsified their data. These investigators usually contracted with the drug companies for their services and were not full-time pharmaceutical company employees. There was little or no concern that the companies had encouraged or known about the data falsifications. But that was of small comfort to the industry. Nor did this go far to appease irate legislative entrepreneurs who knew that they had a "winner" issue. The fact that sophisticated, highly profitable, private organizations charged with a major public responsibility could be duped on such an important matter as the legitimacy of these key studies was more than a major embarrassment–it was a devastating revelation. It certainly could discredit the companies that had accepted the falsified data and had used it as part of their submissions to the FDA.

The senate committee moved skillfully to produce a series of high profile investigative hearings. They called several pharmaceutical companies to testify. Again, while there was little concern for complicity, there was much potential exposure of the companies because of their careless oversight of the clinical investigators. All involved parties knew that the hearing room would be filled with network cameras, reporters, and public interest representatives who, in the industry's view, would be sure to do their part to discredit the manufacturers.

The obvious tact for the pharmaceutical companies was to attempt to deploy their trade association as a shield. One of the first rules of business lobbying is, when necessary and possible, to "hide behind" the trade association. The association produces no products of its own; it does not need to rely on its good name in the same way and to the same extent that an individual company does. So, for the companies under scrutiny by the committee, it made perfect sense for the

Pharmaceutical Manufacturers Association (PMA) to take their place in the congressional hot seat. The companies argued that the PMA was best suited to provide an overview of industry-wide contracting and oversight procedures. A single company could give only a limited perspective, but the association could share a much more comprehensive overview.

The theory was good, but the committee was having none of it.

Committee members, especially the chair, knew they had a good story and that a key component of the story-telling "cast" had to be the individual companies. There would be little public awareness of or interest in the PMA, but there would be considerable interest in the big name pharmaceutical companies–large, multinational, and rich. The committee held firm: the companies would have to testify for themselves. There would be no hiding behind their trade association on this issue.

For the company lobbyists, the committee decision not to permit the association to "take the heat" presented a different sort of challenge from which they were normally faced. The immediate objective was not to convince the committee to pursue a given policy objective. That would come later, when and if the committee considered remedial legislative action–perhaps a new charge to the FDA to establish stricter standards for monitoring clinical investigators. The crisis of the moment was less substantive and more political: how to avoid testifying while not upsetting committee members and staff that had already collected, and were itching to use, much damaging evidence.

One company with a superb record for quality products and high integrity struck upon a simple idea—a sort of plea bargain. In essence, they decided to "turn state's evidence." Their lobbying team knew that, in order to avoid having their executives grilled in public, they would have to deliver something of value to the committee. In this instance, that "something" would be, as it often is in legislative lobbying, good information that the committee did not have, at least, not yet. The company could provide a complete, *firsthand* account of how a highly regarded pharmaceutical company, with virtually unlimited resources, could be duped by a clinical investigator. So, the elements for the deal were clear: the company would provide complete evidence to the committee in exchange for avoiding the need to appear as a witness at the hearings.

The committee accepted. It was a classic "win-win" deal. The company won because it did not have to suffer the bad publicity that would surely follow an ugly public berating by members of the senate. The committee won because it gained added insight into how the investigator scams were executed. And, importantly, both the company and the committee could argue that, should their deal ever become known, they had each served the public well by improving the committee's ability to conduct an important public investigation.

The anecdote provides but one example of a congressional *Soft Behavior Response*. The chair's decision to "do a deal" with the company, and the informal "testimony" that it provided to the committee staff, never appeared–and until this day, has never appeared—in a public record. Nor is there a record of the actual SBR itself. The SBR–important to the company, the committee, and (perhaps) to the general public–is not traceable in any formal sense. There is no record; no contribution to a data base that may be used to chart congressional behavior, lobbyists' tactics, or any other form of legislative-related activity.

The "deal" between the chair and the company, while not necessarily common, is not wholly atypical–not to the extent that the remedial action the company sought and the chair granted was off the record. Secretiveness paid off for both parties. Professional lobbyists, often accused of "dealing in the shadows," and most legislators well understand the wisdom of the political axiom, "one should never attempt to make public policy in public."

What may be of some comfort for those concerned about the maintenance of a well-functioning government and its policy outputs is that the axiom has to do with political processes (as opposed to products). So, working in the "shadows" does not necessarily equate to corruption and/or evil doing. The policies produced by congressional activity that are not seen are seldom different in thrust or political character from those produced by more public deliberations. Perhaps, understandably, most lobbyists and public officials are quick to support this view.[2] Professional lobbyists know (or should know) that, while members may welcome the opportunity to perform an SBR for an interest group they would like to support, and may take a little extra political license in providing this support, the additional latitude provided by the cover of an off-the-record activity is limited. Members will neither appreciate nor be compliant with a request to perform an act which, if it ever should come to light, would be viewed as wholly inconsistent with their past policy positions and legislative actions.   .

In deciding which members to approach and what may be asked of them, lobbyists should consider these parameters for member SBR activity:

1. Members will not be unfaithful to their constituencies, be they geographic, interest group, financial, congressional, or other. Their instinct is to think in terms of how constituencies would respond *if* their actions were to become public. This may seem paranoid, and it may be, but it is also smart politics.

2.   Members will be more inclined to perform an SBR for a lobbyist they know, like, and have learned to trust. Long-term relationships matter. The congressional office is a busy place; staff is limited, as is time. A member is more inclined to comply with a lobbyist's request if s/he believes that the lobbyist can be trusted not to urge a foolish, politically harmful action.

3.   Most members (again, *most* of them) do have political and moral compasses. What they stand for is what they stand for. They will not do violence to the causes with which they have been closely identified. Nor will they knowingly attempt to decieve their congressional colleagues.

4.   Members, like the rest of us, have loyalties based on who they are and what they have done in their "past life." So, a former educator, labor organizer, or business executive may have a strong inclination to respond to requests which emanate from former colleagues–even if these colleagues are not part of what would normally qualify as a constituency.

5.   Also, like the rest of us, members are influenced by past experiences. A family illness, a personal triumph or failure, or a traumatic experience color how a member will respond to a request to do something that s/he might not normally be interested in doing in the routine course of his/her congressional activities. None of these considerations is wholly different from what a lobbyist must consider when requesting a member to take a more public action. The lobbyist who wants to enjoy a long and successful career must know and respect the limits of what a member can and cannot be asked to do–off- or on-the-record. Few acts can be as detrimental to the lobbyist-member relationship as asking the member to do something that is repugnant to him/her. Such a request will be viewed as amateurish behavior at best, and "sleaziness" at worst. In either instance, the lobbyist will likely be *persona non grata* for some extended period of time–maybe forever.

With all of the above understood, the astute lobbyist will examine the following three factors in deciding when a given legislative circumstance is ripe for an SBR: issue salience for the member(s) in question; issue profile; and the level of visibility of the requested act.

Issue Salience: Most members of Congress have a relatively narrow range of issues for which their actions may be highly constrained by principle or constituent (broadly defined) interests. The majority of matters that come before Congress are of relatively little concern for most members. This may even be true of committee agendas. While it is likely that a higher percentage of bills that come before a member's committee will matter in some significant way to him/her, it is still the case that the majority of committee bills will not stimulate much political or professional interest by a member. There is simply nothing at stake about which the member cares.

It is also likely that members will want to spend most of their time and political capital working on issues that, for them, are the most salient. This means that SBRs are frequently best suited to less pressing, less time-demanding objectives, objectives that may not matter much to the member, but may be important to an interest s/he whishes to serve—for whatever reason. (Yes, campaign contributions may be a factor here. But, as provocative as that issue is, it is beyond the scope of this article.)

Issue Profile: There are at least two standards by which to measure issue profile: general and district-specific. Certainly not every issue that comes before Congress attracts broad public attention. *The New York Times, Washington Post*, and CNN, taken together, do not provide a line or a minute of coverage to the vast majority of bills and amendments. Many, if not most, legislative issues are of interest to very narrowly defined communities. And even within these communities, awareness and concern may be relatively low. It is simply not the case that members are besieged by teams of reporters and interest group lobbyists on every issue. Nor are their offices inundated by outpourings of letters, e-mails, and phone calls on the majority of matters.

But national prominence—or lack thereof—is not the sole standard by which congressional offices gauge issue profile. The extent to which an issue is covered in a member's state or district or the extent to which an issue is covered by trade and other specialty journals read by constituents is at least as meaningful to a legislator. Clearly, such coverage will add to constituent awareness and thus to issue salience discussed above. So, what may be a low-profile national issue may well be a high-profile local issue.

Low Visibility Action: Virtually by definition, SBRs are low visibility. But even in the context of SBRs, some acts involve fewer "players" and, if appropriately conceived and executed, less chance of broad public scrutiny than others. Arranging for a meeting with executive branch officials, as low key as that activity may seem, may require a member's office to work with several "go-betweens." The relatively broad exposure expands the margin for error. The chance is increased that someone might perceive the meeting as a "special favor" to a "powerful" interest group and decide to "leak" to a media outlet, or to inform an interest group hostile to the interests of the beneficiary organization.

A long shot? Probably. But scandals can be made of such events.

By contrast, a *prudently* worded insert in a committee report, one that does not attempt to rewrite the bill for which the report is being issued, may require the support and knowledge of only a member or two. In fact, upon occasion, the right staff person may be able to execute the insert with only a *pro forma* communication to his/her boss. Such a modest addition to a bill's legislative history may be important to the "sponsoring" interest, but may attract little or no attention from the broad body of legislators or from other interest groups.

It is not always possible for lobbyists to avoid high profile issues and/or asking members to perform high-visibility acts. Certainly, most lobbyists earn a fair share of their compensation by representing clients on "big-ticket," industry-wide, or even national issues. Daily, the conference rooms of the major national trade associations and Washington law and public affairs firms are filled with teams of lobbyists plotting strategies, divvying up assignments, and otherwise executing alliances formed to affect multibillion dollar issues. Without this work and the issues that drive it, lobbyists' incomes would be significantly diminished and the conference rooms greatly reduced in number and size. So, in many ways, big is good for the lobbying community. High salience and high-profile can be easily and correctly equated with high compensation levels. Said another way: big issues beget big bucks.

This is all true. But for client organizations—those who employ and/or retain professional lobbyists—big is not always better. While it is clearly the case that big issues are often as unavoidable as they are profitable for lobbyists, they are also difficult for even the most politically well connected organizations to control. The bigger the issue, the more likely it will be that several large interests will become involved. This virtually assures that the legislative result—remembering here that a failure to pass legislation is itself a form of a result—will have to reflect a balancing of these interests. Winning—at least, winning decisively—in such a political environment is almost impossible.[3] Even in the context of a single industry, it is not likely that all major "players" will agree upon every legislative objective.

If outcomes of big, multi-player issues are beyond the ability of even the largest organizations to control, it would make sense that a lobbying organization should attempt to create and then pursue a second-level legislative agenda of lower-profile issues. These may be thought of as company- or organization-specific issues. Such issues may not be as "sexy" as the higher-profile matters, but they can result in significant pay outs for "sponsoring" organizations. They are often the stuff of SBRs.

The reasons for this are clear, but are too often overlooked by lobbyists and their clients who seem to have a proclivity for getting caught up in bigger issues. The circumstance may be likened to the "outbox-inbox" dichotomy. Many lobbyists, certainly not all, have a tendency to focus on issues served up to them (put in their "inbox") by the executive branch, Congress, and their trade associations (who are forever seeking to justify the ample dues they charge member organizations). To a certain extent, this is understandable; big issues are big for a reason—they are important to many interests. But organizations with plentiful lobbying resources should be mindful of creating their own legislative agendas (working from their "outbox") when possible.

Even the largest companies can be the beneficiaries of carefully designed, well-crafted legislation or legislative-related acts that address *modest* needs. The key concepts here are *careful design* and *modest objectives*. Lobbyists who know how to think small and avoid raising "red flags" can, on a cumulative basis, produce rich rewards for their clients. The point here is this: *What may produce an important result for a particular company (or other organization) may not affect issues that are important in a broader policy context of broader policy issues.* Thoughtful lobbyists can, upon occasion, define remedies that provide benefits to their clients but do not require significant and/or controversial changes to public policies.

Obviously, not every corporate need is right for this sort of treatment. Some objectives, i.e., reducing pollution controls or compromising safety requirements, are by definition not small public matters. Even a one-phrase insert in a committee report directed to accomplishing these sorts of objectives would become controversial and raise the report's profile. So, modesty is not a function of size and/or policy vehicle; it is a function of objective. Often, the greatest challenge for the lobbyist—who, even if employed (as opposed to retained) by the business organization s/he represents, is not part of the day-to-day business management—is to uncover and recognize these opportunities. Too often, the business managers do not think in terms of a legislative-related remedy for a problem with which they are wrestling. And the lobbyist, often based in Washington and frequently disdainful of "business people," does not know enough about the business to be aware that a remedial problem, and an opportunity to perform a client service, exists. This is the classic "failure to communicate."

Most organizations can and should benefit from identifying objectives unique to them, which may be pursued through low visibility activities that do not necessarily become a matter of public record. (By "low visibility activities" I mean two different, but usually [although not always] related elements. First are those *processes* or *procedures* necessary to accomplish the lobbyist's objective and/or affect a policy-related outcome. What is done—the *process(es)* used—to affect a government policy is what is at issue here, not the language per se. Second is the *substance* of the policy result—the public policy output.)

In contrast to major policy changes which become *high profile* issues and attract many interests and much media attention, issues that are truly small, that have relatively benign policy consequences, may attract little or no interest by any organization other than the one "sponsoring" the activity in question.

It is important here to note that while "pork barrel" amendments to appropriations bills probably meet the above-cited definition(s), especially to the extent that very minor expenditures for "pet" projects have been a long-standing, generally uncontested, and unnoticed mechanism for serving constituent and member interests, they are of a slightly different cast. To the extent that they have a common result, spending federal dollars, their cumulative effect on a single policy area, the federal budget, can be significant. Also, most (if not all) "pork-barrel" provisions can be easily traced to a single member or coalition of members. In recent years, some lawmakers and "watchdog" groups have attempted to call attention to "pork-barreling" and to eliminate the practice. Their efforts have been rewarded with precious little success.

The sort of activity I have in mind is subtler, and is certainly less traceable. In some instances, as in the one recounted above, there is no record of any *activity*. Nor is there any readily identifiable *policy result*. The company's offer to "turn states' evidence" and the chair's decision to spare the company public humiliation, and thus help protect its reputation, were clearly off-the-record acts. While the result for each was meaningful, and the public probably benefitted from the additional information made available to the chair's committee, no one beyond the two principals knew that the event had taken place.

However, not all SBRs can be as stealth-like. Usually, some sort of public record or document is necessary to implement a policy sought by a lobbying organization. Among the most effective of these off-the-record activities is early intervention in the bill writing process. Before a bill actually becomes a bill—that is, before it is ever introduced—there is no record of who adds or deletes any given provision. Members are free to advance any position they would like to see included. Aggressive legislators understand the added leverage gained by getting their "oar in the water" early, and astute, well informed lobbyists continually have their eyes and ears open for opportunities to affect a bill before it is "thrown in the hopper." So, the anonymity which is virtually assured during the early drafting stages serves lobbyists and legislators well; it enables members to have a relatively free hand (in political terms) in representing the needs of interests they deem to be important for political or substantive purposes.

A brief aside is worth mentioning here. The lobbyist-client relationship is not always a "what you are seeing is what you are getting" proposition. Lobbyists can be like double agents. And, while this is especially true of contract (retained) lobbyists who represent many clients, it also can be true when the lobbyist is "in-house." I mention this in the context of early intervention because it is not uncommon for a member, interested in making a lobbyist look good to his/her client (employer), to put a provision in a bill without any intent to protect it at later stages of the legislative process. There is value for legislators and lobbyists in keeping large (primarily business) organizations content, even optimistic, for as long a period as possible—at least through one fundraising cycle.

Lobbyists are anxious to show their clients that they can achieve results within the legislative system—even if these are only short-term results. Getting a provision into a bill, notwithstanding that it is later eliminated, can be seen as evidence that a lobbyist is effective and worth keeping around for another try in a future Congress.

It is not too paranoid or cynical to suggest that lobbyists and legislators well understand that their fortunes are often linked. Each has something the other needs: lawmakers write the laws that lobbyists get paid to affect; lobbyists can provide the information, exposure, and campaign funds members need to further their careers. Each has an interest in making the other look good to the lobbyists' well-heeled clients.

Nor is it too cynical to suggest that lobbyists and legislators, either knowingly or instinctively, play on the naivete of the organizations that lobbyists represent. Lawmaking processes can be complicated and confounding to even the most experienced legislative professionals. This is especially true for major, high profile legislation. The players are many and the strategies and tactics they employ can be complex. Add to this the mores of the House and Senate—which differ markedly—plus the machinations of the executive branch, and it is little wonder that even the most sophisticated business people become confused and disoriented. It is a system in which legislative provisions can easily become lost "in the shuffle" and blame placed on people and powers beyond one's control. Lobbyists and lawmakers play on this confusion and use it to mask their failures: "Well, we got it into a bill this time. That's good. It sends a positive signal for the next Congress."

Well, *maybe.* (And that is being generous.)

Small, company-specific legislative objectives can certainly fall prey to these sorts of complications. But there is little question that the more targeted and modest the objective, and the fewer on-the-record procedures needed to accomplish the objective, the better the chances are to obtain a positive result. SBRs can help to achieve a win-win-win for lobbyists, legislators, and lobby organizations without the need to become embroiled in the full-fledged legislative process. Whether it is an effort to affect a rule issuing from a federal agency—something that in the post-Keating-five era legislators are very careful about doing—importuning another member to vote a certain way in committee, inserting a key phrase in a committee report, or becoming involved at the early stages of the bill drafting process, SBRs offer legislators an opportunity to provide service to lobby organizations.

What is key is that SBRs, to the extent that they are entirely or largely off-the-record, give lawmakers political operating room that might not be available in a more public setting. Again, as noted above, this is not to say that the vast majority of legislators will do something covertly that is fundamentally different from what they would do in the full glare of legislative "sunshine." They will not. The flexibility that is granted through SBRs is more a matter of degree than of kind. The chair, in the example cited above, was able to make a trade off—gaining good information for holding the "witness" harmless—that he might not have been able to make had some of his more zealous supporters been aware that the deal was "going down." In his mind, the chair was not abusing the interests of these "constituents"; he was taking legislative license to better serve them.

Even when members "slip" language into a committee report—one of the most effective and frequently employed SBRs—they are seldom attempting to do something that would drastically alter the content of the bill for which the report is being issued. Nor are they attempting to do something that their constituents would consider a breach of their trust. As noted, members frequently use report language (and other SBRs) to accomplish objectives which have little substantive or political interest for the people in their state or district. Thus, there is no intent to deceive constituents. The goal is to serve an interest that his/her constituents would likely view as benign, but which has substantive or political appeal to the member.

To the purist, these acts may be considered subversions of the legislative process. They are executed in legislative shadows with the intent of drawing as little attention as possible. While it is true that the final product—bill language, committee report, or regulatory content—may often be reflected in a public document, and thus would be broadly reviewable, it is also true that the *process* designed to facilitate democratic representation is being intentionally circumvented by those most closely charged with stewardship of that *process*—the legislators themselves. Does this make SBRs by members wrong? The conclusion here is a resounding, *maybe!* Weak as it may seem, it is not a "copout" answer. It is the right one.

To the extent that legislators remain faithful to their constituents and use SBRs to pursue what they, in good faith, perceive to be appropriate ends, they (SBRs) probably serve a legitimate expediting purpose. But, to the extent that they are used to avoid full public evaluation of policy-related activities, they can be dangerous. After all, one member's understanding of what is a legitimate purpose may be another member's perception of an ill-founded, poorly supported, corrupt policy result.

Lobbyists will continue to seek SBRs when and if they can be deemed to serve their clients' ends. Few lobbyists, even those representing so-called public interest groups, will resist the opportunity to accomplish their objective(s) in the most efficient, least confrontational way. Democratic process is not their worry; it is not what their clients pay them to protect. Only the lawmakers themselves can assure that what happens in the shadows of Capitol Hill could, if need be, withstand the exposure that comes with legislative sunshine.

Notes:

1.Since 1991, the Federal Election Commission has required that contributions made directly to national party "non-federal accounts" must be disclosed. But, by funneling money through PACs and "foundations" registered in selected states, some political leaders and contributors found ways around the reporting requirements. Legislation passed in the 106th Congress has, supposedly, closed that "loophole."

2.This observation is based on interview-based research that I am conducting for presentation in other venues.

3.This point is well illustrated in Jeffrey Birnbaum's book, *The Lobbyists* (Times Books, 1992), which he recounts the efforts of several major lobbyists to affect the 1989-90 deficit reduction legislation. Most of these lobbyists lose outright; a few gain modest results.

Chapter 32

Congress and the Media

Otis Pike (D-New York)

The relationship between Congress and the media is symbiotic, constantly changing, and very, very tricky.

It is symbiotic in that the media need an endless supply of news. They need it 365 days a year, and Congress provides it. Members of Congress need publicity. Good publicity gets them reelected. Bad publicity ends their careers.

The changes in the relationship between Congress and the media over the last 50 years have been dramatic. The criteria by which all public servants are judged are constantly changing. The public today is less interested in what a congressman's or candidate's religious beliefs are or what his military service was, and the media asks about it less and talks about it less. However, the media are far more interested and intrusive about almost all other aspects of a congressman's or congresswoman's personal life. They claim the public has a "right to know" about his or her home life, outside assets, income, tax returns, eating and drinking habits, and marital and extra-marital relationships. The word "ethics" is not even to be found in the index of Congressional Quarterly's comprehensive volume, *Congress and the Nation*, covering the years 1945-1964. Since then, the media, the public, and the Congress have been obsessed with the subject.

It is the task of the media to report news. Since they need some every single day, when the supply of news is low, they create their own. They take polls, and the results of their polls are news. They choose the questions to be asked, thereby giving significance to some issues in which Congress might not be interested. They ignore other issues that members of Congress might find significant. Every day's news gets Congress's interest, and big news usually triggers some kind of congressional action. Really big news will find Congress falling all over itself with duplicate and even quadruplicate hearings all dealing with the same subject.

When the Congress is in session, the media treat some issues the members are dealing with as more important than others. They treat some issues as more important than they should be. Nothing excites some portions of the media (daytime radio talk shows, for example) more than the subject of congressional pay. There will be a frenzy of reporting on any possibility of a pay raise. The Congress will be subject to hostile criticism, will be embarrassed, and probably will vote against something they not only want, but truly believe they deserve.

When the Congress is not in session, the media do think pieces, analyses, projections, and predictions about what the Congress will do when it returns.

The multiple tasks of the Congress, as set out in the Constitution, include writing the laws of the federal union, providing for the common defense, monitoring our conduct with other nations, serving as the conduit through which our citizens petition their government for the redress of grievances, both real and imaginary, and imposing the taxes necessary to pay for all the functions of government, including not only the legislative branch, but the executive and judicial branches as well.

Unfortunately, every congressman or would-be-congressman is constantly and acutely aware that he or she can perform none of these mandatory duties unless he or she is in Congress. Accordingly, and sadly, the priority task for most members of Congress has appeared to be the formidable one of getting nominated and elected in the first place and getting reelected as often as possible thereafter. Always, of course, only so that he or she may most worthily perform the duties entrusted to them by the Constitution. It is in the priority task of winning elections that the relations between Congress and the media are the trickiest. The media can be either an invaluable ally or a mortal enemy.

So, how does a member of Congress best handle this trickiest of relationships? Above all, by being honest with the media. Members must tell the media about any of their actions that they believe are properly the public's business. They must tell plainly and precisely what they did and when they did it. They should report the circumstances surrounding the action, what they said, and what other people present said and did, in committee meetings or on the floor.

Telling the media *why* they did it, as opposed to what they did, is an iffier matter. If a congressman believes that a bill or an amendment is good and can make a plausible, reasonable argument on its behalf, he should vote for it, even if it benefits some person or corporation that has contributed to his or her campaign. Politics is a tough business. An opponent is likely to question a congressman's motives on such an issue, and the media may, too, but a member of Congress who conducts his or her entire career worrying about the next election or the media won't get much done. This former member believes that the best approach to take on any action on which you or your motives may be questioned is to raise the issue yourself. We had a "Sore Thumb" doctrine in our office in which any of the usual items for criticism–voting for a pay raise or a tax raise or taking a trip at the taxpayers expense–stuck out like a sore thumb. The action taken or to be taken was described, the reasons for the action presented. If any opponent or member of the media wanted to criticize, at least you had been straight-forward, had not tried to hide anything, or been furtive. We frequently would conclude a release on such a subject with the words, "Remember, you heard it here first."

However, frequently, the media asks members of Congress about personal or private matters that the member believes are not properly in the public domain. The member on such an occasion should smile pleasantly and say, without profanity, "I don't think that's any of your business."

A member of Congress must recognize the nature of the media's job. They have deadlines, and if the legislator has a story on which he wants good coverage, it is essential that they get the story in plenty of time to develop it before their deadlines. Conversely, if the media are trying to get the member to comment about something on which he or she has no knowledge, it doesn't hurt to admit that, "This is a subject that is outside my area of expertise." But they must be honest with the media, return their calls, and not try to hide. "No comment" will sound better to the public than "Congressman X did not return repeated calls."

Any member of Congress knows, before he arrives in Washington, that certain newspapers in his district will never endorse him no matter how prodigious his performance and exemplary his deportment. He or she should enter into the mental computer the knowledge that the editor (or more likely, publisher) of such a paper is a benighted wretch, lost to the purview of reason and perhaps sanity. This does not mean that all the reporters who labor for that miserable publication are bad people. They might even turn out to be friends. A friendly reporter can do a great deal with adjectives and adverbs in a news story, and a modest application of adjectives like "brave," "honorable," and "decent," or adverbs like "courageously" and "modestly" in the stories about a congressman's legislative activities are worth more than the editorials blasting him at election time.

Reporters are just like congressmen: they are almost completely honest, some are extraordinarily bright, others are just ordinary. Some are aggressive and hard-working diggers after obscure facts; others may be lazier, but also easier for the member to get along with, for they will happily take any press releases the congressional office puts out, accept them just as written, and pass them along verbatim to their readers.

The print media are where the most serious coverage of important issues will be found. Yes, Virginia, there are serious issues that do receive serious coverage. While network TV is more widely seen, it is limited, every night, by its half-hour format that must include, in addition to any issues involving Congress, news of the president's daily doings, major Supreme Court arguments or decisions, fires, floods, drought, tornadoes, hurricanes, plane or train crashes, epidemics, drugs and drug abuse, major criminal activity of all varieties, the stock market, sports, the death of prominent persons, and the weather, always leaving ample time for the purveyors of beer, automobiles, and cures for every form of stress or discomfort caused by the news. It will be a rare night when network TV can find time to give Congress more than two minutes. Most congressional activities are only worth two minutes, but even the most important issues and actions are only skimmed by network TV.

Public TV and public radio are much better. C-SPAN has created a new breed of congressional junkies who get more coverage of Congress than most of the subject matter deserves. When the same faces appear on C-SPAN speaking from the same ideological perspective night after night, they get overexposed. The old epigram, "Nobody ever got beat by a speech he didn't make," is valid, if ungrammatical. Several recent practitioners of the art of hogging special order time on C-SPAN could attest to the fact that no one ever got elected president that way either.

Public radio goes into depth on some subjects Congress is dealing with, so does some public TV, but there is an unreal quality to this programming, because on any issue about which the Congress is 90 percent agreed, they feel compelled to give equal time to the ten percent. In the effort to achieve balance, they lose perspective. When CNN does one of its in-depth studies on any issue, it is excellent, but the issue may not be on the congressional agenda.

For serious coverage on a consistent basis, however, you still have to look to the print media. The best newspapers, *The New York Times, The Washington Post, The Chicago Tribune, The Los Angeles Times*, and a host of smaller, excellent regional newspapers do serious, in-depth coverage of real issues. These are the papers where members of Congress most want their voice heard and their position treated with respect. Unfortunately for the members, the more prestigious a paper is, the more aloof it is and the harder to get into. No congressman should beg for coverage or be obsequious, but it won't hurt to invite some reporter for the best paper in his district to drop around the office for an off-the-record chat from time to time. If the reporter suggests the cocktail hour, so much the better. Unless you are after a very top reporter, he needs the congressman as much as the congressman needs him.

There are several techniques by which a member may get coverage that might otherwise be hard to come by. One is timing. No member should put out his releases when everyone else is doing it. This is usually on Thursday or Friday, at the end of the legislative week. Saturday papers are the least read of the week, anyway. However, Monday's papers start everyone's work week and are widely read. They are put together on Sunday, when even the best and biggest papers have only skeleton staffs working. Such overworked reporters and editors are much more likely to use a statement issued for release on Monday morning. So are the TV and radio reporters.

Former Senator William Proxmire of Wisconsin and his House colleague from the same state, Les Aspin, managed to get magnificent coverage, usually on Mondays, by efficiently timing their releases. A not-very-newsworthy release on a slow news day is much more likely to be reported than one that seems to the congressman to be a blockbuster release on a busy news day.

Another mildly controversial technique that usually works for the congressman in getting coverage he might not otherwise get is the use of humor. He shouldn't use it too frequently or on serious subjects, for it can backfire. The best use he can make of it is not on his adversaries, but on himself. This congressman used to make a weekly radio broadcast on seven radio stations in his district and soon learned that the most popular feature of the radio program was when I read over the air the most abusive letter I had received the previous week that was not profane. At the end of the letter, I didn't try to argue with the writer or otherwise comment. A simple, long drawn out W-E-L-L, in old Jack Benny style, would work, or "The views that you have just heard expressed do not necessarily represent the views of the station to which you are listening." The more abusive the letter, the more listeners will realize that a congressman's job isn't all joy and junkets. Any congressman that doesn't get some abusive letters every week isn't doing his or her job. The best congressional releases and reports put out during my stay in Congress (Mo Udall of Arizona and Bill Hungate of Missouri come to mind) used humor gently and effectively, frequently laughing at themselves.

Humor also can be used effectively against those newspapers or radio stations that a congressman knows are going to endorse his opponent. Early in my term, I sent to all the media in my district, before the campaign, a ten item document labeled "The Handy Quick-Reference Blast Pike Kit." It contained ten things I knew they were going to say about me, anyway: (1) Pike is too liberal; (2) Pike hasn't accomplished enough for his district; etc.

The friendly newspapers, and the big ones, printed it and laughed. When the other ones, during the campaign, printed the stuff, we were at least able to say that they did it just the way we told them to.

Thanks to the franking privilege, a member of Congress is to a very large extent his or her own media machine. The best rule he or she can follow in mailing out releases under the frank is: don't overdo it. Voters will know he is using taxpayer money. The voters will appreciate the opportunity to express their views on public issues in honestly and objectively worded questionnaires, but they will recognize grossly slanted questions and resent them. Any congressman can get any result to a questionnaire that he wants by wording the questions to get the results he wants, but most of his district will recognize what he is doing and it will hurt him rather than help him.

A franked report to constituents should not paint the congressman's positions and accomplishments as the greatest thing since sliced bread and indoor plumbing. Doing so will cause a serious loss of credibility. He should not make easy issues appear difficult, but when issues are close, (and some of them are very close), he should present both sides of the issue, tell where he came down on it, and the reasons for his decision. The constituents will understand, and even if the congressman, in their opinion, came down on the wrong side of the issue, they will appreciate his candor.

Since, in sending out releases under the frank, the congressman is taking over the role of the media, he also should provide what the media does–tough editing.

Usually, the first thing that he should do is go over his draft before it is sent to the printer and take out at least half of the I's. Any document absolutely full of the vertical pronoun will bore one's constituents, rub them the wrong way, and make the congressman appear to be a blowhard.

One of the areas in which both members of Congress and the media have tensions is in the question of what to do with secrets. Very few congressmen, including those serving on the Intelligence, Armed Services, or Foreign Affairs or Foreign Relations committees, learn many secrets that will truly affect national security. Ben Bradlee, the longtime editor of the *Washington Post*, said in his autobiography, *A Good Life* (Simon and Schuster: 1995), "It is a formidable task to convince the public that officials often–more often than not, in my experience–use the claim of national security as a smoke screen to cover up their own embarrassment."

A classic example of such a situation would come about when a member of the Armed Services Committee might learn that a new piece of military equipment, a plane or a tank or a naval vessel, was not performing up to its specifications as well as costing twice as much as it was supposed to. Clearly, the capability of our military equipment is a matter of national security. The cost overrun, however, is largely of concern only to the service that bought it, the contractor who made it, and the taxpayers who are paying for it. Despite the fact that the number of people involved in any defense procurement is so large that the cost overrun has to be widely known by people in the industry (and any "enemies" that are paying attention), the Pentagon will label both the performance problems and the cost overruns as "Top Secret." Sooner or later, a reporter who has heard about the cost overruns will ask the congressman what he knows about it. The congressman will appear stupid if he claims he doesn't know anything about it. He's on the committee that's supposed to know. He will appear almost as stupid if he says, "That's classified information." The reporter already knows. Everybody who cares knows except the taxpayers, whom he's supposed to be representing. This is one of those situations in which, under present law, the congressman has no choice except to suck up his gut and look stupid. If he is asked about the performance failures, it's easy. He says, "That's classified information." He neither looks stupid nor feels stupid, because it ought to be. As stated above, there are very few such situations that a congressman will get involved in, but on those few occasions, it will cause tensions between the congressman and the media.

There will be worse tensions. There are times in the career of any congressman or candidate when he will feel that the media have treated him unfairly. It is more than possible that he is right. No one in public office was ever guaranteed media treatment that he would feel was fair, or even that was fair. There is a substantial amount of hypocrisy in the way the media treat the Congress. The editorial board of *The New York Times*, for example, has more influence on major legislation than almost any individual representative or senator. That same editorial board would never consider revealing their own investments or their tax returns to allow the public to consider whether their own financial interests were affected by their editorial positions. You believe they are not, but there is a double standard. They won't believe it of the Congress. TV commentators have no difficulty editorializing on, and fulminating against, the outside earnings of legislators. Between such commentary, they go off and collect $10,000 a pop making speeches (usually not very good ones) to interest groups and associations of all kinds. Their incomes, investments, holdings, and tax returns are as secret (more secret, recently) as anything the C.I.A. controls.

When a congressman feels that he has been treated unfairly by the media, or when he has had more of their hypocrisy than he can deal with, all he can do is smile, stick it in his mental computer, and not blow his stack. It doesn't hurt to point out to a reporter his errors or possible double standards; most reporters feel some need to keep an image of fairness, and it might do some good. It might do more good to complain to the reporter's boss, but that will make an enemy even more hostile of the reporter. The most difficult and best course for the congressman is to forget it.

When dealing with the print media, no congressman can afford to forget the photographers. The pictures they are taking can help or hurt at least as much as words. If a congressman is making a speech and a photographer he doesn't know is stationed in front of him taking shot after shot, a wise congressman will stop and ask the photographer for whom he's working. If it's a friendly paper, he should tell the audience what a great and enlightened publication it is and proceed with his speech. The photographer is trying to get a good picture of the congressman, one with that quality of statesmanship that he always knew he possessed but rarely found in his pictures. If the photographer is from a hostile paper or declines to say, the congressman should tell his audience that they will probably be treated, within the next 48 hours, to an exceedingly unattractive picture of the congressman with his mouth open and his eyes almost closed. Even the greatest orators in Congress blink sometimes. This announcement may embarrass the photographer enough to make him back off, but probably not. Photographers are a notoriously tough breed. They take pictures of mangled bodies at automobile wrecks. He's being paid to get an unflattering picture. As the executioner said before he pulled the switch, "It's nothing personal."

Let me close with two personal experiences, one showing how bad the media can be, one showing how wonderful.

The media can be this bad. A trusted *Newsday* reporter was given an advance look and some lead time on the biggest legislative accomplishment of my career, the creation of the Fire Island National Seashore. I had the wording and I had the maps. The metropolitan New York papers and TV stations would have been very interested. The reporter promised that, if I would let him copy the language and the maps, he would hold it for 48 hours so the rest of the area media could be informed. It was spread all over *Newsday* the next day. He broke his word. When I blew my stack and asked him how he could do that to me, he said only, "It was too good a story to keep."

The media can be more wonderful than anyone deserves. At the height of the Cold War, Russian bombers were always feared to be lurking just over the horizon, waiting to drop bombs on New York and anything else worth blowing up. We spent billions installing radars to detect them and building fighter planes to intercept them. A new interceptor, the F-106, was to be based close to my home town. The plane was extraordinarily noisy and the locals weren't all that crazy about staying awake all night to protect New York City; they were mildly mutinous. As a buttering-up operation, the manufacturer arranged a three-day junket to San Diego, where the invitees would see their fine propaganda film entitled, "The Sound of Freedom." All the local politicians were invited, the heads of all the service clubs and chambers of commerce, representatives of the clergy and, of course, the media.

No red-blooded young American politician could go to San Diego on a three-day junket without slipping across the border to Tijuana to cement international relations and sample a remarkable potion consisting of a pinch of salt, a bite of lime, and a shot of tequila. Much sampling was required to get it right.

We got back at 4:00 a.m. and when the alarm went off at 6:30, this old Marine couldn't do it. I rejoined the group around 1:00 p.m. and was roundly abused for a lack of valor. This didn't hurt as much as being told that the group picture, the one in front of the wind tunnel, had been taken that morning. Everyone was in it, minus one. The editor of the local paper was a good friend and on the trip home, I begged him not to run the picture. He said 20 other people felt the other way and he had to. Sure enough, on Thursday, there was the picture spread very large across the front page. Beneath the right hand corner, very small, were the wonderful fictional words, "Photo by Pike."

Chapter 33

Dealing with the Press

Lou Frey, Jr. (R-Florida)

In my frequent talks at high schools and colleges, students often ask me if I like the press. The answer is: yes, if they write a favorable story; no, if they don't. However, they are an essential part of our democracy and as a member you have to learn how to live with them. You can't run and hide. You must deal with a normally hostile press. Without press coverage, it is tough to get elected or reelected. The press must deal with a normally suspicious congressman. It is an unholy alliance, both needing the other to exist, but not terribly happy with the prospect.

I tell students that I have two basic rules of politics which involve the press. The first is, "Don't get in a fight with someone who buys their ink by the carload (i.e., the press)." The second is, "If you have to explain, you're in trouble." In political life, there is a continuous war between the press and the member. The member attempts to use the press to favorably present his views so he can remain popular. The press needs the congressman in order to write interesting stories in order to sell newspapers or get high ratings in TV and radio in order to sell advertising.

As we well know, good news does not sell as well as bad or sensational news. When I was campaigning statewide in areas where people had not heard of me (most of Florida), I would kid the crowd saying I knew they had not heard of me although I was in the leadership of Congress and was picked by *Time* magazine as one of the 200 rising leaders of our country. I would add that the reason they had never heard of me was that I was never indicted. People would usually chuckle at that observation, recognizing that, unfortunately, there was a great deal of truth in what I said.

There are, fortunately, many ways to get press coverage without being indicted. For most congressmen not in the leadership, appearances on national news is rare and appearances on local TV infrequent, as most stations cannot afford a crew or a reporter in Washington. The member will receive some coverage when traveling at home and doing something newsworthy. However, most of the time, state and local politicians get more coverage. As a rule, senators command more press than House members. The reason is obvious. There are only two senators in each state, while many states have ten or more House members fighting for press coverage.

CAN YOU EVER TRUST A REPORTER?

No. Their job is to get the news and, in some cases, your job is to see that they don't get the news, or only get your version of what happened. Sometimes you can go off the record with a reporter, or talk just for background. Good reporters usually will keep their word and not use your name, as they want to come back to you again and again for information. But if the story is big enough, you are going to read or hear what you said, no matter whether you were on or off the record.

When I first got to Washington, a congressman who was retiring told me to treat everything, including phone calls, as on the record and I would stay out of trouble. Most people who have been in Washington for a long time say that there was more of a comfortable relationship between the press and the Congress prior to Watergate. For instance, the personal side of a member's life was off limits. Of course, that is long gone. Just ask Gary Hart, among others. When reporters smell blood, such as with President Nixon, Senator Gary Hart, or Speaker Jim Wright, it is like a feeding frenzy of sharks. Each and every day, some item is in the news with each reporter attempting to find a new angle or get an exclusive story. Once you become a part of the feeding frenzy, it is very difficult to survive. The best solution is not to get in the middle.

During the mid-1970s, Koreagate was the in-scandal in Washington. I say the in-scandal because such outbreaks are like the flu, breaking out practically yearly. The question on the lips of every reporter in Washington was, "Do you know Tongsun Park (a Korean national), have you attended any of his parties, and have you received any gifts from him or the Korean government?"

I had no aversion to parties, but I had not gone to any receptions given by Park, nor received anything from anybody involved with Korea. I informed my press secretary of this and she diligently informed the hungry reporters.

On major national stories, the wire services usually divide the country into sections. One reporter, for instance, will be responsible for the southeast. In my hometown paper, *The Orlando Sentinel*, there were approximately 30 paragraphs written about Koreagate, covering all the congressmen in the southeast. The quote from my press secretary appeared, somewhere in the middle of this, stating the facts accurately. It seemed impossible to get negative press from this statement.

If you are in political office, especially on the national scene, you live by your newspaper carrier. When the paper comes to your house and you hear it hit with a thud, you automatically get up and stagger out to see if anything happened while you slept. Reporters will call at any hour. It could be embarrassing if you got a call at 6 a.m. about a major event, such as an assassination of an American leader, and you didn't know it happened.

One morning as I was glancing at the newspaper, the phone rang. My mother lived nearby and was on the phone highly agitated. She said, "Lou, have you seen the headlines?" I said, "Yes, Mom, I've seen the headlines and it is really a shame about Koreagate." My mom said to me, "Is that all you can say? I am really surprised at you," and hung up. Now, there are many times when she could reasonably have been agitated, but this did not seem to be one of them, and it was the first time this had happened. The headlines in my edition of the Orlando paper said, "Congressmen involved in Koreagate" and the brief story about me was accurate. I puzzled a little bit, swallowed a little more coffee, and called my mom back. I said, "Mom, I don't understand the problem." She said "Well, let me read you the headlines." The headlines, which she said were in large bold type, screamed "Frey denies Korean connection."

What had happened was that the night editor, who was friendly with me, had read the story and wanted to make sure that everyone knew that I was not involved in Koreagate, wrote the headline with that end in mind. Apparently, someone at the paper had seen the initial edition, understood the negative implications and called the editor of the paper, who pulled the "Frey" headline and went to the headline that appeared in most of the papers, including mine. Approximately 20,000 papers carried the negative headline. The other 200,000 had the same headline as in my paper.

Obviously, I was upset. As a Republican, I had survived the riots in colleges, Vietnam, Watergate, but I now faced the prospect of everybody thinking I was involved in Koreagate. I met with the editor of the paper after I calmed down enough to discuss the matter. I received a very nice letter from the newspaper explaining what had happened and offering to write a retraction.

Now came the problem and the application of my two political rules. I was faced with the situation where there were approximately 20,000 people in my community who read the headlines and felt I was probably guilty. The other 200,000, whose paper did not have the same headline, had not read about my involvement in Koreagate. A retraction would call attention to the problem, and attacking the newspaper would be absolutely worthless.

Therefore, even though I was right and the newspaper wrong, even though everybody was in agreement as to the truth, I was probably better off not to ask for a retraction. Sometimes, you just have to take the hit and move on. You can gently suggest to the press that it would certainly be acceptable if, in the future, they ran a positive story on something you were doing. As I said when I began, it doesn't make sense to get in a fight with the newspaper, and once you start explaining, you just get into more trouble.

The exception to my rule comes when your political survival depends on explaining your position, even if it means fighting with the press. The bottom line is, in the survival situation, you have no real choice.

HOW CAN YOU GET YOUR MESSAGE OUT?

You can't control the press, but there are many ways to get your message out. Many of you have seen House members talking to an empty House chamber after a regular session has concluded. This is called special order time, and a member can usually talk up to an hour on any subject the member desires. Furthermore, members can hold press conferences in Washington and in the district which will be well-attended, if the subject is important and timely. Press releases are sent out district-wide weekly and are used primarily by weekly newspapers; some are given air time on radio news or talk radio stations. Also, a member will record short messages on newsworthy items aimed mainly at the radio stations in the district. The TV stations never use these. One of the key jobs of the press secretary is to get the member in the news. The press secretary uses the telephone to call and establish a good personal relationship with the various media outlets in the district and national ones covering the member because of committee assignments or leadership positions.

One of the best ways to control the press is to define your own image through a district wide newsletter to all households. This can be done at no cost by using the franking privilege, which each member has. This newsletter is supposed to be for information only and not to promote the member. But this is a very fine line, and most newsletters make the member look good. If my press secretary put out a newsletter that did not make me look good, it would be the last one she ever did.

Another way to control coverage is to send out a questionnaire to all households in the district. The questionnaire can be designed to highlight issues in which the member is involved. Also, questions can be asked about legislation that the member is planning to introduce or issues that are of special concern to the district. Once the questionnaires come back, the answers are tabulated and another opportunity is created to mail the answers back to the district. Also, the tabulation itself can be a plus for the member. I never used a computer to tabulate the questionnaires. I wanted people involved with me, so I used residents of senior citizen housing to do the tabulation. It was a great way to get the job done, get people involved, and as an added benefit, recruit future campaign workers.

Last, you can contact people in a district by sending out congratulations to high school and college graduates, as well as new brides and grooms. I also sent letters to people who accomplished some significant act, or to people on a major birthday or anniversary. Usually, one staff member is assigned to clip the newspapers for these names. In some cases, such as a 50th wedding anniversary, you could get the White House to send a letter from the president.

In conclusion, the best way to control the press is to create your own. Otherwise, you are fair game and you never know what is going to be said or written.

Part Seven

Congress and Policy-Making

The chapters in this section focus on the role of Congress in domestic and foreign policy-making. Inasmuch as all legislative policy-making must operate within the rules of procedure governing the House, this section begins with a review of these rules by Robert S. Walker, who served as chief deputy Republican whip when the Republicans took control of the House in 1995. As Walker explains, the rules of the House are both a powerful tool for the majority and a protection for the rights of the minority.

Next, Lionel Van Deerlin provides a case study of the congressional effort, in the 1970s, to rewrite the Communications Act of 1934. The decision to produce a comprehensive revision of the 1934 act was prompted by AT&T's attempt to secure legislation that would have permanently entrenched its monopoly position in the manufacture and sale of telephone equipment and provision of long distance service. This case features determined and resourceful legislators pitted against a virtual army of corporate lawyers for one of the largest and wealthiest corporations in America. While the eventual result shows clearly the significant advantages major corporations possess in struggles of this sort, we also see how experienced legislators seeking to defend the broader public interest can sometimes deflect a corporate juggernaut.

In parliamentary systems, the legislative agenda is tightly controlled by the prime minister and the cabinet. Within the American political system, by contrast, the executive does not have a monopoly on the initiative; individual members of Congress can and do draft legislation and work to secure passage. In Chapter 36, Lou Frey discusses the strategies and tactics he employed, as a member of the minority party, to succeed in passing legislation on several very different types of issues.

The focus shifts from domestic to foreign policy in the last four chapters in this section. Although Congress' role in formulating foreign policy is well known, its role in implementing foreign policy has received little attention from scholars. John Monagan examines this important, but little understood, contribution of Congress. Lee Hamilton discusses how Congress' involvement in the foreign policy process has changed over the past 35 years with the growth of congressional activism, the rise of television, the collapse of communism, and other developments.

In Chapter 39, H. Martin Lancaster provides an overview of Congress' role in defense policy-making, examining both the defense budget process and the congressional role in decisions to commit troops abroad. Finally, Glen Browder calls for new civil-military relations for the new millennium—one that recognizes the new realities of our post-Cold War environment.

Chapter 34

A Look at the Rules of the House

Robert S. Walker (R-Pennsylvania)

A wag once noted that the rules are the process by which the Congress keeps itself out of trouble which it might never have been in if it had not been for the rules. The rules are a complex set of procedures and precedents which few members of Congress understand in detail, but which govern the legislative actions of every member. Professional parliamentarians must be on constant call whenever the House meets to guide it through the complexities of its own rules process.

One of the first activities of each new Congress is to approve new rules. Actually, the practices and procedures adopted are not really new, but are an updated version of a process used for more than 200 years.

The underlying document used for governing the House of Representatives is the relevant provisions of the United States Constitution. Built upon the constitutional prerequisites are the procedures of Jefferson's Manual, the standing rules, and the precedents which provide interpretations of the meaning of the procedures and rules. There were 53 sections in Jefferson's Manual and 52 standing rules at the opening of the 104th Congress; but the precedents relating to that rather modest number of basic precepts run to thousands of pages.

Jefferson's Manual began as an exercise by Thomas Jefferson to provide guidance to himself in his duties as president of the Senate during the years of his vice presidency, 1797 to 1801. The manual, largely drawn from Jefferson's understanding of English parliamentary practice, was adopted by the House of Representatives as its fundamental rules package in 1837. Revisions and reforms have left little of Jefferson's original language applicable to daily House proceedings, but the manual is still the foundation on which House practice is built.

For the average member of Congress, the history of the rules, the bi-annual revisions, and the precedents have little real meaning. Most representatives want to know little more about the rules than how to keep themselves out of trouble when they are attempting to get something done on the House floor. Many arrive on the floor with written scripts designed to guide them through everything which needs to be said to get their proposition into play. Staff often sit at their side to advise them as the process unfolds. On the average, a representative does not have to be a student of the House rules to survive in the legislative maelstrom.

But for a few members, the rules are a source of fascination. The complexity is a challenge. The precedents provide not only a way to understand the past but an opportunity to find ways of getting things done in the present. Usually, those representatives who choose to establish a regular presence for themselves on the House floor, find that a thorough understanding of the rules is necessary for real effectiveness. Those who understand the rules can control the process.

To watch the House in action is to watch the rules in action. From the moment the gavel comes down to open the House of Representatives for the day to the time a strike of the gavel closes the session, each activity is governed by the rules. In fact, the chief function of the person occupying the Speaker's chair, sitting as the Speaker or Chairman of the Committee of the Whole, is to hold the House accountable to the rules.

At the beginning of a legislative day, the House is called to order by the Speaker. The daily hour of meeting is set by a House Resolution adopted on the opening day of each session. That hour can be changed by an order of the House at any time during the session, usually by unanimous consent after agreement by both party leaderships.

The scheduling of legislative business is the prerogative of the majority leadership. On the final legislative day of the week, someone representing the minority leadership normally will get unanimous consent to address the House for the purposes of asking a representative of the majority leadership about the schedule for the following week. The time is often used by the minority to quiz the majority about the announced program.

But an announced legislative program is not necessarily a firm commitment. As circumstances change, the majority sometimes will decide to pull bills previously scheduled, or even add legislation not previously anticipated.

In addition, many legislative matters are called up for consideration by "unanimous consent." Much business in the House actually takes place because everyone decides that it is non-controversial enough to pass without objection. In recent years, legislation can only be called up for unanimous consent consideration if it has been cleared by both the majority and minority leadership.

The first vote of many congressional days is to approve the journal. The Constitution requires the House to keep a journal of its proceedings, which is actually a summary of the day's actions. The Speaker is responsible for examining and approving the journal of the previous day, but the announcement of his approval can be put to a vote by any member. Many people, including most representatives, regard this vote as a nuisance, and some members refuse to waste their time coming to the chamber to cast this vote. But the reality is that the party leadership, who are anticipating close votes during the upcoming day, use this vote to do some head counting. The vote can be postponed by the Speaker if it has come at a particularly inopportune time.

Votes in the House, when recorded, are cast by electronic device. Each member is issued an individualized plastic card about the size of a credit card. In fact, the cards have been labeled by some as the most expensive credit cards in the world, referring to the national debt and spending programs. The cards are inserted in voting stations scattered around the House floor and members can vote their choice of yes, no, or present. During the 15 minutes of time allotted each vote, one can change that vote, but once the roll call ends and other business begins, the vote is final—no further voting or changing is permitted. In no case can another person or member cast a vote for a colleague.

The legislative day typically will get underway with a series of one minute speeches. Any member may make a speech on a subject of his or her choice, not to exceed one minute in duration. The themes are often political, but a wide range of subject matters usually can be expected.

As was mentioned before, a substantial amount of the work of the House is done by "unanimous consent" (i.e., when a member asks that something be done or permitted by unanimous consent and no other member objects to the request). The request can be as simple as limiting debate time on an amendment or as complex as consideration of whole bills. In most cases, the chair, hearing no one object, says simply: "Without objection, so ordered." And whatever was requested is done.

However, any member may object and stop the action cold. Or, if the exact nature of the request is not understood, a member may inquire by "reserving the right to object." The reservation gives the member control of the House floor for purposes of his inquiry. The time can be used to gain an understanding of what is going on or to ask any other questions. If unsatisfied by the answers, a member can raise an objection.

Most major pieces of legislation are considered under special rules written for that particular bill. Such rules are different from the Rules of the House confer privileged status to consideration of a bill, and set the terms for debate and amendment. Open rules allow unrestricted amendments, while closed rules limit or close off amendment opportunities. Sometimes, these rules also specify the order in which amendments will be considered.

The special rules are written in the Rules Committee and are drafted in accordance with the wishes of the majority leadership, often framed to give the majority political advantage. The rules are, for all practical purposes, not amendable.

When legislation is considered, it is most often done in the Committee of the Whole. The Committee of the Whole, an ancient device derived from the British House of Commons, is used to expedite the work of the House during debate and amendments to bills. In general, it involves less formal procedures, different tests for getting a recorded vote, and fewer numbers to establish a quorum.

The Speaker does not preside in the Committee of the Whole. Instead, he appoints a member of the majority party to preside as Chairman of the Committee of the Whole. The chairman has full authority to keep order, rule on questions, recognize members to speak, and vote.

An easy way to tell if the House is in Committee of the Whole is to look at the position of the ceremonial symbol of authority of the House, the Mace, which sits to the left of the Chair: if it is in a low position, rather than setting on its pedestal, the House is in Committee.

As legislative debate begins, either the manager of the bill moves to resolve the House into Committee or the Speaker, using the authorization of a special rule adopted for consideration of the legislation, simply declares the House so resolved.

The presiding officer now becomes not Mr. Speaker, but Mr. Chairman, and his first duty is to direct that the bill be read in total. Usually, the reading does not occur because there is an immediate call for the reading to be dispensed with or the rule governing the bill's consideration has automatically dispensed with the "first reading."

The chairman then recognizes a member of the majority party to manage the bill, usually either the chairman of the committee from which the legislation emerged or a subcommitee chairman. The debate time is allocated, one half the time to the bill manager and the other half to the minority. Debate time, typically one hour of general debate, has been set by the rule.

Any congressperson wanting to speak on the merits or demerits of the bill must request their time from the majority or minority managers. For example, the manager may give a member two minutes for remarks, and the chair will hold the speech to the time allocated. Additional time can only be granted by the managers. This debate is controlled dialogue, although members having been yielded time can yield to others for questions or comment within their allocation. In other words, while speaking for two minutes, a member can yield to a colleague for a comment, but the colleague's time comes out of the two minute allotment.

There are certain rules of conduct which govern debate. Those doing the speaking cannot impugn the motives of another member, nor can they use offensive language or utter words that are deemed unparliamentary. Inappropriate speech can result in a demand that the speaker's words "be taken down." While somewhat arcane in the days of televised House sessions, the real result is a type of disciplinary action against someone who has stepped beyond the bounds of decorum. The most serious result of such action is that the offending member can be stopped from speaking on any matter for the rest of the legislative day.

Other rules also apply. Speakers must be standing while speaking. They must be appropriately dressed—meaning coats and ties for men and business-type dress for women. Members may be called to order by the chair for speeches which do not address the issue currently before the House. One other thing those speaking must keep in mind is not to call colleagues by their first names, but rather use the salutation of the "Gentlemen from Maryland" or the "Gentlewoman from California." This is done to prevent the debate from becoming personal in nature.

A quorum in the Committee of the Whole consists of 100 members. When there are fewer than 100 Congresspersons on the House floor, the chair can entertain a motion to summon members to record their presence. Depending on circumstances, the quorum call can be either optional or mandatory, but any member can request such a call. Usually, this will be done in conjunction with getting a vote on some matter, and the member will rise and say, "On that question, I demand a recorded vote, and pending that, I make a point of order that a quorum is not present." Bells are then rung throughout the Capitol complex summoning all representatives to come to the House chamber and record their presence and their vote. They have at least 15 minutes to answer the call.

Once general debate has been completed on a piece of legislation, the Committee of the Whole normally considers amendments under the five minute rule. A member offering an amendment is granted five minutes of time to explain the amendment. Anyone wishing to discuss the amendment, pro or con, also is granted five minutes to make his or her case. The time can be extended for each speaker by unanimous consent.

All amendments must be germane to the underlying bill and the section of the bill to which it is offered. An amendment ruled non-germane can be ruled out of order and therefore may not be offered.

Sometimes, members rising to debate under the five minute rule will move "to strike the last word." This is a *pro forma* device to obtain time without having to indicate whether you oppose or support the amendment under consideration. Once the representative speaking under this procedure has finished, the *pro forma* amendment is considered to have been automatically withdrawn and no vote is taken.

When debate on an amendment has been concluded, the author of the amendment or any other member can request a vote on it. The chair puts the question and the yeas and nays are shouted by proponents and opponents. The chairman then declares his opinion of that voice vote, namely that the amendment has either passed or failed. Anyone not satisfied with the voice vote outcome can ask for a division vote—members in the chamber are asked to stand for either the yes position or the no position and the chair counts all members standing—or a recorded vote where representatives are called to the House chamber to cast their votes with the electronic voting cards.

When all amendments have been considered, the Committee rises and reports the bill back to the House with the recommendation that the legislation as amended be passed. At this point, the Committee of the Whole is disbanded and the Speaker resumes the chair.

Now comes a series of actions aimed at moving the legislation toward final passage. Any amendment adopted in the Committee of the Whole can be re-voted in the House. Then the Speaker puts the previous question on the bill and all amendments thereto. After engrossment—putting the bill in its official form—and a third reading of the legislation, the clerk reads the bill's title. A motion to recommit may be offered by any member opposed to the legislation in its present form. This motion may either be straight—which, if adopted, would send the bill back to the subject committee from which it emerged—or with instructions. Here, the legislation is changed in some specific way in the same manner as an amendment would change the bill. Generally, motions to recommit are offered by the minority manager of the legislation.

One may wonder why an opponent would resort to a motion to recommit rather than an amendment. Sometimes, under closed rules, where amendments are limited or non-existent, the motion to recommit is the only way to get the bill changed. In other cases, the motion gives the minority one last chance to make a major change in the legislation.

Following the disposal of any motion to recommit, the House moves to final passage of the measure under consideration. Again, many bills are passed by voice vote, but any representative can demand a record vote. That record vote can be obtained either by suggesting the presence of no quorum if less than 218 members are on the floor, or by getting a sufficient number of members to stand to request such a vote. The number of standees varies depending on how the recorded vote is requested, but for all practical purposes is between 40 and 50.

When the vote is over, the Speaker announces the results. The motion to reconsider the bill is then disposed usually with the statement, "Without objection, the motion to reconsider is laid upon the table." Sometimes, members bent upon slowing down the legislative process will get a vote on the procedural matters, but typically the action is *pro forma*. Once completed, the parliamentary effect is to end any possibility that the bill can be brought up again.

Any general description of House procedures must acknowledge some special circumstances under which legislation gets considered. On Mondays and Tuesdays, the Speaker can entertain motions to suspend the rules and pass legislation. Such motions require a two-thirds vote to succeed and debate is limited to 40 minutes—20 for a proponent and 20 for an opponent. These "suspensions" are unamendable.

Conference Reports are regularly scheduled for House action. The conference report is an agreed-to marriage between House and Senate versions of a legislative proposition. For a bill to be presented to the president for his signature, it must pass both the House and the Senate in the exact same form. Most such agreements are in the form of a conference report that gets one hour of debate time before coming to a vote. These conference reports emerge from conference committees where members of the House and Senate meet to resolve their differences.

While most bills come to the floor after having been approved by a committee, there is a procedure for bypassing the committee process. A discharge petition may be filed after a bill has been introduced and referred to a committee for 30 legislative days or more. If a majority of the House membership (218) signs the petition, the bill must be brought up and considered.

Not all speeches in the House are directly related to pending business. At the end of a day's legislative schedule "special orders" are permitted where a member can discuss any matter or issue he or she wishes for up to one hour. Representatives must sign up for this time in advance.

A legislative day ends with a motion to adjourn. While typically this motion comes when all scheduled business has been completed, it is a highly privileged action and can be used to cut off further action in the House. This device is sometimes used by those unhappy with the House's scheduled activities to disrupt and delay the proceedings.

The rules are a powerful tool for the majority, and they protect the rights of the minority. The majority writes the rules and then uses them to implement its legislative program. The minority uses the procedures permitted under the rules to frustrate the legislative program whenever deemed suitable or necessary.

Without rules, the legislative process would quickly deteriorate into chaos. It does so sometimes even with rules. But the importance of the rules is that they permit all members to exercise their representative functions. This is done by putting their ideas into legislative form and then debating them, by allowing them to interact with other representatives, and by providing them with an orderly format for making their opinions heard.

Thomas Jefferson noted as he began drafting his legislative manual that nothing leads more to an abuse of power than "a neglect of, or departure from, the rules of proceeding." He went on to note that the rules served "as a check and control on the actions of the majority" and as "a shelter and protection to the minority." So it is today. The rules of the House make the House the unique citadel of democracy which it has been and will continue to be.

Chapter 35

Rewriting the Communications Act

Lionel Van Deerlin (D– California)

The first nationwide opinion poll in advance of a presidential election was conducted in 1936 by a magazine called *The Literary Digest*. It showed Kansas Governor Alf Landon leading President Roosevelt by two to one. When Landon subsequently won only Maine and Vermont, the *Digest* went out of business.

Were the *Digest*'s editors guilty of attempted political manipulation? No, theirs was an honest poll, flawed in only one respect. It had been conducted by telephone. And in that era, scarcely two generations ago, fewer than 40 percent of U.S. households had telephones. Inasmuch as they were something of a luxury, phones were mainly in homes of the well-to-do—of people who, then as now, were likely to be Republicans.

Today 95 out of a 100 Americans have a telephone. This isn't just because affluence is more widespread. It's also because the local telephone, thanks to a number of factors, became a bargain. Automatic switching reduced Ma Bell's labor costs. Low-interest government loans made full rural service possible. And finally—goaded by state regulators to hold the price line—the telephone monopoly, American Telephone & Telegraph, presided for many years over a system that soaked it to long-distance callers to provide a subsidy for crosstown service.

As a result of all this, America's communications network became the envy of the world. Where other nations ran their telephone systems as state-owned monopolies, the United States permitted AT&T to become the world's biggest privately-owned corporation, with tightly regulated rates and standards of service. Under a 1934 law, the company was sole provider of all equipment from the basic black phone to gigantic PBX extension systems. Through 22 subsidiaries around the country, moreover, it dominated both local and inter-city service.

Like medieval castle guards, an army of AT&T lawyers stood ever at the ready to repulse any assault on those monopoly rights. No perceived threat was too obscure. In North Carolina, they once prosecuted a dealer for selling plastic covers that wrapped around the phone directory!

Inevitably, monopoly protection dampens innovation. Thus, it was not mighty AT&T, but a small company calling itself "Hush-a-Phone" that marketed a convenient attachment designed to ease telephone conversation in noisy surroundings. No high technology, this—hardly more complex than a cupped hand around the mouthpiece. But Hush-a-Phone knocked the first critical prop from under Ma Bell's legal battlement with a court ruling, in the early 1950s, that its attachment constituted no public detriment. Other imaginative new devices, such as the Carterfone, and next microwave and satellite transmission—cheaper and more efficient than AT&T's landlines—crumbled the castle wall still further. State commissions and the courts combined to open the door for ever greater numbers of competitors. Meanwhile, the Justice Department filed the second of two major antitrust suits against Bell.

The settlement of that eight-year-old case, shortly after Christmas 1981, gave us the most profound change of all. The breakup of AT&T (which, even after divestiture, remained the world's second largest corporation) had its origins in Congress. It marked a reversal of company plans which envisioned a perpetual telecommunications pyramid with private management dictating the rates it would share for interconnection with other companies at home and abroad. (AT&T's "Separation & Settlements" system filled an entire blackboard in our hearing room with arrows tracing cash flow in and out of company coffers, together with myriad discounts. Its arcane provisions purportedly were understood by not more than a dozen insiders.)

It was in 1976, the year of the Bicentennial, that AT&T sent its briefcase brigades storming up Capitol Hill. Massive numbers of prisoners were taken in the first onslaught. A total of 189 House members, plus one-fifth of the Senate, were lined up as cosponsors of a legislative proposal the company was intent on passing.

AT&T's bill may have been the boldest move of its kind since creation of the East India Company in British colonial days. The misnomer, "Consumer Communications Reform Act of 1976," hardly hinted at its purpose, which was to grant this corporation total rights to the manufacture and sale of telephone equipment and the sole right to provide long-distance toll connection. Bell would have exclusive dominion not only in the here and now, but for products and services it might provide in the future.

With just 18 additional House sponsors needed to make a majority, the "Bell bill" might have sailed through as law. Behind it were not only AT&T but also such major independent phone companies as GTE and the politically sophisticated Communications Workers of America.

It couldn't have come at a worse time. The Senate's longtime arbiter of communications policy, John Pastore (D-RI), had announced retirement, and the new leadership was not yet in place. Our veteran House subcommittee chairman,

Torbert Macdonald (D-MA) was wracked by a terminal illness, from which he died in May of that year.

I mention all this because some critics of the communications scene appear to have short memories. They fail to recall where things stood a scant 20 years ago—how close we came to a massive setback for competition and consumer interests generally, and who prevented it.

I like to think I helped somewhat after replacing Macdonald. But there were others—notably the ranking Republican on our subcommittee, Lou Frey of Florida. In an era when Republicans and Democrats may have eyed one another with less suspicion than now seems possible, Frey took the lead—first in manning the barricades against AT&T, later as an advocate of basic change in communications law. Jim Broyhill of North Carolina, then ranking minority member in the full Commerce Committee, was supportive once he was satisfied that Frey and I were not hellbent on "fixing something that ain't broke."

Rep. Tim Worth (D-CO) gave us the only legislative counter to the Bell bill, a pro-competition resolution that attracted a handful of cosponsors against AT&T's legions. (So overwhelming was the company's presence that Wirth on one occasion requested, "Will everyone in the hearing room who works for AT&T please rise?" Except for the press table, it seemed as if the entire audience stood.)

With diametrically opposite proposals on the same subject, I was then able to schedule hearings into "issues raised by competition in telecommunications" rather than on the Bell bill itself. Tennessee's Al Gore, then in his first congressional term, provided stalwart defense for the rights of rural telephone subscribers.

The high point of our early hearings came when the doughty Lou Frey—his mind reeling from the push and pull of testimony by Ma Bell and microwave moguls, by broadcasters, and an "encroaching" cable industry (along with eager advocates, self-anointed, of the public interest)—threw up his hands.

"Seems to me we're swimming upstream here," Frey exclaimed. "TV, cable, microwave, satellites, computers—none of these was known 50 years ago. Yet, here we are in 1976, trying to make sense of a 1934 communications law written to regulate only radio stations and the plain old telephone."

"Wouldn't it make sense to start over? Maybe it's time for a basic overhaul. Why don't we go through that 1934 act, basement to attic? Sure, why not rewrite the whole thing? Why not a new law encompassing the new technologies?"

And so it was that we went to work with an eye to updating the Communications Act of 1934, the Holy Sepulcher from which Bell claimed its monopoly. There followed nearly two years of fact-finding—95 public sessions, covering thousands of pages of testimony as we prepared a detailed record of where telecommunications had wandered since that basic law undertook to regulate the two technologies of its day, "radio" and "wire." A staff headed by chief counsel Harry M. (Chip) Shooshan produced a set of papers setting forth the multiple choices facing us in common-carrier regulation, ranking from the grab-bag dreams of Bell's board chairman, John DeButts, to the shredding of his empire as others proposed. When Frey and I dropped our first rewrite attempt into the House hopper, it proposed the divestiture of Bell's manufacturing arm, Western Electric—this conditioned on the company's keeping its 22 operating subsidiaries. But to assure other carriers reasonable access to those local systems, we proposed replacing the black art of Bell's Separation & Settlements (under which long-distance had subsidized home subscriber rates) with something we were prepared to call a Universal Service Compensation Fund, policed by the FCC.

None of the participants in Judge Harold Greene's historic antitrust settlement of January 1982 seemed ready, when dealing with our subcommittee, to make the concessions his court ordered. Ma Bell still had illusions that she could keep everything. Chairman DeButts said, "We cannot live with divestiture." Rejecting our restructuring proposals out of hand, DeButts committed the corporate equivalent of hara-kiri, taking early retirement. His successor, Charley Brown, told me at the outset that any legislation would have to preempt all pending or future antitrust actions against his company. (To his credit. Brown quickly moderated that position.) Bell's competitors—MCI, Southern Pacific Sprint, burgeoning electronic manufacturers, and a host of "value added" systems carrying voice and data—didn't want the hobbled giant free to compete in new technologies of the computer age. "Break Up Bell" was still the battle cry at Justice. State regulators refused to consider any plan that failed to guarantee low local rates in perpetuity, and other interested parties hovered in the wings: the cable industry, protective of its own rural monopolies; and the nation's newspaper publishers, nervous that Bell's prosperous Yellow Pages might eventually convert to electronic competition for classified ads.

Things rocked along until late 1979. Lou Frey had then left Congress to run for governor of Florida, moving the more conservative but equally collegial Jim Collins of Texas into our subcommittee's ranking minority spot. The bipartisan spirit by this time ran so deep that all subcommittee members of both parties put their names on a new bill aimed at unraveling the competition problem. Bell's enemies had been winning big at the FCC, where a compromise access-rate plan helped all of them gain a larger market share. Savoring prospects of a full antitrust disaster for Bell, they swarmed through members' offices opposing any legislation. Nonetheless, HR 6121 cleared the full Commerce Committee on a 35 to7 vote, opening the way for the first major change in communications law in 46 years.

To obtain that vote margin, it had been necessary to accept three anti-competitive amendments barring Bell or any of its subsidiaries from providing "electronic yellow pages," burglar alarm service, or cable television. Then a funny thing happened. Rep. Peter Rodino's House Judiciary Committee, having taken scant notice of our efforts until HR 6121 was out of Commerce, asked the Speaker to let Judiciary review its antitrust implications. Tip O'Neill gave them 30 days—taking the process so near adjournment that we ran out of time.

Such things work in quietly strange ways. A monolith like AT&T can't always get its way with lawmakers, but it can be deadly effective at stopping something. Though it publicly supported HR 6121, the company may have begun thinking the same thoughts as its competitors—that perhaps a better deal could be won in the courtroom. With such major New Jersey properties as Western Electric, Bell Labs, and Long Lines, I tend to believe AT&T would have come down hard on Rodino if it had been really upset at losing the bill. (Ironically, the Judiciary Committee, though seeming suddenly concerned that we were giving too much to the Big Mother, contained nine members who had obligingly cosponsored the original Bell giveaway back in 1976.)

If a slowdown was indeed company strategy, the deal cut in Judge Greene's antitrust settlement seemed to confirm its wisdom. Bell was permitted to cast loose its least profitable operations, the regional subsidiaries, while retaining those rich inter-exchange tolls as well as getting into data processing, home terminals, and the myriad other technologies of America's exciting information future. The cable industry and newspapers lost, at least temporarily, the protection our committee was willing to give them. Gone too was a three-tiered apparatus by which our bill would have kept local rates from rising more than ten percent a year.

An aphorism of the gridiron holds that when you throw a pass, three things can happen—two of which are bad. Is there solace for members and staff who struggled through the aborted communications "rewrite" of 1976-80?

Well, at least we prevented something bad.

Chapter 36

Legislative Entrepreneurship:
Different Strategies for Different Issues

Lou Frey, Jr. (R-Florida)

As a young congressman, you seek to find a way you can establish yourself as a player among the 434 other members. It is difficult to do, as you usually don't have enough seniority to be the chairman of a committee or subcommittee, and if you are in the minority, you will never be the chairman of a committee or subcommittee. I was in the Republican minority but figured out ways to get legislation passed. I became involved in several issues that were not related to my committees. This chapter will review how I succeeded in getting laws passed on five very different types of issues.

STEALTH LEGISLATION: MOBILE HOME SAFETY

In two cases, I was the only one in the House or Senate who had the original idea and drafted legislation implementing the idea. One bill was the Mobile Home Safety Bill and the other was the Noxious Weed Act. This section will focus on the Mobile Home Safety Bill, which was passed after five years of work without hearings ever being held in the House of Representatives. How it got passed gives one a good look at the way a single member can make a difference.

I did not know much about mobile homes, but a tragic fire in my district during my first term brought the problem of mobile home safety to my attention. During the fire, which started with a space heater, people were trapped in the mobile home because there were no push-out windows and only one exit. Also, the materials in the mobile home were especially flammable. No one survived. I found that, unfortunately, this was not abnormal and that many times people were trapped with flames between them and an outside exit, with bedroom windows high off the floor and often too small to crawl through.

I asked my staff to look into the problem in the district and in Florida. I assumed there were safety standards regulating the industry. After months of research, the staff found that in the early '70s, there had been a huge increase in mobile home production, plugging an important gap in the need for conventional homes. In 1973, mobile home production was approximately 600,000 units as compared to 200,000 in the mid '60s. In 1973, more than seven million people lived in mobile homes. Most importantly, half the single family houses built in the United States in 1973 were mobile homes, and 95 percent of the houses sold under $15,000 were mobile homes.

The research also indicated that, despite the great increase in mobile home production, all levels of government had failed to respond with effective safety regulations. There existed a confusing patchwork of local, state, and federal regulation, which also increased the cost of manufacturing mobile homes. Mobile homes were not subject, for the most part, to local building codes. Even when there was local regulation, it was not effective, as the mobile home was usually constructed outside the local jurisdiction and arrived completed. It made it difficult, if not impossible, for mobile homes to be inspected for conformity with local plumbing, heating, and electric construction codes.

Thirty-six (36) states had adopted varying versions of the mobile home code drafted by the American National Standards Institute (ANSI). There was an expense involved in conducting research and developing standards which states did not want to incur. States had to rely exclusively on the standards developed by ANSI. The code was criticized by many for not requiring usage of the latest technology and therefore providing inadequate protection to the consumer.

The Standards Institute also lacked the resources for its own research and had to rely on that of the industry to develop standards. Furthermore, ANSI had to use a consensus criterion in developing a new standard. In requiring adequate safety and quality levels, requiring a consensus put the emphasis on acceptability. Even in states that used ANSI, the code had been changed, with standards added or deleted. It had not been applied in a uniform manner.

Even more important, variation in enforcement procedures among states which had codes made reciprocity among the states impossible. In a number of states, no state enforcement agency was even designated. In other states, the enforcement agency existed only on paper because no funds had been appropriated to implement enforcement or no procedures were given to the state agency for enforcement. For example, only one inspector was employed, on a quarter time basis, to enforce construction requirements for 3,700 mobile homes sold in Nebraska in 1971. My state, Florida, where more mobile homes and recreational vehicles were sold than any other state in the nation, had only three inspectors from the time the ANSI construction standards were adopted in 1968 until July 1972, when three more inspectors were authorized. The states which had small inspection staffs allowed the manufacturer to self-certify. In essence, the ANSI code was a farce and did not promote mobile home safety.

When our internal research was completed, we were somewhat staggered by the scope of the problem. We spent several months looking for a legislative solution. As a Republican, the last thing I wanted to do was to add more government regulation or start a new government bureaucracy. However, it became clear that the existing patchwork of state, local, and federal regulations had increased manufacturing costs without giving us better safety. It became apparent that, to maximize the economies of mass production, it was essential to minimize needless variation in construction requirements. What was needed was a uniform set of federal standards that would preempt local and state standards and would allow the manufacturer to produce each unit to a single, federal standard. This would create a floor under competition and force out fly-by-night companies. The adoption of such standards would allow for greater sales and more profits for the manufacturer, and hold down insurance costs for the public. Most importantly, it would save lives and minimize injuries.

Now the problem really started. Mobile homeowners were not a powerful force throughout the country. They were low income and typically either very young or very old, unorganized, and unlikely to vote. By contrast, the mobile home industry was well organized and well financed, both in the states and nationally.

I knew it would take some time to build up a consensus, if possible, within the House. What I did was introduce the mobile home bill in 1972 and put it in front of the House with very few sponsors. The original sponsors were close personal friends whom I could talk into giving me a chance to build support for the legislation. The group included people such as Congressman Larry Coughlin (R-PA), Congressman Walter Flowers (D-AL), Congressman Bill Gunter (D-FL), Congressman Peter Kyros (D-ME), Congressman Bill Lehman (D-FL), and Congressman Ron Sarasin (R-CT).

We then began tracking problems of mobile homes nationally which, unfortunately, were many. I called these problems to the attention of fellow House members by making short speeches on the floor during the one minute period, by putting out press releases about disasters, ensuring they also went in the *Congressional Record*, and by writing "Dear Colleague" letters to the other 434 members asking for their support of my bill.

I also used press releases to try to get national attention. For instance, in June of 1972, Hurricane Agnes hit Florida. I sent a press release out which stated, "The high winds and tornadoes associated with Hurricane Agnes have caused considerable property damage and human suffering for the people of my district and throughout the State of Florida. Some of this could have been avoided if my Mobile Home Safety Bill were now law."

I obtained a survey about the hurricane from the Office of Civil Defense, and the Office of Emergency Preparedness, and put it into the *Congressional Record* in 1972. I also looked for opportunities to testify, such as in Los Angeles in front of the National Commission of Fire Prevention and Control. I pointed out to the commission that seven million Americans live in mobile homes, which were built without standardized safety requirements that would decrease the accidents caused by fire. I stated that one study showed the damage from mobile home fires cost an average $1,529, while fire and conventional damages averaged only $350.

On July 3, 1973, I sent a "Dear Colleague" letter to 434 members of the House which stated, "Over the recent Memorial Day weekend, windstorms and tornadoes in Arkansas, Alabama, Georgia, Oklahoma, and Tennessee destroyed 138 mobile homes and did major damage to 140 others. In addition, more than 40 persons were killed in those states. These recent statistics are just further evidence that legislation is necessary to make mobile homes a safer place to live. I have introduced such legislation in both the 92nd and 93rd Congresses, the Mobile Home and Recreational Vehicle Safety Act (HR 5224, 5225). This legislation is now pending before the Interstate and Foreign Commerce Committee, and hearings are scheduled for sometime after the August recess. Sad as it is, one thing that is certain is that more people will be needlessly killed until this legislation is passed. Your cosponsorship can create more momentum for early hearings. Cosponsors of this legislation already include Congressmen Anderson (of Illinois), Ashley, Bafalis, Bell, Biester, Brown (of Michigan), Broyhill (of Virginia), Buchanan, Cronin, Danielson, Donohue, Eilberg, Fascell, Frenzel, Gibbons, Grasso, Hastings, Hicks, Horton, Hosmer, Kemp, McClory, McCollister, McDade, McKinney, O'Hara, Pepper, Pettis, Roy, Roybal, Steele, Whitehurst, Williams, Wolff, and Zwach."

On March 6, 1973, I made a statement in the *Congressional Record* about the need for the bill (page H 1398). "For further information, or if you would like to cosponsor this legislation, please call Rick Knop in my office at x53671. I plan to reintroduce the bill shortly after the Congress reconvenes."

I kept this type of activity up year after year. It took a great deal of patience and tenacity to keep pushing this legislation, which had little public support.

My fight was within the House of Representatives. It was not an issue where the public was involved or really interested, so there was not a great deal of outside pressure on the Congress to act. I did not have to sell 180 million Americans, but only 218 in the House and 51 in the United States Senate.

It was not a bill that was going to defeat or elect someone because he or she had voted for or against it. The mobile home lobby was strong, but it was not strong enough to defeat or elect a person on this single issue. Furthermore, there was very little press outside that which I generated on this issue, both before and after its passage. You can compare this kind of legislation to a legislation that is more controversial and in the public eye, such as the balanced budget resolution or funding for abortion. I would term this kind of legislation "stealth legislation," because the lack of outside pressures and publicity allows a single member to be effective in distinct contrast to the situation on major legislation.

I was fortunate to get a good friend of mine, Bill Brock, who had been recently elected senator from Tennessee, to introduce a parallel bill in May of 1972 in the U.S. Senate. Brock in his press release said, "This bill introduced is similar to a proposal already introduced by Congressman Lou Frey of Florida whose interest and concern about mobile home construction first drew my attention to the great need for effective and reasonable legislation in this area."

It was obvious that the mobile home industry was not wild about my bill. However, I did not ignore them. I spoke in front of their meetings whenever I could. For example, at the 37th annual meeting of Mobile Home Manufacturer's Association at the Washington Hilton, I challenged the group to endorse my bill as other consumer groups had. I had picked up the endorsement of the National Association of Independent Insurers, who had 535 affiliated companies which wrote approximately 85 percent of the mobile home insurance policies in the United States. Civil defense groups, consumers' groups, the National World Cooperative Association, the National Council of Better Business Bureaus, and the International Association of Fire Chiefs also had endorsed the bill.

I continued to send out "Dear Colleague" letters and would get members on the bill from extremely different backgrounds and styles. For instance, in the 93rd session I introduced HR 14445 "To provide a uniform application of safety standards for mobile homes....on April 29, 1974." It had seven cosponsors, Boland (D-MA), Chisholm (D-NY), Kemp (R-NY), Luken (D-OH), Mazzoli (D-KY), Roncallo (R-NY), and Winn (R-KS). The press releases continued to help over a period of time, as did articles in various newspapers and magazines, such as the Rural Electrification magazine.

My emphasis stayed on my fellow House members, reminding them of the problems of mobile homes. But, the biggest problem I faced was that I could not get hearings in the Banking and Currency Committee, where the bill had been sent by the Parliamentarian of the House. The chairman of the committee, Wright Patman from Texas, was not interested in the bill, and despite all my hard work and many additional cosponsors, it was going nowhere.

However, by this time I was in the leadership of Congress and had learned the ropes. The bill did become law in 1975, even though committee hearings were never held in the House. The Senate had passed Senator Brock's bill as part of the 1975 omnibus Housing Bill. Although the House passed the Housing Bill without my mobile home legislation, the bill went to Conference, and I spent my time lobbying the House Republican conferees. The combination of the Senate conferees and the minority House Republican conferees resulted in the Senate Mobile Home Amendment being included in the final bill, even though the Democrat House conferees fought the Senate Bill. The bill reported out by the Conference Committee was then passed by the Senate and House and signed by the president. It became part of Public Law 93-383.

SECTOR LEGISLATION: THE NOXIOUS WEED BILL

The mobile home bill started with a phone call from some of my constituents. This call could have been made to any congressional district office around the country. Sometimes, however, you are called upon to address problems that specifically result from the physical characteristics of your district and state; such legislation should be thought of as "sector legislation." The Federal Noxious Weed Act, which I succeeded in enacting, provides one example of such legislation.

The idea for this legislation came when we attempted a cleanup of a large lake in my district, Lake Apopka, which was dying. The more we studied the lake, the more it appeared that the problems were caused by noxious weeds and that this was also a national problem. Research showed that, in 1973, it cost U.S. farmers $2.5 billion annually to control weeds which were injurious to their crops. In Florida, it was a special problem with many of the lakes, rivers, and streams choked with aquatic weeds, most of which were inadvertently brought into Florida from foreign countries.

It seemed strange to me that we were watching men leave the Kennedy Space Center for the moon, and yet were not able to navigate our lakes, rivers, and streams. I created a Florida federal aquatic weed control and research council plan, which was endorsed by seven participating agencies in departments in Florida and Washington. I found that there was a federal interagency coordinating committee on preventive weed control, which had been working on the noxious weed problem for approximately six years. I worked with both organizations to develop the legislation, which was quickly endorsed by the National Association of State Departments of Agricultures, the Weed Science Society of America, the Northeastern, Southern, North Central, and Western Weed Control Conferences, and many state weed control conferences. Unlike the mobile home bill, from the outset there was a large and powerful constituency for this legislation at both the public and the private (i.e., farmers') level.

The Secretary of Agriculture did not have the authority to designate as noxious those weeds which were new to the United States and not prevalent here, and those weeds which might be injurious to crops or other useful plants, livestock, or poultry, nor those weeds which might adversely impact other interests of agriculture, including irrigation, navigation, or public health. We found a California survey that had shown there were 500 foreign weed species in California alone, of which more than 70 percent were brought from Europe and Western Asia, 10 percent from Eastern Asia, South Africa, and Australia, 10 percent from South America.

The bill was introduced in April 1973. The same day, I put an explanation of the bill in the *Congressional Record* and pointed out that weeds caused a 13 to 18 percent annual reduction in crop yields. I further stated that a 1970 survey indicated that more than 97 million bushels of soybeans were lost to weeds. This loss was equal to the production of 3.7 million acres and valued at $212 million. While the soybean farmer was losing enormous sums of money due to reduced crop yields, he was paying $124 million for herbicides to control these deadly weeds. In my state of Florida, taxpayers were paying $10 to $15 million for programs designed to control and ultimately rid the state of aquatic weeds, but they were losing the battle.

When I introduced the bill, I did not ask for cosponsors, which is very unusual. I knew this was a good issue that had broad support and no known opposition, and I saw no reason to share the credit. The bill moved quickly. On May 16, 1973, the agriculture committee requested executive comments from the agriculture department. I testified on the first day of hearings of the Conservation and Credit subcommittee of the Agriculture Committee on September 13, 1973. The markup of the bill by the subcommittee took place on September 19, 1973. The final day of the subcommittee consideration of the bill took place on October 30, 1973. The bill was reported by the subcommittee with amendments to the full committee and received unanimous approval of the 36-member Agriculture Committee. It then went to the House of Representatives, where it passed on December 18, 1973.

In the Senate, Senator Talmadge, Chairman of the subcommittee on Agriculture, Research and General Legislation of the Senate Agriculture Committee, introduced my legislation. I testified before the Talmadge subcommittee on October 3, 1974. The testimony I gave on Senator Talmadge's bill (S2728) was basically the same as I had previously given before the House subcommittee on behalf of my House legislation. It sailed through the Senate and went to a House/Senate conference, where several minor changes were made. Both bodies passed it in late December 1974, and the president signed it into law.

I issued a press release on December 19, 1974, which said "I am extremely pleased to announce that my federal noxious weed bill will soon be signed into public law by the president. It has just repassed the House today and this will save the American public between $5 and $10 billion annually. It is hard to believe that we have such a problem from weeds. It is not a very exciting subject. It only becomes exciting when we see the amount of acreage it causes to be lost and the amount of money that goes into preventing weeds. We are delighted this went through. I first introduced this in 1973, and I am just so pleased that we finally got this into law."

This legislation, which I earlier characterized as sector legislation, was relatively easy to get through once I isolated the problem, identified the solution, and had all the key players moving in the same direction; farmers are a powerful force in the Congress, as are the committees on agriculture. Normally, when a bill comes out of one of the agriculture committees with a strong majority, or in this case, unanimously, most members go along with it, as they have great respect for the agriculture committees. Furthermore, many do not understand the problems of agriculture and rely on the committees to do what is right. Also, in this case, state governments and federal agencies were for the bill, and were lobbying members from their state or members they worked with where appropriate. There was no opposition to the bill.

The only real problem with the bill, and it was a minor one, was the title. Every time I talked about the bill, or went in front of a committee to testify, there would also be a few laughs about Frey and his Noxious Weed Bill. We had attempted before filing the bill to find a better title which would have more appeal, but never could come up with a good title. During the same time period, I had introduced legislation fighting drugs called "The Drug Pusher Elimination Act." The title alone made members eager to sign on as cosponsors.

In this case, the title was not a serious obstacle to passage, as the subject matter was important to powerful elements of the Congress and the public. I don't believe

I ever sent out a "Dear Colleague" letter asking support from other House members. The only press I got on it was in the Florida papers and national agricultural periodicals. Sector legislation is usually bipartisan or nonpartisan and goes through with little controversy or fanfare. Interestingly enough, Speaker Carl Albert (D-OK), in summing up the achievements of the 93rd Congress, called it one of the "major legislative accomplishments of the 93rd Congress."

SPECIAL INTEREST LEGISLATION: PROMOTIONS FOR POWs

There is a third way to pass a bill and that is to have a close friend on a key committee who is also well-connected in the other body (the Senate). I would entitle this legislation "special interest legislation."

It came about as many legislative initiatives did—by accident. A close friend of mine in my Navy squadron had been shot down in Vietnam in 1965 and was released with the other prisoners in 1973. As he had no family, he came to stay with us in Florida. Sometime thereafter, he called me somewhat upset. It appeared that Title 10 of the United States Code §5573A, restricts Navy Marine Corps Reserve Officers from applying for commissions in the regular service if they achieved the rank of Navy Lieutenant or Marine Corps Captain. There is no comparable limitation for augmentation in the Air Force and Army. In essence, POWs were prevented by law from becoming career officers. There were not many people involved in this situation, only six or seven Navy or Marine officers.

The Rayburn House Office Building has a gym where many members of Congress work out. There are courts there to play paddle ball. I played as often as possible, and my regular partner was Congressman G. V. "Sonny" Montgomery, a Democrat from Mississippi. We called ourselves "The Big Red Machine,"even had tee shirts with The Red Machine stenciled on them. Sonny had been in the service himself and was a key Democrat on the Armed Services Committee. He was well respected and liked on both sides of the aisle. I discussed this problem with Sonny, and at his urging introduced legislation H.R. 8591 to correct the problem.

I testified in front of Subcommittee No. 2 of the House Armed Services Committee on H.R. 8591 on June 11, 1974. I stated, "...there is basically nothing wrong with that provision (§5573A) of the law until we take into consideration the fact that men like Rob Doremus were promoted to Lieutenant Commander or Major while they were prisoners of war. They did not have the opportunity to complete the necessary paperwork while prisoners of war and in fact, most of them did not even know about their promotions until they were released."

My bill authorized the president to make appointments to the active list of the Navy in permanent grades not above Captain and to the active list of the Marine Corps in permanent grades not above Colonel. The authority would be limited to those reserve or temporary officers who were prisoners of war or classified as missing in action during the Vietnam War. As a spokesman for the Navy Department said, "This bill would correct a unique situation for the Navy and Marine Corps. There is no comparable limitation on the augmentation of Air Force and Army officers. Mr. Chairman, acting favorably on this bill will give men like Rob Doremus and the other men —the change actually will affect only a half dozen or so officers—the opportunity to become career officers. They have more than earned the right. Mr. Doremus, who is here to testify, was a prisoner of war for seven and one-half years. I might add that Rob and I flew together for several years in the mid-'50s in the same squadron. Surely, the least you can do for these men is to enact a bill. Thank you, Mr. Chairman."

The bill was scheduled to go to the floor right before the 4th of July recess. The timing was not by accident. I basically made the same statement on the floor that I made in front of the committee, and the bill passed in July of 1974.

However, the bill went over to the Senate and languished. We could not get any action on the bill in the Senate. The House and Senate stayed in session until right before Christmas in 1974, stalled on major tax legislation. This is where the friendship with Sonny Montgomery and his friendship with Mississippi Senator John Stennis, head of the Armed Services Committee in the Senate, came into play. I made a statement on the floor on December 10, 1974, where I said, "Mr. Speaker, a friend of mine who was a POW recently said that the POWs are like hula hoops, they were in season once, and now they are out of season. I was rather proud a short time ago when the House passed legislation helping POWs. It seemed that both the Navy and Marine Corps have rules relative to applying regular commissions that must be done in a certain period of time. However, about seven POWs were not able to apply for regular commissions because they were in a prisoner of war camp. To remedy this situation, the House speedily passed legislation. However, as yet, the other body has not moved on this legislation. There are very few days left in this session, and I hope that the other body will take time out of its very busy schedule to act so that some POWs who spent a great many years in prisoner of war camps for this country can be assisted."

Congressman Montgomery, who was responsible for moving the bill through the Armed Services Committee and managing the bill on the floor, took the time to personally go over and talk to Senator Stennis about the bill. As was apparent, it only affected seven people in the entire country. However, they happened to have been POWs who had paid a very high price.

The Senate has rules totally different from the House. A senator, especially one who is chairman of a powerful committee, can move legislation in miraculous ways, especially at the end of a year. They don't have to deal with a Rules Committee, as in the House, nor is there any Senate rule requiring that amendments be germane. Senator Stennis was therefore able to attach the legislation to a bill that had nothing to do with POWs. However, the bill was one that needed to be passed by the House and Senate before adjournment. On the next to the last day before the Congress adjourned sine die, my bill, included as an "add on" to another bill, was passed by both bodies and was sent to the president, where it was signed. There was no way I could have accomplished this in the Senate. I was a Republican, and there was no Republican chairman in the Senate. I was relatively new in the Congress, and had probably only met Senator Stennis once personally.

I am sure that Congressman Montgomery would have done this for anybody, under any circumstances, but it was much easier for me to get his attention, to get hearings in his committee, and to get it out of the committee to the floor because of our personal friendship. He did not do it because he was a friend, but rather because it was right.

This case also shows that special interest legislation is not just to help fat cats. The Congress can be responsive to the needs of all if you are persistent. Just recently (1998), I talked to Congressman Montgomery about this bill and his help. Sonny said he did not remember helping, but was glad he did.

WHEN A TICKLISH ISSUE IS FORCED ON YOU

Attempting to get legislation through can put you in interesting positions—positions that you don't want to be in. For instance, right after President Kennedy's death, President Johnson issued an executive order changing the name of Cape Canaveral to Cape Kennedy. The late Democrat Senator from Florida, Spessard Holland, told me the story behind the name change. He said he was rushing through the Washington National airport on the way to Tampa when President Johnson called him and asked him what he thought about renaming the Cape. Senator Holland told the president that he ought to check with the people in Brevard County before making any decisions, and the president said "fine." Senator Holland said that, when he reached Tampa, he found news reporters asking his reaction to the name change.

Senator Holland's efforts to restore the name Cape Canaveral began a short time later. The Kennedy Space Center was in my district. Prior to my election, Senator Holland and the entire Florida congressional delegation had been urging the Interior Department's Board on Geographic Names to restore the original name. It was the contention of the Florida delegation that President Johnson's change of the geographic name by executive order was not proper. In fact, the decision to change Cape Canaveral to Cape Kennedy was reached within a 24-hour period without a formal proposal sent to the Board of Geographic Names, without a meeting of the board, and without any investigation or staff reports being made.

Circumventing the procedures by which a name change is normally made, the major criteria of "historic significance" and opinion of the local population were not followed. It was clear that the name Cape Canaveral held a special place in the history of our nation. The discovery of this point on Florida's East Coast in present day Brevard County is credited to Ponce de Leon, the same explorer who discovered this state more than 450 years ago. We also knew for certain that the name appears on a Spanish map printed as early as 1564, and on maps and charts used by world navigators since these early time periods.

Obviously, I was in a tough place. The majority leader of the House, Tip O'Neill from Massachusetts, was close to the Kennedys. While I knew I had to do something, I was not eager to fall on my sword in a hopeless attempt to change the name.

I did talk personally with Majority Leader O'Neill soon after my election, and he indicated sympathy with my position. However, he told me that, as long as Mrs. Kennedy was alive, he would block any change. That was enough for me.

However, the Florida legislature did not let the matter rest. During 1973, the state of Florida enacted a law changing the name of Cape Kennedy back to Cape Canaveral. It was signed by the Governor of Florida on May 28, 1973.

I asked the House Science and Astronautics Committee to have an analysis made of the effect of this state law. They issued an opinion dated June 7, 1973, which concluded as follows: "Florida law changing the name of Cape Kennedy to Cape Canaveral appears to be binding on all state and local agencies in Florida. The Federal Government, however, must continue to use the name Cape Kennedy until the Board of Geographic Names takes action to change the name for Federal official use."

Although the Board requested Congress to resolve the problem by joint resolution, there was no reason for the Board to defer to the Congress any longer in view of the fact that Congress was not involved in the original name change in 1963. Once again, I asked the board to restore the name and got all 16 members of the Florida delegation to join in the request. Political heat on me was beginning to build up in the state, as legislation had passed in the U.S. Senate to restore the name. My legislation in the House continued to be blocked by Majority Leader Tip O'Neill.

Frankly, I was at a loss as what to do. I once again pleaded my case with Tip. By then, he knew me a little better, but the answer was the same, no.

In desperation, I came up with an idea. I drafted legislation changing the name of Cape Cod to Cape Kennedy. I went on a Boston radio station to announce my legislation. The response was immediate—vocal and hostile. The Massachusetts delegation and the people of Massachusetts said you couldn't change a historic name. I pointed out that the name Cape Canaveral was 100 years older than Cape Cod. I then made a speech on the floor regarding this legislation. I said that I felt that the people of Massachusetts should have the same opportunity as the people of Florida to change the name of their most prominent geographic point to honor President Kennedy. I also said that it seemed basically unfair that Florida should have all this honor and opportunity while Massachusetts, John F. Kennedy's home state, should not be included. I concluded "All that we want is for the people of Florida to get the same consideration as the people of Massachusetts. We're going to restore the name either in Congress or by lawsuit." Bob Sikes, the senior Democrat in the House from Florida joined me on this legislation.

This is a case where the legislation did not go through, but the threat of legislation, and the political problems it could cause, made Tip O'Neill withdraw his objections. Soon thereafter, the Interior Department's Board of Geographic Names restored the name of Cape Canaveral, as it remains today.

This is a case where the legislation was not my idea, where I really did not want to push the legislation, but where my political survival within Florida and my district forced me to figure out an answer. I knew that I had not made the majority leader—soon to be Speaker—happy. However, he did not stay angry forever and understood the political box that I had been in.

MAJOR LEGISLATION WITH NATIONAL IMPLICATIONS

The last kind of legislation I would like to discuss is major legislation with national and international implications. The bill H.R. 13015 was the result of the Communications Act. The bill has been discussed in some detail in a chapter by Congressman Lionel Van Deerlin (D-CA), my good friend and chairman of the House Communications subcommittee. That bill, by its very nature, was high profile even when we were only thinking of making minor changes in the communications law. The reason was obvious: proposed legislation would impact radio, television, cable, the Federal Communications Commission, long distance, local, and international telephone, and the fast-growing computer/communication business. At the time of the legislation, AT&T owned or controlled 23 local operating companies, providing 81 percent of the number of telephones in all the exchanges servicing the United States. AT&T was a large group of companies under common ownership with combined assets of $125 billion. The amount of money involved was incredible and was in the process of expanding exponentially.

The hearings went on for many months. Every time there was a hearing, the room was packed to overflowing with interested parties. Every question or statement made by Van Deerlin or me was carefully scrutinized to determine what we really meant and where we were really going. The staff of the committee was constantly besieged with questions and requests for appointments. Interestingly enough, because of the technical nature of the issues, both legal and antitrust, most other members paid little attention to it. When members talked to us on the floor about the bill, we would just tell them that we were working on it, were not sure where we were going, and to keep their powder dry.

From our standpoint, we used the staff to float various ideas to see what the reaction would be and whether there was any chance of putting any coalitions together. The subcommittee was not large, and many times the meetings would be composed of Van Deerlin, myself, and one or two other members. In some ways, it was strange that such an important issue was in essence ignored by other members.

I was a member of the Republican leadership and did my best to keep the other members of the leadership informed of where it was going. Obviously, there was concern on the part of the leadership that the committee would do something dramatic and drastic, which would cause political problems. By this time, however, my reputation was fairly well established in the Congress as someone who was not a bomb-thrower, but rather someone who attempted to put together legislation that would pass.

This legislation and its successors did not pass, although 90 percent of what was in the legislation over the years has become law. This was primarily because the antitrust suit against AT&T was settled and divestiture accomplished. It is important to understand that bills which are not even passed can sometimes have a tremendous impact on the law and economy. The power of the Congress is immense. The pressure of congressional action, or even the threat of congressional action, can force other entities to take action they would not take otherwise.

Chapter 37

Congress in Foreign Affairs

John S. Monagan (D-Connecticut)

The role of Congress in implementing foreign policy is vitally important, but it is a function only vaguely understood by the public. While its role in formulating policy is well known, it is not generally realized that the Congress plays a role in carrying out policies which already have been formulated. In specific matters such as the Fulbright Vietnam investigations, the Kennedy Alliance for Progress program, the Cuban missile crisis, or other spectacular instances, the role of the external affairs committees forcefully gains the attention of the country, but as to their regular, day-to-day functioning, the average American is uninformed. Other committees, such as Ways and Means or Commerce, from the personal issues they treat, have a higher continuing attention from the media, but, while somewhat less outstanding immediately, the relations of the United States with foreign powers remain concerns of vital significance. The functioning of the committees which deal with them has paramount importance for the security and progress of the country.

Unfortunately, there is currently a tendency in the media and, consequently, in the public, to downgrade the importance of forwarding policy by fostering good relations with our world neighbors and associates and even to ridicule and penalize those representatives and diplomats who assume the responsibility of fulfilling this function. Even in this period of galloping globalization, where international contacts are increasingly more intimate and important, the vital national role of diplomacy is not comprehended nor are its activities adequately supported.

Critics have mocked the need for international cooperation as "globaloney," and the foreign travels of members of Congress are customarily derided as "junketing." As to the latter, while it cannot be denied that legislators have indulged in jaunts to noted spas and watering places on occasion, the blanket condemnation fails to recognize the educational influence of well-organized foreign travel and the contribution it makes to the efficient and informed functioning of representatives charged with dealing with international affairs. It is in such activities that the opportunity to implement foreign policy arises. As one whose travels sought the trouble spots, I can testify that no words could adequately describe the actual sight of a Lima slum *barrio* or the depressing feeling of a stay in Moscow before the destruction of the Iron Curtain. In penetrating to these grim areas, we had a chance to forward the national policies of showing concern for Peru and Latin America and in cautiously opening the door to the USSR in time of post-Stalin change. My colleagues and I were better legislators for having had these experiences, and the executive was better served by having our physical support for its policies. It is regrettable that a legislator must today forego foreign travel as a supporting member of the foreign policy team for fear of the uninformed disapproval of constituents.

COMMITTEES INVOLVED

I had the privilege of serving on two committees that were concerned with foreign operations. One was the Committee on Foreign Affairs (now renamed the Committee on International Affairs because of Republican sensitivity to the connotation of "affairs") and the other was the Committee on Government Operations. The former sets foreign policy, as with the 1964 Tonkin Bay resolution of presidential authority, deals with legislation authorizing foreign aid, State Department operations, the construction and maintenance of embassies and consulates, and other such matters. Also, through foreign travel, representation at international conferences, and personal contacts with officials of other nations, its members implement the policies established by the Congress and the executive.

The latter committee is charged with the overview of all departments and agencies of the government to determine the economy and efficiency of their operation and, through the operation of the then-constituted foreign operations subcommittee on which I served, to extend this post-operation audit to governmental programs overseas. This function has its implementing aspect in that it pressures government agencies to hew to the line in correctly carrying out foreign policy guidelines.

It may be illuminating to offer examples of committee involvement with critical matters. I begin with the Gulf of Tonkin Resolution which was passed as a response to the firing on two U.S. destroyers by North Vietnamese torpedo boats in August 1964 during the Vietnam War. We learned of the event when several members of the Foreign Affairs Committee were summoned suddenly to the White House by President Johnson and ushered to the downstairs Situation Room where top military, State, and White House officials were gathered. There we were informed of the confrontation and maps were displayed to locate the incident, as the distance from shore was important. The President quickly thereafter submitted a resolution to the Congress on which the committee held hearings. The resolution was reported and passed unanimously in the House and with only two dissenters in the Senate, Ernest Gruening (D-AK) and Wayne Morse (D-OR). The passage of the resolution was a tribute to the speed with which the Congress could act when motivated, but it later became controversial because of the breadth of the authority given to the president, and questions were raised about the accuracy of the facts which the president provided on the incident. Our involvement was a formulation function, but had its implementation aspect as well.

Another time of stress and emotion for the committee came in the aftermath of the Cuban Bay of Pigs fiasco in 1961 when we held hearings to try to assess the blame for the tragedy. This involved the grilling of Alan Dulles, Director of the CIA, Dean Rusk, Secretary of State, William P. Bundy, Assistant Secretary of Defense, and others, as members expressed the frustration which the country felt at this demeaning and unaccustomed military failure which the Eisenhower administration had planned and which the new Kennedy administration had bungled. This, too, was implementational in its review of the manner in which policy set by the executive had failed to meet a proper standard of excellence in execution.

A few members of the committee who had involvement with Vietnam were at other times called to the White House for counsel by President Johnson during the trying days of the war, and I recall the discussion we had about the advisability of resuming the bombing in 1967 and the anguished frustration which the president expressed, as only he could, at the inability to bring about a conclusion of the conflict. Essentially, this was a continuation of policy making, but it also was an invitation by the president for members of the legislative branch to share in determining the boundaries of the execution of the already-determined controlling policy.

THE REPRESENTATIONAL FUNCTION

Membership on the committee has a representational function as well. In this aspect, we serve as agents of the legislative branch in international meetings convened for various purposes. In the mid-1960s, I served with Assistant Secretary of State Charles Meyer at a U.N. Economic and Social Council meeting in Trinidad, which had been called to discuss problems facing the Americas at that time. Here, in our contacts and conflicts with representatives of other countries, we were definitely implementing the established U.S. foreign policy in these regards.

On another occasion, I was the congressional representative at the U.N. Disarmament Conference in Geneva in the depths of the Cold War when I had the experience of lunch and discussion with the cold-eyed Andrei Vishinski, who had been the agent of Stalin in the rape of Czechoslovakia. This discussion was halting because, at first, Vishinsky pretended not to understand English, but, after a few courses, consented to engage in some exchanges. This meeting and U.S. participation in the conference, in spite of seeming lack of progress, was a small implementing part of the overall U.S. holding policy which eventually outlasted the Soviets and brought us victory in the long confrontation of the mid-century.

PARTICIPATION IN JOINT PARLIAMENTARY COMMITTEES

Bipartisan service on committees convened to discuss parliamentary problems and explore areas of possible cooperation or even of possible conflict is another implementing responsibility of committee members. One such occasion was a gathering of British, Canadian, and U.S. parliamentarians in Bermuda in 1959, where the Commons group included Denis Healey, later Minister of Defense; Lord Hailsham, later Chancellor; and Hugh Gaitskell, then a probable Labor Prime Minister. A similar grouping brought us in 1969 to the inner recesses of the Kremlin, where we met at their invitation with a committee of Russia's purported parliamentarians in discussions which included some moments of heated debate. However, the sessions ended with a valedictory by the Soviet chairman which was doubtless prearranged and which expressed happiness that "capitalists" and "communists" had been able to meet peacefully for a conference. What the motive was in putting out the red carpet we were never sure, although it was possible that sharp, current divisions between China and Russia had caused the Reds to look for an anchor to the windward. At any rate, it was a unique experience to meet in rooms where Stalin had once held sway and to find that the communists, as well as we, included hotheads as well as rationalists in their membership. It was also another implementing policy step in seeking areas of agreement which we hoped might lead to an easing of the cold war tensions. As Winston Churchill said, "to jaw-jaw is better than to war-war."

MEMBERSHIPS IN INTERNATIONAL ORGANIZATIONS

Closer international relations were cultivated through membership in the Interparliamentary Union, a century-old association of members of legislatures, which had been formed to discuss means of improving parliamentary procedures and policies, and which met several times annually in the legislative chambers of various host countries. The controversial admission to membership of communist and satellite countries after World War II had changed the character of the delegates and the context of the issues debated, and by the time of my service in the '60s, Cold War partisanship had been added to democratic fraternizing, but here also there was an opportunity to air differences and for us to defend our national policies in a world-wide forum. In this, we were carrying out a national policy line already established.

One memorable example of such a defense occurred in Teheran in 1966, when hostile delegates attacking U.S. activities in Vietnam and alleging domestic racial discrimination were countered by a brilliant defense by Senator Hiram Fong (D-AK). Obviously an Oriental and self-proclaimed as a member of a minority group, in stirring language, Fong defended our policies in Vietnam, made clear the opportunities which had come to him under our system, and extolled the racial tolerance which, he said, characterized the people of his state and the United States. It was gratifying to find an overwhelming number of delegates breaking into spirited applause at the termination of Fong's speech. This, indeed, was implementation of our foreign policies.

I recall another dramatic confrontation in the Lima meeting of the Union which took place in September 1968, shortly after the Russian invasion of Czechoslovakia. The Russians had not permitted the Czech delegation to come to the conference, and the French Socialist delegates verbally lashed the Russian delegates over the brutal and unwarranted invasion of the Czech homeland. Although as socialists, these French were inured to economic controls, they made clear their hatred of military aggression and the barbarity of the invasion to the Russian delegates, who cowered under their emotional assaults. In supporting the French in their opposition to the Russians, we were at this conference making explicit our national policy.

THE SUPERVISORY FUNCTION

The second committee on which I served was not primarily a legislative committee, but had been created to survey the operations of the government with a view to promoting their economical and efficient functioning. During my service, it was called the Committee on Government Operations and is now called the Committee on Government Reform and Oversight as a result of the Republican revision of nomenclature. I was named to the Subcommittee on Foreign Operations, which had jurisdiction over all departments and agencies engaged in foreign activities. At the time when I joined, under the chairmanship of Rep. Porter Hardy (D-VA), it was primarily concerned with the operation of the massive foreign aid program whose scope was at its peak and whose funds were being disbursed all over the world–in Southeast Asia, in South America, in Europe–in hundreds of projects and localities. The theorists who conceived the programs believed that the provision of capital through funds or through public works would assist poor countries to raise themselves to a more secure economic position. This aid would thus raise the standard of living of the beneficiaries and deprive the communists of a basis for infiltration. Of course, there was an element of urgency involved since the Russians were continuing their world-wide policy of aggression and were bent on seizing influence wherever possible. In the face of this aggression, our planners considered that our policy was protecting the freedom of these weak nations, as well as holding back the Russians and maintaining our own position in the world.

As so frequently is the case with U.S. programs, speed was the watchword and funds were appropriated first, while the planning and controls came afterward.

Our subcommittee initially directed its attention to the aid program in Laos. The communist influence there was active and threatened a take-over of the country itself and also a penetration into Vietnam and other countries of the area, ostensibly allied with the free world. Adjoining a west-oriented Thailand, Laos had been hastily assembled and established as a free country by the Geneva Conference of 1954. It was our national policy objective to keep it in the western orbit and to sustain it as a buffer against communist advances. In frantic haste, we were pouring funds and commodities into this small, primitive, mountainous, and landlocked country, and, as a result, the economy was in a shambles. As an intriguing sidelight, for American probers, the very ambience was the height of exoticism. The names of the characters were strange and foreign to our ears. The basic unit of currency was called a *kip* and the prime actors had names such as Souvana Pouma, Suphanouvong, and Phoumi Nosavang; the capitol was called Vientiane and the neighboring area, Luang Prabang. The proletarian opposition was known as the Pathet Lao.This Somerset Maugham atmosphere, plus the remoteness from the American scene, in spite of is critical aspect, lent an air of unreality to the whole scenario.

U.S. intervention was ineffectual and disruptive. Our subcommittee, through our hearings showed the harmful effects of our expenditures on the primitive Lao economy. In addition, it demonstrated the inability of the program to cope with officials playing off the contending major powers as well as its failure to achieve the political objective of developing a western-oriented government. As time passed, Vietnam, whither our interest shifted from Laos, gradually came to assume predominant importance for the United States, while the Pathet Lao joined with the Viet Cong in forming our opposition in that new field of conflict. At the same time, Laos was taken over by the proletarian element. Through our subcommittee, we were forwarding U.S. policy by seeking to make its operation more effective.

A more satisfying subject of review was the operation of the Peace Corps, where we found dedicated and effective workers getting demonstrable results. In Senegal, Iran, Chile, and India, we found selfless Americans who, in what were often harsh surroundings, at little cost to the country and with peons' wages, were bringing practical assistance to impoverished people, brightening our image, and creating vast good will for the United States. Here again, our supervision was supportive and productive.

COMMERCIAL ASSISTANCE

As we members of these two committees pursued our various studies, we had an opportunity to fulfill another important function i.e., rendering assistance to U.S. companies which were involved in the rapidly increasing globalization of commerce. For example, during a visit to Argentina, we were told by concerned U.S. businessmen of the advantages which German competitors had achieved through support by their government of favorable lending terms offered to purchasers. They believed there was a need for comparable governmental support on our part. We were able, on our return, to illustrate the need for credit guarantee programs to maintain jobs and stimulate economic activity in our industries.

In Chile, we learned of the probably impending governmental expropriation of U.S. industries, such as the Anaconda Chuquicamata copper mining complex, the paucity of compensation, and the need for insurance against loss from the governmental taking of such vast investments. In these instances, it was possible to forward the interests of companies engaged in perfectly legitimate trading whose corporate health was important for workers and economic stability generally in our home communities.

SUMMARY

These, then, are examples of the manifold activities engaged in during my service on the congressional committees responsible for guiding the foreign affairs of the nation. In this chapter, I have sought to illustrate the implementation function, since this aspect of committee activity has been less known than its role in formulation. In all cases, we prepared and filed reports of our studies. In some, our recommendations were placed in the files and had no lasting effect. In others, they provided an object study of practices to be avoided in the future. Many times, they furnished support for effective programs and brought about progressive changes which were beneficial to the country. In all instances, they embodied a vital functioning of the legislative branch of the government in which members of Congress were dedicating thought, time, and energy to activities directed at serving, advancing, and securing the common welfare.

Chapter 38

Changes in the Role of Congress in Foreign Affairs

Lee H. Hamilton (D-Indiana)

Some people wonder how an Indiana man like myself got involved in foreign affairs. Today, it might not seem unusual since Americans of all backgrounds are involved in international politics. But when I first entered Congress in 1965, foreign policy tended to be directed by an elite circle of experts and officials who came primarily from the Northeast.

I had no intention of becoming involved in foreign policy. It happened purely by accident. I wanted to get on the House Public Works Committee, but I couldn't, and was placed instead on the Foreign Affairs Committee. I then discovered that I enjoyed working on foreign policy. Some years later, I turned down a spot on the powerful Ways and Means Committee, which nearly everybody in the House wants to be on, so that I could continue working on foreign affairs.

Looking back now at my years of service in Congress, I am very grateful that I was given the opportunity to contribute to American foreign policy. Congress has a special role to play in formulating U.S. foreign policy, yet this role is not always well understood.

The president is the principal architect of foreign policy. But Congress has important responsibilities as well. The Constitution delegates foreign policy powers to both branches, so cooperation between them is essential. The appropriate role of Congress is to investigate and to provide oversight over foreign policy, and to help formulate general principles. The executive branch must implement our foreign policy, but it needs congressional support in order to be most effective. At its best, Congress should be a partner in the development of America's foreign policy, with an obligation to work critically, but respectfully, with the president.

These fundamental characteristics of our system are as true today as they were in 1965. But the actual roles played by each branch have changed dramatically since then. This change is natural because the Constitution does not give clear authority to one branch or the other in many areas of foreign policy. As a result, the balance of power between the branches can vary with the spirit of the times.

During my years in the House, I noticed four major changes in the role played by Congress in foreign affairs.

First, Congress is more involved in many aspects of foreign policy than it was 35 years ago. When President Truman was asked who makes foreign policy, he said, simply, "I do." No president could make that kind of statement today.

This change started with reaction to the Vietnam War in the 1960s. The Senate Foreign Relations Committee began educating—and changing—public opinion about the war. Both the House and Senate moved to cut off funds for the war, and eventually our policy changed.

Congressional activism continued in the 1970s, when members began to accumulate larger and highly professional staffs with increased expertise. This greater involvement of Congress in foreign policy now appears permanent. Members of Congress simply do not accept the view that foreign policy is the sole province of the executive branch. Neither do their constituents.

Second, the number of actors involved in foreign policy-making has increased. In 1965, the important foreign policy players were few—the president, the secretaries of State and Defense, the national security adviser, the chairmen of the House and Senate Foreign Relations committees, and a small number of others. To consult with Congress, the president and his advisers simply needed to call up the key committee chairmen. Today, power in Congress is more diffuse, and consultation means talking with as many members as possible. Every member of Congress takes an interest in foreign policy at one time or another, and every member wants to be heard.

There are also many more groups outside of government seeking to influence foreign policy today: trade groups, non-profits, international organizations, ethnic groups, academic institutions, foreign countries, former officials, and others. Special interest groups have always played a role in American foreign policy, but their impact has grown over the past three decades. There are more of them, they are more sophisticated, and they have a lot of money. They lobby vigorously and effectively on Capitol Hill.

Third, the information revolution has changed the way Congress operates in foreign policy. More information flows today to foreign policy-makers—both in Congress and the executive branch—than they can possibly use. Some of it is official intelligence—we certainly have more of that, and it is more precise and voluminous than ever before. But official intelligence is just one source. There are now many more specialized news broadcasts and publications, as well as Internet sites.

Television in particular has the ability to set the foreign policy agenda through the power of its images. Television drove us into Somalia, and television drove us out. During the Gulf War, we learned more from CNN's correspondent in Baghdad than we learned from our own government.

With all this information, it is harder for the government to keep secrets—not impossible, but more difficult. That is good news for human freedom, and I welcome it. But the glut of information also means that the process of making foreign policy is far less orderly or predictable.

The great speed with which the media operates today also puts a higher premium on quick reactions. On many occasions in my later years in Congress, I spent the entire day responding to press inquiries. The news media want reaction now, not an hour or two from now, and they have no interest at all in reaction a day or two after the event.

Fourth, the important issues in foreign affairs have changed substantially since I entered Congress. In the early 1960s, our foreign policy was dominated by one concern: the containment of the Soviet Union and communism. President Kennedy said in his inaugural address that the United States would "pay any price, bear any burden" to defeat communism. What president would make such a claim about any foreign policy issue today?

Since the collapse of communism, no single rationale has driven our foreign policy. Our focus ranges from economic and security interests in Asia, to ethnic conflicts in southeast Europe, to threats to peace in the Middle East, to prospects for political and economic reform in Russia.

Economic issues are much more important to our foreign policy than they were in the 1960s. International trade agreements have proliferated, and economic sanctions on other countries have been the source of some of our most vigorous debates.

Human rights is a far bigger issue than it used to be. Members of Congress call today for major changes in policy based solely on human rights abuses in other countries. In recent years, Congress has taken a particular interest in the issue of religious persecution, adding it to the list of human rights conditions considered in formulating our foreign policy.

Additionally, we now have a number of new transnational issues on our foreign policy agenda. Worldwide proliferation of weapons of mass destruction, international terrorism, global warming, population growth: these issues have taken on an importance they didn't have three decades ago.

Along with the changes in the issues dealt with by Congress, there has been a change in our conception of the national interest. The national interest used to be defined as protecting the free world from the communist threat. Today, members of Congress define the national interest in different ways. To some members, it means promoting U.S. economic interests abroad. To others, it means promoting democracy and human rights. To still others, it means focusing more resources on the fight against the international drug trade.

The changes I have described are neither simply good nor bad. Most of them have both benefits and drawbacks.

The stronger role of Congress in foreign policy means that the executive branch must be more accountable and consider other views. But it also means that our foreign policy sometimes becomes a muddle of conflicting initiatives.

The greater number of actors involved means that our foreign policy is more representative of the entire population. But it also means that our policy is sometimes influenced by special interests rather than the national interest.

The information revolution means that much more information about the world is available to Congress and the population at large. But it also means that Congress reacts erratically to some of this information, and our foreign policy suffers as a result.

The changing issues of foreign policy happily show that we won the Cold War and no longer face a communist threat. But they also indicate that we now face a more complex and uncertain world.

We cannot predict how the practice of U.S. foreign policy will develop in the future, but Congress will most likely continue to play an important role. Perhaps when our president in 2035 is asked who makes foreign policy, he will think about the role of Congress, and say, "We do."

Chapter 39

The Legislator's Role in Defense

H. Martin Lancaster (D-North Carolina)

After empowering the president as commander-in-chief, the founding fathers vested the Congress with the power to "provide for the common defense," and specifically with the powers to declare war and raise and support the armed forces. Congress generally exercises both of these powers through its control of the federal purse, and thus the president must submit his recommendations for the defense budget to the Congress for approval.

Congressional examination of the defense budget falls under the jurisdiction of the Armed Services committees, which provide policy guidance and authorize the use of funds for particular programs, and the Defense subcommittees of the Appropriations committees, which provide the funds for authorized uses.

There are 55 members of the House Armed Services Committee and 21 members of the Senate Armed Services Committee. Forty-nine (49) House members are on the Appropriations Committee and 28 senators sit on their Appropriations Committee.

Each of these congressional committees is divided into subcommittees with jurisdiction over specific portions of the defense budget. For example, the House Armed Services Committee, of which I was a member, has six subcommittees. I served on three of those, overseeing research and technology, military personnel, and the operations, training, and maintenance budgets.

The committees, either at full committee or at subcommittee level, undertake careful review of the defense budget. This oversight process includes convening hearings, during which testimony is taken from witnesses who then respond to questions from committee members. Customarily, witnesses are called from the executive branch defense agencies to justify that portion of the budget for which they are responsible, although other knowledgeable parties are on occasion invited to appear before the committees. In addition to hearings convened to justify budget requests, committees have hearings after the money is spent to insure that it has been used wisely for authorized purposes.

Not only do the president and Congress establish funding levels through the budget process, they also set other military policies. Sometimes, those policies are strongly opposed by the military leadership and the rank-and-file. An issue early in President Clinton's first term that illustrated this conflict was the effort of the president to allow homosexuals to serve openly in the military, something which had been precluded by military policy for many years. Public and congressional response to this proposal was so strongly negative that the president modified his position significantly even before submitting it to Congress. Congress made further changes in the policy. As ultimately adopted, a military person who is homosexual may not publicly declare his homosexuality and the military may not actively pursue investigations of non-declaring homosexuals.

Congressional committees have large staffs which exercise an important role in defense oversight work. The tenure of members of Congress varies widely, and while many members of defense committees have served in that capacity for several years and are familiar with military issues, many members are new to the committees and do not share that same level of knowledge. Staff compensates for this variance by providing expertise on issues that transcend the election-year cycle of two years in the House and six years in the Senate.

On the House side, the Armed Services Committee has a staff of 32, and the Defense Appropriations Committee has a staff of 17. On the Senate side, the Armed Services Committee has a staff of 15. In addition, each member of these respective committees has a personal staff person concentrating on defense matters. This means that approximately 170 staff members devote full time to analyzing defense budgets, defense programs and weapons systems, and general defense policy.

Congressional staff interact with staff in the executive branch to discuss programs and collect information important to making defense funding and policy decisions. Their institutional knowledge allows them to intelligently question the military on key issues and programs and report back to members of Congress.

After two or three months of hearing and staff work, the defense subcommittee chairmen make adjustments to their portion of the budget and bring the result to a vote at the subcommittee level. Those packages are then forwarded to the full committee for debate and vote on the entire defense bill. Amendments may be offered at either the subcommittee or full committee level to change the budget, and they will be included in the budget package if a majority votes in favor of the amendment.

At this point, members of Congress have an opportunity to bring their own thoughts, philosophies, priorities, and those of their constituents to bear on the final product. Never does a presidential budget make it through this process without changes by the subcommittees or committees.

Once the budget has passed through the full committee, it is forwarded for consideration by the whole House or Senate. Members of Congress, including many who are not on the Armed Services or Defense Appropriations committees, openly debate and question the administration and committee positions on defense and funding. Many floor amendments are offered to change priorities, delete programs, reduce funding, and occasionally increase funding. A number of these amendments are passed each year. Compromise between the administration and the Congress is the order of the day, with intense negotiation preceding any vote.

The House and Senate always pass their defense authorization and appropriations bills in dramatically different forms, based on differing philosophies and priorities in the two chambers. A joint Conference Committee is then appointed to work out the differences between the two versions and to take into account requests from or priorities of the president which have been rejected or modified by one or both houses of Congress. Wheeling and dealing is elevated to an art form with compromises being reached that ultimately reflect a synthesis of priorities of the president and the two houses of Congress. The final version then goes to the floors of the House and Senate for action.

When the final defense bill passes through both chambers of Congress, it is then sent to the president for his signature, whereupon it becomes law.

CIVILIAN CONTROL AND THE COMMITMENT OF TROOPS

The budget process represents an important element of civilian control of the military, as composition of the military and its support establishment is shaped by civilian leadership. Similarly, the military is subject to constitutionally-based executive and legislative branch power with respect to the employment of U. S. military forces.

Many believe that Congress' finest hour in the second half of the 20th century was our debate of the question put to us by President George Bush: Should we commit U. S. troops to repel the Iraqi invaders of Kuwait? This is an excellent and recent example of the role of our Congress in setting defense policy.

The Goldwater-Nichols Act, passed in the early 1980s, has had a profound impact on how our military works and works together. First of all, it reduces the authority of the Chiefs of Staff of the respective services and strengthens the control of the chairman of the Joint Chiefs of Staff and, secondly, it requires more joint planning and joint operations to insure a unified defense posture as opposed to each service going its own way.

This was a congressionally developed and imposed defense policy, which the Defense Department opposed when it was being considered. Congress adopted this policy because it could observe independently the infighting and competition between the Army, Air Force, Navy, and Marines and felt that this was weakening our defense posture and costing billions in redundant spending. The military establishment now sees the wisdom of this policy in addressing these concerns.

Other committees have jurisdiction over certain aspects of the military, such as the Intelligence committees for military intelligence-related matters and the Foreign Affairs committees for arms control agreements with other nations and specific activities pursuant to those treaties.

During the first two years of the Clinton administration when Democrats also controlled Congress, and to some extent during the last two years of the Bush administration, significant downsizing of the military had begun in recognition of the end to the Cold War and a significant change in the threat the United States and its allies in Europe faced. In addition to dramatic cuts in defense personnel, the missile defense system, which was a Ronald Reagan initiative, was eliminated; the B-2 bomber was seen without a mission (which had been to evade Soviet air defenses and drop bombs on that adversary) and was, therefore, capped at 20 planes; investments were made in dual-use technologies with significant federal assistance to private companies doing research in areas that might benefit both military and civilian sectors; and a greater emphasis was placed on peacekeeping and multilateral defense programs.

With the Republican Party gaining a majority in the House and Senate, all of those changes came under attack. However, each of these conflicts over the direction of defense policy and spending will be resolved by civilians as various pieces of legislation move through the House and Senate and ultimately to the president's desk for signature. The House and Senate will almost certainly pass their respective bills in very different forms and those differences will have to be resolved in a joint House and Senate Conference Committee. Once the differences have been ironed out and both houses pass identical legislation, the various bills will be sent to the president for his signature. Where the president has not been able to work out compromises with congressional leadership in the legislative process, he will have no choice but to veto the legislation and send it back to the Congress for further work.

The Constitution grants the Congress the power to declare war, but the employment of forces during conflict is directed by the president as commander-in-chief. Even when war is not declared, such as in Desert Shield/Desert Storm, congressional debate and subsequent votes by Congress significantly impact the use of troops by the president. Knowing that the defense budget and policies are all subject to ultimate congressional approval, presidents are generally reluctant to pursue a course of action which does not have the support of the U.S. population as reflected in congressional debate and votes.

While debate about the role of the president and Congress during war remains a subject of military constitutional debate, the military is removed from this discussion. The Constitution establishes the military as an instrument of power directed by the commander-in-chief and raised and supported by the Congress not as an executor of power in its own right. The military, sworn to uphold the Constitution, understands this fact and stands ready to execute assigned missions when so directed by appropriate civilian authority.

CONCLUSION

In the United States, the separation of powers as provided by the Constitution has provided for effective civilian control over the military. This has been successful in our country since power is not concentrated in any one branch of government and the branches of government respect this separation and distinction in their respective roles.

But our system is not without its flaws. Overlapping responsibilities lead to duplication of effort. The huge bureaucracy associated with the military and its oversight at times restricts our ability to change course quickly when necessary. Disparate congressional interests in particular programs interfere with decision-making based purely on policy considerations, as evidenced by "pork-barrel" spending and the continuation of defense programs for political reasons long after their defense purpose has been served and the military has recommended their termination.

Our career military officers, unfettered by most of these machinations, participate in a rigorous professional military education system which instills in its students doctrine based on respect for military history and for the principles on which the U. S. military was founded. This effort to train our professional soldiers in such a way is often cited as one reason the civil-military relationship in the U.S. is so entrenched among our armed forces.

The civil-military provisions of our Constitution have been carried out since George Washington, citizen-soldier and soldier-statesman, led the executive branch as the first U. S. president. Considered against the backdrop of U. S. strength and stability for over 200 years, our method of civilian control of the military must be measured a success by any standard.

Chapter 40

Congress and the Pentagon:
Civil-Military Relations for a New Millennium

Glen Browder (D-Alabama)

While civilian supremacy is an essential, constitutional protection against executive ambition and military dictatorship, over the course of two centuries, this principle has become an "icon" that we need to re-examine as we enter the new millennium. I am not suggesting that we dispense with civilian control; however, today's leaders must rethink how they debate national security in a drastically changed environment. In short, we need to focus on bridging the gap between Congress and the Pentagon in the 21st century.

This chapter will promote the idea of more responsible interaction among America's legislators and military leaders by discussing: (1) the normal process of legislative control through defense budgeting; (2) contemporary challenges to this normal civil-military relationship; and (3) some suggestions for responding to these challenges and improving relations between Congress and the Pentagon in the future.

THE MANY FUNCTIONS OF THE DEFENSE BUDGET

What civilian control means in American democracy is that civilians—preferably elected public officials—exercise extensive control, both procedurally and substantively, over the defense establishment. Therefore, civilians run the operating system of government, civilians sit atop a clear chain of military command, civilians establish military policy, and civilians control prevailing power against the military.

In textbook language, a budget is "a statement of the financial condition of an administration for a definite period of time based on estimates of expenditures during the period and proposals for financing them." That general definition is acceptably descriptive of defense budgeting, with one qualification—the defense budget actually consists of numerous legislative documents and actions that, collectively, represent an important statement of America's defense position. A more substantive understanding of the "power and purse" authority can be gleaned from a review of the purposes and functions of the defense budget as a public document:

A Public Policy Statement. The defense budget is essentially a public policy statement of national security. It allows Congress to express our values and interests and concerns as a nation. It also communicates to the Pentagon "how much" we are willing to spend to achieve our national security objectives.

A Statement of Priorities. The defense budget also establishes our security interests and objectives by prioritizing general programs and specifying line-item dollar appropriations. For example, every year, the budget directs the Pentagon to enlarge or reduce or reshape force structure; it emphasizes favored weapon systems over others; and it simply "zeroes out" some programs and initiatives.

A Planning Document. The defense budget represents a formal plan for the coming year and future years. Annual congressional budgets (and multi-year plans) include policy directives and revenue projections by which the Defense Department schedules its activities accordingly.

A Management Tool. The defense budget plan thereby provides the basis for managerial direction of the military bureaucracy. Congress and the Pentagon vigorously track and adjust military performance in compliance with legislated assignments and proper management principles.

A Mechanism for Accountability. Finally, the defense budget enhances accountability. At the end of the day (or fiscal year), the American people have a right to ask whether their national government faithfully fulfilled its constitutional responsibilities to provide for the common defense. It is through rigorous budget review that Congress holds the commander-in-chief, the defense establishment, and itself accountable.

THE BUDGET PROCESS FOR DEFENSE

Just as the defense budget is a central statement of public policy, the defense budgeting process is a vital tool of congressional control over the military. Defense budgeting is a fairly open, continuous, detailed, almost tortuous process of defense policy-making and oversight.

Defense budgeting can be viewed as a three-step process: (1) origination with the president; (2) debate and passage by Congress; and then (3) back to executive agencies for implementation. I am going to present and comment on some interesting elements of the legislative process (but don't expect any neat, logical presentation because defense budgeting is not a neat or logical process).

The Budget Calendar. From a broad, congressional perspective, the defense budget process begins in January when the White House sends to Congress the president's total budget proposal and supportive material (a joint project packaged by the White House Office of Management and Budget). Executive branch leaders (including defense secretaries and top military officers) testify before Congress and answer questions regarding their requests for the coming year. Congress then passes a budget resolution setting the overall budget figure and allocating appropriate parts and amounts to committees of jurisdiction. Once the defense-pertinent committees complete their hearings and pass proposed legislation (usually by mid or late summer), the varying defense bills come to the floor for debate, amendment, and passage by the full membership. Then it's on to the White House for presidential approval (ideally before the start of the new fiscal year on October 1) and implementation by executive agencies (most notably the Pentagon).

A Dual Track, House and Senate, Process. As most people know, Congress is divided into two bodies—the House of Representatives and the Senate. Every defense budget (and all successful legislation) must pass both bodies in the same form before becoming law; so, usually, defense bills of dual substance and different procedural tracks eventually are resolved through the conference process before going to the president. (To simplify discussion in this chapter, I am abbreviating the House and Senate duality into a singular "congressional" reference).

Authorization and Appropriation. The defense budget involves two kinds of legislative fiscal action—authorization and appropriation; and its provisions must be both authorized and appropriated with some consistency. For people who find the difference between authorization and appropriation tricky and confusing, I am not going to be of much help. I have studied countless academic and congressional definitions, and I have talked at length with colleagues and staffers—without sufficient resolution to my satisfaction. So I'll stick with my own simple working distinction—that "authorization" means granting authority to do something and "appropriation" means approving specific dollar amounts for authorized activities.

Multiple Forums: Defense Budgeting as a "Fussy-Messy" Process. There are multiple forums and opportunities for conducting defense budget business within Congress. There are numerous leaders, staffs, committees, subcommittees, authorizations and appropriations, formal and informal relationships—in both the House and Senate. In the House where I served, the primary official arenas are the Budget Committee, the National Security Committee, the Appropriations Committee (Defense Subcommittee), the Intelligence Committee, and the Foreign Affairs Committee—and all five are paralleled in the Senate. I call them the "Big Ten of National Security."

All of this is a complex process, but our Founders reasoned (and most subsequent theorists and practical leaders generally agree) that all proposed governmental action—especially that involving military force—should be thoroughly scrutinized and deliberated before becoming public policy. Besides, this complicated process gives just about everybody—inside and outside Congress—a shot at influencing and affecting America's National Security.

Therein lies an inherently troublesome aspect of American democracy. The downside of congressional control is the fact that elected legislators are political animals. The American system puts politicians in charge of national security, politicians who often lack sufficient defense experience and expertise and who face other-than-defense pressures (such as competing spending priorities and electoral imperatives). Sometimes, unfortunately, petty politicians raucously mix partisan interests, political pork, and personal aggrandizement with national defense policy. We legislators fuss and squabble—among ourselves and with the military establishment—on serious defense matters; and we make a political mess of the defense policy process. Constantly. Openly. Shamelessly. I call it the "fussy-messy" approach to national security.

As a result, the politics of national defense policy in the United States inevitably involves a certain amount of incoherence, irrationality, and irresponsibility. What we end up with, if we are not careful, is blatant parochialism, micro-management, fiscal inefficiency, short-term focus, and disjointed security policy.

CIVILIAN CONTROL THROUGH INDIVIDUAL MEMBERS

Legislators also exert institutional control over the defense establishment individually; and creative lawmakers often develop personalized styles and techniques of influence over their military counterparts.

Both the legislative branch and the executive branch operate within a constantly hanging and unruly environment of constituents, political supporters, organized interests, news media, and a vast universe of independent policy players (academic, research, and advocacy individuals/institutions)—and, of course, the judiciary.

Within Congress, I drew upon the resources of (in no particular order) the formal congressional leadership (particularly the speaker's office and committee chairs), my political party (Democratic floor leaders), other colleagues (friends in influential places or with special expertise), the defense and budget committees, my personal and committee staff, congressional caucuses (such as the Democratic Caucus, Democratic Study Group, and Defense Depot Caucus), and congressional support agencies (such as the General Accounting Office and Congressional Research Service). Despite this array of congressional resources, I often felt outgunned by a defense establishment whose headquarters—the Pentagon—approximates a bustling city of about 25,000 personnel during the course of a workday.

I defined my responsibilities as an individual policy-maker within a framework of three kinds or levels of representational activity that linked me to the military establishment. I thus exercised civilian control through a variety of representational linkages that formed a continuum from relatively personal and passive influence to more official and dynamic leadership.

At the most elementary level, I employed the instrument of personal relationships between myself and the military. Quite often, we could exercise influence simply because I (or someone on my staff) knew somebody in the military establishment with whom we could resolve our problems and differences informally.

My next approach would be to exercise the operational power of my office as a member of Congress. Pursuing the interests of my constituents through official communications or my votes on the floor of the House sent a direct message to (and sometimes elicited productive response from) the Pentagon.

But the most effective instrument of legislative control was the third, dynamic dimension—going beyond personal relationships and operational options to aggressive leadership on defense policy. I found that I could exercise influence very effectively and appropriately by taking a seat on the pertinent defense committee, participating in defense initiatives, speaking out on defense matters, and pushing my own defense legislation.

The best real-world examples of my efforts at civilian control, institutionally and individually, dealt with the Department of Defense's process for closing military bases, its chemical defense program, and its controversial handling of the "mystery illnesses" afflicting veterans of the Gulf War.

In the first case, I engaged very aggressively as a constituency-conscious member of Congress on the issue of how best to reduce America's post-Cold War defense infrastructure—the volatile issue of base-closures. Because one of the bases targeted by the Secretary of Defense for closure (Fort McClellan) was in my Alabama district, I worked with the House Armed Services Committee on legislation to limit the Secretary's authority and to expand the work of a base closure commission that had been successful in the 1980s (Defense Base Closure and Realignment Act of 1990). Furthermore, I organized an informal "Fairness Network" to work with other members to make sure that our military installations were treated fairly in process of base closure. Closing military bases is an inherently painful ordeal for everyone involved, but we established and implemented a course of action that was as fair and effective as possible.

In the second case, as an aggressive member of the House Armed Services Committee, I grilled Pentagon officials in public hearings about the dangers of proliferating chemical weapons around the globe; and I concluded that the Pentagon was not adequately preparing for these so-called "weapons of mass destruction." Therefore, I chaired a Special Congressional Panel on "Countering the Chemical and Biological Threat in the Post-Soviet World"; and I followed up that report with legislation requiring the Department of Defense to strengthen significantly its chemical defense program and to report to Congress on its efforts ("Title XVII—Chemical and Biological Weapons Defense" in the FY 1994 National Defense Authorization Act). Now, Congress exercises effective oversight of this increasingly important aspect of our national defense.

A third example of my civilian-control activities involved the problem—unexplained medical ailments—experienced by many American military personnel returning from service in the Gulf War, or "Desert Storm," of 1991. I found myself, along with several other representatives and senators, having to fight a guerilla war against our own military establishment which showed very little sensitivity to the suffering of sick veterans. I do not know—and we may never know—what happened to these healthy young men and women in that desert conflict, but they deserved better from their government. Of all my interactions with the Pentagon, this would prove to be the most personally frustrating—and unresolved—because of the intransigence of the Pentagon in the face of our institutional and individual pressures (and our inability to engage the Congress fully and effectively on this issue). Fortunately, some legislators have persevered, and affected veterans are receiving help. But the controversy will continue for years to come.

These examples show that the American concept of civilian supremacy can work and has worked well—institutionally through the defense budget process and individually through member-to-military initiatives—throughout our history. Congress—armed institutionally with the "power and the purse" and aggressively challenging the military as individual legislators—has enjoyed variable but effective civilian control. However, as the following section will show, the requisite conditions of civilian supremacy are changing; and Congress must adapt to these changes.

THE COLLAPSE OF THE OLD ORDER

I became concerned about the deteriorated relationship between U.S. legislators and the military establishment early in my congressional experience. I had been elected to Congress as a replacement for the late Rep. Bill Nichols, a decorated World War II veteran, solid defense reformer, and respected friend of the military. When I came to Congress in 1989, I discovered that things were changing dramatically in Washington as well as Moscow. After decades of military expansion during the Cold War, the defense establishment began breaking apart. Budget-balancing and defense downsizing took their toll on our national defense, and unpleasant experiences such as base closures strained political and personal relationships between military officials and legislators. Despite my pro-defense record, I found myself increasingly at odds with the Pentagon; and I am sure that those in the Pentagon resented my aggressive role in defense policy and politics.

My subsequent tenure at the Naval Postgraduate School has not lessened my concern about the relationship between legislators and the military. I was not surprised to find that there are differences between my perspective as a former lawmaker and the ideas of the future military leaders in my "Congress and the Pentagon" seminar. What worries me is my young military students' questions about where they stand with America's political leadership. They have committed themselves to a lifetime of service and sacrifice to a nation that appears, to them, increasingly disinterested in a long-term, positive relationship.

But the problem goes beyond strained feelings. There is growing distrust and disagreement between politicians and military people over questions of both opinion and fact; and I detect a significant deterioration of the integrity of the civil-military relationship. Neither Congress nor the Pentagon has dealt very well with the new order of the universe; and I am convinced that, as a result, the public has lost some of its confidence in these two important national institutions.

Consequently, a full decade after the end of the Cold War, United States still has not defined a satisfactory national security strategy and is struggling, with mixed results, in its role as the world's reigning super power.

Therefore, I believe that we must re-examine our approach to civil-military relations in general and civilian supremacy in particular. Revising our notion and practice of civil-military relations to incorporate constructive interaction is urgent and timely for several reasons.

First, America has lost its enemy. The Soviet Union, the Warsaw Pact, Communism, the so-called "Evil Empire"—they're all gone. The external threat that dominated American life for most of the 20th century no longer exists. But, as is so often mentioned, the post-Cold War world is still a dangerous and unstable place. The American military establishment is expected to continue its capability for fighting major wars while being called upon increasingly often and in different and unconventional capacities—for peacemaking, peacekeeping, and humanitarian missions—throughout the world.

Second, the defense budget is shrinking. Even with prospective increases in actual dollars, real defense expenditures will not keep pace with inflation and international demands. America's military in the foreseeable future will have to be relatively smaller and, at the same time, better.

However, the most important reason for civil-military cooperation is a fundamental, systemic development—something that I call the "demilitarization" of America—as we leave the 20th century. Our country generally is drifting away from historic military loyalties and interests, shifting its attention toward domestic, economic, and social priorities. This drift has been obvious for several years in the declining proportion of civilian policy-makers with military experience and knowledge. More problematic is the fact that U.S. society and the military communities are moving in opposite directions socially and politically. In short, we are experiencing a serious estrangement between civilians and the military that points toward potential disaster for American democracy.

Let me try to summarize, then, where we have been and where I think we are going in terms of our civil-military relationship. There is no disputing the fact that the traditional model of civilian supremacy served us well throughout the 20th century, a time during which the United States waged two world wars and a Cold War against powerful enemies threatening our lives and very survival as a nation. The U.S. government (both Congress and the White House), buttressed throughout with large numbers of military veterans, generally was pro-defense in politics and policy during this period, and the American people—both civilians and military personnel—shared not only pro-defense perspectives but also relatively compatible social values, political views, and personal lives.

Those were favorable conditions for healthy civil-military relations. The defense budget process brought together knowledgeable legislative leaders and responsible military officials to debate enormous military expenditures and weapons systems for an American populace that valued national security in an international environment of cataclysmic potential and dread. The contentiousness of our defense debate was justified not only by the stakes involved but also by broad national consensus, which accepted such contention; and the defense cornucopia allowed a certain level of political pork and inefficiency. Congress exercised "the power and the purse" vigorously and effectively.

But times have changed. America is not just ending the Cold War—we are entering a totally different era, with no clear threat, with increasingly complex missions, and with relatively less money for the military. Too many elected officials lack sufficient experience and knowledge to understand and appreciate the defense requirements of the new world order. Our military corps seems politically isolated and increasingly anxious. Most importantly, the American people are drifting in directions that complicate and, conceivably, could jeopardize our future national security. In short, the historic, requisite conditions for civilian supremacy are strained in contemporary America. We still have the same constitutional foundation; but the international threat to U.S. security has changed drastically, and our country seems unsure about its military mission. Furthermore, our civilian leadership, military establishment, and civic culture are evolving in an important, disconcerting manner.

The "fussy-messy" model of civil-military relations is a luxury that we can no longer afford. Thus, we in the legislative-military leadership—while maintaining the principle of civilian supremacy—need to explore new ways of working together more effectively. In other words, it is absolutely necessary that all of us understand our different but complementary responsibilities. We need to constructively integrate our efforts in order to participate more positively in the redefinition, re-prioritization, and reshaping of America's national defense and international security policy during these historic and difficult times.

ELEMENTS OF NEW CIVIL-MILITARY RELATIONS

We need to re-examine our historic approach to defense policy. The "fussy-messy" model of civil-military relations, which has served our nation well over many years, is now out of date and dysfunctional.

My ideas may be controversial (and in some cases somewhat radical), but my purpose is non-partisan and non-ideological. I am not pushing a pro-defense, anti-defense, or any other political agenda. Democrats and Republicans, liberals and conservatives, all should be concerned about the future of civilian supremacy.

I should note that my recommendations are directed toward Congress rather than the Pentagon, partly because I come from a legislative background, but mainly because civilian supremacy is a congressional duty. Our Constitutional Founders placed primary responsibility for the common defense and civil-military relations on the legislative branch.

To begin, my general recommendation is that Congress take bold steps to redesign its defense policy process in the new millennium. More specifically, I believe that the following institutional adjustments would enable Congress to deal with the realities of the "new world order," develop a positive relationship with the Pentagon, and contribute to a sound national defense for America's future:

1. *Acknowledge the New Realities.* Congress first should officially recognize, somewhere in its formal deliberations, that the post-Cold War environment is one of: (1) uncertain military threats and missions; (2) changing domestic, economic, and social priorities; and (3) the demilitarization of American society.

2. *Create a Civil-Military Relations Commission.* Secondly, in conjunction with this official affirmation, Congress should establish a congressional commission on civil-military relations—an advisory body of knowledgeable leaders from the congressional community, the military establishment, and broader society—that will address civil-military relations in the "new world order."

3. *Establish a Formal System of Congressional Education on Defense.* Simultaneous with this affirmation of the new world order and creation of a civil-military commission, Congress should institute a formal educational program for legislators (especially those serving on defense-related committees). Prior military service is not a necessary requirement for defense policy leadership, but it is clear that the decreasing presence of veterans deprives Congress of valuable experience and knowledge. All legislators should understand the historic nature of civil-military relations in American democracy; and those in key defense positions may have to be prepared professionally for dealing with national security policy in the "new world" environment.

4. *Enhance Congressional Staff Capability.* Congress also must strengthen its staff capabilities, with particular emphasis on acquiring additional personnel with military service and knowledge. This advice runs counter to popular feelings about "big government"; but the fact is that, with declining numbers of veterans among the elected membership, America's national defense requires more military experience and expertise in support personnel.

5. *Reform the Defense Policy Process.* Congress should take a close look at how it conducts defense politics— including its budgetary, jurisdictional, and committee practices—to lessen the level of contentiousness and add some rationality to the defense policy process. Byzantine arrangements of the congressional process hamper healthy civil-military relations and overly politicize and complicate national defense policy.

For openers, it may be time to look favorably on some long-contemplated reforms—such as implementing multi-year defense budgets, clarifying the distinction between defense authorizations and appropriations, and constraining the multiplicity of committees dealing with national security. More fundamentally, Congress might want to expand or revamp its internal structure of defense policy leadership. Perhaps the current arrangement of defense fiefdoms (driven in great part by partisan, provincial, and self-selecting participants) could be enhanced by creating a House-Senate Select Defense Oversight Committee—composed of experienced, knowledgeable members from both chambers—for more comprehensive, cooperative, and accountable direction on defense matters. An even more radical suggestion is that the defense committees and subcommittees establish experimental panels of active legislators and representatives from the defense establishment to participate in the conventional committee process. Incorporating broad input at an early stage of the process might improve both the politics and policy of national security.

6. *Individual Responsibility for the Civil-Military Relationship*. Finally, I would suggest that defense legislators re-orient themselves toward greater outreach and cooperation as individuals. Their personal relationships, operational activities, and dynamic leadership can be used extensively for improving civil-military relations in the future.

In closing, let me repeat, I am not suggesting that Congress ignore its constitutional responsibilities; and I doubt that civilian control will ever be a neat, pleasant process. However, I feel strongly that today's leaders should think about how they debate national security in a drastically changed environment. In that reflective process, I believe Congress will conclude that it is in our national interest to forge a less fussy, less messy, and more productive relationship with the military establishment.

The relationship between Congress and the Pentagon has always been and, as long as the current Constitution prevails, will forever be one of civilian supremacy and vigorous legislative control. Elected lawmakers and professional military officers cannot be, and should not become, a partnership of political equity and rigid rationality. But perhaps it is time to re-examine our notion of civil-military relations as we enter the 21st century.

American democracy must respond to important developments in the new millennium—changing defense threats and missions, shifting national priorities, and a disturbing estrangement between civilian society and the military community. Now, and increasingly in the future, our legislative and military leadership must find ways to work together for national and international security.

Part Eight

The Evolution of Congress

The chapters in this concluding section discuss how Congress has changed over time. The opening chapter, by Bud Brown, traces the development of the United States Congress from the first representative assemblies, created to respond to initiatives of the colonial governors, through the First and Second Continental Congresses and the Articles of Confederation, to the more powerful legislative body we are familiar with today, whose powers were described in Article I, Section 8 of the U.S. Constitution.

In the second selection, Don Sundquist gives his reflections, from his current vantage point as Governor of Tennessee, on how the Congress measured up in addressing the problems facing the country during his tenure in the House. He also laments how Congress has changed for the worse in recent years with a rise in partisanship and a decline in collegiality.

Eugene McCarthy echoes this theme, suggesting that Congress used to work much better than it does now. He calls for a return to many of the practices that characterized the Congress in the 1950s, when (he believes) it was better equipped to deal expeditiously and effectively with national problems.

The volume concludes with a comparison of two impeachments: the impeachment proceedings against President Richard Nixon in 1973-74, and the more recent impeachment of President Bill Clinton. Drawing on responses from many former members who participated in the Nixon inquiry, Lou Frey and I find a sharp difference between the recollections of Democratic and Republican members. More importantly, we find that the Watergate investigation was intensely partisan from the outset and remained so until convincing evidence of President Nixon's guilt led almost all Republicans on the Judiciary Committee to join with the Democrats in voting for articles of impeachment. Because the Nixon impeachment tends to be remembered as more bipartisan and cooperative than it actually was, Democrats were able to deny legitimacy to the Clinton impeachment by maintaining party unity in voting against impeachment at every stage.

Chapter 41

Early History and Development
of the U. S. Congress

Clarence J. "Bud" Brown (R-Ohio)

The philosophic and organizational roots of the United States Congress go back to the pure democracy of Athenian Greece and the representational concepts of the Senate of Rome and beyond. These two idealized national histories were familiar to most of the Founding Fathers of the United States of America. However, the single most immediate and influential factor was the parliamentary system of government wrested from the King of England 300 years earlier in 1456. In the United States, that process would be turned on its head. Rather than negotiating to themselves some portion of imperial and parliamentary control over their part of the empire, the new Americans separated entirely, created a new nation, and designed the most democratic republic to date.

In English history, some of the powers of governance had been taken from an almost omnipotent king by his knights and princes when they forced him to sign the Magna Carta. The powers of caesars, kings, and czars over their common folk began when the crown of command was placed on the imperial head without effective objection. But even after the Magna Carta, peers were controlled by the sovereign in many ways, and the common people still had little say in their governance—except by acquiescence to the "upper classes"—until the 20th century. With a new nation on a "new" continent, however, the U.S. Congress—an Americanized ideal of a hated Parliament—came first, created by the very first article of the new Constitution. There would be no king, of course. Only, later in the Constitution is there mention of an executive who would carry out the will of the Congress as expressed in laws passed by that representative body. How the new nation came to give governing authority in the form of a pure republic to a more or less democratically-elected assembly is explained by its earlier history.

With discovery of new lands in the Western hemisphere, popes, kings, and entrepreneurs commissioned envoys to expand their hegemony and gather wealth from the region. Cut off for long periods from their European homelands, resident governors, the selected authorities of kings or corporate patent holders, prudently named prominent citizens as their advisory councilors. In time, governors' councils were supplemented or replaced by assemblies of the free local gentry when their interests were not sufficiently represented to achieve their concurrence or control. To gain approval for executing actions mandated from far away, or to raise funds or mobilize labor to accomplish local projects or common defense, governors eventually found it politic to allow their suggestions to be modified by their appointed advisors or assemblies and eventually even to have the assemblies elected. The next logical step followed soon when elected assemblies began originating projects or governmental ideas of their own by petition to the governor or his council. Ultimately, the petitions became legislation.

The governors found their representative assemblies particularly helpful when enlisting local militia for defense of new resident populations from attacks by natives who had previously held communal ownership of the continent and did not have the Homeric European appreciation for the concept of individual private property. As the numbers of new immigrant Americans increased and the frontier moved further inland, native American reaction grew more hostile. After a century, stimulated by the French, who controlled sparsely populated Canada and were trading in the unsettled territory beyond the mountains, warfare between natives and colonials moved from sporadic to general. When hostilities became pervasive along the western frontier, the now predominantly English European settlers pressured the advisory assemblies of their various colonial governments to undertake some common defense. In 1754, a first "continental" gathering of those disparate colonies (New Hampshire, Massachusetts, Rhode Island, Connecticut, New York, Pennsylvania, and Maryland) met in Albany to discuss a plan for common defense. Whether it was because these were largely English colonies or because England had the greatest national military power in Europe and America in that era, professional military assistance under centralized control was solicited and granted from London.

As any command organization would, the British-American Expeditionary Force saw its authority emanating from its king and his parliament, who exercised power through colonial governors, not the local public assemblies. As emigres, British colonists in America still held ingrained loyalty to their nation's monarch. But they were increasingly aware that they had no representation in Parliament—even though they had some champions there, frequently among the king's "loyal opposition." To an increasing degree, local representative assemblies were petitioning local governors—or, when frustrated, over the governors' heads to King or Parliament in London—regarding local problems and grievances. And the colonial assemblies began to communicate their common concerns with each other. Assembly responses to governors' initiatives became assembly-initiated petitions; petitions became resolutions; and resolutions became legislation. The function of the assemblies shifted from merely accepting or negotiating modification of gubernatorial (or London government) proposals, to vetoing such initiatives, and finally to initiating their own petitions, resolutions, and legislation to which the governor or London would be obliged to react.

After seven years of war, the British captured Canada from the French, leading to war between the two powers and their allies in Europe. The result in America was that native incursions were now limited to the new lands British colonials were starting to settle west of the Appalachians. By 1763, the situation was made more fractious from London, where the Parliament sought revenues through taxes and duties on English imports into America to recoup costs of the recent war there, by the continued stationing of troops in the colonies (which led to the "Boston Massacre" in 1770), and by military "administration of justice and support of civil government."

Americans reacted to these developments with boycotts of taxed imports, demonstrations such as the 1773 "Boston Tea Party," hostility toward British troops quartered in the colonies, and petitions and resolutions from assemblies in many colonies objecting to what were seen as actions smothering economic, social, and political development in America. Communications on these subjects among the colonial assemblies set the stage for the First Continental Congress—56 delegates from 12 colonies (sans Georgia)—which met in Philadelphia on September 6, 1774. Benjamin Franklin had proposed such colonial unity at the Albany Congress, but it had been rejected by all the legislatures to which it had been referred. Now, unity came naturally in reaction to the acts of the British government in London. Congress (its official title) chose Peyton Randolph of Virginia as its leader, agreed to a formula for representation (two representatives from smaller states and seven from the largest, with each state bound to vote as a unit), and began petitioning London for a redress of grievances and restoration of cordial and considerate relations.

Radicals in that first 51-day Congress passed and publicly disseminated resolutions declaring "unconstitutional" the so-called Coercive Acts of the British Parliament. They further recommended stringent economic sanctions against Britain, and urged people in Massachusetts to form and arm their own militia. More adept now than the British army at fighting native Americans, the colonials began to see the British troops quartered among them as more oppressive than supportive. They also found, in taxation without representation, their rallying cry for liberty from unpopular rule from London that was increasingly seen as "foreign."

Conservatives in the Congress attempted to paper over the developing hostility with a plan for "proposed Union between Great Britain and the Colonies." The plan called for a president-general, named at the pleasure of the king, and a grand council, chosen for three-year terms by the assemblies of each colony, to be an "inferior and distinct branch of the British legislature." Then, either Parliament or its American branch could initiate laws to govern America, although both would have to concur for enactment. The plan failed by a six to five unit vote of the member colonies.

The Second Continental Congress convened May 10, 1775, three weeks after the battle of Lexington. The climate had changed. Congress would no longer be petitioning for recovery of the British rights of colonial citizens or the renewal of cordial relations with throne and Parliament. It started taking actions appropriate to the government of an independent nation. It asked Canada to join its ranks in putting the colonies in a defense posture, and named George Washington to take command of the forces around Boston as a continental army.

After the unsuccessful battle of Bunker Hill, Congress adjourned on August 2nd, but not before professing the people's allegiance to George III (and formally rejecting independence), petitioning the king to take no further hostile action against the colonies, and asserting that Americans would rather die than be enslaved. Reconvened September 12th (now with Georgia as the 13th member), Congress learned that the king had refused to receive the petition and proclaimed the colonies to be in open rebellion. Parliament followed suit, rejecting reconciliation on November 7th. On December 6th, Congress disavowed its allegiance to Parliament, while at the same time disclaiming any intention to deny the sovereignty of the king. A royal proclamation in December closed the colonies to commerce effective March 1, 1776. In an effort to get supplies for an increasingly likely war with Great Britain, Congress sent emissaries to Europe.

The final break came with the July 2nd Declaration of Independence, formalized by Jefferson's elegant closing language signed July 4th: "We, therefore, the representatives of the United States of America, in General Congress assembled,...do, in the name, and by the authority of the good people of these colonies, solemnly publish and declare, that these United Colonies are, and of right ought to be free and independent states...and that, as free and independent states, they have full power to levy war, conclude peace, contract alliances, establish commerce, and do all other acts and things which independent states may of right do...."

That language was still ambivalent as to whether the United States of America was a single nation governed by a Congress of 13 delegations from various colonial assemblies or 13 "free and independent states." The Articles of Confederation, the first framework of our national government, were not concluded until November 15, 1777, and ratification by the 13th colonial assembly did not come until March 1781. This ambivalence would continue until a unifying national Constitution was ratified in 1787. Not until then, would an executive branch of the new government be established.

The Continental and Confederation Congresses were held together by the war and the common agonies of their own failures and occasional successes. The delegates (two to seven from each state, depending on population—including Canada, if it so chose), were annually elected, qualified, and paid by the states, with terms (no more than three years in any six) set by the Confederation Articles. State delegations still voted as a unit as a concession to small states, and all amendments would have to be approved unanimously—which is to say not often! The power to declare war, enter treaties and alliances, raise an army and navy, regulate coinage and borrow money all required the assent of nine of the thirteen delegations. Congress could otherwise establish a postal service, adjudicate disputes between states, and regulate Indian affairs. As to adjudication of state disputes, the final ratification of the Articles was held up at Maryland's insistence until it was agreed that state claims to western lands would be given over to the central government.

The mistrust of a strong (and distant) central government was evidenced by the fact that there would be no single executive authority and no power to tax or levy tariffs. The central government would be financed through contributions and the promissory credit of the various colony states. Congress could appoint "such other committees and civil officers as may be necessary for managing the general affairs of the United States." In this way, Robert Livingston was named Secretary of Foreign Affairs, Robert Morris Secretary of the Treasury, and General Benjamin Lincoln Secretary of War. Everything was negotiated and negotiable among the disparate and changing personalities involved. Committees of delegates undertook what would otherwise have been executive management responsibilities—providing for the common defense, establishing justice, insuring domestic tranquility, and promoting the general welfare.

If the central governing authority was weak and ineffective at times, it was sustained by the common support of the cause of national independence and individual liberty. But no one successfully argued that any of the sovereign powers of the various colonies be given over to a central government. However, even before the Declaration of Independence, the Second Continental Congress had urged each colony to form new, independent state governments. Massachusetts did so in the autumn of 1774, New Hampshire in January 1776, and South Carolina the following March. Some were drafted by the state assemblies without formal authorization and put into effect without popular consent. Others were authorized but never submitted to voters for approval. Three were authorized and ratified by voters and only two elected state constitutional conventions and submitted them for voter ratification.

All had some form of a bill of rights including freedom of speech, press, and petition; the rights of habeas corpus; and trial by jury. All cited the separation of powers between the legislative, executive, and judicial branches; but all lodged strong powers in their legislatures, ten of which were bicameral (the exceptions were Pennsylvania, Georgia, and Vermont). The power of the executive branch was weaker than the colonial governor had been in all states except New York, Massachusetts, and New Hampshire, and only two states gave the governor the right to veto. Most states gave the legislature the right to appoint the judiciary. Pennsylvania, the most democratic, even set up a three-member governing council as its executive, members of which could serve no more than three years in seven. State assemblymen could serve no more than four years in seven, and there were no qualifications for voting or holding office. Otherwise, most states maintained their pre-revolutionary requirements for voting and holding office: ownership of some property to vote at all with higher values required for various offices (1,000 pounds to be a state senator in New Jersey and Maryland, and 2,000 pounds in South Carolina). Most states also imposed religious qualifications!

As the Revolutionary War progressed, the flaws of the Continental Congress and later, the Articles of Confederation, for governing a diverse, growing, and economically complicated nation became more and more apparent. Inability to raise the means to finance the war was the first bad sign. When the American forces enjoyed victories, weapons and military supplies were delivered in timely fashion and creditors showed patience. But as suppliers failed to receive compensation and the tide of war ran against the Americans, military supplies and equipment also slowed. As the war ended successfully, the belated adoption of the Articles of Confederation did little to improve the situation. Of ten million dollars requisitioned by Congress from the states from 1781 to 1783, only $1.5 million was forthcoming. Many states issued worthless scrip to pay off paper debt instruments that Congress had used to finance the war and other national activities. Resulting inflation saw banks foreclose on farmers across the land and merchants insist on hard coin payment for goods, causing declines in imports and exports. To pay their obligations, states raised taxes and tariffs, further depressing markets. Congress could not levy import duties without unanimous consent, which it could not get. And it could not force states to return property confiscated from British loyalists during the war, as it had promised in the treaty ending war, because it lacked the authority. Besides, much of that confiscated property was being used to finance the states' war debts.

The traders and merchants of the coast towns and the manufacturers of the cities wanted a central federal government whose credit was backed by power to generate revenue. Political leaders feared that the nation created by the blood of fighters for independence could not survive internal economic dissension and the pressures of foreign interests. Alexander Hamilton successfully urged the New York Assembly to ask Congress to call a convention to revise the Articles. The Massachusetts Assembly seconded that idea. Then Virginia and Maryland worked out a plan to resolve navigational and commercial issues between the two states and called for a convention at Annapolis to extend this agreement to Pennsylvania, Delaware, New Jersey, and New York. But Hamilton and Madison persuaded the Annapolis meeting to seek a meeting of all the states. Congress, not wanting to lose its authority, finally issued a call for a convention in Philadelphia in May of 1787 for the "sole and express purpose of revising the Articles of Confederation and reporting to Congress and the several Legislatures."

With the resulting Constitution, a new republic was born with a democratically elected House of Representatives, apportioned on population, and a Senate (elected by state legislatures) that would have two separate votes for each state regardless of population. There would also be an independent executive whose separate election Congress would certify and whom it could remove only by impeachment in the House and conviction by two-thirds of the Senate. There would be one Supreme Court and "such inferior courts as Congress shall from time to time ordain and establish." While the new president would be able to propose laws, only Congress could enact them. Although the president had the power to veto acts of Congress, two-thirds of the Congress could override that veto, and the president would then have to execute those laws. As it later developed, if the Supreme Court were to decide a law passed by Congress violated the Constitution, it could strike down that law; but Congress could initiate an amendment to the Constitution overriding the Supreme Court decision if three-fourths of the states ratified it.

The House of Representatives was left to decide its own organization and rules of its operation, and it decided, in large measure, to adopt the procedures, officers, and nomenclature of the British Parliament. The Speaker would preside and declare the results of actions taken. The Clerk would read to the illiterate when appropriate and maintain records of proceedings. The Sergeant at Arms would maintain order and protection of the legislative body with his symbol of authority, the Mace. And the Doorkeeper would maintain the sanctity of the Chamber and its gallery for public observers.

The proportionality of state representation in the House of Representatives is set in the Constitution. Court decisions have since refined the distribution of the representatives within the state to assure the citizens of each state equal representation (one man, one vote). The committee structure of both the House and Senate is an outgrowth of the constitutional guarantee of the right of citizens to petition their national legislature, as Congress, from its earliest days, referred such petitions to committees for reading and action. Jurisdictions of committees and assignment of members to committees are confirmed by each Congress and thus have been subject to considerable change over the years.

One of the more fundamental amendments has been the shift to statewide popular election of senators, replacing the original constitutional provision for senators to be chosen by the legislatures of the various states. The designation of senators by state legislatures in the early days of the republic brought many very distinguished statesmen onto the national stage at a critical time while the popular election of House members by a rustic population of little education failed to produce a distinguished membership within that body. Conversely, with the spread of public education and the economic expansion of the country following the Civil War, the composition of the House began to reflect improvements in the educational level of the general electorate, while the state legislatures were sending men to the Senate who were distinguished more by their wealth than by political sensitivity and leadership. The amendment to the Constitution in 1913 requiring the popular election of senators has had a salutary effect reflecting the improvement in the educational level of the whole population today.

Chapter 42

A Governor's Reflections
on Life in the U.S. House

Don Sundquist (R-Tennessee)

I never intended to make Congress a career. When I first ran, I said I would only serve for 12 years and then come back home. I imposed my own term limits, and I was coming home in 1994, whether I ran for governor or not.

As governor of Tennessee, I agree with what's happening in Washington now in terms of giving responsibility back to the states. We've been given more responsibility for welfare reform. In Tennessee, we've reformed health care and welfare prior to the changes federally. In the process, we've proven that you can do more with less money if the federal government will give us the flexibility to do it, and I think we've shown that states, left to their own best instincts, will not engage in a "race to the bottom," as some critics contend, but rather, will make a race to see who reaches the top, who does the best for their citizens.

My experience as governor has strengthened the conviction I had as a member of Congress that government works best at a level closer to the people. If anything, I would have been an even more forceful advocate for shifting responsibility back to the states. Likewise, my experience in Washington as an opponent of unfunded federal mandates on states has made me very careful as governor not to impose unfunded state mandates on local government.

I always felt that a member's contribution shouldn't be measured just by how many bills Congress writes and passes. As a conservative, I looked for opportunities to simplify regulation, cut red tape for taxpayers, and simply to prevent what I regarded as bad bills from becoming law.

I think that one of the failures of Congress, under both Democrats and Republicans, has been the huge debt we ran up for a long period of time, starting with the Depression and World War II. Many people just assume that you have to have a deficit every year. I'm happy to see that being challenged now.

When I first went to Congress, we had high inflation, high interest rates, and high taxes, and there were experts who said we had to live with those things, that this was going to be a fact of life in the future. In fact, we didn't have to live with double-digit inflation. We don't have to live with high interest rates. We don't have to live with high taxes. I'm glad we've reached a point where most people believe that we don't have to live with federal budget deficits.

On the whole, I loved the institution and was proud to serve. Congress can work. You can affect change. The best example of that, I think, are the votes on defense and foreign policy during the 1980s that helped bring about the collapse of communism and the end of the Cold War. I was southern whip for Trent Lott and then briefly for Dick Cheney. One of the things we accomplished in the '80s was the building of bipartisan support among southern representatives for some very, very tough votes on defense, on Nicaragua, and the Contras. I truly believe that because we prevailed and supported President Reagan's policy of strength, it demonstrated to the Soviets that we were going to match them dollar for dollar, project by project. They finally gave up. The Cold War didn't end—America won it. I credit President Reagan for strong leadership, and I credit the Democrats and Republicans in the House and the Senate who were able to fight for a strong defense, new weapons, and for the military.

They were tough votes at the time, but we were proven to be right by events, and we did change the course of history.

I don't miss Washington, but I miss my former colleagues and the camaraderie we enjoyed. If I have one regret, it's that I never had the chance to serve in the majority. My heart breaks for Bob Michel; he was there for 42 years and never did serve in the majority, only to see Republicans gain control of the House in the year he stepped down. Bob would have been an excellent and honorable Speaker, and I'm sorry he never got that chance. In fact, we had a number of promising House members who became discouraged in the minority and left the House for Senate races or cabinet positions; Trent Lott and Dick Cheney come to mind.

I never served in the congressional majority; I was elected governor the year the Republicans won control of the House. I found it interesting, though, to hear Democrats complaining about how the Republican majority operates. From what I can tell, the Republican majority is dealing with the Democrats exactly the way the Democrats usually dealt with us when we were the minority. My former colleague, Sam Gibbons of Florida, for example, complained about committee Republicans meeting and approving a bill without consulting the committee's Democrats. Well, I remember when Sam Gibbons was the acting chairman and he and the Democrats went into a back room and approved a bill that hadn't even been written—they approved it "in concept." I'd never heard of such a thing. Not only did they not consult with us, we had no paperwork. They approved a bill that they described to us but hadn't even written! I take a lot of the Democratic complaints about life in the minority with a grain of salt. Democrats had great fun with the rules when they worked to their benefit.

It would have been nice to be part of the majority, and I am a little bit envious of those who, instead of being ranking members, are now chairmen. Instead of acting on someone else's agenda, it's now our agenda. It's been a big adjustment for some of my former colleagues, who had been in the minority for a long time. It's a difficult transition, but I think the Republicans handled it very well in the last couple of years in terms of setting an agenda and passing legislation.

I love the House of Representatives, but I'm disappointed that it has gotten as partisan as it has. When I first went to Congress, there was more camaraderie; the tone was better. Speaker Tip O'Neill and President Reagan would be competitive and partisan in their business dealings and cordial after hours, and the same was true for most of the rest of us. After the House adjourned, everybody was decent to each other and could share a laugh. That changed. Toward the end of my service in Congress, it was much more partisan. Members would call for votes just to put opponents on the spot. I deplore the direction the Congress has taken. I'm disappointed that some people seem to be interested only in getting elected and reelected, sometimes by grandstanding at the expense of the institution.

The whole subject of congressional pay is a good case-in-point. I served on the bipartisan Task Force on Ethics Review that wrote and passed the Ethics Reform Act of 1989. We eliminated honoraria, we ended the practice of allowing members to retire with their leftover campaign cash, and we put in place a system for cost of living adjustments (COLAs). Although ours were less than the COLAs everyone else gets, they would keep congressional salaries at a level where people without independent wealth could afford to serve without sacrifice to their families. We thought that we had solved the problem, but right up to the present, someone grandstands every year, trying to force a procedural vote to deny the COLA to Congress. It's an easy way to score political points, but I worry that it will do long-term damage to the institution and discourage good people from offering themselves for public service.

Congress as an institution has taken some cheap shots from people who serve in Congress or who aspire to serve in Congress. Much of the debate over the supposed congressional perks is exaggerated, petty, or just plain wrong. You almost wonder why anyone would want to be part of a body whose own members delight in discrediting it to the public. If the quality of members has decreased, as some have suggested, well, that's a big part of the reason why.

In my era, there was a bipartisan sense of camaraderie and historical perspective. I remember when I was first elected, it annoyed me that Bill Green, a Republican from Manhattan, didn't vote with us very often. I said to Bob Michel, who was the Republican leader, "Can't you do something about Bill Green?" Bob said, "Let me ask you a question: Bill Green replaced Bella Abzug. He represents a very liberal district in downtown New York City. Would you rather have Bill Green or Bella Abzug?"

Every member has to serve his or her own district and the philosophy of the people who elected him/her. You have to be respectful of other members. So I may not have agreed with Bill Green, but I came to recognize that he was doing what the people of his district wanted him to do, and I found later that he was a very decent human being, very bright and articulate. That was a good lesson for me to learn.

Chapter 43

Congress—It Used to Work

Eugene J. McCarthy (D-Minnesota)

In the roughly two and a half decades preceding the reforms of the 1970s (and also preceding the founding of Common Cause), Congress operated largely under the provisions of the Legislation Reorganization Act, passed in 1946. The major provisions of the act dealt with two matters: committee numbers and structure, and the budget process. Standing committees were reduced from 33 to 15 in the Senate and from 48 to 19 in the House of Representatives. Provisions were included to improve professional and clerical staffs, and salaries were increased from $10,000 a year to $12,500 a year. Members of Congress were brought into the Civil Service Retirement Program.

The second major matter addressed by the act was the budget. The act provided that the House of Representatives Ways and Means Committee, the Senate Finance Committee, and the Appropriations Committees of both houses should act as a joint budget committee and each year prepare a government-wide budget. The report was to be accompanied by estimates of total expenditures and receipts. The law prohibited Congress from appropriating more than the estimated receipts without authorizing an increase in the public debt. A proposal to require that the president reduce all appropriations by a uniform percentage if expenditures exceeded receipts (a kind of early Gramm-Rudman Act) was rejected.

In its first test, in 1947, the budget procedure died in a House-Senate conference. The provisions were deemed unworkable and were suspended. In 1950, Chairman Clarence Cannon of the Appropriations Committee tried to control the budget by putting all appropriations ($37 billion was the amount that year) into a single bill. In 1951, the Appropriations Committee returned to the traditional method of Senate appropriations bills for each government department and agency.

Cannon held that the $37 billion budget was too big and too complicated to be handled in one package. No such modesty has been expressed by current members of Congress, who now take on in one appropriation expenditures in excess of $1 trillion.

In any case, without complying with a controlling budget procedure, without reforming Congress, without codes of ethics, without the purifying effect of the Federal Election Act, without Common Cause, Congress—sometimes in support of presidents, sometimes in opposition—between 1947 and 1970 paid off the World War II debts, met the costs of the Korean War, initiated and financed the Marshall Plan, extended Social Security to include nearly all U.S. citizens, established and financed Medicare and Medicaid, built and paid for the interstate highway system, financed the hospital-building program and the development of nuclear power and weapons, balanced the budget in most years and allowed an increase of less than $150 billion in the federal debt in a period of more than 20 years, and kept inflation within a range of two percent to three percent annually—a rate increase generally favored, even by conservative economists.

All of this was done with the powerful House Rules Committee in place, with the seniority rules generally operative, and with members returning to their districts and states when Congress was out of session, some to work in law offices (risking conflict of interest), on their farms, or in their businesses. These members of Congress ran in campaigns in which there were no limits on expenditures or personal contributions, with little or no regulation beyond requirements that contributions and expenditures be reported.

Scandals were few, limited largely to personal misconduct, and none seriously prejudiced or affected the operations of the House or the Senate. Throughout these two decades, the traditional efforts of the Senate to have more power over appropriations (mostly to increase them) continued, but those efforts were largely rejected.

Between 1952 and 1967, bills to create a joint budget committee, composed of members of both the House and the Senate, were passed eight times in the Senate, but were never accepted in the House. The issue came to a head in 1962, when the House Appropriations Committee refused to go to the Senate wing of the Capitol for a conference.

The primary responsibility for taxes, constitutionally assigned to the House of Representatives, also was recognized and honored. All revenue bills originated in the House. In practice, the claims of the House went further than the right to originate bills. Tax bills in the House were offered to the membership under very strict rules. The revenue bills passed in these decades by the House were essentially what the Ways and Means Committee offered. The Senate, especially under the Finance Committee chairmanship of Sen. Harry Byrd, Sr., honored this distinction and seldom attempted any major modification of the tax bills sent to it by the House of Representatives.

The separation of power and of responsibility between the House and the Senate on foreign policy was not as clearly maintained as was that on taxes and appropriation. Encroachment in this case was not from the Senate but from the House of Representatives.

Before, during, and in the years immediately following World War II, foreign-policy responsibilities were restricted largely to the Senate and to the executive branch, with little interference from the House of Representatives. When foreign-policy programs, following the war, required authorization and appropriation of money, the House inevitably became involved. For example, whereas the United Nations Charter was approved by the Senate only in 1948, the United Nations Participation Act of the same year was passed and approved by both the Senate and the House. The Greek-Turkish aid program was passed by a vote of 67 to 23 in the Senate and by a vote of 287 to 108 in the House. Similarly, both the House and the Senate participated in formulating and approving the European Recovery Act, thus setting precedent (with the exception of the approval of treaties) for participation of the House in foreign policy matters on a basis roughly equivalent to that of the Senate.

The growing use of joint resolutions by the House and the Senate on foreign-policy issues further blurred the lines distinguishing the powers of the House and the Senate on foreign-policy matters. The most significant example of such resolutions was, again, the Near East Resolution passed during the Eisenhower administration, which did two things: it gave the House equal standing with the Senate in foreign-policy determinations and made the resolutions, because the House participated, a kind of declaration of war, as did the joint actions on the Tonkin Gulf Resolution in 1964, as later interpreted by the Johnson and Nixon administrations.

Once involved in foreign-policy decisions, the House had to take responsibility for them. The House was under pressure to prove itself right within the allotted two years of a House term, while senators have a range of six years before being called to account. It is almost impossible to conduct foreign policy, or even to understand it, in a two-year cycle.

The principal instrument for House meddling in foreign policy was the rider attached to appropriations and other bills, such as the one carrying the name of Rep. Edward Boland of Massachusetts. This prohibited aid to anyone seeking to overthrow the government of Nicaragua.

In recent years, Congress—both the House of Representatives and the Senate—has attempted to micromanage foreign policy. Both houses, with greater and greater frequency, have attempted to give detailed directions, impose restrictions, and require reporting on foreign assistance and other legislation relating to foreign policy. A quantitative indicator of the extent of such interference is the great increase of reporting requirements on such programs: from 200 in 1973 to more than 700 by 1988.

A more formal action on the part of Congress to further control executive power in international affairs was the passage of the War Powers Act in 1973 (a kind of closing-the-barn-door-after-the-horse-has-fled action by members of Congress who had supported the Vietnam War). The act probably involved an unconstitutional concession of power over foreign policy not only from the president to Congress but also one within Congress, from the Senate to the House of Representatives.

While the House was taking on foreign policies that structurally and functionally it was not constituted to carry out, it was subjected to attacks by reformers strongly supported, if not led, by Common Cause, with help from the League of Women Voters and most of the press. This made it difficult for the House not only to carry out its new responsibilities but also to accomplish its traditional and constitutional responsibilities.

The principal result of the reforms of the 1970s was that power and responsibility, which had been exercised and accepted by the Speaker of the House, the Rules Committee, committee chairmen, and ranking members of various committees, was widely dispersed among a growing number of committees, subcommittees, and caucuses. Committee staff members were increased. By the end of the 1970s, the Democratic leaders of the House acknowledged that their position of leadership had been seriously eroded. Each congressional office had become a separate political party.

In 1974, the House took responsibility for taking committee assignments away from the Ways and Means Committee. During the same year, Congress approved the Congressional Budget and Impoundment Control Act, which largely repeated what was acknowledged to be a mistake in the 1946 Reorganization Act. The 1974 act established a joint budget committee and a complicated process for comprehensive treatment of spending and tax policies, a process that eroded the House of Representatives' basic and primary responsibility for expenditures.

In 1975, supported by a large number of new members, the junior members of the House attacked seniority as a basis for picking chairmen. In 1977, the House adopted a code of ethics, which limited outside earned income and required elaborate reports on gifts, honoraria, and so forth. No limits were imposed on unearned income. The limitation on earned income has been cited as the reason for the bookselling devices that brought Speaker of the House James Wright and Senator David Durenberger so much trouble, leading to the resignation of Wright from the House of Representatives and the censure of Durenberger by the Senate.

Having failed to bring about good, effective, pure, and Platonic government through reorganizations, budget reform, or codes of ethics, the reformers turned to the electoral process as the source of the trouble, and money as the source beyond the source. Common Cause did, and does still, cite money as the root of all political evil, unmindful or indifferent to the fact that the Bible holds that there are two temptations of a higher order, and both more dangerous. One is the desire for power and the other is pride. In politics, pride is expressed by trying to make one's mark on history.

The 1970 campaign finance reforms, culminating in the revised (under Supreme Court orders) 1976 act, changed the way in which House members, in particular, financed their campaigns. The revised legislation limited individual contributions, allowed people of great wealth to spend as much of their own money as they wished (as in the Perot presidential campaigns), and made members increasingly dependent on funding of their campaigns by political action committees, especially those organized by corporations.

During the years in which these changes in legislative and policy responsibilities were effected, burdening individual House members with more and more responsibilities, the length or number of days that Congress is in session annually increased dramatically. Once again, we see that Congress is now essentially in continuous session, which is bad for Congress and bad for the country. This leaves members with fewer days to spend with their constituents, forcing them to spend more money on impersonal communications, much of it concentrated during campaigns, and leaving them more and more dependent on the mass media, which in turn sends them back to the PACs for funding treatment.

Members of the House are less and less representative of the nation as a whole and of their particular constituencies. There is less time and opportunity for the *process* of representation. And the House has little of the democratic and populist nature that the Founders intended.

The House also has suffered from the great increase in the number of constituents in each district. The Founding Fathers worried that districts of 30,000 might be too large. When I ran for Congress in 1948, the average district size was approximately 340,000—about the number Lewis Mumford said was the maximum for a manageable political unit. The average congressional district size today is about 600,000—20 times greater than that held to be reasonable by the Founding Fathers and twice what Mumford believed was a workable political unit. And the size of House districts is growing every day.

What should happen is a return to smaller districts. The objection is that this would make the House too large. But this might not be so bad. Today, Germany's Bundestag has 662 members, the British House of Commons has 651 members, the National Assembly of France has 577 members, and the Diet of Japan has 512 members.

Yet in Japan, the ratio of constituents to each representative is approximately 238,000 to one, in Germany 120,000 to one, in France 96,000 to one, and in Britain 87,000 to one. With all of the responsibilities a member of the House carries for domestic programs, added foreign-policy chores, casework service to more than a half-million people, getting reelected every two years, giving some attention to private and family matters, and so on, it is not surprising that what was called a House banking service (it was not; it was really a check-cashing service) might have been abused a few years back.

What should be done to make the House a respected and effective legislative body once again?

1. The House of Representatives should be "disorganized" or reorganized to about what it was in the 1950s.

2. The full power of the Speaker, the Rules Committee, and of the Ways and Means Committee should be restored, along with the seniority system and the strong-chairman tradition.

3. The budget process now in effect should be abolished, and the process followed under Chairman Clarence Cannon in the 1950s be restored.

4. Sessions of Congress should be shortened so that members of the House can spend more time with their constituents, thus freeing themselves in some measure from the need to spend large amounts of money to communicate with these constituents both during sessions and in campaigns.

5. The House of Representatives should reassert its dominance over appropriations, and the Ways and Means Committee should assert its authority over taxes. The House should yield to the Senate primary responsibility over foreign policy relative to the House and not participate in joint foreign-policy resolutions. The House should stop or control the offering of riders on legislation affecting foreign policy.

6. The federal election laws either should be repealed or significantly modified by removing the limitations of individual contributions and outlawing contributions from both labor and corporate political action committees as now constituted.

7. House members should retain their parking privileges at the airport in Washington and their gyms. It's good for the country to try to keep sane as many members of Congress as possible.

8. The number of staff members should be reduced by at least 50 percent.

9. The number of citizens in each district should be reduced by 50 percent and House membership doubled.

10. The code of ethics should be revised to require reporting of income, but set no limits on outside earned income. A person should be able to run for office and serve in office without being continuously in danger of acting illegally.

Chapter 44

Partisan Memories:
Watergate Revisited

Lou Frey, Jr. (R-Florida)
with Michael T. Hayes

I had the privilege to serve in the United States Congress during Watergate and was one of the five elected Republican leaders in the House of Representatives. Even after 25 years, it is painful to think about and discuss. President Nixon was not involved in any way in the break-in. Yet, he and his chief advisors went to great lengths to cover it up. This incredible stupidity was compounded by the fact that, at the time, Nixon was leading the Democratic candidate, George McGovern, in nearly every state and in November 1972, won nearly every state in the general election. Furthermore, there is never anything of importance in any political headquarters.

It is my recollection that the impeachment of President Nixon was extremely partisan from the very beginning and remained that way until the tapes were released showing that Nixon, in the view of most members, had indeed committed an impeachable offense. One of my earliest memories of Watergate is of a subway ride I took from the Rayburn Building to the Capitol with Congressman Phil Burton, a liberal Democrat from California. Phil intensely disliked Nixon and had been at odds with him for many, many years.

As we sat together in the train for the brief 30-second ride, Phil said to me, "Lou, we're gonna get Nixon, wait and see. Nixon is gonna be impeached." This comment was made several months after the Watergate break-in, well before Congress had given any thought to impeachment proceedings. I remember looking at Phil and asking him what he was smoking. I put it out of my mind for some time. I thought it was just Phil's dislike of Nixon showing through, but it proved to be prophetic.

However, rather than trusting my judgment and memory, I wrote a letter to a number of members who were in Congress in 1973 and 1974, both Democrats and Republicans. The letter went to members of the Judiciary Committee, such as Peter Rodino, Tom Railsback, Caldwell Butler, Bob Kastenmeier, and over 50 other members who served during these tumultuous times. I also looked at several video tapes and did some research through the Internet.

The letter I wrote asked these former members to compare the Nixon impeachment proceedings with the recent impeachment of Bill Clinton. I expressed my sense that few people remember accurately what happened during Watergate. While the impeachment of President Clinton has been characterized as intensely partisan, the Nixon impeachment has come to be viewed as having been almost idyllically bipartisan.

My memory is somewhat different. The impeachment of Richard Nixon may have ended up being a bipartisan exercise, but for many months, Watergate was a partisan struggle. To test whether that memory was accurate, I asked these former House members for their recollections of Watergate. I have received many answers and found out so many interesting sidebars that it would be impossible to cover them all in this chapter; the remarks included here reflect a mere sampling of their responses.

No one will be surprised to find there was not unanimity of opinion. The comments by these former members from both sides of the aisle allow us to understand how decent, honest people who are trying their best can have a totally different view about an extremely important subject.

DEMOCRATIC MEMORIES

Most Democratic former members remember Watergate as a shining example of bipartisanship from the very beginning. John Conyers (D-MI), who is one of the few members to have voted in both impeachment hearings, took this view in an editorial in the *Washington Post* on September 27, 1998:

> In sharp contrast to recent events, 24 years ago, members of both parties worked together with mutual respect and devotion to our constitutional duties as we considered the awesome responsibility of the possible impeachment of our nation's Commander-in-Chief.
> There were differences in opinion, of course, and partisan shots and volleys along the way. But at every turn, we achieved bipartisan consensus and maintained a deliberative and judicious approach to the task at hand. We voted unanimously to adopt procedures governing confidentiality. We voted unanimously to adopt procedures for the presentation of evidence. Requests for additional evidence were bipartisan.[1]

Similarly, William Hungate of Missouri, another Democrat on the Judiciary Committee that investigated Watergate, said, "I would never assert any action of Congress was totally nonpartisan. However, this one was as close as any I saw in my seven terms there." In support of this conclusion, Representative Hungate stressed the extent of Republican support for the articles of impeachment reported out by the Judiciary Committee in July 1974.[2]

REPUBLICAN RECOLLECTIONS

By contrast, most Republicans I contacted felt strongly that Watergate was intensely partisan from the very beginning, only becoming bipartisan very late in the process when the "smoking gun" tapes came out showing conclusively that President Nixon had participated in the cover-up and thus was guilty of obstructing justice. As Congressman Bill Frenzel (R-MN) put it: "Watergate certainly started out in a partisan matter. Until the famous televised Judiciary Committee hearings starring Tom Railsback and a cast of dozens, Republicans were just spectators, observing the Democrats doing everything they could to chew up a president they hated."[3]

Representative Caldwell Butler (R-VA) explicitly challenged John Conyers' rosy characterization of the Watergate investigation as bipartisan and procedurally fair in an editorial reply to Conyers published in the *Washington Post*. Butler cited several actions taken by the Rodino Committee that can only be characterized as partisan:

1. Between August 1973 and January 1974, the Judiciary Committee staff produced two massive committee prints (one roughly 700 pages long and the other 900 pages long) on impeachment materials and procedures. Republicans were not consulted in the production of either of these documents.
2. No Republicans were invited to the strategy meeting on October 22, 1973, at which Speaker Carl Albert, Majority Leader Tip O'Neill, and other Democratic leaders decided to refer all impeachment resolutions to the House Judiciary Committee.
3. John Doar was named special counsel to the Judiciary Committee on December 20, 1973. Operating in secret, Doar and his staff made a study of past presidential abuses. While this report was made available to Chairman Rodino, Republicans on the committee were never told of its existence.
4. On January 31, 1974, the committee met to consider House Resolution 803, which would give the committee the powers it required to conduct an impeachment inquiry. Republican attempts to amend the resolution to limit the scope of the inquiry or place a time limit on the inquiry were defeated along party lines.
5. On February 21, 1974, the committee released a staff study on the constitutional grounds for impeachment. Judiciary Committee chairman Peter Rodino and the Republican ranking member, Edward Hutchinson of Michigan, publicly differed on the key question of whether criminal conduct should be required for impeachment. Hutchinson argued that evidence of actual criminality should be required for impeachment; Rodino disagreed.

6. Chairman Rodino sought to end the long tradition of permitting each member of the committee five minutes to question witnesses, reserving for himself the right to decide how long each member should ask questions; members would have to pass their questions in writing to the counsels. Republican David Dennis (R-IN) ultimately had to seek a resolution before the full House in order to reestablish the fundamental right of committee members to question witnesses.

"The message here," Butler concluded, "is to remind all that impeachment, by design of the Founding Fathers, is a political process, not a legal one. That is not an excuse not to use every effort to build consensus on these issues, but an acknowledgment of reality."[4]

Congressman Lawrence Hogan (R-MD), whose recollections of Watergate are reviewed in Chapter 15 of this volume, echoes this characterization of the investigation of President Nixon as very partisan:

> The Nixon inquiry was very partisan. Jerome Waldie (D-CA), Robert Drinan (D-MA) and several others were ready to impeach him before the votes were counted...Peter Rodino (chairman of the House Judiciary Committee), who posed as the objective, bipartisan statesman, was not.
>
> I fought very hard against the unfairness of the inquiry and fought openly with Rodino... They were not going to allow Nixon's lawyer to sit in the hearings. They were not going to allow him to question witnesses, and they were not going to allow him to put up a defense. I fought with Rodino in the well of the House over these three points, and eventually they gave in and did allow these concessions.
>
> I fought with my fellow Republicans on the committee, urging them to fire Albert Jenner, our Republican counsel, who was vehemently anti-Nixon and worked hand-in-glove with Doar and the Democrats against Nixon. They ignored me, and eventually when it was too late, they did fire him. By that time, the damage had been done.
>
> Your memory is correct: it was very partisan, more so than the Clinton case. On the whole, the inquiry ended up being fair, but only after some very vigorous fighting with the Democrats.[5]

Representative Tom Railsback, another Republican member of the Judiciary Committee that investigated Watergate, recalls that:

> ...we fought strenuously about many of the same issues that confronted the Clinton inquiry, e.g., What should be the time limits on the investigation? How many staff persons should be hired? What should be the ratio of majority to minority staffers? What latitude will be given to the chairman to issue subpoenas? What will be the standards used in determining whether the president should be impeached? Shall the president be permitted counsel who will be permitted to participate? Will live witnesses be called? And many others as well.[6]

Railsback praised Henry Hyde's handling of the impeachment inquiry, noting that Hyde had ensured that President Clinton's counsel could participate and have access to evidence and committee proceedings. Moreover, under Hyde's leadership, Democrats on the Judiciary Committee were given a better ratio of minority staffers than Republicans had in the Watergate inquiry. Chairman Rodino hired an additional 134 attorneys to investigate the Watergate affair; only 12 were assigned to the Republican members. By contrast, chairman Hyde hired an additional 21, with seven (one-third of the total) assigned to the Democrats.[7]

Railsback's recollections are particularly valuable inasmuch as he was one of four Republicans on the Judiciary Committee who were undecided from the outset. (The others were Hamilton Fish of New York, Caldwell Butler of Virginia, and William Cohen of Maine.) This group of four undecided Republicans agreed to meet, review the evidence, and share concerns with three undecided Democrats on the committee, Walter Flowers of Alabama, Jim Mann of South Carolina, and Ray Thornton of Arkansas. This bipartisan group of seven helped draft the first two articles of the impeachment that were reported out of the committee.

DIFFERENCES BETWEEN THE TWO IMPEACHMENTS

There are some obvious differences between the two impeachments. For one thing, the Judiciary Committee under Peter Rodino was politically closer to the center than the committee chaired by Henry Hyde. Moreover, Congress was not as polarized in the 1970s as it had become by the late 1990s. Two additional differences between these impeachments are particularly significant, however, in my view.

First, the Nixon White House made a deliberate decision not to lobby members of the Judiciary Committee, while the Clinton White House was directly and daily involved in developing strategy with House Democrats, including the Judiciary Committee. Tom Railsback emphasizes the very different strategies pursued by the two presidents in response to the impeachment inquiries:

> When I reflect on the two proceedings, several differences jump out. Back in 1974, you didn't have the spin-doctors that were on television every night attacking the special prosecutor and Congressional investigators. You didn't have direct White House involvement, orchestrating the defense. If the Nixon White House had tried to influence the Republicans on the committee, we would have warned them to stay away. The Clinton White House got involved and went on the attack, and in my opinion, caused the partisan divisions that the Democrats complained about.[8]

Second, most Republicans met their constitutional responsibility, voting for Nixon's impeachment in the end. This brings to mind a second vivid memory I have of Watergate. In early August 1974, many months after Phil Burton's prophetic comments to me, I was in the Republican cloak room having a cup of coffee. There are a number of phone booths in the Republican cloak room. Congressman Charles Wiggins (R-CA), who was the major Nixon defender on the House Judiciary Committee, burst out of one of the phone booths and said to everybody in the room, "It's all over; there's a smoking gun." Republican support for the president evaporated, both on the committee and in the House, and he was forced to resign a few days later.

In the same op-ed piece cited earlier, written in the midst of the Clinton impeachment inquiry, Caldwell Butler explained why Republicans felt compelled to vote for impeachment when faced with clear evidence of President Nixon's complicity in the Watergate coverup:

> For years, we Republicans have campaigned against corruption and misconduct in the administration of the government of the United States by the other party. ... And, somehow or other, we had found the circumstance to bring these issues before the American people in every campaign. But Watergate is our shame. These things happened in the Republican Administration while we had a Republican in the White House. It is we, not the Democrats, who must demonstrate that we are capable of enforcing the high standards we have set for them.[9]

By contrast, in the impeachment of President Clinton, the overwhelming majority of Democrats remained loyal to the president all the way through the process. Not surprisingly, there is an almost universal feeling among the Democratic former members I contacted that the Clinton impeachment was intensely partisan from the very start. The Democrats who participated in the impeachment of President Clinton maintained this line throughout the impeachment process in the House and the subsequent trial in the Senate.

Because the Watergate investigation has come to be remembered as more bipartisan and cooperative than it really was, the Democrats could undermine the legitimacy of the Clinton impeachment by merely maintaining party unity. By voting together as a bloc in opposition to the impeachment inquiry, House and Senate Democrats could convincingly characterize the Clinton impeachment as a partisan witch hunt, devoid of any real legitimacy. As former Congressman Bill Frenzel observed to me, when the "smoking gun" was found showing conclusively that President Nixon had in fact committed impeachable offenses, all the Republicans in the House (with the one exception of Earl Landgrebe of Indiana, who remained a Nixon loyalist to the end) came to the view, albeit reluctantly, that the president should be removed from office. As Frenzel observed, this Republican support for impeachment made that process "bipartisan." By contrast, Democratic opposition to President Clinton's impeachment, despite conclusive evidence that he had perjured himself and obstructed justice, made that impeachment appear partisan.[10] Orval Hansen (R-ID) echoed this assessment:

> An impeachable offense is in the eye of the beholder. Members can look at the same evidence and reach different conclusions. While many Democrats condemned Clinton's conduct in the strongest possible terms, they were not prepared to take the step that many Republicans did in the Nixon impeachment by voting against their own president. The solid Republican support for impeachment was viewed as proof of their partisanship. The Democrats' solid support of their president was not seen as partisan.[11]

Thus, the Clinton White House and contemporary Democrats in Congress had learned two valuable lessons from the Nixon impeachment. First, President Nixon made a serious mistake by not taking the affair seriously from the outset and thus failing to do everything in his power to mobilize his party behind him in the House. And second, to be legitimate, the impeachment of a president must ultimately be a bipartisan decision. This basic and indisputable fact gave the Democrats leverage, both to block a conviction and to deny the entire effort legitimacy.

I think the message of Watergate is that we have a rule of law in this country, that no one is above the law. The most moving experience of my political life took place during this terrible period when I was invited to the White House by Gerald Ford to see this good and decent man, who had never run for national office, sworn in as president of the United States. To me, Watergate, more than any other event, proved that our system works. It proved that our institutions of democracy are strong and stable. Like a sailboat buffeted by strong winds, we may heel to the port or starboard, but somehow we manage to come back upright. Our system worked when it had to in response to Watergate. Whether it worked as well in the Clinton impeachment, each reader will have to decide.

Notes:

1. John Conyers, Jr., "Republicans Don't Care to Play Fair," *Washington Post*, September 28, 1998, p. A. 25.

2. William L. Hungate, personal letter to Lou Frey, March 15, 2000. Representative Hungate addresses the Watergate investigation at more length in his book, *It Wasn't Funny at the Time*, published by Hungate Research Consulting, St. Louis, Missouri.

3. Bill Frenzel, personal letter to Lou Frey, March 13, 2000.

4. M. Caldwell Butler, "The Good Old Days of Consensus," *Washington Post*, October 5, 1998, p. A. 21.

5. Lawrence J. Hogan, e-mail to Lou Frey, March 20, 2000.

6. Tom Railsback, "Revisionist History, Watergate, and the Clinton Impeachment," unpublished letter to the *New York Times*, September 23, 1999, p. 2.

7. Tom Railsback, "Revisionist History," p. 3.

8. Railsback, "Revisionist History," pp. 2-3.

9. Butler, "The Good Old Days of Consensus."

10. Frenzel, personal letter to Lou Frey, March 13, 2000.

11. Orval Hansen, personal letter to Lou Frey, March 21, 2000.

Contributors

Lou Frey, Jr., a distinguished graduate of Colgate University, served in the U.S. House of Representatives from the Orlando, Florida area from 1969 to 1979. He served as chair of the Republican Research Committee during the 93rd and 94th Congresses. He served on a variety of committees in the House, including the Interstate and Foreign Commerce Committee, where he served as ranking member of the Subcommittee on Communications, and the Science and Technology Committee. He currently is an attorney in Orlando.

Michael T. Hayes is Chairman of the Political Science Department at Colgate University. He is the author of three books, in addition to this volume: *Lobbyists and Legislators, Incrementalism and Public Policy,* and *The Limits of Policy Change: Incrementalism, Worldviews, and the Rule of Law* (forthcoming, Georgetown University Press). His works have won the E. E. Schattschneider Award and the Jack Walker Award.

Joe Bartlett, presently retired, was a veteran staff official of the U.S. House of Representatives. He was both the youngest Chief of Pages and the youngest Reading Clerk, and he is the only person nominated by the House to attend the Federal Executive Institute, where he returned in 1982 as Distinguished Scholar. Bartlett was first elected Minority Clerk, the senior Republican staff office, in 1970, and was re-elected unanimously five times.

Glen Browder is currently the Eminent Scholar in American Democracy at Jacksonville State University in Alabama as well as the Distinguished Visiting Professor of National Security Affairs at the Naval Postgraduate School in Monterey, California. He represented Alabama in the U.S. House of Representatives from 1989 to 1997, serving on the House National Security Committee and the House Budget Committee.

Clarence J. "Bud" Brown, currently retired, was a member of the U.S. House of Representatives from Ohio's seventh district from 1965 to 1983, succeeding his father, who had represented that district from 1938 to 1965. Representative Brown rose to be the second ranking Republican on the House Commerce Committee and the ranking Republican on its Fossil and Synthetic Fuels Subcommittee.

Barber B. Conable, Jr. retired in September 1991 after serving for more than five years as President of the World Bank. A Republican from New York state, he served as a member of the U.S. House of Representatives from 1965 to 1985. During his tenure in the House, he served on the Ways and Means Committee for 18 years, the last eight as ranking minority member. He served in various capacities in the House Republican leadership for 14 years.

R. Lawrence Coughlin is senior counsel in Government Relations Practice in Washington, D.C. He served in the U.S. House of Representatives for 24 years, representing parts of the city of Philadelphia and its Montgomery County suburbs until January 1993. He was a senior member of the House Appropriations Committee and served for 12 years as ranking member of its Transportation Subcommittee. For five years, he was also ranking member of the Select Committee on Narcotics Abuse and Control.

William C. Cramer is an attorney practicing in Washington, D.C. and Tampa, Florida. He is an adjunct professor of political science at the University of South Florida and St. Petersburg Junior College. He served in the U.S. House of Representatives from 1955 to 1971. He was elected to the House leadership from 1963 to 1970, was ranking minority leader of the Public Works Committee and member of the Judiciary Committee. He drafted and co-sponsored: the Federal Aid Highway Act, which established the interstate highway system; the Anti-Riot Act; the Voting Rights Act; and the 23rd, 24th, and 25th amendments to the U.S. Constitution. He also served as Republican National Committeeman from Florida from 1964 to 1984, and as General Counsel to the Republican National Committee from 1973 to 1980. He served as chief counsel to Gerald R. Ford in the Vice Presidential confirmation hearings, and his law firm represented President Ford in the Nixon pardon proceedings.

Tom Downey is Chairman of Downey-McGrath Group Inc., a government affairs consulting firm in Washington, D.C. He served in the U.S. House of Representatives from 1975 to 1993, representing New York's second congressional district on Long Island. He served on the House Armed Services committee and was an adviser to both the SALT and START arms control negotiations. He also served on the House Ways and Means Committee and was chief House architect of the 1988 welfare reform legislation, the Family Support Act, as well as landmark child care legislation.

John N. Erlenborn served in the U.S. House of Representatives from 1965 to 1985. While in Congress, he served on the Education and Labor and Government Operations committees. From 1984 to 1994, he was a partner in a national law firm where he specialized in employee benefit law and served as an expert witness in employee benefit litigation. Since 1994, he has been an adjunct professor in the graduate program of the Georgetown University Law Center.

Eugene A. Forsey, who died in 1991, was widely regarded as one of Canada's foremost constitutional authorities. He taught political science at McGill University, Carleton University, and the University of Waterloo, and he served as Chancellor of Trent University from 1973 to 1977. He also authored the definitive work on the Canadian constitution, *How Canadians Govern Themselves*, from which the material in this volume is drawn. A political activist as well as a scholar, Mr. Forsey also served as director of research for the Canadian Congress of Labor and its successor, the Canadian Labor Congress. He ran for public office four times for the Co-operative Commonwealth Federation (CCF), and was appointed to the Canadian Senate in 1970 and the Privy Council in 1985.

Robert Garcia served in the U.S. House of Representatives from 1979 to 1991. He served on the Banking, Housing, and Urban Affairs Committee and the U.S. Postal and Civil Service Committee, chairing subcommittees on international banking and trade, census and population, and postal operations. He was coauthor of the Garcia-Kemp bill, creating urban enterprise zones (enacted in 1993 as "empowerment zones") and the Civil Service Reform Act. He was also floor manager of the bill establishing Martin Luther King's birthday as a national holiday. Representative Garcia was co-founder and chairman of the Congressional Hispanic Caucus. Currently an attorney in Washington, D.C., Representative Garcia serves on the board of directors of both the Salvation Army and Prison Fellowship Ministries.

Lee H. Hamilton is Director of the Woodrow Wilson International Center for Scholars in Washington, D.C. He served in the U.S. House of Representatives from 1965 to 1999, serving on the Committee on Foreign Affairs (now the Committee on International Relations) throughout the entire 34 year period. Representative Hamilton chaired that committee during the 103rd Congress and subsequently served as its ranking Democrat. He also chaired or co-chaired the Joint Economic Committee, the Permanent Select Committee on Intelligence, the Joint Committee on the Organization of Congress, and the Select Committee to Investigate Arms Transactions with Iran.

Orval Hansen served in the U.S. House of Representatives, from Idaho, from 1969 to 1975. While still serving in the House, Representative Hansen began a program of studies leading to a Ph.D. in political science from George Washington University, which he obtained in 1986; his chapter in this volume is drawn from his doctoral dissertation. He is currently President of the Columbia Institute for Political Research in Washington, D.C.

George J. Hochbrueckner currently heads a Long Island consulting firm. He served in the U.S. House of Representatives from 1987 to 1995, representing New York's first district. Representative Hochbrueckner specialized in issues of environmental protection and defense conversion, serving on the Merchant Marine and Fisheries and Armed Services committees. He authored landmark legislation to encourage recycling by creating markets for recycled materials and helped write strong legislation to prevent oil spills after the Exxon Valdez incident. He also helped organize the congressional India Caucus in order to improve relations between India and the United States.

Lawrence J. Hogan, an attorney, served in the U.S. House of Representative Representatives from 1969 to 1975. He served on the House Judiciary Committee when it was compelled, by Watergate and other events, to recommend impeachment of President Nixon; his decision to vote for impeachment was a critical factor in the president's eventual decision to resign from office. Representative Hogan ran unsuccessfully for Governor of Maryland in 1974 and was the Republican Party's nominee for the U.S. Senate in 1982. Hogan has been a consultant with the Federal Emergency Management Agency since 1982. He has also served on the faculty of the University of Maryland for many years, teaching courses in law for both the School of Journalism and University College.

Elizabeth Holtzman, currently an attorney in New York City, is the youngest woman ever elected to the U.S. Congress, serving in the U.S. House from 1973 to 1981. She served on the House Judiciary Committee during the Watergate episode, winning national attention for her role in the impeachment hearings as well as her questioning of President Ford about the Nixon pardon. She also chaired the Subcommittee on Immigration, Refugees, and International Law, authoring the rape privacy act, the bill to extend the deadline for ratification of the Equal Rights Amendment, the nation's first refugee law, and legislation barring Nazis from the United States and authorizing their deportation. She is the author of *Who Said It Would Be Easy* (Arcade Press, 1966).

Harry A. Johnston, an attorney in West Palm Beach, Florida, served in the Florida State Senate from 1974 to 1986 and the U.S. House of Representatives from 1989 to 1997. During his years in the House, Representative Johnston served on the Budget, Interior, and Science and Space committees. He also served on the House Foreign Affairs Committee for all eight years of his tenure in the House, chairing the Africa Subcommittee. He negotiated a cease fire in Southern Sudan and has lectured on African issues at both Harvard and Princeton.

H. Martin Lancaster represented North Carolina in the U.S. House of Representatives from 1987 to 1995, serving on the House Armed Services Committee for his entire tenure there. After leaving Congress, Representative Lancaster served as Assistant Secretary to the Army (Civil Works) and Special Advisor to the President on Chemical Weapons. He became President of the North Carolina Community College System in 1997.

Christine Bideganeta LaRocco is currently an educational consultant working with academic and vocational schools across the nation. She is the co-author of six literature anthologies and the recipient of two national innovation-in-teaching awards for her work with at-risk students. Her spouse, Larry LaRocco, represented Idaho in the U.S. House of Representatives from 1991 to 1995.

William M. Lehman represented Florida in the U.S. House of Representatives from 1973 to 1993, serving on the Select Committee on Children, Youth, and Families, as well as on the Appropriations Committee. In 1982, he became Chairman of the Transportation Subcommittee of the Appropriations Committee. He is author of *Mr. Chairman: Journal of a Congressional Appropriator*, also published by the University Press of America.

Bert Levine served as Vice President of Federal Government Relations and State Government Relations during nearly two decades with Johnson and Johnson. Prior to becoming a lobbyist, he was a counsel to a congressional subcommittee for the 92nd and 93rd Congresses. He is co-author of the second edition of *Lobbying Congress* (Washington, D.C.: CQ Press, 1996) and has taught at Rutgers, Colgate, and Drew Universities. He is currently a visiting assistant professor of political science at Bucknell University and is completing his Ph.D. dissertation at Rutgers.

Romano L. Mazzoli represented the third district of Kentucky from 1971 to 1995. He was Chairman of the Subcommittee on Immigration, Refugees, and International Law and co-author of the Simpson-Mazzoli immigration reform legislation. He also served on the House Small Business, Intelligence, and District of Columbia committees. He is currently the Senior Distinguished Fellow in Law and Public Policy at the Louis D. Brandeis School of Law at the University of Louisville.

Eugene J. McCarthy represented Minnesota in the U.S. House from 1949 to 1959. Following his five terms in the House, McCarthy served two terms in the United States Senate. Senator McCarthy ran for president in 1968 in order to challenge President Johnson's handling of the Vietnam War, nearly defeating the president in the New Hampshire primary and forcing his withdrawal from the presidential race. He ran for president again in 1976 and 1992. He is the author of more than 20 books.

Paul N. "Pete" McCloskey, Jr. is currently an attorney in Redwood City, California, specializing in land use and condemnation. He was elected to the U.S. House of Representatives in a special election in 1967 and was reelected seven times representing the San Francisco Peninsula area. He initiated the effort to repeal the Gulf of Tonkin Resolution in 1969, and ran for the presidency in 1972, challenging Richard Nixon's Vietnam policies. In June 1973, he made the first House speech suggesting the impeachment of Richard Nixon for obstruction of justice. He played a leading role in enacting the Capital Gains Tax Reduction Act in 1977 and in abolishing the Renegotiation Board in 1978, the first government agency abolished in 22 years. He has written four books, including *Truth and Untruth: Political Deceit in America.*

John S. Monagan represented the fifth district in Connecticut from 1959 to 1973. He served on the House Committee on Foreign Affairs and the House Committee on Government Operations. He authored the International Drug Control Resolution of 1972 and the drug control provisions of the Foreign Assistance Act. He also served as Official U.S. Observer to the Disarmament Conference in 1962, and participated in Study Missions to Moscow, Prague, Budapest, and Warsaw between 1962 and 1964.

G. V. "Sonny" Montgomery is the President of the Montgomery Group, a consulting firm based in Alexandria, Virginia. He represented Mississippi in the U.S. House of Representatives from 1967 to 1997. He served as Chairman of the House Veterans' Affairs Committee for 12 years and authored the Montgomery G. I. Bill.

Peter A. Peyser represented New York (his district encompassed Westchester County and parts of the Bronx) in the U.S. House of Representatives as a Republican from 1971 to 1977 and as a Democrat from 1979 to 1983. Peyser was a political maverick whose moderate liberalism enabled him to function within both parties while always remaining independent of the party leadership. He served on the Education and Labor, Government Operations, and Post Office and Civil Service committees and was Chairman of the ERISA Task Force.

Otis Pike represented the first district of New York as a Democrat from 1961 to 1979. Since his retirement, he has written a political column for the Long Island newspaper, *Newsday*, as well as a syndicated column, mostly about politics, for the Newhouse News Service.

John J. Rhodes, II graduated from Harvard Law School and in 1952, became the first Republican elected to the House from Arizona; he served there longer than anyone else in Arizona history, representing Arizona's first district from 1953 to 1983. After being Chairman of the House Republican Policy Committee, Rhodes was unanimously chosen by his colleagues to be House minority leader in 1973, succeeding Gerald R. Ford, who had been appointed Vice President under the 25th Amendment to the Constitution, replacing Spiro Agnew. The first Republican in 40 years to be elected unanimously as minority leader, Rhodes was unanimously reelected at the beginning of the 94th Congress after guiding his party during the period of the Watergate impeachment inquiry.

John J. "Jay" Rhodes, III also represented Arizona's first congressional district, serving in the House from 1987 to 1993. He served on the Interior and Insular Affairs and Science, Space, and Technology committees. He currently is an attorney in Washington, D.C.

Carlton R. Sickles is Senior Vice President of Carday Associates, Inc. in Beltsville, Maryland. He represented Maryland as congressman-at-large from 1963 to 1967, serving on the Education and Labor and District of Columbia committees. Sickles left Congress to run for governor of Maryland in 1966, losing narrowly in the Democratic primary. After this defeat, Sickles was appointed to the board of directors of the Washington Metro system, which he had helped create as a member of an interstate commission charged with studying the passenger carrier facilities in the metropolitan Washington area. Sickles' tenure on this commission began while he served in the Maryland state legislature and continued during his tenure in the U.S. House of Representatives.

Denny Smith was first elected to the U.S. House of Representatives in 1980, upsetting 12-term incumbent Al Ullman, Chairman of the House Ways and Means Committee. The Oregon Republican served in the House for ten years, from 1981 to 1991. He served on the House Budget, Interior and Insular Affairs, and Veteran's Affairs committees. He was co-chairman of the Congressional Military Reform Caucus and founder and co-chairman of the Congressional Aviation Forum. He is currently Chairman of the Board of Eagle Newspapers, Inc.

Don Sundquist is Governor of Tennessee, having been elected in 1994 and re-elected in 1998. He served in the U.S. House of Representatives from 1983 to 1995, representing Tennessee's seventh congressional district. In Congress, he specialized in issues involving tax policy and international trade; he served on the House Ways and Means Committee in his final six years in Congress and chaired the Republican Task Force on Trade. Sundquist helped write and pass the landmark Ethics Reform Act of 1979.

James W. Symington represented Missouri in the U.S. House of Representatives from 1969 to 1977, serving on the Science and Technology and Interstate and Foreign Commerce committees. Like his father, the former United

States Senator from Missouri, Stuart Symington, he held a number of important administrative posts in a Democratic national administration before returning to Missouri to run for elective office. He currently is an attorney in Washington, D.C.

Lionel Van Deerlin, a former print and broadcast journalist, served nine terms as a Democratic congressman from California, chairing the House Communications Subcommittee from 1976 to 1980.

Robert S. Walker is Chairman and CEO of the Wexler Group. He represented Pennsylvania in the U.S. House of Representatives from 1977 to 1997. He served as Chief Deputy Republican Whip and chaired the Science Committee when the Republicans took control of Congress in 1995. He also served as Vice Chairman of the Budget Committee.

G. William Whitehurst represented Virginia in the U.S. House of Representatives from 1969 to 1987. His committee assignments included Armed Services, the Select Committee on Intelligence, and the Ethics Committee. Representative Whitehurst kept a diary of his 18 years in Congress, which has been published in two volumes: *Diary of a Congressman* and *Diary of a Congressman, Volume II: Abscam and Beyond.* He is currently the Kaufman Lecturer in Public Affairs at Old Dominion University.

Jim Wright represented Fort Worth, Texas in the U.S. House of Representatives from 1955 to 1989. He served as House Majority Leader for ten years prior to being sworn in as Speaker in January 1987. He was reelected Speaker in January 1989. Following his resignation in 1989, he began teaching political science at Texas Christian University. He has written numerous newspaper columns, articles, and books, including *Balance of Power: Congress and the Presidents from the Era of McCarthy to the Age of Gingrich.*